TRANSFORMING
MISSION
THEOLOGY

Beyond loving God, what is more important than loving our neighbor? If today our neighbors are global—as shown by the labels in the clothes we wear, the food we eat, the components in our electronics—then hardly anything is more important than missions. It is through missions that we live out God's love for our global neighbors. This book distills the wisdom of a lifetime in missions. It is biblical, showing how Moses, David, Isaiah, and Paul explored God's love for the nations. It is theological, because without theology faith will be flat, superficial, and soon skewed and bent. It is the grassroots mission of dusty feet and sweaty students, tears and abrazos and roars of laughter. It is stewardly mission that recognizes better and worse ways to do the work, and critiques strategies so as to find the best. This book is the culminating work of one of the preeminent missiologists of our time. Read it and learn.

Miriam Adeney, PhD

associate professor of missiology, Seattle Pacific University

author, *Kingdom Without Borders and Wealth, Women, and God*

To my knowledge, Charles Van Engen at the School of Intercultural Studies of Fuller Theological Seminary was the first professor of Biblical theology of mission in North America, and his influence is worldwide. In this volume, we have a harvest of the fruit from his career of teaching and writing about mission theology. This work should be a standard textbook for courses in world mission and missiology.

Gerald H. Anderson, PhD

director emeritus of the Overseas Ministries Study Center, New Haven, CT

former editor, *International Bulletin of Mission Research*

This book is the product of not only many years of thinking theologically about mission, but also actually doing it. Chuck Van Engen writes with his usual passion, creativity, and clarity. These pages come alive with his deep faith and wide-ranging theological wisdom. To read this book is to sit at the feet of a teacher who has himself sat long at The Master's feet and has walked long ways with him.

Stephen Bevans, SVD, PhD

Louis J. Luzbetak, SVD Professor of Mission and Culture, emeritus,

Catholic Theological Union, Chicago

Transforming Mission Theology is the book I have been waiting for, vintage Van Engen. This volume integrates much of what Chuck has been teaching over many years, but takes it to deeper places. Mission in the world confronts us with many complex, challenging situations. The methodology outlined using the four domains of mission theology is a tremendously helpful tool for reflecting thoughtfully on the complex realities in the world.

Jude Tiersma Watson, PhD
InnerChange, a Christian Order Among the Poor
associate professor of urban mission, Fuller Seminary

Van Engen, drawing on forty years of studying, critiquing, and living out his theology of mission, has written what will likely become a classic in missiology of the stature of David Bosch's *Transforming Mission*. It's historical depth, ecumenical breath, evangelical spirit, cross-cultural awareness, and deep personal commitment to God's mission in the world, make this book an outstanding contribution to mission theology. It will become and remain a classic for many years to come.

Darrell Whiteman, PhD
missiological anthropologist
former editor, *International Bulletin of Mission Research*
former professor of anthropology and dean of the E. Stanley Jones School of
World Mission and Evangelism, Asbury Theological Seminary

TRANSFORMING
MISSION
THEOLOGY

CHARLES VAN ENGEN

WILLIAM CAREY
LIBRARY

Published by William Carey Library
Pasadena, CA 91104 | www.missionbooks.org

Joanne Liang, graphic design

William Carey Library is a ministry of
Frontier Ventures
Pasadena, CA | www.frontierventures.org

Printed in the United States of America
21 20 19 18 17   5 4 3 2 1 BP100

Library of Congress Cataloging-in-Publication Data
Names: Engen, Charles Edward van, author.
Title: Transforming mission theology / Charles Van Engen.
Description: Pasadena, CA : William Carey Library, 2017. | Includes bibliographical references. | Description based on print version record and CIP data provided by publisher; resource not viewed.
Identifiers: LCCN 2017003561 (print) | LCCN 2017011933 (ebook) | ISBN 9780878086511 (eBook) | ISBN 9780878086351 (pbk.) | ISBN 0878086358 (pbk.)
Subjects: LCSH: Missions. | Theology, Doctrinal.
Classification: LCC BV2061.3 (ebook) | LCC BV2061.3 .E54 2017 (print) | DDC 266--dc23
LC record available at https://lccn.loc.gov/2017003561

CONTENTS

PART I
THE SOURCES OF MISSION THEOLOGY

PART II
THE MEANING OF MISSION THEOLOGY

PART III
THE METHODS OF MISSION THEOLOGY

PART IV
THE GOALS OF MISSION THEOLOGY

PART V
SAMPLES OF MISSION THEOLOGY

LIST OF FIGURES

PREFACE

A Biblical Theology of Missions

Teaching missiology is both a privilege and a challenge. As one who served many years as a missionary, I count it a sacred trust to help the current and next generation of missionaries know and obey Christ's commission to all disciples to be his witnesses to the ends of the earth. I also realize that missions are a dynamic field of study as we adjust to the rapid changes in culture and peoples globally. Responding to these two has been a characteristic of missiology at Fuller School of Intercultural Studies (formerly School of World Mission) since its inception in 1965.

The foundational discipline of missiology is the biblical theology that approaches the whole of Scripture as the story of God's redemptive mission to the world. We base our work on the Bible, Old and New Testaments, to understand the message in order to know the mission of God. I embraced this wonderful discipline at the feet of Arthur Glasser, whose biblical basis for mission was published as *Announcing the Kingdom: The Story of God's Mission in the Bible.* When it came time for him to retire, the faculty of the School of World Mission wanted a person whose track record as a missionary and theologian would build on Glasser's foundation with a view of taking us into the next millennium. They chose Charles (Chuck) Van Engen as a worthy successor.

I met Chuck soon after taking up a position in missiology at Wheaton College. Walking across the campus together was like finding a long-lost friend whose experience and insights were a complement to my own. Chuck was full of life and energy inspired by the gospel and fully committed to exploring the mission of the kingdom of God through the Church and beyond in this rapidly changing world. I was thrilled to be a colleague, if even at a distance, and even more to follow his insights as they were developing through his work on the Biblical Theology of Missions, a core course of the missions programs at Fuller. Later that decade I was hired as a faculty member at the school, cementing my relationship and tremendous respect for Chuck Van Engen.

Through the years, particularly 1990–2010, Van Engen continued to refine his knowledge of the biblical theology of mission. His influence expanded both through his writings and his irrepressible energy. This was particularly evident in Latin America and Korea. But as he worked with other mission theologians, for example on the theology task force leading up to the LCWE conference in Cape Town 2010, his thinking was refined as well as influential in the global conversation. Van Engen's contribution is seen in many publications as well as his class notes from years of teaching.

As one who uses Van Engen's material in all of my classes, I often wished for a single volume that would bring together his insights in conversation with the significant work of other mission theologians. This volume, *Transforming Mission Theology,* provides exactly what many of us wanted in a single volume. Taking its position next to works by David Bosch, Christopher Wright, Andrew Kirk, and many others, this volume is the fruit of careful scholarship mining the rich resources of missiology and theology. Evident in the pages are the influences of his mentors, Johannes Verkuyl and Arthur Glasser. Profoundly biblical in his orientation, Van Engen also has the sensitivities of a systematic theologian; this volume is a tremendous resource to the missions' community.

Transforming Mission Theology is an exploration of the praxis (theory and practice) of mission and the broader field of missiology as an integrative discipline. As a teacher, Van Engen provides clear rationale for what mission is and isn't, building on the works of many others; the volume approaches the work of doing mission theology in a globalizing world. Each of the five parts addresses a major concern of missiology by breaking down the issues into chapters dealing with the elements, for example addressing mission theology as part of contextualization and transformation in Part II and some of the more timely responses to contextual issues in mission theology in Part V.

This volume represents the effort of one of the leading mission theologians of this generation. It provides an accessible, well documented, integration of missiology and theology as they intersect in mission theology.

Doug McConnell
provost, Fuller Theological Seminary

INTRODUCTION

There are numerous assumptions regarding mission and missiology that under-gird, circumscribe, and help to define the focus and purpose of mission theology within the larger discipline of missiology. In this introductory chapter I will briefly summarize some of those assumptions in order to introduce and clarify the per-spectives offered in the rest of the book. At the risk of over simplification, I will suggest a number of assumptions in mission praxis and missiology as a discipline about which many others have written. There is not enough space here to explain at length these concepts that have been foundational in the Church's missiological reflection of the past hundred years and about which I have written in other works. But it is important that we remember them here, because they influence the way we do mission theology. By mentioning them at the outset of this book, I hope to clarify for you, the reader, where I am coming from and why I develop mission theology as I do.

This is a book about doing mission theology. During more than twenty-five years of teaching biblical theology of mission in the School of World Mission (now the School of Intercultural Studies) at Fuller Theological Seminary, I sought to learn how to do theology of mission and how to teach others. For many years, I used the term "theology of mission" to refer to the activity that this book seeks to describe.[1] But Andrew Kirk[2] and others have convinced me that the term we need to use in the future is "mission theology."[3] Mission theology is something the followers of Jesus the Christ do. *World* *The Church* *dynamic relationship*

David Bosch said it this way. *Authentic Theology*

> Authentic theology . . . only develops where the Church moves in a dialectical relationship to the world, in other words, where the Church is engaged in mission, in the wider sense of the word. Internal renewal of the Church and missionary awakening belong together. (Bosch 1980, 2006, 25) *Church Renewal and* *Missionary awakening*

Belong Together

Another way to say this, in the words of Andrew Kirk would be,

---

1.   See, e.g., Van Engen 1996, 17–31; Van Engen 2000, 949–51; Van Engen 2008, 551–62; Van Engen 2011, 57–98; Van Engen 2012, xi–xvii. As I have mentioned elsewhere, Gerald H. Anderson's edited collection in *The Theology of Christian Mission* (Gerald H. Anderson, ed., 1961) marked the beginning of this subdiscipline in Protestant missiology. In the foreword to that work, Lesslie Newbigin wrote, "Even the good Christian congregation which faithfully gave its yearly offering to foreign missions finds itself having to face for the first time the question whether it is really true that there is salvation in no other name than that of Jesus. We live in one world in which the competing faiths, no longer separated and insulated by distance, jostle one another in every city and even in the minds of ordinary Christians. Today the question of the theology of the Christian mission is a question that—whether recognized or not—knocks at the door of every congregation" (Newbigin 1961, xiii).

2.   The interface of theology and missiology in Andrew Kirk's thought can be appreciated in the following definition of "theology" he offered in 1997. "My thesis is that it is impossible to conceive of theology apart from mission. All true theology is, by definition missionary theology, for it has as its object the study of the ways of a God who is by nature missionary and a foundation text written by and for missionaries. . . . Theology should not be pursued as a set of isolated disciplines. It assumes a model of cross-cultural communication, for its subject matter both stands over against culture and relates closely to it. Therefore, it must be interdisciplinary and interactive" (Kirk 1997, 50–51).

3.   The reader may wish to consult the following: G. H. Anderson et al 1970, 594; David J. Bosch. *Witness to the World: The Christian Mission in Theological Perspective* 1980, 2006, 21–27; David J. Bosch 1991, 489–98; A Scott Moreau, Gary Corwin, Gary McGee 2004, 74–89; Christopher J. H. Wright 2006, 33–69 (focused on the relationship of biblical hermeneutics and mission); A . Camps, L. A. Hoedemaker, M. R. Spindler, edits 1995, 5–6; Stephen B. Bevans and Roger Schroeder 2004, 35–72; Francis Anekwe Oborji 2006, 52–56; H. Armstrong, M McClellan, D. Sills 2011, 11–32, 53–77; John Mark Terry, Ebbie Smith, and Justice Anderson, edits 1998, 9–12; Jan A . B. Jongeneel 1997, 9–18; John Corrie, ed., 2007, 237–44, 380–84; Craig Ott, Stephen J. Strauss, with Timothy C. Tennent 2010, xi–xxx.

The theology of mission is a disciplined study which deals with questions that arise when people of faith seek to understand and fulfill God's purposes in the world, as these are demonstrated in the ministry of Jesus Christ. It is a critical reflection on attitudes and actions adopted by Christians in pursuit of the missionary mandate. Its task is to validate, correct, and establish on better foundations the entire practice of mission. (Kirk 1999, 21)[4]

Justice Anderson said it this way.

The starting point of all missiological study should be a missionary theology. The dynamic relationship between systematic theology and academic missiology (involves them as being) mutually interdependent. The missionary enterprise needs its theological undergirding; systematic theology needs missionary validation. Missions is systematic theology in action, with overalls on, out in the cultures of the world. The missionary is the outrider of systematic theology. (Anderson 1998, 9)

Mission is Systematic Theology In Action

Or as Ott, Strauss, and Tennent stated in *Encountering Theology of Mission,*

Missional theology seeks to delineate more clearly the missional aspects of theology as a whole, placing God's mission as a central integrating factor. In the words of [David] Bosch, "We are in need of a missiological agenda for theology rather than just a theological agenda for mission (Bosch 1991, 494)." Missional theology is thus concerned with providing an interpretive frame of reference by which we understand the message of scripture and the mission of the church in its entirety. (Ott et al. 2010, xviii)[5]

---

4.   Cathy Ross cites this definition with approval in her survey of Kirk's missiological works in John Corrie and Cathy Ross, eds., 2012, 11–12. Scott W. Sunquist cites Kirk's definition seemingly with approval in Sunquist 2013, 11.

5.   Ott, Stauss, and Tennent add a caution. "Missional theology is dependent on the other theological disciplines, learning from them and building upon them, and then bringing them into relation with God's mission in the world. Missiology apart from a sound theology is a dangerous and speculative undertaking. Not only does theology help us to correctly interpret the scriptures, but it also provides the larger framework of biblical understanding with which a theology of mission must be in harmony" (Ott et al 2010, xix).

Over my years at Fuller I was often asked to teach a doctoral-level methods course that we called then, "Theologizing in Mission." As I learned and taught others how to do this activity, I came to understand that there was no one methodology that could encompass doing theology in mission and doing missiology in theology. In a sense, "theologizing in mission" is not in itself a method at all. Rather, I began to suspect that mission theology involves a close intertwining of content and method—and each affects the other. Because mission is first and foremost God's mission (understood in Trinitarian perspectives),[6] theological reflection must be permeated by missiological understanding and our missiology must be permeated with theological reflection. As Christopher J. H. Wright put it,

> There should be no theology that does not relate to the mission of the church—either by being generated out of the church's mission or by inspiring and shaping it. And there should be no mission of the church carried on without deep theological roots in the soil of the Bible. (Wright 2010, 20)

The two endeavors need to be given concrete reality in—they need to be lived into—mission action-reflection (that is, praxis) that participates in God's mission working primarily, but not exclusively, through the Church in God's world. Like a DNA molecular helix, missiological understanding, theological reflection, and missionary action intertwine around each other, connected by a host of issues, ideas, and learnings, to make one integrated whole that I have learned to call "mission theology." The chapters of this book constitute multiple and varied samples of doing mission theology. None of them are the only way to do mission theology. None of them represent the whole endeavor of doing mission theology. But my hope is that something in these samples will stimulate the readers to explore ways to create and transform their own mission theology in their participation in God's mission, in their contexts, in their time and space.

AFFIRMATIONS ABOUT MISSION

Let me begin by affirming the following.

---

6.   One of the best brief discussions regarding a trinitarian understanding of God's mission may be found in D. Bosch 1980, 2006, 239–42. Lesslie Newbigin beautifully articulated the contours of a trinitarian mission theology in *The Open Secret* (Newbigin 1978).

A. Mission is not the purview of the king, queen, nation state, or church institution. *conquered + colonized - Planted/imposed their religion*

Although this matter differed widely from nation to nation, generally speaking, from the fifteenth into the eighteenth centuries, in Western Europe and North America, there was a pervasive assumption that mission was the purview of the king, queen, and/or nation state. Wherever the Western European nations extended their military, political, and economic power throughout Latin America, Africa, and Asia, they also "planted"—or one might say, imposed—their form of Christian faith and church. The principle of *cuius regio eius religio* (whose reign, their religion) that had dominated European nations for centuries was assumed to be something to be followed also as they conquered and colonized parts of other continents. In the US, the idea of "manifest destiny" was used to support a similar concept of mission. There were those who knew then, and we know now, that this idea of mission is unacceptable, is unbiblical, and is missiologically and theologically untenable. A student interested in this topic can consult the rather substantial literature regarding "mission and colonialism," especially works written by mission theologians in the global South and East.

B. Mission is not merely church extension, expansion, church multiplication that seeks merely to create new branch offices of the sponsoring religious corporation. *Like Branch offices*

From the fifteenth century until now, the Church of Jesus Christ has been tempted to think of mission as an activity focused primarily on starting new local manifestations of the religious institution sponsoring the activity. Church planting has too often been reduced to essentially opening branch offices of the institutional church, the denomination, the mission organization, or (more recently) the megachurch that has funded, directed, sent its emissaries, and controlled the establishment of new local congregations that look like exact copies of the mother institution. The essentially forced conversion by conquest of Latin America in the sixteenth century by the Roman Catholic Church of that day is an example of this view of mission. This understanding of mission as planting branch offices of the denomination in new locations around the globe persists even today in almost every Christian tradition. See, for example, *Toward a Theology of Mission Partnerships* (Van Engen 2001) for a brief initial reflection on this matter. This view of mission must be carefully reexamined and reevaluated. In the Gospels and in Acts, mission is described numerous times with these words: "Jesus went about the

towns and villages announcing the good news of the kingdom of God and healing"
(Matt 9:35–36; Luke 4:43; 5:15; 8:1; 9:1–2). Luke's narrative in Acts is essentially
the story of the followers of Jesus (with Paul's mission at center stage) going about
the towns and villages of their world, preaching the good news of the kingdom
of God and healing. The Church in its many local forms is important—in fact,
essential—for our understanding of mission. But we need to be careful today not
to allow mission to become too narrow, ecclesiocentrically imprisoned, or controlled. The emergence of the church is to be understood as a fruit of mission,
not as the goal of mission, a caution expressed by mission thinkers as disparate as
Roland Allen, J. C. Hoekendijk, Johannes Verkuyl, Orlando Costas, and others.
This matter is beyond the scope of this book, but it needs to be kept in mind as we
attempt to "transform mission theology."

C. Mission is God's mission.

A strongly ecclesiocentric view of mission dominated Western European and
North American Protestant mission theology during the 1920s and 1930s. Mission
was seen as the responsibility no longer of separate mission associations (as was the
case during most of the nineteenth century), but rather of the church. This view
was especially strong at the International Missionary Council (IMC) meeting in
Tambaram (Madras, India) in 1938. Mission was the activity of younger and older
churches together, but World War II changed all that. Fueled especially by the
deep pessimism caused by the silence of the churches with regard to the atrocities
that occurred during the war, mission came to be seen more as an action of God
(missio Dei) than as an activity of the church. At the Willingen (Germany) conference of the IMC in 1952 this view of mission began to grow. This view of mission
was helped along by Georg Vicedom's book entitled *The Mission of God* (1965)
which was associated with the 1963 Mexico City conference of the Commission
on World Mission and Evangelism (CWME) of the World Council of Churches
(WCC). Over time, the concept was reshaped to include everything God does in
the world. Promoted by mission thinkers like J. C. Hoekendijk who was deeply
disenchanted and pessimistic about the church, by the time of the Uppsala Assembly of the WCC in 1968, this more secularized view of mission had little or no
relationship either with the church or with world evangelization. Its proponents
were right in rescuing mission from the suffocating control of the churches, but
in so doing, they threw out the baby with the bathwater and essentially lost both
church and mission (cf. Van Engen 1996, 145–56).

The origin of Mission is discovered in the Nature of God

D. "The Living God is a Missionary God."[7]

In the late 1950s and early 1960s a conviction grew among missiologists that the origin of mission was to be found in the nature of God. In Roman Catholic, conciliar (related to the World Council of Churches), and Protestant evangelical circles, this conviction grew such that by the 1970s it was shared by all three of these major strands of Christian thought. By the middle of the 1970s one can find Orthodox and Pentecostal mission thinkers also affirming that the foundation, meaning, and parameters of mission originate in the heart and purposes of God. Later in this book I will deal more specifically with the related concept of *missio Dei* that was eventually expanded and secularized in conciliar circles to such a degree as to become unacceptable for many other mission thinkers.

WHAT MISSION IS NOT

Based on the positive, general affirmations offered above, we may also state some preliminary assumptions as to what mission is not.

1. It is not what we in the Christian church want it to be.
2. It is not what our surrounding culture or our world wants it to be.
3. It is not determined only by the needs of persons or structures.
4. It is not merely acts of compassion for the needy.

There seems to be a trend today in evangelical churches to assume that mission is mission when it involves acts of kindness from those who have to those who have not; from those in power and strength to those on the margins in weakness, from those who know to those who do not know, and so forth. Biblically, this is insufficient. The Bible's call to compassion and kindness is clear, but there is another broader and deeper issue here. As the Apostle Paul emphasized, God often does mission in exactly the opposite way. God often uses the weak, the ignorant, and the poor in God's mission (1 Cor 1:18–30). By way of example, we could note that Jesus emphasized this viewpoint in what is virtually a constitution of Jesus' mission in Luke 4. In that passage, Jesus states that the Holy Spirit has anointed him for mission. Following that statement, and speaking to those gathered in the synagogue in Capernaum, Jesus offers two Old Testament examples of God's mission: the widow of Zeraphath and the little girl who spoke of her faith to Naaman the Syrian, commander of the Syrian army, who was healed of his leprosy. It is not

Naaman

---

7.   John Stott 2009, 3–9.

surprising that such talk made the folks in the synagogue in Capernaum furious, yet they should have known better. All through the Bible one can find numerous illustrations of how God chooses so often to work through the weak to influence the strong, through the ignorant to correct the wise, through the powerless to challenge those in power. On their way to transform their mission theology, I think evangelicals need to rethink their assumptions about God's mission.

5. It is not all good things the churches do in the world.

6. It is not merely joining what God is doing the world.

7. Is not any agenda or action that is good for humanity.

WHAT MISSION INVOLVES

Given the affirmations stated above, we may affirm that *God sends the church to the world!*

A. God sends the Christian Church to the world.

From the 1960s through the 1980s, the conciliar reconceptualization and secularization of mission involved changing the traditional order of "God working through the church to the world" to "God-world-church." Strongly advocated by J. C. Hoekendijk and others in the conciliar movement, this view of mission was an appropriate post-WWII concern that God's mission be relevant to all of life. God's mission is supposed to change the state of things in the world. It is supposed to improve the human condition. Where God's mission happens, the context should register changes for the better. However, emerging from the Second World War, Hoekendijk and others in the state churches in Europe were deeply pessimistic about the church in general. Thus, in his major work, *The Church Inside Out* (1966), Hoekendijk essentially called for the euthanasia of the church as we know it or, at very least, he affirmed the church should exist only as an instrument of sociopolitical and economic change to bring in God's *shalom*. However, by overemphasizing the sociopolitical and economic ramifications of the Church's mission, this view of mission moved away from the more comprehensive view seen in the Bible that preserves the order of mission as "God-church-world." Even so, as we examine God's mission action throughout the Bible and in the history of the church, we must also consider the fact that at times God works alongside, and sometimes in spite of, or even over against, the institutional forms of Christian churches.

Def inition

B. The origin, authority, message, means, and goals are God's and must be consistent with God's mission.

The Greek word *apostello* and its associated synonym, *pempo,* are the primary biblical words and concepts for mission in the Bible. The secondmost prominent word for mission in the Bible is *diakonia.* Later in this book, we will have an opportunity to think more in-depth about this matter.[8]

C. Therefore, mission theology is an activity that seeks to discern what God wants to do primarily through God's people at a specific time, place and context in God's world.

IMPLICATIONS FOR DOING MISSION THEOLOGY

Drawing from the assumptions mentioned above about mission generally, we could state the following regarding mission theology (MT).

1. MT is revelationally grounded and circumscribed by what we are taught in the Bible concerning God's mission. The Bible is like an "operator's manual" of mission.

2. MT must be biblically permeated in all aspects of its reflection so that the Church's understanding of God's mission is consistent with the Bible's presentation of such.

3. MT does its theological reflection about and in the midst of contextually grounded mission praxis.

4. Doing MT involves both word and deed through a continuous hermeneutical spiral.[9]

5. MT is not complete until and unless it translates into mission action.

6. MT is not mindless activism disassociated from reflection, evaluation, thought, analysis, critique, or creativity.

As my mentor, Johannes Verkuyl, affirmed in his *magnum opus, Contemporary Missiology,* "Missiology may never become a substitute for action and participation. God calls for participants and volunteers in his mission. In part, missiology's

---

8. See Van Engen 2008 and Van Engen 2010.

9. The issue of theological reflection as a process that follows a hermeneutical spiral will be discussed later in this book.

goal is to become a "service station" along the way. If study does not lead to participation, whether at home or abroad, missiology has lost her humble calling" (Verkuyl 1978, 6).

In my view, one of the best summaries of mission theology's reflective task now and into the future was offered by David Bosch in *Transforming Mission* (1991, 368–519). Here Bosch offered thirteen "Elements of an Emerging Ecumenical Missionary Paradigm" that constitute a challenge and assignment for us today in mission theology. In his summary of summaries, he says,

> The mission of the church needs constantly to be renewed and reconceived. Mission is not competition with other religions, not (merely) a conversion activity, not expanding the faith, not building up the kingdom of God; neither is it social, economic, or political activity. And yet, there is merit in all these projects. So, the church's concern *is* conversion, church growth, the reign of God, economy, society and politics—but in a different manner! The *missio Dei* purifies the church. It sets it under the cross—the only place where it is ever safe. The cross is the place of humiliation and judgment, but it is also the place of refreshment and new birth . . . As community of the cross the church then constitutes the fellowship of the kingdom, not just "church members"; as community of the exodus, not as a "religious institution" it invites people to the feast without end . . . Looked at from this perspective, mission is, quite simply, the participation of Christians in the liberating mission of Jesus, . . . wagering on a future that verifiable experience seems to belie. It is the good news of God's love, incarnated in the witness of a community, for the sake of the world. (519)

Great !

MT is like the axle of a wheel, the central anchor for all mission praxis. Missiological thought, analysis, critique, and creativity are to be connected to the axle in order to make up the spokes of the wheel. The people of God gathered in local congregations of followers of Jesus are the rim and rubber of mission action that meet the road in their contexts of mission.

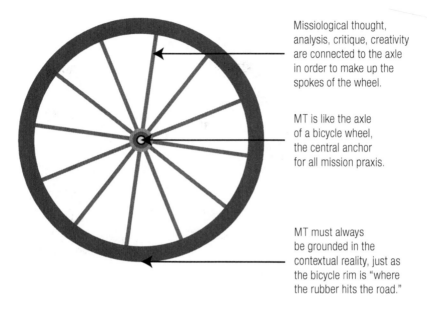

Missiological thought, analysis, critique, creativity are connected to the axle in order to make up the spokes of the wheel.

MT is like the axle of a bicycle wheel, the central anchor for all mission praxis.

MT must always be grounded in the contextual reality, just as the bicycle rim is "where the rubber hits the road."

FIGURE 1: Missiology Viewed as a Wheel

PART I
THE SOURCES OF MISSION THEOLOGY

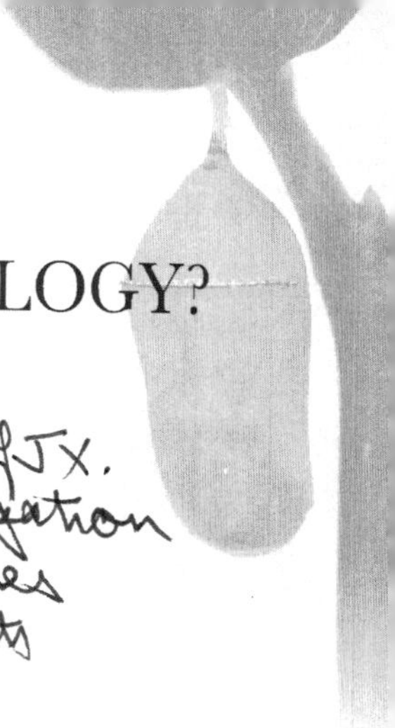

CHAPTER 1
WHO DOES MISSION THEOLOGY?

[handwritten: Each does MT.]

[handwritten: 1 The H.S, 2 The Chrch of JX. 3 Local Congregation 4 The sent ones 5 The recipients]

THESIS

In this chapter I will suggest five different agents who do mission theology: the Holy Spirit, the Church of Jesus Christ, the local congregation, the sent ones who participate in God's mission, and the recipients of the church's mission praxis.

INTRODUCTION

In this chapter, we are asking the question, who does mission theology (MT)? In the previous chapter, I characterized MT as an activity to be done, not a static set of propositions with which folks may or may not agree, nor a set of verbal affirmations that can promptly be forgotten.[1] MT is an activity of reflection and action—of praxis.[2] It is, therefore something the whole church does, not the domain of a single professional "missiologist." God's mission is too extensive, too complex, and too profound to be encompassed by the thought of one person. Rather, MT is an activity of the Church of Jesus Christ seeking to understand more deeply why, how, when, where, and wherefore the followers of Jesus may participate in

---

1. In mission theology today we need to keep in mind the words of James in James 1:23–25: "Any one who listens to the word but does not do what it says is like someone who looks at his face in a mirror and, after looking at himself, goes away and immediately forgets what he looks like. But whoever looks intently into the perfect law that gives freedom, and continues in it—not forgetting what they have heard, but doing it—they will be blessed in what they do."

2. The term "praxis," though not new at the time, was popularized—and the concept expanded—by Latin American theologians of the 1970s, especially by those who followed Paulo Freire's perspectives on education and by a number of Latin American proponents of Liberation Theology of the day. Generally, it refers to a spiral-like process of action-reflection-new action-new reflection in which action transforms reflection and subsequent reflection leads to new, transformed action. How this process may work itself out in mission theology will be dealt with later in this book.

God's mission, in God's world. Professional "missiologists" are invited and needed to stimulate, examine, summarize, draw out the assumptions, and reflect on the implications of the Church's MT—both that which has been articulated and that which has not yet been expressed. A description of those who do MT would include at least the following five agents.

THE HOLY SPIRIT

Since Jesus' ascension, the first and primary agent of mission theology has been— and is—the Holy Spirit. Prior to his passion and resurrection, Jesus had explained this matter to his disciples. In his farewell discourse, Jesus told his followers that, "When the Counselor comes, whom I will send to you from the Father, the Spirit of truth who goes out from the Father, he will testify about me. And you also must testify, for you have been with me from the beginning" (John 15:26–27; see also John 14:16–17, 26; 16:7–16).

These words of Jesus have often been understood as referring to orthodoxy, to the Holy Spirit's illumination that would enable the disciples to understand the teachings of Jesus concerning God's revelation in Jesus the Christ, including a new understanding of their Scriptures, the Old Testament. That is one element of what Jesus was teaching his disciples, but there is another aspect of Jesus' teaching that we sometimes miss. Although a missiological reading of this passage is beyond the scope of this book, it is important to note that throughout Jesus' discourse in John 14–17, the concept of *sending* is a dominant theme. The chapter has to do with Jesus' mission and therefore the mission of the disciples once Jesus has "gone to the Father." The key to the passage is the role of the Holy Spirit. The Holy Spirit will teach the disciples about Jesus' mission and empower them to "bear witness" (John 15:27), a clear reference to their mission, so I believe it was no surprise to the disciples to hear the resurrected Jesus tell them, "Peace be with you! As the Father has sent me, I am sending you" (John 20:21).

In Luke 24:49, Jesus tells the disciples to wait in Jerusalem for the coming of the Holy Spirit. Luke repeats this in Acts 1:4, where Jesus tells the disciples that they will be baptized with the Holy Spirit and they will receive power when the Holy Spirit comes upon them to be witnesses of Jesus Christ in Jerusalem, and Judaea, and Samaria, and to the ends of the earth (Acts 1:8).

Throughout the book of Acts, the Holy Spirit's actions and revelation provide the content for the disciples of Jesus to construct a mission theology. This is clearly seen in the way Luke tells the story about the first Jerusalem Council where the radical decision was taken by those gathered there that the gospel was for all peoples and the Gentiles did not need to become Jews in order to follow Jesus. The mission theology foundation for such an earthshaking decision? Four times (an intentional emphasis) Luke mentions the coming of the Holy Spirit to the household of Cornelius in Acts 10 as the basis—the mission theology, as it were—for the decision of the Jerusalem Council. The episode of Acts 10 is retold by Peter in Acts 11:5–17, again in Acts 15:7–11, and referenced again by James in Acts 15:13–17.

Since then, throughout the history of revivals and awakenings of the Church, one can perceive the work of the Holy Spirit not only in mobilizing and energizing the Church in mission, but also guiding, teaching, illuminating, and transforming the Church's understanding of its mission—its mission theology. The traditional Pentecostal movement, born at the beginning of the twentieth century, had it right. The coming of the Holy Spirit is inseparably intertwined with the mission of the Triune God, and the mission of the Triune God is mobilized, expounded, and shaped by the presence and work of the Holy Spirit.

Harold Dollar said it this way.

> The Holy Spirit is the missionary Spirit, sent from the Father by the exalted Jesus, empowering the church in fulfilling God's intention that the gospel become a universal message, with Jews and Gentiles embracing the Good News. The Spirit leads the mission at every point, empowering the witnesses and directing them in preaching the gospel to those who have never heard, enabling them with signs and wonders. (Harold Dollar 2000, 451)

Another way of saying this would be as follows: the Church is the Body of Christ, the physical presence of the risen Jesus on earth (e.g., Rom 12; 1 Cor 12, Eph 4). That being the case, the mission of the Church today is to participate in Jesus' mission, the Head of the Church. The mission does not belong to the Church. The Church participates in Jesus' mission. Therefore, Jesus' mission defines the motivation, message, means, agents, and goals of the Church's mission. How does this come about? By the presence, action, illumination, and transformation of the Holy Spirit, the one sent by the Father and the Son. One way to illustrate these relationships might be to state that Jesus Christ is the head of the Body; the Church as the Body comprises the muscles, arms, legs, face, etc. that do the mission; and the Holy Spirit is the nervous system that communicates the commands of the Head to the muscles of the Body and mobilizes the Body to action. Thus, one may say that the Holy Spirit is the first and primary agent in the process of transforming mission theology. How this happens will be a matter of interest throughout the rest of this book.[3]

THE CHURCH OF JESUS CHRIST

Earlier we mentioned that God's mission works primarily (though not exclusively) through the Church to the world. Beginning with God's call to Abraham (Gen 12:1–3)[4] through whom all the nations would be blessed, God's mission has primarily worked through God's people.[5] Although Israel often missed the point and too often wanted to keep God's grace for itself rather than be an instrument of God's grace to the nations, yet God's clear intention, repeated time and again from Genesis to Revelation, was that Israel was to be God's instrument to bless all peoples.[6]

---

3.   The relationship of pneumatology to mission theology is an important issue. One of the early Protestant mission thinkers to reflect on this relationship was Roland Allen (1868–1947), Anglican missionary to China at the beginning of the Twentieth Century. A classic work in this regard that drew from Roland Allen's thought is Harry Boer 1961. Rob Gallagher did his PhD dissertation in missiology at the School of World Mission of Fuller Seminary on this topic. His research, coupled with a number of recent publications in mission theology by Pentecostal and Charismatic scholars, has helped churches and missions around the world grasp more deeply the essential role of the Holy Spirit in clarifying, directing, and empowering Christ's mission. See, for example, the works of Gary McGee. The works of J. Edwin Orr in the history of revivals and awakenings are important in this regard because they show the intimate relationship between revivals and mission. A. T. Pierson (1837–1911) was an important American pastor and mission thinker who closely associated spirituality and mission theology in his preaching and extensive writing.

4.   Concerning the "Abrahamic Blessing" theme that courses its way throughout the Bible as a primary motivation and shaper of biblical mission theology. See Sarita Gallagher 2014.

5.   Helpful resources to inform a missiological reading of God's mission as it flows throughout the Bible include, Arthur Glasser et al. 2003; Christopher Wright 2010; Michael Goheen 2011.

6.   It is beyond the scope of this book to develop this major biblical theme that is foundational for mission theology. For many years I taught a course that I inherited from Arthur Glasser concerning the "Biblical Foundations of Mission." In that course we examined this theme and its many profound implications for mission theology. Arthur Glasser et al. 2003 grew out of and became the basic text for that course.

Following Augustine of Hippo, we may say that the Church of Jesus Christ is made up of everyone who everywhere, always, has believed in, and been followers of, Jesus Christ. This great company of believers, spread over the entire globe in many different cultures and contexts, has carefully and thoughtfully expanded, deepened, developed, and refined its understanding of God's mission and mission theology over the past twenty centuries. As the Body of Christ, the Church has not only done mission activities, for better and sometimes for worse, but has also constantly reflected on that mission and sought to articulate its understanding of such over time. Today, this includes more than 1.5 billion believers who think, speak, and act with reference to mission theology in a multitude of languages, drawing from a myriad of cultures around the world. Though they read the same Bible and are illuminated and guided by the same Holy Spirit, their understanding of mission theology differs markedly, as that is influenced by their particular historical, cultural, and linguistic contexts, as well as their experiences over time, as they participate in God's mission. Andrew Walls has been very instructive in helping us more clearly understand these developments in mission theology around the world, over time, something he called "the Ephesian Moment."[7] See, for example, Andrew Walls 1996, 2002.

In the twenty-first century, we seem to be tempted—on all continents—to assume that our mission theology is new and possibly superior to that which was articulated in earlier centuries. Maybe we need to reexamine that presumption and ascribe greater wisdom and importance—and listen more intently—to what we can learn from those who have gone before us. The Church of Jesus Christ has been doing mission theology for a very long time and has much to teach us. There is much for us to critique and many unbiblical, heretical, and destructive thoughts and actions that did not honor Jesus the Christ, but there were many other expressions and much praxis that did honor our Lord and can serve to guide us into the future.

THE LOCAL CONGREGATION OF FOLLOWERS OF JESUS

The Church (capital "C") that includes everyone, everywhere and always, who have followed Jesus is a wonderful idea, but no person experiences the capital-C

---

7.   Andrew J. Walls, "The Ephesian Moment: At a Crossroads in Christian History," in A. J. Walls, *The Cross-Cultural Process in Christian History* (NY: Orbis) 2002, 72–81. 2002, 72–81.

Church. Rather, we all experience the fellowship of the followers of Jesus in local congregations. We participate in the Church to a lesser or greater degree as and when we participate in a group of followers of Jesus. Thus, from its very birth in Jerusalem at Pentecost, the Church took concrete shape, visible form, in the local group of believers described in Acts 2:42–47. Here, amidst the faces, names, stories, experiences, and interaction of persons, the local congregation of believers developed their mission theology.[8]

Paul developed this idea further through his use of the "Body of Christ" image. In Romans 12, 1 Corinthians 12, and Ephesians 4, with a focus on the "gifts" (the charisms) which each member of the Body has, Paul stressed the life of the local gathering of followers of Jesus, the local congregation.[9] Throughout his letters written to these local groups, one might generally say that Paul sought to broaden and deepen their mission theology.

Mission theology is an essential element—and should be a natural fruit—of the life of a local congregation. The members of a local church (small "c") are called to discover, learn, and develop their mission theology as together they live out their lives, experience God's grace, study the Bible together, reflect together on God's mission, and discover their calling as God's missionary people in their place and in their context.[10]

This congregational foundation and location of mission theology may be found throughout the history of church, including in the early years of many

---

8.   It is beyond the scope of this chapter and this book to develop the ecclesiology being summarized here. See, for example, Van Engen 1981, 78–190; and Van Engen 1991a *in loco*.

9.   One's ecclesiology of the "local church" will differ according to whether one approaches the issue from the perspective of a predominantly Anabaptist "believers' church" viewpoint, or a congregational view, or a view based on presbyterial polity, or a more Episcopal "parish" perspective, or a "people movement" viewpoint. There are important differences between these viewpoints that influence the way one understands the "mission of the local congregation." However, this matter is beyond the scope of this book.

10.   One of the intentional attempts in Latin America to live out what is described above involved the Base Ecclesial Communities in Brazil during the 1970s and 1980s. For an evangelical treatment of this phenomenon, see, e.g., Guillermo Cook 1985. Sadly, many of these groups eventually stepped away from a careful reading of the Bible in context, lost much of their ecclesial and theological focus and became mostly cell groups focused primarily on certain political agendas. From small Pentecostal and Charismatic storefront churches found in cities the world over to very large megachurches also spread around the globe, the potential, function, and unique role of local congregations in constructing mission theology is a matter waiting to be seriously researched.

monastic movements. See, for example, *God's Missionary People* (Van Engen 1991a) for an initial attempt in this direction.[11] As a group of believers lives out its faith over time, and as those followers of Jesus experience God's grace and express their understanding of God's mission in their context, their mission theology takes shape. We need much more careful listening to, and intentional learning from, the mission theology that emerges in and through the life of local congregations, in the power of the Holy Spirit.

THE MESSENGERS WHO DO MISSION THEOLOGY AS THEY PARTICIPATE IN GOD'S MISSION

Down through the centuries, from the earliest beginnings of the Christian Church, the Holy Spirit has called women and men from among the faithful followers of Jesus, members of local believing communities of faith, to dedicate a significant portion of their lives to specific missionary action. For example, in Acts 13 the Holy Spirit made it plain to the followers of the Way that they were to set apart Saul and Barnabas for a specific task to which the Holy Spirit was calling them. This same pattern can be seen throughout the history of the Church.[12]

THE DIACONATE AS A WINDOW TO THE MESSENGERS WHO DO MISSION THEOLOGY

One of the ways the New Testament teaches us how women and men were called and empowered to participate in God's mission—and to do MT—is by describing them as "deacons." Elsewhere I have discussed the fact that the primary word in the New Testament for mission is *apostello* (with its synonym, *pempo*), to send. The

---

11. In 2011 Mark Fields wrote an important PhD dissertation for the School of Intercultural Studies of Fuller Theological Seminary entitled, "Contours of Local Congregation-based Mission in the Vineyard Movement, 1982 to 2007." I had the joy of accompanying him in this research as the mentor. I learned a lot from Mark.

12. This theme is especially fascinating, broad, and complex when it is infused by the stories of women and men specifically called in this way. What an inspiration and blessing it is to read the missionary biographies to learn how God worked through the lives of such people. Missionary biographies are a marvelous source of mission theology. A wonderful source for this mode of doing mission theology is Gerald Anderson, ed., *Biographical Dictionary of Christian Missions*, 1998.

second most prevalent word for mission in the New Testament is *diaconia,* also used in the noun form as *diaconos* and in the verb form as *diaconeo.* A brief overview of the concept of the *diaconate* as it develops in the New Testament may serve as an example of a mission theology taking shape in the midst of the participation by specific women and men in God's mission to the world so loved by God.

In the appendix, the reader will find a thematic concordance covering the various occurrences of the Greek words *DIAKONEW, DIAKONIA,* and *DIA-KONOS.* Our English translations (as well as translations in many other languages) have not been consistent at this point, and they fail to show us the richness of the concept of the DIACONATE which covers a verb (to diaconize), a concept (as a role or function—the diaconate), and a subject (deacon). The Greek use of this concept in the New Testament is very concrete and follows a specific pattern that serves to demonstrate to us a clear picture about the Church in mission. In what follows I have sought to bring out the Greek sense of the concept by using the transliterated Greek term.

The Church is the loving communion of the disciples of Jesus. As such, it is profoundly the communion of the Crucified One. In his ministry, Jesus developed in his person and in his teaching a life of diaconal service, a ministry that he then transferred to his disciples as a commandment and a commission. So Jesus declared that, "The Son of Man did not come to be DIACONIZED, but to DIACONIZE and to give His life as a ransom for many" (Matt 20:28; Mark 10:45).

As an example of this truth, Jesus washed the disciples' feet the last night before his death, and then proceeded to teach them the significance of the act: "I am among you as one who DIACONIZES" (Luke 22:27). "You call me teacher and lord, and rightly so, for that is what I am. Now that I, your Lord and Teacher, have washed your feet, you also should wash one another's feet. I have set you an example: you should do as I have done for you" (John 13:13–15). Thus, in the new kingdom which Jesus brings, authority and greatness are completely reversed so that those who would "be great among you," Jesus says, "shall be your DEACON" (Matt 23:11). "The chief among you (shall be) like the one who DIACONIZES" (Luke 22:26–27). "Whoever wants to become great among you must be your DEACON" (Matt 20:26).

The disciples experienced this new way of life throughout their association with Jesus' ministry. He walked with sinners, the sick, the hungry, the ones in need—and he gave them counsel, health, new sustenance, and help. It is precisely this ministry of the diaconate which Jesus took as His commission for ministry.

The Spirit of the Lord is upon me, because he has . . . anointed me to proclaim good news to the poor. He has sent me to proclaim freedom for the prisoners and recovery of sight for the blind; to set the oppressed free, to proclaim the year of the Lord's favor. (Luke 4:18–19, Isa 61:1–2)

Later when John the Baptist sent his followers to Jesus to ask if he was the Coming One, the Messiah, Jesus answers by giving his Messianic credentials, and these credentials are the elements of the DIACONATE. "The blind receive sight, the lame walk, those who have leprosy are cleansed, the deaf hear, the dead are raised, and the good news is proclaimed to the poor . . ." (Matt 11:5). Thus, precisely in the ministry of service and assistance—that is, in the DIACON-ATE—Jesus teaches His disciples and models for them the means by which they also might have the opportunity to participate in the messianic mission of God. The angels enjoy the privilege of DIACONIZING Jesus (Matt 4:11; Mark 1:13). Then, taking the place of the angels, Peter's mother-in-law also enjoys this privilege (Matt 8:15; Mark 1:31; Luke 4:39); as do the women of Galilee (Matt 27:55), Joanna and Susanna (Luke 8:3), Martha the sister of Lazarus (Luke 10:40), and even Judas Iscariot (Acts 1:17).

Jesus attributed such an importance to the DIACONATE that he promised his disciples that they would have the honor of sitting at the Lord's table in His kingdom (Luke 22:30), and it will be the Lord Himself who will DIACONIZE them, if they have been faithful servants (Luke 12:37). At this banquet the Lord will take the place of the DEACON, the one who serves the table (Luke 17:8).

Based on the importance given to the diaconate in His ministry, Jesus went a step further and made the diaconate one of the major criteria for being His disciples. "Whoever DIACONIZES me must follow me; and where I am, my DEACON also will be. My Father will honor the one who DIACONIZES me" (John 12:26).

However, the diaconate has its price.

Anyone who loves their father or mother more than me is not worthy of me; anyone who loves their son or daughter more than me is not worthy of me. Whoever does not take their cross and follow me is not worthy of me. Whoever finds their life will lose it; and whoever loses their life for my sake will find it. (Matt 10:37–42; cf. Luke 12:49–53; 14:26–27)

> Whoever wants to be my disciple must deny themselves and take up their cross and follow me. For whoever wants to save their life will lose it, but whoever loses their life for me will find it. What good will it be for someone to gain the whole world, yet forfeit their soul? Or what can anyone give in exchange for their soul? For the Son of Man is going to come in his Father's glory with his angels and then he will reward each person according to what they have done. (Matt 16:24–27)

This vision of the final judgment brings out the tremendous importance of the diaconate in the mind of Jesus. In Matthew 25, in the last major teaching portion of Matthew, we find the allusion to, the promise of, and the prophesy concerning this judgment. "When the Son of Man comes in his glory, and all the angels with him, he will sit on his glorious throne. All the nations will be gathered before him, and he will separate the people one from another as a shepherd separates the sheep from the goats. He will put the sheep on his right and the goats on his left . . ." (Matt 25:31–32).

On what basis will the judgment be made? On the basis of the diaconate. It will be based on those who have carried out a diaconal lifestyle in relation to the people around them—in relation to the hungry, the thirsty, the strangers, the naked, the sick, the imprisoned. These are the same people who figure so large in the messianic credentials of Jesus himself, those who are the recipients of Jesus' diaconate. When the Lord tells those on His left, "Depart from me . . . for I was hungry and you gave me nothing to eat . . ."; they also will answer, "Lord, when did we see you hungry or thirsty or a stranger or needing clothes or sick or in prison and did not DIACONIZE you?" (Matt 25:41–44) And Jesus will answer, ". . . whatever you did not do for one of the least of these, you did not do for me" (Matt 25:45).

Obviously, the diaconate is given major stress in the Gospels. It is an essential element of ministry itself, and of the very commission of Jesus—an absolutely essential element of discipleship for those who follow Jesus the Christ. Thus, in the extended discourse in John 13–16 Jesus tells his disciples, "As the Father has loved me, so have I loved you. Now remain in my love. If you keep my commands, you will remain in my love, just as I have kept my Father's commands and remain in his love. . . . My command is this: Love each other as I have loved you . . ." (John 15:9ff).

It is not surprising to find Paul naming Jesus the Christ as a deacon. In Romans 15:8 Paul states that "Christ has become a servant (DEACON) of the Jews on behalf of God's truth, so that the promises made to the patriarchs might be confirmed and, moreover, that the Gentiles might glorify God for his mercy" (Rom 15:8–9).

The disciples of Jesus took this command very seriously and accepted it as their lifestyle. So much so that since Judas Iscariot was no longer with them after the resurrection and ascension of Jesus, they took it upon themselves to elect someone in his place precisely because they wanted to look after the diaconate. Thus, they prayed, "Lord, you know everyone's heart. Show us which of these two you have chosen to take over this DIACONIA which Judas left to go where he belongs" (Acts 1:24–25).

During the next weeks and months, the disciples experienced the coming of the Holy Spirit, the conversion of the first 3000 believers to Christ, the rapid growth in the number of followers of Jesus, and the rapid increase in the needs which must be met among the faithful. It was precisely on the basis of the example, model, and teaching of Jesus that the diaconate became the pattern of the ministry of the apostles who sold their possessions, distributed them among the needy, ate together from a common table, and served one another. In those first months of the life of the Church, we see a very strong desire on the part of the disciples (including the new believers) to live according to the model which Jesus had shown them (Acts 2:43–47). Peter and John healed a lame man (Acts 3:1–10). The disciples asked the Lord for power "to heal and cause signs and wonders to be done through the name of thy holy servant Jesus" (Acts 4:30). They demonstrated great spiritual power because they also lived out their faith, selling their lands and giving the price to the apostles to distribute among the needy (Acts 4:32–25). The Church continued to grow, the signs and wonders continued to be done by the apostles, just as they served one another in mercy to the sick and demon-possessed (Acts 5:12–16). The issue with Ananias and Sapphira was so very serious precisely because it undermined the diaconal nature of this community of disciples of Jesus (Acts 5).

Thus, we see that the twelve apostles took Jesus' model for themselves and that this new community of believers was in fact a communion of the Crucified One, just as Jesus had demonstrated, taught, and commanded. The diaconate was an essential element of the life of the disciples of Jesus. In fact, the very importance of this pattern augmented the scandal of the Greeks who saw their widows being neglected (Acts 6). In that first Christian community everyone expected assistance because that was the pattern of the community's life together. Following the ethics of Deuteronomy, the first and foremost who were to be cared for were the widows, along with the orphans, aliens, and strangers (Deut 10:18; 14:29; 24:17,19,20,21; 26:12,13; 27:19). The community as a whole and the number of those in need had grown beyond the means, beyond the resources, of the twelve apostles. They could not care for everyone equally. What was being neglected was the daily DIACONATE, and this was very serious (Acts 6:1). This pushed the twelve to divide their DIACONATE into two complementary aspects. They had the people select seven for the DIACONATE OF THE TABLES (Acts 6:2), so that they could better serve the DIACONATE OF THE WORD (Acts 6:4). Both groups were DEACONS, but the sphere of their work differed.

Seven were elected for the DIACONATE OF THE TABLES. They were seven specially chosen persons, all with Greek names, who received a special commission and task with reference to the Greek-speaking part of the Jerusalem church, although their function was still not clearly defined. The office of deacon had still not taken shape, and would not do so for quite a few years to come. The seven did not receive any special title in Acts 6, yet their ministry, their diaconate, was very clear and can be clearly understood by looking at the lives of a couple of those first seven.

Stephen was the first example given in Acts. Jesus had already spoken about the diaconate saying, "whoever loses their life for me will save it" (Luke 9:24), and that was precisely the price, the ultimate sacrifice, that was required of the first deacon. Stephen was stoned to death (Acts 7).

In Acts 8:1, at the scene of the death of Stephen, Luke points out the presence of the man who would later serve in the Church as a deacon of God's grace for the Gentiles: Saul of Tarsus. Saul's first task for the Christian community was clearly a DIACONAL one. In Acts 11:29–30 this man, now converted, joined Barnabas to take an offering from the believers in Antioch to the persecuted believers in Judea. He was probably chosen as someone who could do this task in the midst of the persecution, because of his Roman citizenship and his prestige in the Roman and the Jewish communities in Jerusalem. Having completed this financial DIACON-ATE, Barnabas and Saul began their ministry of missionary DIACONATE, (Acts 12:25; 19:22; 20:24; 21:19) and, together with others, they were called to be DEACONS of the gospel.

Paul very intentionally called himself a DEACON of the mystery of the gospel for the Gentiles. I count sixteen times that Paul used DEACON to refer to himself in six of his letters.[13] Where Paul most clearly and succinctly associated his

---

13. Sixteen personal references on the part of Paul as being a "deacon" are the following: Romans 11:13; 15:25; 15:31; 1 Cor 3:5; 2 Cor 3:3; 2 Cor 3:6; 2 Cor 4:1; 2 Cor 5:18; 2 Cor 6:4; 2 Cor 8:4; 2 Cor 8:19; 2 Cor 8:20; Eph 3:7; Col:23; Col 1:25; and 1 Tim 1:12.

diaconate with God's mission to the Gentiles in Jesus Christ is found in Ephesians 3. Here is the way Paul said it.

> This mystery is that through the gospel the Gentiles are heirs together with Israel, members together of one body, and sharers together in the promise in Christ Jesus. I became a servant [DEACON] of this gospel by the gift of God's grace given me through the working of his power. Although I am less than the least of all the Lord's people, this grace was given me: to preach to the Gentiles the boundless riches of Christ, and to make plain to everyone the administration of this mystery, which for ages past was kept hidden in God, who created all things. (Eph 3:6–9)

At the same time Paul was developing his diaconate, there were others whom Luke signals. We find Philip, presumably one of the seven who earlier had been elected to the DIACONATE OF THE TABLES, who exercised his diaconate in evangelization—first in Samaria (Acts 8:5ff) and later with the Ethiopian (Acts 8:26ff). Then we find Dorcas "who filled her days with acts of kindness and charity" to the extent that when she died, it was necessary to bring her back to life again for the sake of the poor who were complaining to God that they could not exist without her help. Of her it was true to say, "whoever loses her life for my sake, shall find it" (cf. Acts 9:36ff).

In the following decades, the diaconate began to take a more defined shape as a calling in the church. Paul developed this aspect of the ministry in 1 Corinthians 12:5, where he spoke of a diversity of DIACONATES, but the Lord is the same. Once the deacon formed part of the group of church leaders, it was by means of various DIACONATES that the Church could express its discipleship as the community of the Crucified One. In 2 Corinthians 8 and 9 Paul describes the congregations in Macedonia who wanted "to be allowed to share in this generous DIACONIA to their fellow Christians" (2 Cor 8:4), an idea which the Greek renders literally, "the grace and the *koinonia* of the DIACONIA of the saints." The beauty of the diaconate among the poor churches of Macedonia inspired Paul to write his letter of appreciation to the Corinthians who had sent a special offering. He wrote the following to the Christians in Corinth.

> Now he who supplies seed to the sower and bread for food will also supply and increase your store of seed and will enlarge the harvest of your righteousness. You will be enriched in every way

> so that you can be generous on every occasion, and through us
> your generosity will result in thanksgiving to God. This service
> [DIACONIA of LEITOURGIA] that you perform is not only
> supplying the needs of the Lord's people but is also overflowing
> in many expressions of thanks to God. Because of the service
> [DIACONIA] by which you have proved yourselves, others will
> praise God for the obedience that accompanies your confession
> of the gospel of Christ, and for your generosity in sharing with
> them and with everyone else. And in their prayers for you their
> hearts will go out to you, because of the surpassing grace God
> has given you. Thanks be to God for his indescribable gift!
> (2 Cor 9:10–15)

Here we find the diaconate firmly established in the work and life of the Church—in the very nature of the community of the Crucified One. In fact, the diaconate remained such a significant part of the life of the Church that later when Paul wrote his pastoral instructions to Timothy in relation to the selection and ordination of the officers of his church, we find two functions expressed there: the bishops were set alongside the deacons—each with their characteristics, responsibilities, and ministry.

The diaconate, then, is clearly an essential element in the life of the disciples of Jesus. The importance of the diaconate is such that James would state that pure and undefiled religion is found precisely in the exercise of the diaconate. "Religion that God our Father accepts as pure and faultless is this: to look after orphans and widows in their distress and to keep oneself from being polluted by the world" (James 1:27).

In fact, James was emphasizing one of the most important aspects of the life of the people of God as found in the Old Testament.

> At the end of every three years, bring all the tithes of that year's
> produce and store it in your towns, so that the Levites [who have
> no allotment or inheritance of their own] and the foreigners, the
> fatherless, and the widows in your towns may come and eat and
> be satisfied, and so that the Lord your God may bless you in all
> the work of your hands. (Deut 14:28–29; cf. also Job 31:16,17,21;
> Ps 146:9; Isa 1:17, 23)

What James wanted us to understand is that the ministry of the diaconate is one of the essential and irreplaceable expressions of the nature of the Church as the community of the Crucified One, as servants of Jesus Christ. When we confess "Jesus is Lord" it is impossible for us to escape active participation and strong commitment to what that implies in Christ's call to service and to the diaconate that Jesus demonstrated and commanded. We see the semblance of the Crucified One in the face of "the least of these my little ones," in the lives of those who suffer want. It is in this sense that the Church of Jesus Christ cannot exist or live without DIACONIA . . . without its deacons, who are in fact the whole people of God.

Moreover, obedience to the Lord is to be expressed concretely and to be determined essentially by means of the service of the diaconate. When the Church of Jesus Christ is obedient to the mandate of Jesus to love one another, when the reality of the communion of the Crucified One is in fact a reality in the Church's taking up the cross and presenting it in the world of the here and now, then expression is given to the ministry which we understand to be the DIAKONIA of the Church. Only in the DIAKONIA will we find what James calls "true and undefiled religion." This constitutes a mission theology shaped, expressed, and lived out by the followers of Jesus.

THE RECIPIENTS OF THE CHURCH'S MISSION PRAXIS

A fifth agent of mission theology involves the hearers, the recipients of the message proclaimed by Christ's followers. Luke highlights this group in Acts 13 at the end of Paul's first major sermon that constitutes an outline of his mission theology. "When the Gentiles heard this, they were glad and honored the word of the Lord, and all who were appointed for eternal life believed. The word of the Lord spread through the whole region" (Acts 13:48–49).

Throughout the rest of the Book of Acts, Luke offers numerous summary comments regarding the hearers of Paul's message, stating that some believed and others did not. The hearers were themselves doing mission theology, judging whether they would—or would not—accept Paul's revolutionary message of the gospel of Jesus Christ offered to all peoples.

As the recipients of Paul's message considered it and lived out their understanding of the gospel, Paul calls them his "letter." "You yourselves are our letter, written on our hearts, known and read by everyone" (2 Cor 3:2). Thus, over time, each church in each place (Jerusalem, Corinth, Ephesus, Colossae, Galatia, Rome) would begin to develop their own mission theology, and that was merely the beginning of the story. As the gospel spread and the Church of Jesus Christ expanded to other places among diverse cultures, unexpected, unanticipated, new understandings of the gospel would begin to develop. Andrew Walls called this growth the expansion and development of knowing God in *The Cross-Cultural Process in Christian History* (2002). Around the world and over the centuries, one can appreciate the way new understandings of God and new visions of God's mission spring up and flourish each time the gospel takes shape in a new place and a new culture. The hearers of the gospel themselves are also agents of mission theology. Yale missiologist Lammin Sanneh has emphasized the role of the hearers in adapting and adopting the infinitely translatable gospel in relation to the receptors' cultures and worldviews.[14]

CONCLUSION

We have briefly surveyed five agents who do mission theology. In doing so, we have begun to understand that MT is a verb, not a noun. It is something we *do*, not something we *have*. As I have learned from many Latin American theologians, we *do* theology in the midst of life and ministry. This activity is broader, deeper, more pervasive, and more thoroughly transformational than merely stating a set of propositions that we hope folks will accept. This is also the case with MT. As Hendrikus Berkhof said it, in doing theology—and thus also mission theology—we "seek to love God also, and particularly, with [the] mind and thus grow in fellowship with [God]" (H. Berkhof 1985, 14).

Over time, all of God's people are called to do MT in the power of the Holy Spirit. The more God's people share their biblically grounded and Holy Spirit-inspired discoveries with each other—across languages and across cultures—the broader and deeper our understanding of, and participation in, God's mission in a lost and hurting world, so loved by God, may become. In the next two chapters, I will describe what constitutes mission theology. Following that, the chapters in the rest of the book are offered as examples, as a variety of illustrations, of how we may do mission theology today.

---

14. See, e.g., L. Sanneh 1989 and his subsequent publications.

CHAPTER 2
WHAT IS MISSION THEOLOGY?

This chapter was originally published as Charles Van Engen, "Mission, Theology of," in William Dyrness and Veli-Matt i Kärkkäinen, eds., *Global Dictionary of Theology*. Downers Grove: IVP, 2008, 550–62. Adapted and used by permission.

THESIS

During the past fifty years, Christian thinkers have been reexamining the theological presuppositions that underlie the mission enterprise. The discipline that has learned how to reflect biblically, theologically, philosophically, and missionally on these presuppositions is known as mission theology. In this chapter I will describe what mission theology is and then proceed to examine seven characteristics of mission theology: it is multidisciplinary, integrative, biblical, praxeological, definitional, analytical, and truthful.

INTRODUCTION

Prior to the 1960s, a number of important scholars influenced Christian missionary reflection on the theological issues impacting mission practice. These included folks like Gisbertus Voetius (1589–1676), Gustaf Warneck (1834–1910), Martin Kähler (1835–1912), Josef Schmidlin (1876–1944), Karl Barth (1886–1968), Karl Hartenstein (1894–1952), Helen Barrett Montgomery (1861–1934), Roland Allen (1868–1947), Hendrik Kraemer (1888–1965), Johan H. Bavinck (1895–1964), Walter Freytag (1899–1959), W.A. Visser t' Hooft (1900–1985), Max Warren (1904–1977), Bengt Sundkler (1910–1964), Carl Henry (1913–2003), Harold Lindsell (1913–1998), and John Stott (1921–2011). Mission theology as a subdiscipline of missiology with its own parameters, methodologies, scholars, and foci began in the early 1960s through the work of Gerald H. Anderson, who compiled a collection of essays into what I consider to be the first primary text of the discipline entitled, *The Theology of Christian Mission* (Anderson 1961).

Ten years later, in *The Concise Dictionary of the Christian Mission*, Gerald Anderson defined what he called then the theology of mission as, "concerned with the basic presuppositions and underlying principles which determine, from the standpoint of Christian faith, the motives, message, methods, strategy and goals of the Christian world mission." Anderson considered there were

> three points [that were] especially important for understanding contemporary theology of mission: "The Basis: The source of mission is the triune God who is himself a missionary. . . . The Scope: In this "post-Constantinian" age of church history, mission is no longer understood as outreach beyond Christendom, but rather as "the common witness of the whole church, bringing the whole gospel to the whole world"[15] . . . The Task:

---

15. In this article in the *Concise Dictionary of the Christian Mission,* Anderson attributed this phrase to the 1963 gathering of the Commission on World Mission and Evangelism of the World Council of Churches (CWME-WCC) in Mexico City. Since the 1989 conference in Manila, the Lausanne Movement has made extensive use of this phrase, drawing inspiration from it and including it in the planning and emphases of the Lausanne III conference in Cape Town, South Africa in 2010. The Manila Manifesto concluded with these words. "Our manifesto at Manila is that the whole church is called to take the whole gospel to the whole world, proclaiming Christ until he comes, with all necessary urgency, unity, and sacrifice. (Luke 2:1–7; Mark 13:26, 27; Mark 13:32–37; Acts 1:8; Matt 24:14; Matt 28:20)." (www .lausanne.org/content/manifesto/the-manila-manifesto; downloaded Oct 3, 2016. Website inactive.) The evangelical mission movement has seemed to ignore the fact that the phrase was originally created in World Council of Churches (WCC) circles long before the Lausanne Movement began to use it.

In fact, with reference to mission and the unity of the Church, the phrase appears to have first been expressed by the Central Committee of the World Council of Churches in Rolle, Switzerland in 1951. (See John A . Mackay, *Ecumenics: The Science of the Church Universal,* N.J.: Prentice-Hall, 1964, 13–14.). It subsequently appeared in numerous WCC publications and documents during the 1960's. See, e.g., W. A . Visser 't Hooft, ed., *The New Delhi Report: The Third Assembly of the World Council of Churches 1961,* N.Y.: Association Press,1962, 85–86; J. C. Hoekendijk, *De Kerk Binenste Buiten,* W. Ten Have N.V.: Amsterdam, 1964. *The Church Inside Out,* Isaac C. Rottenberg, translator to English, Philadelphia: Westminster Press, 1966, 108–109; Ronald K. Orchard, ed., *Witness in Six Continents: Records of the Meeting of the Commission on World Mission and Evangelism of the World Council of Churches held in Mexico City, December 8th to 19th, 1963.* London: Edinburgh House, 1964, 173–75; See also Charles Van Engen, *The Growth of the True Church: An Analysis of the Ecclesiology of Church Growth Theory,* Amsterdam: Rodopi, 1981, 379–85. See also John A. Mackay, *The Latin American Church and the Ecumenical Movement.* N.Y.: NCCC, 1963,13, 16 and David Bosch, *Witness to the World,* London: Marshall, Morgan and

Evangelization is humanization.... Through witness and service to humanity, assisting them in struggles for justice, peace and dignity, Christians share in God's mission of restoring men and women to their true, God-intended nature." (Neill, Anderson, and Goodwin 1971, 594)

Mission theology is simultaneously missiological action-in-reflection and theological reflection-in-action. In 2007, InterVarsity Press published the *Dictionary of Mission Theology*, edited by John Corrie. Corrie explained the purpose of the dictionary.

In recent years, the integral nature of the relationship between theology and mission has been increasingly recognized.... It is acknowledged that missiology should not be seen merely as an outpost of theological investigation, compartmentalized in the curriculum and tacked on alongside biblical theology, hermeneutics, ecclesiology, and so on. It is rather that all theology is intrinsically missiological since it concerns the God of mission and the mission of God. This means that all theological categories are inherently missiological and all missionary categories are profoundly theological. (Corrie 2007, xv)

"Theology of Mission," writes Andrew Kirk, "has the task of keeping under review and validating best practice in all areas of missionary obedience." (Kirk 1999, 21)

MISSION THEOLOGY IS MULTIDISCIPLINARY

Mission theology is complex because its object of study and reflection is the entire field of missiology which itself is a multi- and interdisciplinary enterprise. For the sake of brevity, in this section I will offer a series of short propositions that describe the way mission theology interfaces with missiology as a multidisciplinary endeavor.

Scott, 1980, 178–81,187–95 for an informative, brief description of the broader missiological issues surrounding the use of the "whole church taking the whole gospel to the whole world" phraseology. See also Lausanne Committee for World Evangelization,*The Manila Manifesto*. Pasadena: LCWE, 1989; J. D. Douglas, *Proclaim Christ Until He Comes: Calling the Whole Church to Take the Whole Gospel to the Whole World*, Minneapolis: World Wide Publ., 1990; Van Engen, *Mission on the Way: Issues in Mission Theology*, Grand Rapids: Baker, 1996, 150.

A. Missiology is a unified whole. It is a discipline in its own right, centered in Jesus Christ and his mission. As the Church participates in the mission of Jesus Christ, it participates in God's mission in God's world, in the power of the Holy Spirit.

B. While missiology is known to be a unified discipline, it is a multidisciplinary field. Missiology draws from many skills, cognate disciplines, and bodies of literature. There is a long list of cognate disciplines from which missiology draws to describe, understand, analyze, and prescribe the complex nature of mission. Missiology draws from all the traditional areas of theological studies (biblical studies, theology, history, ministry, and so forth) to understand God's intention in mission, examines the historical and present theories and practices of the church's participation in God's mission, and utilizes all the social sciences at its disposal to understand the contexts in which the church's mission occurs.

C. Mission theology helps us clarify our proximity or distance from the center, Jesus Christ. It asks us whether there is a point beyond which the diverse cognate disciplines may no longer be helpful or biblical.

D. Mission theology helps us reflect on the center that integrates our missiology. Missiologists have differed concerning the integrating idea they have chosen to use as the center of their missiology. Examples of such integrating ideas would include Gisbertus Voetius (the conversion of the heathen, the planting of the church, and the glory of God); William Carey (the Great Commission drawn from Matt 28:18–20); Pietism (the lostness of humanity); Orthodox missiology (the praise of God); Vatican II (the people of God); Donald McGavran (make disciples of *matheteusatepanta ta ethne*); David Bosch (God of history, God of compassion, God of transformation); Arthur Glasser (the kingdom of God); the World Council of Churches at Uppsala, 1968 (humanization); along with concepts like "the pain of God," "the cross," "bearing witness in six continents," "ecumenical unity," "the covenant," "liberation," and so forth.

E. Mission theology helps us interrelate who we are, what we know, and what we do in mission. It helps us bring together our faith relationship with Jesus Christ, God's presence, the Church's theological reflection throughout the centuries, a constantly new reading of Scripture, our hermeneutics of our contexts, and our understanding of the ultimate purpose and meaning of the Church in relation to missiology.

F. Mission theology helps us move continually between the center and the outer limits of the multiple cognate disciplines of missiology. It leads us to constantly seek integration, deepened understanding, and mutual enrichment of the various disciplines.

G. Mission theology serves to question, clarify, integrate, and expand the presuppositions of the various cognate disciplines of missiology. As such, mission theology is a subdiscipline in its own right that fulfills its function only as it interacts with all of the other subdisciplines of missiology.

MISSION THEOLOGY IS INTEGRATIVE

Mission theology seeks to bring together four sources of data or domains from which the mission theologian draws understanding: the Bible, the church, the context, and the unique personal pilgrimage of the human agents of God's mission. Over the past three decades, there has been a significant consensus in mission theology on the need to integrate three of those domains in a dynamic, interrelated whole: *Word* (the primacy of the Bible in all mission theology), *church* (the primary agent of God's mission in the world), and *world* (the impact of culture, socioeconomics, political realities, and all other arenas of human life in the reality of a given context). Some would call this the interaction of text, context and faith community. The tripartite structure of these three (Word, world, church) constitutes a basic framework of the missiology followed and taught by a significant number of mission thinkers and theologians of the past several decades. These include, for example, Eugene Nida, Louis Luzbetak, José Miguez-Bonino, Shoki Coe, Harvie Conn, Arthur Glasser, Charles Kraft, Paul Hiebert, Robert Schreiter, C. René Padilla, Mark Lau Branson, Alan R. Tippett, David Hesselgrave, Lamin Sanneh, Charles Van Engen, William Dyrness, and Stephen Bevans, among others.[16]

---

16. See, e.g., Steven Bevans, *Models of Contextual Theology.* Maryknoll: Orbis, 1992; reprinted and expanded 2002; Jose Miguez-Bonino, *Doing Theology in a Revolutionary Situation.* Philadelphia: Fortress, 1975; Branson, Mark and Rene Padilla, eds., *Conflict and Contexts: Hermeneutics in the Americas.* Grand Rapids: Eerdmans, 1986; Shoki Coe, "Contextualizing Theology" in *Mission Trends No. 3,* Gerald Anderson and Thomas Stransky, eds., Grand Rapids: Eerdmans, 1976; Harvie Conn, "Contextualization: A New Dimension for Cross-Cultural Hermeneutic" *Evangelical Missions Quarterly* XIV: 1 (January, 1978) 39–46; Harvie Conn, *Eternal Word and Changing Worlds: Theology, Anthropology and Mission in Trialogue.* Grand Rapids: Zondervan, 1984; Harvie Conn. "A Contextual Theology of Mission for the City," in *The Good News of the Kingdom,* Charles Van Engen, Dean Gilliland, and Paul Pierson, eds., Maryknoll: Orbis, 1993, 96–106; Harvie Conn, "Urban Mission," in *Toward the 21st Century in Christian Mission,* James Phillips and Robert Coote, eds., Grand Rapids: Eerdmans, 1993, 318–37; Robert Coote and John Stott, eds., *Down to Earth: Studies in Christianity and Culture,* Grand Rapids: Eerdmans, 1980; William A . Dyrness, *Learning About Theology from the Third World,* Grand Rapids: Zondervan, 1990; Bruce Fleming, *The Contextualization of*

Recently, I began to understand that I was missing a fourth domain or arena that is important for constructing a full-orbed mission theology. I had neglected to include the arena of the personal pilgrimage of the human beings who are the agents of God's mission. Once I began working with all four domains in the construction of my mission theology I had several of my Wesleyan students point out to me that what I was doing looked to them to be similar to what is popularly known as the Wesleyan quadrilateral, with "context" replacing the quadrilateral's emphasis on "reason." Thus a four-domain approach to mission theology would include (1) the Bible as the exclusive source text of God's mission; (2) the church's

---

Theology, Pasadena: WCL, 1980; Dean S. Gilliland, "New Testament Contextualization: Continuity and Particularity in Paul's Theology, in Dean Gilliland, ed., *The Word Among Us: Contextualizing Theology for Mission Today,* Waco: Word, 1989, 52–73; Arthur Glasser, "Help from an Unexpected Quarter or, The Old Testament and Contextualization," *Missiology* VII: 4 (Oct., 1979), 401–10; Stanley J. Grenz, *Revisioning Theology: A Fresh Agenda for the 21st Century,* Downers Grove: IVP, 1993, 93; David Hesselgrave and Edward Rommen, *Contextualization: Meanings, Methods, and Models,* Grand Rapids: Baker, 1989; Paul Hiebert, "Conversion, Culture and Cognitive Categories," *Gospel in Context* I.3 (July, 1978), 24–29; Paul Hiebert, "Critical Contextualization," *International Bulletin of Missionary Research* XI: 3 (July, 1987) 104–11; Paul Hiebert, "Evangelism, Church, and Kingdom," in *The Good News of the Kingdom.* Charles Van Engen, Dean Gilliland and Paul Pierson, eds., Maryknoll: Orbis, 1993, 153–61; Donald Jacobs, "Contextualization in Mission," in *Toward the 21st Century in Christian Mission,* James Phillips, and Robert Coote, eds., *Toward the 21st Century in Christian Mission,* G.R.: Eerdmans. 1993, 235–44; Charles Kraft, *Christianity in Culture: A Study in Dynamic Biblical Theologizing in Cross-Cultural Perspective,* Maryknoll: Orbis, 1979; Charles Kraft, *Communication Theory for Christian Witness,* Maryknoll, NY: Orbis, 1991; Charles Kraft and Tom Wisely, eds., *Readings in Dynamic Indigeneity,* Pasadena: WCL, 1979; Louis Luzbetak, *The Church and Cultures,* Maryknoll: Orbis, 1988; Eugene Nida, *Message and Mission,* N.Y.: Harper, 1960; Lamin Sanneh, *Translating the Message: The Missionary Impact on Culture,* Marykoll: Orbis, 1989; Robert Schreiter, *Constructing Local Theologies,* Maryknoll: Orbis, 1985; Daniel Shaw, *Transculturation: The Cultural Factor in Translation and Other Communication Tasks,* Pasadena: WCL, 1988; Wilbert Shenk, eds., *The Transfiguration of Mission: Biblical, Theological & Historical Foundations,* Scottdale: Herald, 1993, 153–77; Tite Tiénou, "Forming Indigenous Theologies," in: James M. Phillips and Robert T. Coote, eds., *Toward the Twenty-First Century in Christian Mission.* Grand Rapids: Eerdmans, 1993, 249–50; Alan Tippett, *Introduction to Missiology,* Pasadena: WCL, 1987; Charles Van Engen, *God's Missionary People.* Grand Rapids: Baker, 1991; Charles Van Engen, Dean S. Gilliland, and Paul Pierson, eds., *The Good News of the Kingdom,* Maryknoll: Orbis, 1993.

Leonardo Boff, Orlando Costas, David Bosch, Johannes Verkuyl, John V. Taylor, Donald McGavran, Max Warren, Lesslie Newbigin, James Scherer, Gerald Anderson, Carl Braaten, Howard Snyder, Jürgen Moltmann, among others, also utilize a three-arena approach in their theology and missiology, though they may not speak of all three at once in the same place.

theological and missiological reflection about God's mission over time; (
sonal, spiritual, and experiential pilgrimage of the human agents of Goc
and (4) the cultural context as the stage where the drama of God's mission takes
place (see Figure 2 below). Each domain is a sphere of knowledge, influence, activity
and relationships. The overlap of the various domains with one another represents
an increased level of integration and continuity between them. Conflicting and
sometimes contradictory views of God's mission may become evident when one
compares the perspectives of the various domains. In the following paragraphs I
will briefly outline the content of each of these four domains.

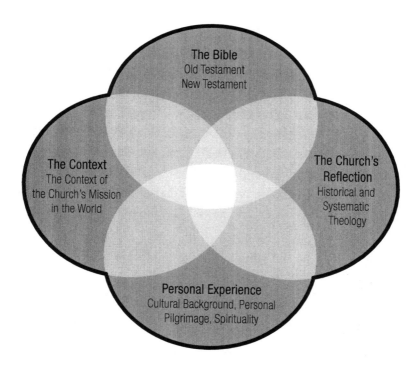

FIGURE 2: Integration of Four Domains of Mission Theology

A. The Bible

The exclusive source text for the process of theologizing in mission is the Bible. The
Bible is the unequaled and essential missionary manual of the church's mission. It
is the revelation of the missionary God. The Bible tells of the inbreaking of God
throughout human history. The Bible informs us about the mission of God (the *missio*

Dei) and provides the missiological examples to follow Jesus Christ in mission. The Bible informs, shapes, and critiques the other three domains. A number of helpful works that deal with reading the Bible through a missiological lens and allowing the Bible to transform the way we understand mission would include, for example, the titles found in the bibliography at the end of this book under names such as Helen Barrett Montgomery, Gerald Anderson, D. Bosch, Charles Van Engen, C. René Padilla, Christopher Wright, Walter Kaiser, Johannes Nissen, Timóteo Carriker, James Chukwuma Okoye, Kenneth Gnanakan, Andreas J. Köstenberger and Peter T. O'Brien, Rob Gallagher and Paul Hertig, John Piper, Sarita Gallagher, Shawn Redford, Richard Bauckham, Michael W. Goheen, and Scott Sunquist.

B. The church's reflection

The church's theological and missiological thinking has impacted the lenses (or hermeneutical approaches) that have been used throughout history to understand the Bible, theology, and the mission of the church. Historical theology and systematic theology are examples of lenses used over time to read Scripture, reflect theologically, and view mission from a particular viewpoint, often based on Western assumptions and methodologies. Churches and Christians in the majority world of Africa, Asia, and Latin America are examining critically the theology received from the West, studying how it does or does not interface with their reality and how it has impacted their understanding of God's mission in their contexts. This domain also includes the history of the church's theological reflection on mission and the history of mission conferences and gatherings as they have sought to articulate and influence the church's understanding of God's mission over time.

Thus you will find some scholars dealing with the history of theology of mission. See, for example, Rodger Bassham (1979); David Bosch (1980, 1991); James Scherer (1987, 1993a, 1993b); Arthur Glasser (1985); James Stamoolis (1987); Beth Snodderly and A. Scott Moreau, editors (2011); and Scott Sunquist (2013) among others. These mission theologians are concerned about the effects that mission theology—the way Christians have thought about mission—has had upon mission activity in particular contexts. They examine the various pronouncements made by church and mission gatherings (Roman Catholic, orthodox, ecumenical, evangelical, pentecostal, and charismatic) and ask questions about the results of these for missional action. The documents resulting from these discussions are part of the discipline of mission theology.

C. Personal experience

Those who approach the Bible and examine the story of God's mission bring their own set of cultural, personal and individual strengths, weaknesses, experiences, and spiritual pilgrimage. These affect the way in which scripture and mission is understood and perceived—and the ways in which God's mission is incarnated through the life of each person. The Bible, the church, the context, and God's mission are all understood through personal ethnohermeneutical, existential, and experiential lenses. Each person's particular spiritual gifts, natural abilities, experiences, knowledge, and personality create a unique mix. God's mission is carried out through the life of particular persons in unique ways that cannot, and should not, be reproduced or repeated (Rom 12; Eph 4; 1 Cor 12). The extensive literature on leadership and mission produced during the past forty years contributes to our understanding of this domain. The teaching and writings of J. Robert Clinton are especially helpful in this regard.

D. The context

Each unique context shapes the understanding of mission and the process of theologizing in mission. All mission action and reflection need to be contextually appropriate. Thus all relevant tools of the social sciences need to be brought to bear upon the way mission theologians research their contexts. All theologies are local theologies (Schreiter 1985), and the impact of the context on one's theological understanding cannot be underestimated. This domain of mission theology will be developed and explained more completely in subsequent chapters in this book and do not need to belabored here.

E. Integration of the four domains

When mission happens, all the various cognate disciplines are occurring simultaneously. Mission theologians must study mission not from the point of view of abstracted and separated parts, but from an integrative perspective that attempts to see the whole, while at the same time taking into consideration the unique contribution of each of the four domains.

An overarching theme that unites all four of the domains is the centrality of Jesus Christ. The mission about which we theologize is God's mission. It is not owned, controlled, or determined by the church or by individual Christians or Christian organizations. God's mission is supremely given in Jesus Christ. Jesus Christ must, therefore, be at the center of all the domains of a contextually appropriate mission theology. The church's mission is the mission of Jesus Christ. The disciples of Jesus Christ participate in the *missio Christi*. Their authority, their mandate, their methods, and their goals in mission are influenced by their understanding of Jesus Christ (their Christologies), illumined by the Holy Spirit who is sent by the Father and the Son. Jesus told his disciples, "As the Father has sent me, so I send you" (John 20:21; cf. John 17:18).

Because of the complexity of mission theology, mission theologians have found it helpful to focus on a specific integrating idea in particular contexts at specific times. The integrating idea serves as the hub through which to approach a rereading of Scripture, an analysis of the church's thinking, an appreciation of the persons as agents of God's mission, and the unique contextual issues impacting God's mission at a particular time and place. This integrating theme is selected on the basis of being contextually appropriate and significant, biblically relevant and fruitful, and missionally active and transformational. The integrating idea serves to focus the mission theologian's understanding of mission centered in Jesus Christ as the only true Center of all the church's missional action and reflection, but also applied in such a way as to interface with the mission theologian's reading of all four domains. The integrating idea expresses the interconnecting paradigm, the central theme, perception, and thinking pattern that draws from the four domains and combines them into a cohesive whole, a more or less integrated concept of mission in a specific local setting at a particular time.

In 1987, the Association of Professors of Mission discussed at length what missiology is, and how it does its reflection. In a subsection dealing with theology of mission, it was said that,

> The mission theologian does biblical and systematic theology differently from the biblical scholar or dogmatician . . . The mission theologian is in search of the "habitus," the way of perceiving, the intellectual understanding coupled with spiritual insight and wisdom, [that lead] to seeing the signs of the presence and movement of God in history. . . . Such a search for the "why" of mission forces the mission theologian to seek to articulate the vital integrative center of mission today. . . . Each formulation of the "center" has radical implications for each of the cognate disciplines of the social sciences, the study of religions, and church history in the way they are corrected and shaped theologically. Each formulation supports or calls

into question different aspects of all the other disciplines. . . . The center, therefore, serves as both theological content and theological process as a disciplined reflection on God's mission in human contexts. The role of the theologian of mission is therefore to articulate and guard the center, while at the same time to spell out integratively the implications of the center for all the other cognate disciplines. (Van Engen 1987, 524–25)

MISSION THEOLOGY IS BIBLICAL

Because of its commitment to remain faithful to God's missional intentions, mission theology shows a most fundamental concern over the relation of the Bible to mission, attempting to allow Scripture not only to provide the foundational motivations for mission, but also to question, shape, guide, and evaluate the missionary enterprise. One of the most basic aspects of mission theology has to do with the relation of the Bible to mission theory and practice.

Determining the scriptural understanding of mission is not as simple as we might think. According to David Bosch,

> We usually assume far too easily that we can employ the Bible as a kind of objective arbitrator in the case of theological differences, not realizing that [all] of us approach the Bible with (our) own set of preconceived ideas about what it says . . . This means that it is of little avail to embark upon a discussion of the biblical foundations of mission unless we have first clarified some of the hermeneutical principles involved" (Bosch 1978, 33).

In a similar vein, Senior and Stuhlmueller end their work on *The Biblical Foundations of Mission* stating that they did not mean to,

> imply that the biblical style of mission is absolutely normative for mission today. There is no definite biblical recipe for proclaiming the Word of God. . . . Nevertheless there is a value in reflecting on the biblical patterns of evangelization (Senior and Stuhlmueller 1983, 332).

For too long, both biblical scholars and mission practitioners have contributed to the confusion by ignoring each other. Lesslie Newbigin (1986, 1989) helped us to see that Western culture's preoccupation with the origin of the created order and human civilization brought with it a degree of blindness to questions of purpose, design, and intention. To a large extent biblical scholars have followed this same path in their examination of the biblical text in relation to God's mission. With notable exceptions, their analysis of Scripture has seldom asked the missiological questions regarding God's intentions and purpose.

On the other hand, the activist practitioners of mission have too easily super-imposed their particular agendas on Scripture, or ignored the Bible altogether. Thus Arthur Glasser called for a deeper missiological reflection on the biblical message. "All Scripture," he said,

> makes its contribution in one way or another to our understand-ing of mission. . . . In our day evangelicals are finding that the biblical base for mission is far broader and more complex than any previous generation of missiologists appears to have envi-sioned. . . . In our day there is a growing impatience with all individualistic and pragmatic approaches to the missionary task that arise out of a prooftext use of Scripture, despite their pop-ularity among the present generation of activistic evangelicals. (Glasser 1992, 26–27)[17]

Johannes Verkuyl advocated a change in hermeneutical approach. "In the past," he wrote,

> the usual method was to pull a series of prooftexts out of the Old and New Testaments and then to consider the task accom-plished. But more recently biblical scholars have taught us the importance of reading these texts in context and paying due regard to the various nuances. . . . One must consider the very structure of the whole biblical message (Verkuyl 1978, 90).

The basic contours of a broader missiological hermeneutic were explored thirty years ago in Part I of *The Theology of the Christian Mission*, edited by Gerald Anderson (1961, 17–94). Here G. Ernest Wright, Johannes Blauw, Oscar Cull-mann, Karl Barth, Donald Miller, and F. N. Davey surveyed a wide range of

---

17. See also Bosch (1980, 42–49); Verkuyl (1978, 89–100); and Scherer (1987, 243), as well as the authors mentioned earlier in this chapter who have written regarding "Bible and mission."

biblical material, deriving from the Bible what the Church's mission ought to be. At about the same time, the missiological reflection of the Second Vatican Council on the role of Scripture in mission thinking (for example, in *Lumen Gentium* and *Ad Gentes Divinitus*) closely followed this model as well (see Flannery 1975, 350–440, 813–62). Subsequent papal encyclicals like *Evangelii Nuntiandi* and *Redemptoris Missio* appealed to Scripture, though this appeal at times appeared like elaborate prooftexting to buttress predetermined ecclesiastical agendas (Bevans 1993).[18]

Thus over the last several decades a significant global consensus has emerged with regard to the Bible and mission. As David Bosch explains it,

> Our conclusion is that both Old and New Testaments are permeated with the idea of mission. . . . [But] not everything we call mission is indeed mission. . . . It is the perennial temptation of the Church to become (a club of religious folklore). . . . The only remedy for this mortal danger lies in (the Church) challenging herself unceasingly with the true biblical foundation of mission (1978, 18–19).

Traditionally, the Bible has been examined to see how the Bible supports, informs, and critiques mission, what has been called "the Bible basis of mission" (see, for example, Padilla, ed., 1998).[19] However, during the past couple of decades a second equally important question has been explored: How does a missiological reading offer a more complete understanding of the Bible itself, deepening and broadening our hermeneutic of the biblical text? Among those exploring a missional hermeneutic of the Bible are Ken Gnanakan (1989); Timothy Carriker (1992); Johannes Nissen (1999); Walter C. Kaiser (2000); Arthur Glasser (2003); Christopher Wright (2006); and James Chukwuma Okoye (2006).

Mission theology is theological. Most fundamentally, it involves reflection about God. It seeks to understand God's mission, God's intentions and purposes, God's use of human instruments in God's mission, and God's working through God's people in God's world. See, for example, Niles (1962); Vicedom (1965); Taylor (1972); Verkuyl (1978); Stott (1979); and Spindler (1988).

---

18. During the past several years, Pope Francis has sought to address this matter in relation to a number of thorny theological and ecclesiological issues, but that discussion is beyond the scope of this work.

19. Examples of this approach can be seen in, for example, Robert H. Glover 1946; H. H. Rowley 1955; A. de Groot 1966; and George Peters 1972.

Mission theology deals with all the traditional theological themes of systematic theology—but it does so in a way that differs from how systematic theologians have worked down through the centuries. The difference arises from the multidisciplinary missiological orientation of its theologizing. Mission theology is an applied theology. At times, it looks like what some would call pastoral or practical theology, due to this applicational nature. This type of theological reflection focuses specifically on particular issues, those having to do with the mission of the Church in specific contexts. In *Mission as Transformation* Vinay Samuel and Chris Sugden called for "doing theology in Transformation."

"First," they wrote,

> mission is the mother of theology, and theological and biblical reflection arises out of engagement with the context, experience and questions of mission. Second, theology and biblical study is inherently a cross-cultural and intercultural exercise as people from different cultures share their insights on the biblical text. Thirdly, theology is a team (effort), developed as iron sharpens iron wrestling with issues raised by the call to the obedience of faith (Samuel and Sugden 1999, xiii–xiv).

Mission theology draws its incarnational nature from the ministry of Jesus, and always happens in a specific time and place. Neither missiology nor mission theology can be allowed to restrict itself to reflection only, or to merely historically interesting story-telling of mission endeavors in the past. As Johannes Verkuyl stated,

> Missiology may never become a substitute for action and participation. God calls for participants and volunteers in his mission. In part, missiology's goal is to become a 'service station' along the way. If study does not lead to participation, whether at home or abroad, missiology has lost her humble calling . . . Any good missiology is also a *missiologia viatorum*—"pilgrim missiology" (Verkuyl 1978, 6,18).

MISSION THEOLOGY IS PRAXEOLOGICAL

Mission theology must eventually emanate in biblically informed and contextually appropriate missional action. If our mission theology does not emanate in informed action, we are merely a "resounding gong or clanging cymbal" (1 Cor 13:1). The intimate connection of reflection with action is absolutely essential for missiology. At the same time, if our missiological action does not itself transform our reflection, we have held great ideas, but they may be irrelevant or useless, sometimes destructive or counterproductive.

In mission theology, we borrow from sociology, anthropology, psychology, economics, urbanology, the study of the relation of Christian churches to followers of other faiths and religious perspectives, the study of the relation of Church and state, and a host of other cognate disciplines to understand the specific context in which we are doing our reflection. Such contextual analysis offers us a deeper understanding of the particular context in terms of a hermeneutic of the reality in which we are ministering. This in turn helps us hear the cries, see the faces, understand the stories, and respond to the living needs and hopes of the persons who are an integral part of that context.

A part of this contextual analysis today includes the history of the way the church in its mission has interfaced with that context down through history. The attitudes, actions, and events of the Church's mission action and reflection that occurred in a particular context prior to the arrival of the mission theologian will color in profound and surprising ways all present and future missional endeavors.

One of the most helpful ways to interface reflection and action is by way of the process known as "praxis." "Missiology," Orlando Costas wrote,

> is fundamentally a praxeological phenomenon. It is a critical reflection that takes place in the praxis of mission. . . . [It occurs] in the concrete missionary situation, as part of the church's missionary obedience to and participation in God's mission, and is itself actualized in that situation. . . . Its object is always the world, . . . men and women in their multiple life situations . . . In reference to this witnessing action saturated and led by the sovereign, redemptive action of the Holy Spirit, . . . the concept of missionary praxis is used. Missiology arises as part of a witnessing engagement to the gospel in the multiple situations of life (Costas 1976, 8).

The concept of "praxis" helps us understand that not only the reflection, but profoundly the action itself is "theology on the way" that seeks to discover how the church may participate more fully in God's mission in God's world. The action is itself theological and serves to inform the reflection, which in turn interprets, evaluates, critiques, and projects new understanding in transformed action. Thus the interweaving of reflection and action in a constantly spiraling pilgrimage offer a transformation of all aspects of our missiological engagement with our various contexts.

A praxeological approach to mission theology grew out of attempts around the globe to discover new ways to contextualize the gospel in differing cultural contexts. Shoki Coe (1976) from the Phillippines, along with a number of Latin American theologians, were among the first to suggest the contours and methodologies, which they called contextualization. "Contextualization," writes J. Andrew Kirk,

> recognizes the reciprocal influence of culture and socioeco-
> nomic life. In relating gospel to culture, therefore, it tends to
> take a more critical [or prophetic] stance toward culture. The
> concept . . . is intended to be taken seriously as a theological
> method which entails particular ideological commitments to
> transform situations of social injustice, political alienation and
> the abuse of human rights" (Kirk 1999, 91; see also Bosch 1991,
> 420–32).

The impact of contextualization theory on mission theology will be explored in a later chapter in this book.

In Acts 15, Luke highlights this praxeological way of doing mission theology in the way he tells the story of the decision on the part of the Aramaic-speaking church in Jerusalem to allow Gentile believers in Jesus to remain essentially Gentile (with some requested behavioral changes). The theological foundation of this momentous decision was the event of the Holy Spirit's pentecostal outpouring on Cornelius in Acts 10, retold in Acts 11, and referenced two more times by Peter in Acts 15:7–11 and James in Acts 15:13. The point here is that the events themselves, the Holy Spirit's action itself, was the theological basis for this unprecedented decision on the part of the Jerusalem church.

Clearly we are trying to avoid superimposing our own agendas on Scripture. This was a mistake made by liberation theologians from which they did not recover. Rather, what is being sought is a way to bring a new set of questions to the text, questions that might help us see in the Scriptures what we had missed before. David Bosch called this new approach to Scripture "critical hermeneutics" (Bosch 1991, 20–24; see also Bosch 1978 and 1993; see also the works of Paul Hiebert).

Conceptually we are involved here in something that philosophy of science has called "paradigm construction" or "paradigm shift." A paradigm is a conceptual tool used to perceive reality and order that perception in an understandable, explainable, and somewhat predictable pattern. A paradigm consists of the total composite set of values, worldview, priorities, and knowledge that makes a person, a group of persons, or a culture look at reality in a certain way. David Bosch helped us to see paradigm formation as a powerful way to reconceptualize our understanding of God's mission in differing communities, in varying contexts (see Bevans and Schroeder 2004).

Thus we find that mission theology is a continual process of reflection and action leading to renewed reflection leading to renewed action. This involves a movement from the biblical text to the faith community in its context. By focusing our attention on an integrating theme, we encounter new insights as we reread Scripture from the point of view of a contextual hermeneutic. These new insights can then be restated and lived out as biblically informed, contextually appropriate missional action of the faith community in the particularity of time, worldview, and space of each specific context in which God's mission happens. This process will be explained more fully in later chapters of this work.

MISSION THEOLOGY IS DEFINITIONAL

One of the most interesting, significant, yet difficult tasks of mission theology is to assist missiology in defining the terms it uses. Within this enterprise, a central question has to do with how one may define "mission" itself. What is mission? What is not mission? Over the past hundred years a host of differing definitions have been offered. I discuss this in Chapter 4. Among the various Christian traditions there has been a heated debate over an acceptable definition of mission. The smoke continues to rise from the fire of profound disagreements over what is mission.

For the sake of brevity, let me offer my own preliminary definition of mission, by way of illustration.

> God's mission works primarily through the people of God intentionally crossing barriers from the people of God to all peoples of the world and from faith to the absence of faith in settings of nominal Christianity, to proclaim by word and deed the coming of the kingdom of God in Jesus Christ through the Church's participation in God's mission of reconciling people to God, to themselves, to each other, and to the world and gathering them into the Church through repentance and faith in Jesus Christ by

> the work of the Holy Spirit with a view to the transformation of
> the world as a sign of the coming of the kingdom in Jesus Christ.

Various aspects and issues that impact our definition of mission will be developed in later chapters in this book.

MISSION THEOLOGY IS ANALYTICAL

The mission enterprise is complex in both its theory and its practice. It becomes more complex when we begin to examine the host of theological assumptions, meanings, and relations that permeate that practice. For this reason, mission theologians have found it helpful to partition the task into smaller segments. We noticed earlier that Gerald Anderson defined mission in terms of "faith, motives, message, methods, strategy, and goals," along with "basis, scope and task." Jim Stamoolis followed a similar methodology in *Eastern Orthodox Mission Theology Today* (1986, 2001) by organizing his research around questions dealing with "the historical background, the aim, the method, the motives, and the liturgy" of mission as that took place among and through the Eastern Orthodox.

To organize their questions, mission theologians begin with the recognition that mission is most fundamentally *missio Dei*. It is God's mission. Mission derives from God's nature and God's intention. One finds a number of mission theologians reflecting on "God's mission" (*missio dei*). Georg Vicedom brought this to the attention of the world church before and during the Mexico City meeting of the CWME/WCC in 1963. The book he wrote for that congress was published in English in 1965 as *The Mission of God*. H. H. Rosin summarized the history of the term in H. H. Rosin 1972. I will discuss this more at length in a later chapter in this book.

God does not act alone, nor does God's mission occur in a vacuum. Beginning with Noah and Abraham and their families, and continuing to the present day, God's mission has taken place through the instrumentality of humans (*missio hominum*). God's mission has also taken many forms through the endeavors of the diverse social groupings created by the people of God and their surrounding cultures (*missiones ecclesiae*). The *missio Dei* is singular—is pure in its motivation, means and goals—for it derives from the nature of God, but God's decision to use human instruments (*missio hominum*) involves working through fallen human beings who are simultaneously just and sinful. *Missio hominum* is always mixed as to its motivations, means and goals (see Verkuyl 1978, 163–75). In God's grace, God seems to delight in carrying out his mission through the instrumentality of human social groups and social organizations. Thus *missiones ecclesiae* are plural because of the multiplicity of the activities of the churches, the lack of unity of the churches, the mixture of centripetal (gathering) activities with centrifugal (sending, joining, and identifying) activities of the churches, and because their shape is influenced so much by what is going on in the churches, among the Christians, and in the surrounding contexts at the time. Finally, God's mission interacts with, and exerts influence upon, global human civilization (*missio politica oecumenica*—see, e.g., Verkuyl 1978, 394–402). *Missio politica oecumenica* deals with God's concern for the nations and God's interaction through God's people with the civilizations, cultures, politics, and human structures of this world. Christ's kingdom mission always calls into question the kingdoms of this world. From the standpoint of a trinitarian approach to mission theology, we would want to also consider the concepts of *missio Christi* and *missio Spiritu Sancti*. A full-orbed trinitarian mission theology will include reflections on the significance of diverse christologies upon mission theology as well as the impact of pneumatological perspectives on mission theology. In *The Open Secret* (1978) Lesslie Newbigin laid the foundation for a trinitarian approach to mission theology. We are all in his debt.

These are important distinctions. A final one needs to be made. Mission is both *missio futurum* and *missio adventus*. *Missio futurum* has to do with the predictable issues of God's mission as that takes place in human history. Thus *futurum* is the movement into the future that involves the natural and human extrapolation and results of the missions of the churches in the midst of world history. But the story of mission is always incomplete if it stops there. We must also include *missio adventus*. This is the *adventus* of the inbreaking (the advent) of God, of Jesus Christ in the Incarnation, of the Holy Spirit at Pentecost, of the Holy Spirit's mission in and through the Church. God's mission brings unexpected surprises, radical changes, new directions, and at times radical transformation in the midst of human life: personal, social, and structural. God works in the world through both *futurum* and *adventus*. Mission theologians need to be constantly asking about the difference between, and the interrelation of, *futurum* and *adventus*, sorting out their implications for mission theology.

Once we have seen the two ways of organizing our questions in mission theology, we can bring the two types of questions together. I have attempted to do this in Figure 3. I have called this a "Working Grid of Mission Theology."

Foundational Categories of Mission Theory	Missio Dei	Missio Hominum	Missiones Ecclesiarum	Missio Politica Oecumenica	Missio Christi	Missio Espiritu Sancti	Missio Futurum / Adventus
God's Missional Action	*The Mission of God*	*Missional Use of Human Agents*	*Missions Through the Corporate People of God*	*Missional Action in Global Civilization*	*Messianic Mission Through Jesus Christ*	*Mission Through the Holy Spirit*	*Kingdom Mission in the Predictable Future and Surprising Advent*
The Context of Mission							
The Agents of Mission							
The Motives of Mission							
The Means of Mission							
The Methods of Mission							
The Goals of Mission							
The Results of Mission							
Hope/Utopia of Mission							
Prayer in Mission							
Spiritual Power in Mission							
Structures for Mission							
Partnerships in Mission							
Presence, Proclamation, Persuasion, Incorporation							

FIGURE 3: A Working Grid of Mission Theology

In the grid, I have sought to represent in a diagrammatic form the interaction of the various theological categories of mission theory with several illustrative aspects of missional action. The interfacing of the mission categories (placed along the horizontal axis) with the aspects of missional action (placed along the vertical axis) yields a host of new questions for mission theology. Each square in the grid constitutes a specific question for appropriate mission theology in a local context.

Notice in the grid below that each horizontal level (for example in terms of "motivation for mission"), provides at least seven different types of questions to be asked: God's motivation, human motivation, the motivations of the churches and mission organizations, the motivations in mission in relation to global civilization, Christological motivations for mission, the role of the Holy Spirit in motivating the Church in mission, and motivation in terms of *futurum* as distinguished from *adventus*. Notice, also, that each vertical column, for example if we ask about *missio Dei*, informs the motivation, means, agents, goals, etc. of mission.

Clearly no one missiologist can do all that is represented by this grid. That is not necessary. Only one or two of the many boxes may in fact be appropriate to investigate in a particular context, at a particular moment, and in relation to specific actions of mission. However, I have been discovering that the grid can offer us both (1) simplicity of analysis by differentiating the questions and (2) the complexity of the whole enterprise in terms of the entire grid. My students and I have begun to see that almost every master's thesis or doctoral dissertation in missiology naturally falls into one or two of the squares. Yet, when the person begins to reflect in terms of mission theology as related to the question of that square, the investigation leads naturally to ask about all the other issues represented by the larger grid.

An example of this kind of analysis may be seen in the extended discussions that occurred in the late 1960s in the World Council of Churches and centered on whether they should use "mission" or "missions" in the title of the *International Review of Mission(s)*. That discussion had to do with the distinction between God's mission which is one, and the enterprises of the churches seen as "missions" that are many. So in its April 1969 issue, the oldest Protestant missiological journal in the world dropped the "s" in its name to become *The International Review of Mission*. In that issue's "Editorial," William Crane wrote,

> Missions in the plural have a certain justification in the diplo-
> matic, political, and economic spheres of international relations
> where their nature, scope, and authority are defined by the

interests of both those who initiate and those who receive them.
But the mission of the Church is singular in that it issues from
the One Triune God and His intention for the salvation of all
[human beings]. His commission to the Church is one, even
though the ministries given to the Church for this mission, and
the given responses of particular churches in particular situations to the commission, are manifold. . . . The various studies
and programmes initiated by the Division of World Mission and
Evangelism in the past few years since integration into the life
of the World Council of Churches, also reflect this concern for
the one mission of the Church in six continents rather than the
traditional concern for missions from three continents to the
other three. (Crane 1969)

MISSION THEOLOGY SEEKS TO BE TRUTHFUL

This brings us to the seventh characteristic of the mission theology. In the social
sciences, as also in all scholarly enterprises, one of the most important questions
has to do with the basis on which one can determine the validity and reliability of
the results of that discipline's investigation.

In the social sciences that have heavily impacted missiology, normally the
concept of validity has to do with the question, "How can we be sure that we
are collecting the right data in the right way?" The concept of reliability is normally understood to address the question, "How can we be sure that if the same
approach were taken again the same data would be discovered?"

However, in mission theology these questions are not the right ones. The
mission theologian is neither concerned about the quality of the empirical data nor
the repeatability of a process that may yield identical results. In fact, the opposite is
true. Given the fact that the mission theologian studies God's mission, the data will
always be new (and will sometimes call into question earlier data), and the results
will often be surprising and different. Repeatability is not a value here. Mission
theology, therefore, must seek another way to recognize acceptable research. The
question of reliability must be transformed into one of *trust*, and the matter of
validity must be seen as one of *truth*. Thus the methodological questions facing the
mission theologian are the following:

A. Trust

- Did the researcher read the right people, the trusted authors and sources?
- Did the researcher read widely enough in a breadth of perspectives on the issue?
- Did the researcher read other viewpoints correctly?
- Did the research understand what was read?
- Are there internal contradictions either in the use and understanding of the authors or in their application of the issue at hand?

B. Truth

- Is there adequate biblical support for the statements being affirmed?
- Is there an appropriate continuity/discontinuity of the researcher's statements with theological affirmations made by other thinkers down through the history of the church?
- Where contradictions or qualifications of thought arise, does the mission theologian's work adequately support the particular theological directions being advocated in the study?
- Are the dialectical tensions and/or seeming contradictions allowed to stand (as they should), given what we know and do not know of the mystery of God's revealed hiddenness as that impacts our understanding of *missio Dei*?

These methodological questions lead to specific criteria of acceptability in mission theology's research, as these interface with missiology as a multidisciplinary discipline.

C. Criteria of acceptability

- Revelatory—It is grounded in Scripture.
- Coherent—It holds together, is built around an integrating idea.
- Consistent—It has no insurmountable glaring contradictions, and is consistent with other truths known about God, God's mission, and God's revealed will.
- Simple—It has been reduced to the most basic components related to God's mission in terms of the specific issues at hand.
- Supportable—It is logically, historically, experimentally, and praxeologically affirmed and supported.

- Outside agreement—Are there other significant thinkers, theological communities and/or traditions that lend support to the thesis being offered?
- Contextual—Does it interface appropriately with the context?
- Doable—Can the concepts be translated into missional action that in turn is consistent with the motivations and goals of the mission theology being developed?
- Transformational—Would the carrying out of the proposed missional action issue in appropriate changes in the status quo that reflect biblical elements of the *missio Dei*?
- Demonstrating appropriate consequences—Are the results of translating the concepts into missional action consistent with the thrust of the concepts themselves and with the nature and mission of God as revealed in Scripture?

CONCLUSION

Mission theology is prescriptive as well as descriptive. It is synthetic (bringing about synthesis) and integrational. It searches for trustworthy and true perceptions concerning the Church's mission based on biblical and theological reflection, seeks to interface with the appropriate missional action, and creates a new set of values and priorities that reflect as clearly as possible the ways in which the Church may participate in God's mission in specific contexts at particular times. When mission theology is abstracted from mission practice it seems strange and can be too far removed from the concrete places and specific people that are at the heart of God's mission. Mission theology is at its best when it is intimately involved in the heart, head, and hand (being, knowing, and doing) of the Church's mission in the world. Mission theology is a personal, corporate, committed, profoundly transformational search for always new and more profound understanding of the ways in which the people of God may participate more faithfully in God's mission in a lost and broken world so loved by God.

CHAPTER 3
DOING MISSION THEOLOGY IN A GLOBALIZING WORLD

This chapter was originally published in a book honoring Paul Hiebert: Van Engen, "The Glocal Church: Locality and Catholicity in a Globalizing World," in Craig Ott and Harold Netland, eds. *Globalizing Theology: Belief and Practice in an Era of World Christianity*. G. R. Baker, 2006, 157–79. Used by permission.

THESIS

The thesis of this chapter is that a healthy local congregation of disciples of Jesus lives out its catholicity by intentionally and actively participating in Christ's mission as a **glocal** *entity. It is active simultaneously in global and local mission, global and local world evangelization, that dynamically fosters the glocal interaction between the global and the local. The world church is always local; the local church is always global. A healthy local congregation in the twenty-first century is globally connected and locally involved. In this chapter, I have chosen to use the word "glocal" as a way to signal a kind of simultaneity in the nature of the Church of Jesus Christ that is at once global and local in a number of senses. I will suggest that in the twenty-first century the Church of Jesus Christ needs to become what it is: glocal in its essence, glocal in its theologizing and glocal in its missional calling. I will draw from the way the internet functions to illustrate the glocal nature of the Church.*

INTRODUCTION

During the past twenty years or so, the word *glocal* has been one of several new words coined to express a new interweaving of the global and the local.[20] When I

---

20. In a helpful footnote, James N. Rosenau, University Professor of International Affairs at George Washington University, gave us an excellent summary of similar terms, including the term *glocal*, that seek to describe the various ways in which the global and local are interconnected. He prefers the word "fragmegration," . . . "Intended to suggest the pervasive interaction between fragmenting and integrating dynamics unfolding at every level of community . . . Other single-word labels designed to suggest the contradictory tensions

began to consider the concept of glocal as appropriately describing the nature of the Church in the twenty-first century, I decided to search for the term in Google. Much to my surprise I was offered 347 entries (mostly books) in which the term *glocal* appears. These represent a wide-ranging diversity of areas of investigation including

- education;
- organizational management;
- advertising and economics;
- communication, cinema and computers;
- globalization studies as such;
- human rights and social work;
- the internet
- banking—e.g., VISA
- religion; and
- missions

A primary arena of interest in the interweaving interaction between the global and the local seems to be in the study of cities. Examples can be found in such works as Saskia Sassen's *Global Networks, Linked Cities* and Allen J. Scott's *Global City-Regions: Trends, Theory, Policy*. What I found most impressive was extensive information on "The Glocal Forum" and its Global Metro City network, founded by Uri Savir. With offices in Zurich, Switzerland and Rome, Italy, the network's website (www.glocalforum.org—website inactive) affirms the following.

> Global Metro City—The Glocal Forum is a nonprofit orga-
> nization working to build a new relationship between the city
> and the global village with the aim of contributing to peace and

---

that pull systems toward both coherence and collapse are *chaord*, a label that juxtaposes the dynamics of chaos and order; *glocalization*, which points to the simultaneity of globalizing and localizing dynamics; and regcal, a term designed to focus attention on the links between regional and local phenomena. The chaord designation is elaborated in Dee W. Hock, *Birth of the Chaordic Age* (San Francisco: Berrett-Koehler, 1999); the *glocal*ization concept is developed in Roland Robertson, "Glocalization: Time-Space and Homogeneity-Heterogeneity," in Mike Featherstone, Scott Lash, and Roland Robertson, eds., *Global Modernities* (Thousand Oaks, CA: Sage, 1995), 25–44; and the "regcal" formulation can be found in Susan H. C. Tai and Y. H. Wong, "Advertising Decision Making in Asia: 'Glocal' versus 'Regcal' Approach," *Journal of Managerial Issues*, Vol. 10 (Fall 1998), 318–19. I prefer the term *fragmegration* because it does not imply a territorial scale, and it broadens the focus to include tensions at work in organizations as well as those that pervade communities." (Rosenau 2003)

development. Founded in 2001, the organization encourages global powers to have broader respect for local powers and cultural diversity in a process defined as glocalization. . . . The Glocal Forum aims to create a more equitable balance between the global and the local throiugh a new pattern of diplomacy— the diplomacy of cities. (info@glocalforum.org 2005, see also www.wearethefuture.com.)

My search led me to a denomination and a local congregation that seem to be ahead of their time. The Virginia Baptist Mission Board has named its entire mission program "Glocal Missions and Evangelism." The related website states,

We who are united by a shared sense of Mission face a renewed and fresh challenge as our world moves headlong into the 21st century. The Glocal Missions and Evangelism Team envisions all Virginia Baptists being on a mission to fulfill God's call in their lives. Our purpose is to mobilize, train, and equip individuals and churches, in cooperation with other ministry partners, to carry the witness and ministry of Christ to Virginia and to the ends of the earth. (www.vbmb.org/glocalmissions/default .cfm, 2005; link no longer active)

I also found a large local church that seeks to embody a similar vision. NorthWood, pastored by its founder, Bob Roberts, has created the "Glocalnet" that includes three other churches planted by NorthWood in Las Vegas, Nevada; Hiram, Georgia; and Oakville, Ontario, Canada. In their website they explain that

Our goal at NorthWood is to glorify God through ongoing transformation. . . . We believe transformation is an ongoing process. It is a result of a constant, growing, interactive relationship with God that includes corporate and personal worship. It is a result of community. God didn't design us to be islands. That's why nearly every day of the week you will find groups or teams of people from NorthWood meeting together to encourage, challenge, and support each other.

Transformation is also a result of *glocal* (local and global) impact as we serve others. At NorthWood, we do not believe that it's all about us. We believe actions speak louder than words when it comes to sharing God's love. That's why we are committed not only to meeting the needs of Northeast Tarrant County, but also to meeting needs around the world. As the NorthWood family reaches out and serves together, individual, community and *glocal* transformation takes place. To learn more about NorthWood's *glocal* outreach, check out the *glocal* section of our site. (Northwood Church 2005)

Five years before the Indonesian tsunami of 2004, Leonard Sweet published his earthshaking book *Soul Tsunami* in which he described the turn of the century transformations that mark some of the greatest transitions the world has seen at least during the past 500 years. (Sweet 1999) Sweet entitled one of the chapters of that book, "Life Ring # 8: Get Glocal." Sweet builds on Peter Drucker's words, "Every organization of today has to build into its very structure . . . organized abandonment of everything it does" (Drucker 1993; Miller 2004; Sweet 1999).

Sweet suggests that one's proactive life response to tsunami-size transition should include an effort to, "Get Glocal." (Sweet 1999) Nowhere in this chapter can I find a definition of "glocal." However, when one considers the issues that Sweet presents in the rest of this chapter, and although he uses the word "global" and "globalization," Sweet is describing the glocal when he says

Before you leave the house in the morning, you experience how global (glocal?) this world has become. You make that first cup of coffee—but only with the help of four states and six foreign countries.

Who owns Firestone? Japan's Bridgestone.

Who owns Dr. Pepper? Britain's Cadbury/Schweppes.

Who pushes the buttons of the Pillsbury Doughboy? Diageo, a company created by Guinness (what country owns Guinness?) and Grand Metropolitan.

"Globalization" is more than the preeminent economic trend of the 21st century, with a thriving global investment culture. It is also a new way of living and being in the world.

The coming together of the new biology and the new physics is providing the basic metaphors for this new global civilization that esteems and encourages whole-brain experiences, full-life expectations, personalized expressions, and a globalized [or glocalized?] consciousness.

It is hard to underestimate the unprecedented nature of this global civilization. We have an interdependent, interlocked economic system in which everybody in the world participates. Global integration is becoming almost universal, with the Net the main medium . . . (Sweet 1999, 121–22)

I believe that Sweet was emphasizing the glocal here, that is, the interrelationship between the local and the global in their multifaceted, multidirectional, interactive dynamic influence one upon the other: So his challenge is this. "Let others talk about making a difference in the world. It's time for the church to make a different world. Don't make a difference in the world. Make the world different. Redeem and redream your world" (Sweet 1999, 126).

A glocal perspective of the universe recognizes that the smallest stone thrown into a pond causes ripples that shake the earth. And the smallest shift in the tectonic plates of the planet causes a wave that changes the course of human history. In ecclesiology broadly conceived and in missional ecclesiology in particular, we have been accustomed to set the local, national and global over against each other. For example, we tend to speak of a local congregation's local or neighborhood context of outreach, ministries, or mission. And a local church will have a task force or committee specifically targeted toward the local needs of the church's closest contexts. Until recently, denominations in North America have typically had some kind of "home mission board" and another "board of world/global mission." This local-global split is in fact worsening in many (especially mainline) denominations (including the author's) in the United States. Many local churches in the U.S. are now devoting the lion's share of their time, attention, personnel, and money to the needs of the people located closest to the church's building, and doing so by reducing and in some cases curtailing altogether their involvement in national or global ministries and mission. The primary exception to this might be some short-term mission trips by the church's members, trips that may be more a kind of Christian tourism than mission. The concept of "globalization" has not seemed to counteract this trend. To the contrary, much of the discussion of "globalization" seems to set the global over against the local and then analyzes the impact that global forces are having on local realities—often with a rather protectionist attitude.

In contrast to this, a glocal perspective may help us move beyond discussions of modernity versus postmodernity (Van Engen 1996); beyond questions of post-colonial global mission (Hiebert 1991); and possibly beyond the controversies over globalization as such (see, e.g., Tiplady 2003). Glocalization, rather, seeks to perceive the world through the lens of the simultaneous interaction; the interweaving influences; the dynamic, always-changing, multidimensional interrelatedness of the global and the local. This dynamic interaction recognizes that what was once known as the "local" is itself an aspect of the "global" in the same way as a quark or an electron is part of the entire universe. And the glocal recognizes that what we once knew as the "global" can only be expressed concretely in and through the local. In fact, mission in the twenty-first century involves an ascending, never-ending spiral or "boomerang effect," as Willem Saayman has suggested.

> I would like to argue that an adequate missionary ecclesiol-
> ogy demands a rethinking of the concept of linear process in
> mission. I think the process and progress from church to mission
> to church should rather be seen as cyclical, and specifically as
> an ascending, never-ending spiral. From the very beginning,
> therefore, the progress is not in a straight line *away* from the
> "sending" church *to* some faraway unreached "mission field,"
> but rather curving back to it throughout. If we stick to the
> injunction of Acts 1:8, I would argue that the movement is from
> Jerusalem to Judea and back to Jerusalem, to Samaria and back
> to Jerusalem, to the ends of the earth and back to Jerusalem, etc.
> Such an understanding, to my mind, better expresses the role
> of mutuality and interdependence as essential preconditions for
> the churches to carry out their missionary responsibility. This
> implies that the evangelizers must always be evangelized anew;
> to use a well-known metaphor: the missionary chickens must
> always come home to roost. Or, to change my metaphor: this
> is the essential "boomerang effect" of Christian mission. The
> "sending" church(es) can and may never be left unchanged
> by its mission, not if the church is truly missionary by its very
> nature. (Saayman 2000)

Quantum physics has taught us that matter is one of the manifestations of energy. We now know that eternity is found on the head of a pin. In biblical language, all heaven rejoices when one lost sinner repents (Luke 15:7). I originally wrote this chapter during Holy Week. As I walked through the story of the passion and resurrection of Jesus the Christ, I was struck by the glocal significance of the crucifixion and resurrection of our Lord. The whole universe in time and space was transformed in the instant when Jesus, hanging on a Roman cross near Jerusalem in that "first" century, proclaimed, "It is finished" (John 19:30). And all of life and human existence was changed when the resurrected Jesus Christ whispered to his disciples on that Easter Day, "Peace be with you" (Luke 24:36). In both time and space, the local and the global are folded in upon each other and are interwoven through each other into themselves—and glocal eternity is forever in an instant totally transformed. How can I grasp this?

I find that thinking about the nature of the Internet helps me get my mind around this new vision of reality. Every illustration or analogy has its limits and limitations. But I beg the reader's indulgence to imagine the Internet as an analogy of the glocal Church of the twenty-first century. In looking at the Internet in this way, I do not mean to be examining the Internet as a location and pathway for communicating the gospel—or for attraction and advertising by creating web pages. That is a different matter and Shawn Redford, among others, has challenged us all to rethink the mission of the Church in relation to the Internet, a missional process that he called, "Facing the Faceless Frontier" (Redford 1999). In what follows I want to suggest something different. What would the glocal Church of Jesus Christ look like in the twenty-first century if we were to examine it in terms of its structure and organization, through the kaleidoscope of the Internet?

Gazing through this looking glass (Alice in Wonderland), I think of each local congregation, each group of disciples of Jesus—"where two or three gather in my name, there am I with them." (Matt 18:20)—as a desktop PC. This local-congregation-as-PC, like the laptop on which I am presently writing this chapter, may have a cable or phone line through which it could be connected to the Internet. This, the small "c" church (represented by my desktop computer), may involve 5, 50, 500, or 5000 disciples of Jesus.[21] In computer terms, my computer may differ from other PC's in terms of the PC's memory capacity, storage space, brain power, interfacing capabilities and so forth. But no matter the size, it is fundamentally a PC. Similarly, no matter the size of the local church, in its theological and biblical

---

21. I consider one the most insightful and practical analyses of the impact on leadership, structure, organization, administration, and communication of the varying sizes of congregations is Lyle Schaller, *Looking in the Mirror,* 1984.

essence it is still basically the corporate congregation *(kaleo)* of those who gather as disciples of Jesus Christ.[22]

Moving to a second level of organization, I also have my PC networked in my home with two other desktop computers and a laptop. I have done this by connecting each computer to a wireless network. When all four computers are up and running, I can access all the data on all the hard drives of all four computers simultaneously. But each PC has its own hardware and software structures.[23] This is analogous to a regional group of churches, or a regional judicatory. Such a group of like-minded local congregations need networking hardware and software, an ecclesiastical structure and personal relationships that hold them together and facilitate their interrelations and intercommunications. Each local congregation has its own leadership, governance, structure, and other internal systems, but there is some level of cooperation, fellowship, accountability, recognition, and empowerment among them. In computerese, they are a "local network." The networking hardware may be as organizationally loose as a clergy association or a pastors' prayer group in a town, or it can be as tight as a Roman Catholic diocese or Methodist district. The extent, depth, and structural cohesion of this "network" depend, of course, on the ecclesiastical polity to which that network of congregations belong.

This takes us to a third level of organization. Some years ago, when the Internet was in its infancy, many of us became greatly enamored with the idea of email. I was among the first fifty thousand or so to subscribe to America Online (AOL). I remember the year that AOL was faced with a classaction lawsuit brought by hundreds of thousands of subscribers because the local "servers" that AOL was using were not being expanded fast enough to meet demand. AOL is, of course, now only one of many companies that offer access to their "server." And now most universities everywhere in the world have set up their own "servers" to facilitate communication on their campuses. My wife, Jean, worked for a number of years in a large cancer research institution called City of Hope in Duarte, California. City of Hope has its own internal "server" that integrates the communication and

---

22. A local congregation is in fact more than the sum of its parts and is more than merely the total of the individuals who gather. How one associates the sum of the individuals with the larger corporate entity that is the church is an important question.

23. I could do this if I had the right software installed in each computer, and herein lies an analogy to various forms of ecclesiastical organization: Roman Catholic, Orthodox, and Protestant: Episcopal, Presbyterial, Congregational, or New Apostolic Reformation.

facilitates all the organizational, administrative, and interpersonal relations necessary to run an institution with nearly 3000 employees. In computerese this is an "intranet." I think of Western European state churches, American denominations, and "national churches" that arose in Asia, Africa and Latin America during the twentieth century as types of "intranet" systems. Looking at the Roman Catholic Church globally one might say that it is like a huge "intranet." In Protestantism, although there are world federations, alliances, fellowships, councils and conferences that bring together various denominations and national churches that share similar ecclesiastical traditions, these do not function, in my mind, in a structurally tight fashion enough to be thought of as intranets. The Anglican/Episcopal network centered in the Lambeth Conferences might be considered a type of Protestant intranet, but even that has begun to unravel in recent years.

Global banking was transformed by the internet. Visa is a glocal reality. When I access my bank account with an ATM card I may be physically located at my bank's local branch a few blocks from my home. But when I trigger that access with my ATM card, I become part of a global network to which my local branch belongs. I may use my VISA card in the ATM of another bank. In that case, also, I am accessing the internet banking system, a glocal reality that is both local and global simultaneously.

As we deepen and broaden our thinking about the global catholicity of the church, we may begin to see the Church of Jesus Christ as being a kind of glocal internet. The internet is something ontologically different from anything I have described thus far. Especially after the invention of internet computer languages, the internet became the invisibly visible organically structured pathway of glocal communication. In my home office where I am writing, I use a cable/modem that is essentially always connected to the internet. When I call up an internet communication software, something almost miraculous happens. Instantaneously my computer becomes itself a part of the internet. And I, through my computer, become one small component in a phenomenally huge glocal electronic system. My desktop PC is no longer an autonomous, individual computer, neither is the internet merely the sum of such individual computers. Rather, my PC is now an integral part of a much, much larger whole: I and my computer are the Internet. In other words, when I log into the internet, my PC sitting on my desk becomes instantly glocal—it is simultaneously local and global. It is a glocally integrated part of the interaction between the local and the global.

This is the level at which I believe we need to think of the Church of Jesus Christ in the twenty-first century as glocal. Analogous to my PC's relationship with the internet, when I gather with other Christians in the name of Jesus, I am in that instant gathering with the family of God that includes over 1.5 billion followers of Jesus, the very large family of which Paul speaks in Ephesians 3:14–21. Like my PC, my local "congregation" is now hooked in spiritually, organically, temporally and spatially to all those who everywhere, always, have believed in Jesus Christ. As we gather to worship our Lord Jesus Christ, we are instantly interconnected with all other Christians around the globe who are in Christ. This is the glocal Church that exists "in the power of the Spirit" (Moltmann 1977). This glocal reality recognizes that the small "c" church is in fact an integral part of the large "C" Church. This fact transforms our understanding of the missional life of the local congregation. Such a local congregation is not only *pars pro toto* (a part for the whole) as this has been expressed, for example, in Orthodox ecclesiology; it *is* the whole in which it participates. The whole Church is there in that local congregation—and that local congregation exists precisely because it is part of the whole. The concept of the glocal, then, may offer us a new way of understanding the catholicity of the Church. In what follows, I will explore this by considering that the Church is glocal in its essence, in its extension, and in its mission.

The glocal Church is a twenty-first century way of expressing the catholicity of the Church. But in order to affirm that, we need to review what the Church has understood when it says that it is "catholic" or "universal."

IN THE TWENTY-FIRST CENTURY THE CHURCH OF JESUS CHRIST IS GLOCAL IN ITS ESSENCE[24]

From its birth after Peter's Pentecost sermon, continuing in Paul's Gentile mission, demonstrating astonishingly rapid numerical and geographical expansion during its first century of life, and acquiring explicit expression in the Apostolic Fathers, the Apologists, and the Post-Nicene Fathers, the Christian Church demonstrated a commitment to gather men and women from the whole world into its fold. For twenty centuries the Church has defined its essential nature by using four words to describe its attributes, with one of these having to do with its universality: "I believe in the one holy *catholic* and apostolic Church" (emphasis added).

Because of the universal scope of God's intention, because of the universal scope of Christ's lordship, because of the universal scope of the kingdom of God, the Church of Jesus Christ has always understood itself as nothing short of

---

24. Parts of this section have been adapted from Van Engen 1981, in loco.

universal. Because the Great King, Jesus Christ, has dominion over all nations, the Church has understood the scope of its missional task as including all nations. As Kenneth Cragg once said, "The gospel has no native country."[25] The universal nature of the gospel has meant that the Church could find its true self only as it became a global village, open to, including, calling, and embracing all humans. "The source of the missionary movement is the great heart of God," Robert Glover said.[26] In fact, the source of the Church's catholicity itself is the great heart of God. The universal rule of Christ has universal implications for the nature of the Body of Christ.

The universal motif of the offer of salvation to all persons and the incorporation by faith of all peoples, families, tribes and nations in the people of God (as in the Book of Revelation) has been reiterated again and again in the history of the Church. The New Testament Church, the early Church Fathers, the monastic movement, and the Second Vatican Council, each in its own way has sought to give expression to the same basic truth. It is the will of God that all peoples should become increasingly related to Christ and his Body, the Church. This universal purpose is built into the very essence of what the Church is as the people of God. They are the people of God gathered from the whole world. As such, it is essential to their being that they participate in that gathering. As the people of God, the Church participates in Christ as and when it participates in Christ's universal salvation, gathering people from all four corners of the earth to be His Body, the Church.

From its beginning, this Christian community which called itself the Church, had some very distinctive features. Prominent among these was the conception of the Church as the "communion of the Holy Spirit" emphasized in the apostolic benediction, that could be understood as an early definition of the Church: "The grace of the Lord Jesus Christ, and the love of God, the fellowship of (*koinonia*) the Holy Spirit" (2 Cor 13:14).[27]

Kenneth Scott Latourette posed the question as to the factors that might have been responsible for the Church's amazing growth as a communion of the Holy

---

25. Quoted by D. T. Niles 1962, 248.

26. R. H. Glover 1946,13.

27. S. Minear points this out in *Images of the Church in the New Testament*, 133–35. See also J. G. Davies 1965, 55, where Davies makes the comment, "From the Pneumatological (aspect) the Church is dynamic, stretching out to its final destiny, through the present and future action of the (Holy) Spirit."

Spirit. At the outset, he enumerated various factors external to the early Church and concluded, "Never before in the history of the race had conditions been so favorable for the acceptance of any one faith by so large a proportion of (human-kind)."[28] Latourette pointed out that alongside these external factors one must take into consideration a very important internal one. Christianity was inclusive, he wrote:

> Whence came these qualities which won for Christianity its astounding victory? Careful and honest investigation can give but one answer, Jesus. It was faith in Jesus and his resurrection which gave birth to the Christian fellowship and which con-tinued to be its inspiration and its common tie. . . . The early disciples unite in declaring that it was from the command of Jesus that the gospel was proclaimed to all, regardless of sex, race or cultural background.[29]

"From the outset [Christianity] possessed a strong sense of the essential unity of all believers and a desire to give that unity tangible expression in a body bound together by a common faith and by love."[30] This is the astounding quality of the early Christian Church. The Christian Church was not anything like the secret mystery religions of the day that were exclusivist and introverted. Rather, Christianity from the very earliest times, as in Peter's Pentecost sermon (Acts 2), perceived itself as a radically inclusive religion that aimed to proclaim its message and extend its fellowship to both men and women, slaves and free, Romans, Jews, Greeks, Barbarians, and all persons who would receive it.[31] The Church under-stood its growth in catholicity as an expression of its essential nature.

One of the earliest references to the early Church's self-awareness in this vein can be found in the Didache.

> As this broken bread [of the Eucharist] was scattered upon the mountains and was gathered together and became one, so let thy Church be gathered together from the ends of the earth into

---

28. K. S. Latourette 1967, 364.

29. K. S. Latourette 1953, 106–7.

30. K. S. Latourette 1967, 364.

31. Cf. the New Testament Table of Nations in Acts 2:9–11, as well as Paul's statements of this thesis in Romans 1:14; 1 Cor 12:13; and Gal 3:28. David Bosch emphasized this in 1980, 94–95.

thy Kingdom: for thine is the glory and power through Jesus Christ for ever and ever.[32]

As we can see in the New Testament Table of Nations in Acts 2, the earliest notions concerning the nature of the Church include some kind of universal or catholic idea. Theirs is not a Church of only one race, one nation, or one language. It is a Church "gathered together from the ends of the earth."[33]

This idea of the universality of the Christian Church must be understood as the substance behind the word "catholic," first used by Ignatius (c. 35–107)[34] in his Epistle to the Smyrnaeans. J. N. D. Kelly remarks,

> As regards "Catholic," its original meaning was "universal" or "general" and in this sense Justin can speak of "the catholic resurrection." As applied to the Church, its primary significance was to underline its universality as opposed to the local character of the individual congregations.[35]

At that time there was still no difference in the minds of the early Church fathers concerning the visible in contrast to the invisible Church. This universal fellowship or communion was almost always conceived of as an empirical, visible society. It was not a Platonic idea, nor was it an "invisible" reality possible only in heaven, or in the realm of wishful thinking. This was the real, existing fellowship of Christ, called by the Holy Spirit, open to all people in the world.[36] The Church of the Apostolic Fathers is the "holy and universal Church sojourning in every place" to which the Smyrnaeans wrote to tell about the martyrdom of Polycarp around A.D. 155 or 156.

Prior to the Council of Nicaea, the apologists talked about the unity of the Church as a quality that was to be seen in the earthly, empirical Church. Cyprian, for example, stated, "Baptism is one, just as the Holy Spirit is one, just as the

---

32. Henry Bettenson 1956, 70.

33. J. Pelikan 1971, 156.

34. For the origin of the word "catholic," see, e.g., J. C. Brauer, 1971, 423. See also H. Küng 1971, 297 and Phillip Schaff 1950, 145.

35. J. N. D. Kelly 1960, 190.

36. Ibid. 1960, cites Clement of Rome, Justin, Ignatius, 2 Clement, and Hermas in this regard, 190–91.

Church is one."[37] And again, "He cannot possess the garment of Christ who tears and divides the Church of Christ.[38]

In making such an issue of the empirical unity of the church, Cyprian was expressing the conviction of the church catholic from the beginning.[39] This view of the unity of the empirical Church in both Irenaeus and Cyprian, (as the spokespersons for their era) was directly related to the catholicity or universality of the visible Church. Cyprian, for example, used the illustration of the sun with many rays, and the tree with many branches to show that "The Church is one which with increasing fecundity extends far and wide into the multitude . . ."[40] As preface to stating the creed, Irenaeus said, "The Church, though scattered through the whole world to the ends of the earth, has received [the faith] from the Apostles and their disciples."[41] By the end of the fourth century a definition had emerged that had been preserved surprisingly intact to this day. The Nicaeno-Constatinopolitan Creed stated, " . . . And I believe in the one holy *catholic* and apostolic Church" (emphasis added).[42]

This early definition of the Church spelled out four signs that at the outset were "commentated and explained, but not used apologetically."[43] In order to gain an understanding of the Church's self-awareness as expressed in the creed, we must observe carefully, then, how they were explained and used by those contemporary with it.

One of the most explicit of the Nicene Fathers on this point was Cyril of Jerusalem (315–386). Cyril expressed the belief that the Church was Catholic, meaning universal thus to be distinguished from heretical gatherings.[44] But this is not given in a sense of exclusivity, from which the heretics are withheld. Neither did this mean for Cyril that it necessarily was the institutional hierarchy which is "Catholic." That came later. For Cyril of Jerusalem, the witness of the Cross reached out to the whole world (Lect. xii; 40).[45]

37. Roy Defarrari, ed., 1958.

38. Ibid., ocit., 102.

39. J. Pelikan, ocit., 159.

40. R. Deferrari, ocit., 99.

41. Schaff 1877, 13. Cf. also H. Bettenson 1956, 17 & 121–26.

42. See, e.g., Schaff, 1877, vol. I, 28; Schaff & H. Wace, 1974, vol XIV, 163; H. Bettenson, 1947, 1963, 25–26, and Schaff, 1950, vol II, 536–37; as well as W. Bright, 1892, in loco.

43. H. Küng, 1971, 266.

44. See, e.g., Schaff & H. Wace, 1974, 140; G. Bromilev, 1978, 132.

45. Schaff & H. Wace, 1974, 93.

This meant also that the gifts and blessings of the Holy Spirit were to be spread over the whole world (Lect. xvi, 22).[46] This universality of grace had ramifications for the catholicity of the Church (Lect. xviii, 23 & 24).

> It is called Catholic then because it extends over all the world, from one end of the earth to the other; and because it teaches universally and completely one and all the doctrines which ought to come to men's knowledge . . . and because it brings into subjection to godliness the whole race of mankind . . . and because it universally treats and heals the whole class of sins. . . . And it is rightly named (ecclesia) because it calls forth and assembles together all men.[47]

Thus it is of the essential nature of the true, Catholic Church that it should extend its blessings to all people, over the whole world. Cyril of Jerusalem's conviction was shared by many of his Eastern contemporaries, including, for example, John Chrysostom (347–407). "The Church," he affirmed, "is Catholic, that is to say, spread throughout the whole world . . ."[48]

Augustine of Hippo (354–430) was "the most influential of the fathers of the Western Church."[49] In fact, "in a manner and to a degree unique for any Christian thinker outside the New Testament, Augustine has determined the form and the content of church doctrine for most of Western Christian history."[50] His influence was no less determinative in ecclesiology as it was in other aspects of church doctrine. Augustine's idea of the Church was a very large one. "For Augustine the Church comprises not just the part that journeys here on earth, but also that part which in heaven has always from creation held fast to God, that is, the church of the holy angels."[51] Augustine's Church is a universal community, a sort of "congregation of the human race."[52] His is a dynamic view of the Church as the *communio sanctorum*, "the eschatological community of salvation sent into the world. She is also, the 'City of God' on earth, the kingdom, the institution of salvation."[53]

---

46. Ibid., 121.
47. Ibid. 139–40.
48. J. N. D. Kelly 1960, 402.
49. J. C. Brauer 1971, 72.
50. J. Pelikan 1971, 293.
51. Geoffrey Bromiley 1978, 113.
52. Juan Luis Segundo 1975, 6.
53. David Bosch 1980, 105.

We must keep in mind that for Augustine the Church was the people—the elect on earth and in heaven. The Church had not yet been reduced to hierarchy and institution quite as strongly as it would be later. Augustine wrote about all people in the whole world. He made the distinction, though not as radically as did the Reformers later, between the invisible Church of the elect whom only God knew, and the more visible Church that was "an admixture of good and bad alike and will remain so until the final consummation . . . the *corpus permixtum*."[54] This did not, however, negate for Augustine the fact that there is, has always been, and always will be only one Church, one Body, one Communion of Saints. So when Augustine spoke of the vast numbers of Christians in the Catholic Church and used that as a defense of his own church over against the heretics, he was speaking primarily of people in the here-and-now, of the *communio sanctorum* in the world as he knew it.

One of Augustine's contemporaries was Vincent of Lérins (d. before 450). He is credited with having formulated the Vincentian Canon: *quod ubique, quod semper, quod ab omnibus creditum est* ("What has everywhere, always, by all been believed.").[55] The "all" to which Vincent referred was not to be restricted exclusively to the clergy and hierarchy of the church. Augustine also included the laity, especially in relation to the prayers of the entire church, which often reflected and gave expression to the apostolic tradition.[56] Thus in Augustine's thought the "all" who seek theological consensus must be as broad as the Church itself.

Jumping ahead, centuries later, Martin Luther affirmed that, ". . . Christian church" is a name and "Christian holiness" an entity common to all churches and all Christians in the world; therefore it is called "catholic."[57]

Thus for Luther the Church universal was the Church spread over the whole world:

> I believe that here below and throughout the world, there is
> only one Christian Church, the Church universal, and that this
> Church is identical with the universal fellowship of the saints,
> i.e. the devout believers everywhere on earth. This Church

---

54. J. G. Davies 1965, 258. See also Maurice Wiles & Mark Santer, eds., 1975, 164–65; J. N. D. Kelly, ocit., 413.

55. J. C. Brauer, ocit., 849–50. Jaroslav Pelikan helpfully summarizes this discussion in 1971, vol. 1, 334–41.

56. Cf. Pelikan 1971, 339.

57. Martin Luther 1955, 41 (*On The Councils and the Church*), 145.

is gathered, sustained and ruled by the Holy Spirit . . . and strengthened day by day through the sacraments and the Word of God.[58]

And John Calvin echoed this by saying,

Often, too, by the name of Church is designated the whole body of mankind scattered throughout the world who profess to worship one God and Christ . . . The Church universal is the multitude collected out of all nations, who, though dispersed and far distant from each other, agree in one truth of divine doctrine, and are bound together by the tie of a common religion.[59]

The idea of catholicity contains much more than simply the notions of geographical and numerical extension. It has also to do with cohesion, with doctrinal continuity, and with catholicity in a temporal sense.[60] Here, however, we should notice the theme that courses through the Scriptures from the time of Abraham: that the salvation of God is meant for all people, spread over the whole world. Further, it is important to notice that with the restoration of the notion of the Church as a people of God, the Communion of Saints, the Reformers again gave this geographic and numerical universality its proper weight in ecclesiology. And the Reformers were followed in this by all of Protestantism. The fact that the Church is the communion of saints and includes all races and languages spread over all

---

58. Lee Woolf, ed., *Reformation Writings*, vol. 1, 87 (quoted by C. C. Eastwood 1958), 26.

59. John Calvin 1975, IV, 1, 7 & 9.

60. Karl Barth emphasizes this: "The adjective 'catholic' means general, comprehensive . . . Applied to the Church it means that it has a character in virtue of which it is always and everywhere the same and always and everywhere recognizable in this sameness, to the preservation of which it is committed . . . Where it does not exist and is not recognizable in this sameness, where it is not concerned to preserve it, where it is not 'catholic,' it is not the true Church, the Church of Jesus Christ. The term 'catholic' speaks explicitly of the true Church activating and confirming its identical being in all its forms . . ."

From the geographical meaning of the word there had derived and still derives the wider sense in which the reference is to the relationship of the Christian community to the other natural and historical human societies. In essence the Church is the same in all races, languages, cultures and classes, in all forms of state and society." (*C. D.,* IV, 1, 701–3) Cf. also H. Küng, *The Church,* 298–302.

the world was also stressed, for instance, in several of the evangelical creeds.[61] And remarkably, even though some of these creeds are set forth by strongly separatist groups, they still emphasize this facet of the essence of the Church. Thus for the Reformers and their progeny, the Church as the communion of saints is composed of people of every race, spread over the whole world who believe in Jesus Christ— and thus, further, the Church is for all peoples everywhere in all the world.

Both G. Warneck and Samuel Zwemer made a point of this. For them this meant that "The Reformation certainly did a great indirect service to the cause of missions to the heathen . . ."[62] In fact Luther laid the very foundation of Protestant missions in this regard.

Luther maintained the universality of Christianity and its elevation above all kinds of limit, whether of place, time, rank, or nation. He was quite certain also that, according to the promise, the gospel must speed through the whole world and reach all nations . . ." All the world does not mean one or two parts," Luther said, "but everywhere where people are, thither the Gospel must speed and still ever speeds, so that, even if it does not remain always in a place, it yet must come to, and sound forth in, all parts and corners of the earth.[63]

The Reformers viewed the Church as being essentially created from and looking toward a gathering of people into the communion of the gospel. Martin Luther first expressed this in thesis number sixty-five of his ninety-five theses, by presenting the gospel as a net. "Thus the Gospel treasures are nets, with which of old they fished for men of riches."[64]

John Calvin developed this idea a little further. He presented the Church as a net and stressed that when one is at first fishing with the net, all kinds of fishes are caught, and it is only after having brought them in that they are separated.[65] This sets in bold relief the aspect of the Church's nature as a gathering and as a gatherer. Thus, "The Church universal is a multitude collected out of all nations."[66]

The gathering motif taught by Luther and Calvin was given prominence in several of the creeds of the Protestant church, such as the Two Helvetic Confessions,

---

61. See, e.g., *The Belgic Confession, The Confession of the Waldenses, and the Second Helvetic Confession* (Schaff 1877, in loco).

62. G. Warneck 1901, 11. See also Samuel Zwemer 1950, 208–11.

63. Ibid., 12.

64. H. Bettenson 1947, 190.

65. John Calvin 1975, IV,I, 13, 292. Cf. also *Calvin's Commentaries* re: Acts 2:47.

66. Ibid., IV, 1, 9 & 20. See also IV, I, 2.

the Scottish Confession, the Heidelberg Catechism, the Westminister Confession, the Savoy Declaration of the Congregational Church, and the Baptist Philadelphia Confession of 1688.[67] In fact, the Presbyterian Church North (Presbyterian Church in the United States of America) in its 1903 revision of the Westminster Confession made this motif one of the major additions. Not only is the indicative universality of God's salvation mentioned ("God in Christ offers a way of life and salvation sufficient for and adapted to the whole lost race of men . . ."), but the imperative dimension is derived from it ("Christ hath commissioned His Church to go into all the world and to make disciples of all nations").[68]

The numerical universality of the Church should be understood as part of the gift of catholicity that has been bestowed upon the Church—a gift which in itself constitutes a task. The numerical growth of the Church is seen as a quality of the Church turned inside out, a dynamic energy directing the Church toward the world. The numerical growth of the church in this way of thinking is precisely the universal, Catholic Church seeking to be what is. This is not triumphalist self-aggrandizement. Rather, it is a characteristic of the very essence of the Church as the gathering of the community of the Holy Spirit, open to all peoples, to the whole world, in all time. As Hans Küng put it, the Catholic Church must "keep on becoming Catholic."[69]

The Church should never become fixed at any one place in the world. She must be on her way to the ends of the earth in the certainty that Christ's time is pressing. In this manner mission calls forth the end, the coming of the Lord himself. Mission theology is its goal. Then it also becomes adoration of the Triune God.[70]

---

67. See Schaff 1877, III, 219, 874, 458, 324, 657–58, 721–23, and 738–41. This obviuos element in the creeds was for some reason negated by Richard de Ridder. He said "Times and circumstances have changed. The heathen, the pagan, the 'not-mv-people'are no longer oceans away, but all around the disciples todav . . . And, unfortunately, at this critical point where the Church of Christ is dispersed in the world (a minority, it must be remembered), confessional statements are silent where they ought to be most articulate. The Reformation definitions take little or no account of the New Testament viewpoint which points the Church outside of itself." (Cf. R. de Ridder 1971, 213–14.) But if the Protestant churches around the world that hold to the above-mentioned credal statements would take seriously the "gathering" motif that they clearly state, De Ridder's criticism would not hold water.

68. Ibid., 919–22.

69. Hans Küng 1963, 377.

70. W. Andersen, "Further Toward a Theology of Mission," in Gerald Anderson, ed., 1961, 313.

G. C. Berkouwer pointed out that the Great Commission is actually an expression of the Church's catholicity.[71] It is for this reason that the Church must take the lead, and does take the lead, in being accessible and open to all people.[72] The Church cannot be truly the Church without a movement outward to all people. The Church's universality is the intentional, centrifugal, totally outward movement of the Church. The Church's meaning, life, and existence are spelled out by this outward movement. Her place in the world and her participation in Christ is demonstrated by this outward movement. The Church is less than church when there is a loss of this outward directedness of the people of God.[73] The Church can do no other than to deeply desire greater universality. Ernest Best said, "Catholicity is of the essence of the nature of the Church without which it is not recognizable as Church."[74]

G. C. Berkouwer echoes this:

> The riches of the Church cannot be understood unless the Church is in motion in the "going forth" (Matt 28:19) that Jesus commanded as "the most profoundly necessary step." Therein it is clear that God loved the world (John 3:16), that He was in Christ reconciling the world to Himself (if Cor 5:19), and that Christ is the Savior of the world (John 4:42). This is a continuing reminder of the *missio Dei*, the "mission of God," which radically excludes every religious or cultural absolutizing.[75]

The nature of Church's universality means that it exists for all people, for the whole world, and it is called to be in every place, among every language, tribe, family and culture. Thus we must conclude that the universal Church can be recognized by its deep desire, its profound commitment to extend its joy, love, and fellowship to as many persons, peoples, cultures and nations as possible.

---

71. G. C. Berkouwer 1976, 106.

72. Cf. Theodore Eastman, *Chosen and Sent: Calling the Church to Mission,* 131.

73. Cf., e.g., Karl Barth C.D. IV, 3, 2, 767–772; G. C. Berkouwer *The Church,* 392ff and 123; "The Missionary Obligation of the Church," in Norman Goodall, *Missions Under the Cross,* 188–91; R. de Ridder, *Discipling,* 214–18; H. Bavinck, *Our Reasonable Faith,* 526–28; G. Peters, *A Biblical Theology of Missions,* 27; Johannes Blauw, *Missionary Nature of the Church,* 115–18; and John Piet, *Road Ahead,* 18; John Piper 1993.

74. E. Best, *One Body in Christ,* 193.

75. G. C. Berkouwer, *The Church,* 394–95. Berkouwer quotes here from K. Barth, C.D., IV, 3, 2, 874.

The Church which has lost this burning desire has lost something of its universality under God.[76]

IN THE TWENTY-FIRST CENTURY THE CHURCH OF JESUS CHRIST IS GLOCAL IN ITS THEOLOGIZING

In the twenty-first century, we find ourselves living in a new world. Acts 1:8 is now a reality. The Church of Jesus Christ, numbering more than 1.5 billion are now literally witnesses of Jesus Christ everywhere in their Jerusalems, Judeas, Samarias and their ends of the earth. We are all aware that the center of gravity of the Christian Church has shifted from North to South, from West to East. This shift does not only impact the numbers of Christians in the world, the languages they speak, and the locations where they may be found. This shift also means that mission-sending is now polycentric: cross-cultural missions send their missionaries from everywhere to everywhere. Some estimate that a larger number of cross-cultural missionaries are being sent and supported today by the churches and missions in Africa, Asia and Latin America than the total of those sent and supported from Europe and North America. For example, in India alone there are over 400 Protestant mission agencies sending and supporting over 4000 cross-cultural missionaries within and beyond the borders of India. In Latin America it is estimated that there are over 600 Latin American mission agencies that send and support around 9000 cross-cultural missionaries.

But the shift in the center of gravity of today's Christian churches and missions also means that the center of gravity of the Church's makeup and the Church's doing of mission theology have also shifted. Christianity is longer a Western religion. This fact should not surprise us. Christianity was originally not a Western religion: it was Middle Eastern, North African and Near Asian.[77] The Church is no longer the monocentric and mostly monocultural enterprise concentrated in Western Europe or North America. The Christian Church of the twenty-first

---

76. See "Lumen Gentium" in A. Flannery, ed., *The Documents of Vatican II*, 350; and J. Blauw, *Missionary Nature*, 111.

77. Philip Jenkins (2002) helped us all take seriously what David Barrett (1982) had been saying for twenty years prior to the turn of the century. It was unfortunate that Jenkins chose to use the word "Christendom" in his title. The last thing that the Church of Jesus Christ need in Asia, Africa, Latin America, Oceania—and even in Europe and North America—is to create a new "Christendom."

century registers a monumental shift with regard to the appropriate agendas, categories, agents, methodologies, worldview assumptions, types of rationality, perspectives, and modes of articulation that influence its thought and life around the globe. The Church is now a global/local (glocal) reality. The glocal Christian Church of the twenty-first century consists of everyone, always, everywhere who confess with the mouth and believe in the heart, who proclaim in word and deed, that "Jesus Christ is Lord" (Rom 10:9–13; 1 John 4:1–3).

Although the glocal Church is one, it is made up of a multiplicity of radically different contexts locally and globally. We are now a world church comprised of many members globally. Yet, we are one church. In Ephesians, Paul's primary letter dealing with a missional ecclesiology, Paul writes, "There is one body and one Spirit, as there is also one hope held out in God's call to you; one Lord, one faith, one baptism; one God and Father of all, who is over all and through all and in all" (Eph 4:4–6).

The Christian Church does not confess "holy catholic church*es*," or "famil*ies* of God" or "bod*ies* of Christ" or "New Israel*s*." In the biblical view of the church the plural only refers to geographical location of churches, not the existential being of the Church. In its essence there is only one Church. In Ephesians *ekklesia* appears only in the singular.

As Karl Barth put it, we cannot justify, spiritually or biblically, "the existence of a plurality of churches genuinely separated . . . and mutually excluding one another internally and therefore externally. A plurality of churches in this sense means a plurality of lords, a plurality of spirits, a plurality of gods."[78]

Yet we are also many members. Paul affirms the Church's oneness as a preamble to describing the pluriformity of the gifts of the Spirit that are each a part of the one Body. "But to each one of us grace has been given as Christ apportioned it. . . . So Christ himself gave the apostles, the prophets, the evangelists, the pastors and teachers, to equip his people for works of service (*eis ergon diakonias*), so that the body of Christ may be built up until we all reach unity in the faith and in the knowledge of the Son of God and become mature, attaining to the whole measure of the fullness of Christ" (Eph 4:7–13).[79]

---

78. See Van Engen 1991, 49; quoting from Karl Barth 1958, 675).

79. It is unfortunate that leaders and churches in the New Apostolic Reformation movement chose to misread and misinterpret this passage. They have read this passage in an extremely individualistic fashion that takes Paul's description of a "five-fold ministry" and assigns a hierarchical priority to the list, with "apostles" being first in authority over the

So there is one Church that is one Body, but there are many members, many charisms, and many ministries given for the Church's mission in the world. This pluriformity and polycentricity of the one church necessitates our learning to be a glocal Church involving the simultaneous, constant, dynamic interaction between the local and global. We seem to still not fully appreciate the far-reaching implications of this dialectical tension of diversity within unity in a globalizing world. Let me point out two illustrative implications of this new reality.

A. Both theology and theologies

Doing mission theology in a globalizing world will necessarily entail theologizing that affirms both the oneness of the Church and the multiplicity of gifts that make up that glocal Body of Christ. We will be led astray if we affirm only one or the other of these twin truths. Unfortunately, down through the centuries the Church has in fact accepted only one or the other of them. On the one hand, since Constantine the Christian Church has tended to do its theology from a predominantly monocentric and monocultural perspective. The Medieval Synthesis was just that: the articulation of a set of theological dogmas that were assumed to be universally true for everyone, everywhere, always. This produced the concept of "theology" as a singular noun understood to be the systematic aggregate of a set of unchanging propositions.

This monocentric view of doing theology dominated not only the Roman and Eastern churches, but the various branches of Protestantism after the Reformation as well. And this perspective also permeated Protestant missions in their theologizing for over 150 years during the time of colonial missions, a time that Paul Hiebert called, "The Era of Noncontextualization" in his article, "Critical Contextualization" (see, e.g., Hiebert 1994, 76–81).

In reaction to the hegemony of the Western church over theology, theologians from Africa, Asia, and Latin America have affirmed a polycentric perspective of theologizing. This view provided the impetus for the first Protestant use of the concept of "contextualization." The multiform and polycentric nature of the process of doing theology was emphasized by Shoki Coe and stressed through the

---

other four ministries. This reading of the passage flies in the face of Paul's overall organic ecclesiology in Ephesians—including in this passage itself—that presents the Church as a unified Body. I understand Paul as mentioning "apostles, prophets, evangelists, pastors and teachers" as illustrative of many charisms given to the members of the Body in which all are ONE body and there is no priority to be assigned to any one gift or ministry.

publication in 1972 of *Ministry in Context* on the part of the Theological Education Fund of the World Council of Churches (see, e.g., Coe 1976; Thomas, ed., 1995, 175–76; and Bevans 2002, 153 nn 45 and 46.).

Tite Tiénou has described it as thus:

> The word "contextualization" was . . . chosen with the specific purpose of conveying the idea that theology can never be permanently developed. Everywhere and in every culture Christians must be engaged in an ongoing process of relating the gospel to cultures that are constantly changing. As long as the world endures, this process continues. For many people contextualization, not indigenization, is the term that best describes this never-ending process (Tiénou 1993, 247; see, e.g., Kirk 1999, 91; and Van Engen 1989, 97 nn 18, 19.).

The perspective of contextualization as local theologizing represents a constantly changing reciprocal interaction between church and context, between global and local. It is a process of glocal reflection that begins with an analysis of the historical situation, proceeds to a rereading of Scripture which in turn leads to interactive theological reflection concerning the context. This involves an act of theologizing that propels the Christian to active engagement with the cultural, socioeconomic, and political issues extant in the context, in conversation with Christians in all other contexts.

Locating the theological task in the local context implies an epistemological approach to being a glocal Church. It questions what we do and do not know about God in the local situation. This epistemological perspective of contextual theology received added impetus after 1976 when "twenty-two theologians from Africa, Asia, Latin America and representatives of minority groups in North America founded the Ecumenical Association of Third World Theologians (EATWOT) in Dar es Salaam, Tanzania . . . By 2002 EATWOT's membership had grown to over 700 members . . . (Mbiti 2003, 91). The conferences, papers, and published books flowing from EATWOT during the past twenty-five years have provided strong support for an epistemological approach to doing contextually appropriate theology, especially in and from the two-thirds world.

"Contextualization," writes J. Andrew Kirk,

> recognizes the reciprocal influence of culture and socioeconomic life. In relating Gospel to culture, therefore, it tends to

take a more critical [or prophetic] stance toward culture. The concept . . . is intended to be taken seriously as a theological method which entails particular ideological commitments to transform situations of social injustice, political alienation and the abuse of human rights.[80]

So the multiplicity of contexts and worldviews representing a diversity of cultural assumptions and agendas that constitute the world church today makes it necessary to speak in the plural, to talk of "local theologies." But let me hasten to repeat here the complementary truth: there is only *one* Church of Jesus Christ. Our dilemma is that neither of these two options alone is acceptable. To view the doing of theology as the construction of one monolithic "theology" superimposed on all Christians everywhere violates the truth that God's revelation took place "at many times and in various ways" (Heb 1:1) and has always been received within the categories of specific cultural contexts. As David Bosch said it, "Interpreting a text is not only a literary exercise; it is also a social, economic, and political exercise. Our entire context comes into play when we interpret a biblical text. One therefore has to concede that all theology (or sociology, political theory, etc.) is, by its very nature, contextual" (Bosch 1991, 428).

On the other hand, the atomization of a plurality of local "theologies" violates the oneness of the Church, the unity of the Holy Spirit, the singularity of the gospel, and the unity of all Christians who read the same Bible (see Bosch 1991, 427). Thus, neither monolithic uniformity nor atomized pluriformity are satisfactory approaches to doing theology in a globalizing world today. So the challenge before us in the twenty-first century is to find a way to know God in context, that is, we must learn to do critical theologizing in a glocal fashion through reading the same Bible in the midst of multiple cultures.

B. Epistemological Recontextualization

The global shift in the center of gravity of the Christian Church worldwide offers a second implication that profoundly impacts the way we do mission theology in the twenty-first century. In addition to our seeking to reconcile "one theology–many theologies" we also must consider how we shall go about recontextualizing the gospel of Jesus Christ in situations where there are multiple Christian groups

---

80. J. Andrew Kirk 1999, 91. Kirk quotes from Miguez Bonino 1971, 405–7; cited also in Norman Thomas 1995, 174 and David Bosch 1991, 423 & 425.

involved in theologizing, where there are multiple generations of believers, and where one may find a growing nominalism and secularization of the Church and its theology.

The world of this new century has undergone radical changes that significantly alter our approach to contextualization, changes that call for an epistemological approach of the glocal Church involved in "critical theologizing." With more than one-quarter of the earth's population claiming to be Christian in some fashion, and with two-thirds of that Christian population to be found in the South and East of the globe, the process of contextualization must also include an epistemological effort. That is, contextualization now involves some Christian churches sharing with other Christian churches the way they, in their context, read the Bible and understand the gospel (cf., e.g., Phan 2003). Christians from everywhere need to share with other Christians everywhere how they are coming to know God in context. Each step forward, each "translation" (cf. Sanneh 1993, 31; Walls 2002, 72–81) of the gospel offers the possibility of discovering something about God as revealed in the Bible that no one had previously seen. "As the gospel continues to take root in new cultures, and God's people grow in their covenantal relationship to God in those contexts, a broader, fuller, and deeper understanding of God's revelation will be given to the world church" (Van Engen 1996, 88–89).

This is what Andrew Walls has called "the Ephesian moment," drawing from a historical and cross-cultural reading of Ephesians.

> The Ephesian moment, then, brings a church [to be] more cul-
> turally diverse than it has ever been before; potentially, therefore,
> nearer to that "full stature of Christ" [Eph 4:13] that belongs
> to his summing up of humanity. The Ephesian moment also
> announces a church of the poor . . . The Ephesian question at the
> Ephesian moment is whether or not the church in all its diversity
> will demonstrate its unity by the interactive participation of all
> its culture-specific segments, the interactive participation that is
> to be expected in a functioning body (2002, 81).

Tite Tiénou suggests that,

> Accepting difference [in contextual theological formulations]
> raises [an] important issue related to the formation of indige-
> nous theologies, namely the polycentric nature of Christianity.
> If we believe that Christians from other cultures can enrich our

faith or help us correct our mistakes, we are in effect saying that Christianity is not permanently wedded to any human culture. Put another way, the acceptance of difference means that the Christian faith can be at home in any culture. Consequently Christianity has as many centers as the number of cultures of its adherents (Tiénou 1993, 248–59).

This deepening, broadening, enriching of our understanding of God's revelation in the Bible is only possible if there is an ongoing conversation between the local congregations and churches and the church globally by way of a mutually enriching process of critical theologizing. An epistemological approach to contextualization in this new situation of ecclesial diversity has to do with the second, third, and fourth generations of believers in each location. In most of the cases where contextualization was seen as a communicational process the intent was for Christians to communicate their understanding of the gospel in culturally appropriate ways to those who were not yet followers of Jesus. This involved an initial contextualization or indigenization of the gospel message.

But our world has changed. In almost every country in the world one can find the children, grandchildren and great grandchildren of the first Christian believers. This involves a recontextualization of the gospel, a rereading of Scripture in the midst of a new and changed reality being faced by the second, third, and fourth generations of Christians. And this must be done in conversation with the glocal Church. Without such an intentional recontextualization, without a careful critical theologizing in that context, it is highly probable that the children and grandchildren of the church will become Christian *in name only* (Gibbs 1994, 17–38) and eventually either mix pre-Christian concepts with their inherited Christian ideas, or become post-Christian nonbelievers. This matter will be dealt with more completely in a later chapter of this book.

The present search by many in the West to articulate the faith in a fashion that will be understandable and acceptable to postmoderns is an example of this kind of recontextualization. Such recontextualization necessitates an epistemological model of contextualization that is deeper, broader, higher and farther-reaching than a communicational model would be. Recontextualization closely follows a pattern common to the Old Testament where the periodic renewal of the Covenant on the part of Israel involved essentially a recontextualization of the Covenant for a new time and place in the life of Israel.

To recontextualize the gospel in a changed context calls for the Christians in that context to participate in an emic process that Paul Hiebert called "critical contextualization" with its four steps: (1) exegesis of the culture, (2) exegesis of Scripture and the hermeneutical bridge, (3) a critical response to past customs, and (4) the corporate discovery of new contextualized practices (Hiebert 1994, 88–91).[81] Parenthetically, I would add a fifth step to Hiebert's four steps mentioned above. I believe the glocal Church's process of critical contextualization is possible only if the members of the one Body are willing to do their theologizing in a relational and worshipful manner that Hiebert called "centered set" thinking.[82]

---

81. Hiebert's concept of "Critical Contextualization" appeared in at least four places: Hiebert 1984; Hiebert 1987; Hiebert 1994a; Hiebert 1994b.

82. In *On Missiological Issues,* Hiebert develops the "characteristics of centered sets."

"First," Hiebert says, "a centered set is created be defining the center or reference point and the relationship of things to that center. Things related to the center belong to the set, and those not related to the center do not. . . .

Second, while centered sets are not created by drawing boundaries, *they do have sharp boundaries* that separate things inside the set from those outside it—between things related to or moving toward the center and those that are not. Centered sets are well-formed, just like bounded sets. They are formed by defining the center and any relationships to it. The boundary then emerges automatically. Things related to the center naturally separate themselves from things that are not. . . .

Third, there are two variables intrinsic to centered sets. The first is membershiAll members of a set are full members and share fully in its functions. There are not second-class members. The second variable is distance from the center. Some things are far from the center and others near to it, but all are moving toward it. . . .

Fourth, centered sets have two types of change inherent in their structure. The first has to to with entry into or exit from the set. Things headed away from the center can turn and move toward it. . . . The second type of change has to do with movement toward or away from the center. Distant members can move toward the center, and those near can slide back while still hearded toward it." Hiebert goes on to demonstrate that "Hebrew Culture" was structured as a centered set, based on relationships, especially in terms of a covenantal relationship of the people of Israel to the God of Abraham, Isaac, and Jacob.

Hiebert then asks,

What happens to our concept of *Christian* if we define it in centered-set terms? First, Christians would be defined as followers of the Jesus Christ of the Bible, as those who make him the center or Lord of their lives. . . . Second, there would be a clear separation between Christians and non-Christians, between those who are followers of Jesus and those who are not. The emphasis, however, would be on exhorting people to follow Christ, rather than on excluding others to preserve the purity of the set. . . . Third, there would be a recognition of variation among

IN THE TWENTY-FIRST CENTURY THE CHURCH OF JESUS CHRIST IS GLOCAL IN ITS MISSIONAL CALLING

We might summarize the first two parts of this chapter by means of two comple-mentary observations about doing mission theology. In the first part we considered the fact that in its essence, the glocal Church is universal—and universally incar-nated in specific times and places. In the second part we considered the fact that the Church is glocal in its extension, a fact that implies two dialectical realities: (1) although there is one Church, yet there are many churches; and (2) although there is one Bible, yet there are many readings. Building on this reality, we could make two complementary observations.

The glocal Church's mission theology is to be critiqued by the global Church and is to be informed, shaped, and critiqued by local churches. All universal truths about God can only be lived out by a particular people and by specific congre-gations locally and the local congregation derives its meaning as it is the local manifestation, the local concrete expression of the universal glocal Church of Jesus Christ. It would appear that such a glocal perspective was affirmed by the Apostle Paul, the master contextualizer par excellence. He stated that,

> Though I am free and belong to no man, I make myself a slave
> to everyone, to win as many as possible. To the Jews I became
> like a Jew, to win the Jews. . . . To those not having the law I
> became like one not having the law . . . so as to win those not

---

Christians. . . . Fourth, two important types of change would be recognized in centered-set thought. First, there is conversion, entering or leaving the set. . . . The second change is movement toward the center, or growth in a relationship. A Christian is not a finished product the moment he or she is converted. Conversion, therefore, is a definite event followed by an ongoing process. Sanctification is not a separate activity, but a process of justification continued throughout life."Hiebert then proceeds to look at the Church as a centered set and missions as a centered set, following the four characteristics he mentioned earlier. (1994, 123–31 emphasis is Hiebert's).

Paul Hiebert's idea of "centered set" is especially important as a hermeneutical guide to our reading of Scripture in evangelical mission theology. It provides a means by which we can be firmly and tightly anchored in truth in Jesus Christ, yet simultaneously open to differing worldviews, different cultural glasses with which we read the Scriptures, all within the same world Church comprised of the disciples of the one Center, Jesus Christ.

having the law. To the weak I became weak, to win the weak. I have become all things to all people so that by all possible means I might save some." (1 Cor 9:19–22)

Earlier in the same passage in 1 Corinthians Paul also said, "Woe to me if I do not preach the gospel!" (1 Cor 9:16)

In Galatians Paul wrote,

I am astonished that you are so quickly deserting the one who called you to live in the grace of Christ and are turning to a different gospel—which is no gospel at all . . . As we have already said, so now I say again: If anybody is preaching to you a gospel other than what you accepted, let them be under God's curse! (Gal 1:6–7, 9)

How do we walk between these two seemingly contradictory views? How does the glocal Church maintain the dialectical tension between faithfulness to the revelation and contextual appropriateness in our mission theology? How do Christians and Christian churches from different contexts representing such diverse global contexts listen and learn from each other in order to know the same God better each in their own contexts? I believe Paul gives us an indication of a way forward in the way he develops his thought in Galatians 3 through 6. Here I am rereading Galatians not from the point of view of law and grace (though certainly that is a major theme) but rather from the standpoint of Paul's thought as a glocal mission theologian: as a missionary writing a missionary letter to a mission church. And I think the principle he offers us in Galatians is this: affirm commonalities and acknowledge differences in a trinitarian process of theological reflection in mission. Let me offer the reader a brief outline.

A. God the Father: Common Humanness, Diverse Cultures

Having made his case that Jews and Gentiles alike are "not justified by the works of the law but by faith in Jesus Christ," (Gal 2:16) Paul proceeds to offer a trinitarian viewpoint that can hold in tension twin truths: one gospel (Gal 1:6–9), many perspectives. And the first stone in this trinitarian foundation has to do with God the Father. So Paul harks back to Genesis and speaks of God's choosing of Abraham and his descendants who are chosen precisely so that in them "all the Gentiles" will be blessed.

So also Abraham "believed God, and it was credited to him as righteousness." Understand, then, that those who have faith are children of Abraham. Scripture foresaw that God would justify the Gentiles by faith, and announced in advance to Abraham: "All nations will be blessed through you." So those who rely on faith are blessed along with Abraham, the man of faith. (Gal 3:6–9)

Paul is drawing our attention to the first twelve chapters of Genesis where two complementary facts are spelled out. On the one hand, Genesis affirms three times that God created all humans. All humanity descends from Adam and Eve, all humanity descends from Noah, and all humanity derives from Babel. Thus, all the "nations" in the Genesis account are described in the "table of nations" of Genesis 10: "From these the nations spread out over the earth after the flood" (Gen 10:32). So all humans are cousins, descended from the same family, all are created by the same God.

Yet in the same breath, Paul reminds his readers also that Abraham is specially chosen so that in him and in his descendants all the "ethne," all the "nations" will be blessed. Because the complementary truth of the story in Genesis is that this same God who created all humans is also the one who in judgment and mercy by divine intervention confused the languages at Babel and thus created the multiplicity of cultures in the world. The phenomenal diversity of languages and cultures around the world is also attributed to the direct work of this same God of all who wishes to bless all the nations through the instrumentality of Abraham. Thus, following Paul's logic, on the basis of creation, we can simultaneously affirm commonalities and acknowledge differences.

B. God the Son: Common Faith, Diverse Faith Stories

Paul now takes the second step in developing his trinitarian viewpoint that can hold in tension the twin truths: one gospel (Gal 1:6–9), many perspectives. And this second stone in Paul's trinitarian foundation had to do with God the Son, Jesus Christ.

Now that this faith has come, we are no longer under a guardian. So in Christ Jesus you are all children of God through faith, for all of you who were baptized into Christ have clothed yourselves with Christ. There is neither Jew nor Greek, neither

> slave nor free, nor is there male and female; for you are all one
> in Christ Jesus. If you belong to Christ, then you are Abraham's
> seed, heirs according to the promise. . . .
>
> But when the set time had fully come, God sent his Son,
> born of a woman, born under the law, to redeem those under
> the law, that we might receive adoption to sonship. Because you
> are his sons, God sent the Spirit of his Son into our hearts, the
> Spirit who calls out, "Abba! Father!" So you are no longer a
> slave but God's child, and since you are his child, God has made
> you also an heir. . . . (Gal 3:25–29; 4:4–6)

Paul wants to shout from the rooftops that in Christ the dividing wall is
broken, a new humanity has been created, and all peoples of all cultures are
brought together to become members of the same family (cf. Eph 2:11–3:19). In
fact, in Christ, even the Gentiles become "seed of Abraham!" In Jesus Christ, all
peoples from all cultures (Jews and Gentiles alike) can call God "Abba!"

Yet in the midst of asserting this almost unbelievable truth, Paul also makes
reference to the ways in which Paul's hearers and their society subdivided and separated humans in terms of culture, socioeconomics and gender. So Paul recognizes
that there are differences between Jew and Greek, slave and free, male and female.
In spite of such social and human differences, all are brought together and created
into a new family, the offspring of Abraham. Thus, on the basis of salvation in Jesus
Christ, we can simultaneously affirm commonalities and acknowledge differences.

C. God the Holy Spirit: Common Fruit, Diverse Gifts

Paul goes on to take the third and final step in developing his trinitarian viewpoint that
can hold in tension the twin truths: one gospel (Gal 1:6–9), many perspectives. And
this third stone in Paul's trinitarian foundation has to do with God the Holy Spirit.

> But the fruit of the Spirit is love, joy, peace, forbearance,
> kindness, goodness, faithfulness, gentleness, and self-control.
> Against such things there is no law. Those who belong to Christ
> Jesus have crucified the flesh with its passions and desires. Since
> we live by the Spirit, let us keep in step with the Spirit. Let us
> not become conceited, provoking and envying each other. . . .
>
> Do not be deceived: God cannot be mocked. A man reaps
> what he sows. Whoever sows to please their flesh, from the flesh
> will reap destruction; whoever sows to please the Spirit, from

the Spirit will reap eternal life. Let us not grow weary in doing good, for at the proper time we will reap a harvest if we do not give up. Therefore, as we have opportunity, let us do good of all people, especially to those who belong to the family of believers. (Gal 5:22–6:15)

The Holy Spirit comes to all believers in Jesus Christ without any distinction. And the fruit of the Holy Spirit is given to all equally. In Ephesians Paul will say, "There is one body and one Spirit just as you were called to one hope, one Lord, one faith, one baptism" (Eph 4:4–5). Thus, in Acts 2, at Pentecost, the many tongues of flame came from one fire. All together receive the same fruit of the Holy Spirit and are one "family of believers." (In Ephesians and 1 Corinthians Paul uses the analogy of the one Body to demonstrate this unity.)

Yet even here while affirming the unity of the Church in the one Holy Spirit Paul interjects the concept of multiplicity and diversity. "Each one should test their own actions. . . . Each one should carry their own load. . . . Let us [each] do good to all people. . ." (Gal 6:4,5,10). Paul alludes to a problem that the readers of Galatians have: "provoking and envying each other" (Gal 5:26). So Paul wants his readers to recognize the differences that exist between believers. Thus, following Paul's logic, on the basis of the Holy Spirit's creation of one Church, we can simultaneously affirm commonalities and acknowledge differences.

So how do we manage to hold in dialectical tension the twin truths of one theology, many perspectives? I believe Paul would answer by pointing to Jesus Christ. In the final analysis the glocal Church of the twenty-first century must be centered in the cross and resurrection of our Lord. Only there is it possible to have a "new creation" in which we learn to simultaneously acknowledge differences and affirm commonalities.

May I never boast except in the cross of our Lord Jesus Christ, through which the world has been crucified to me, and I to the world. For neither circumcision nor uncircumcision means anything; what counts is a new creation. (Gal 6:14–15)

CONCLUSION

In the twenty-first century, the Church of Jesus Christ needs to become what it is: a glocal Church. The thesis of this chapter has been that a healthy congregation of disciples of Jesus lives out its catholicity by intentionally and actively participating in Christ's mission in a glocal fashion. It is active simultaneously in global and local mission that dynamically fosters the glocal interaction between the global and the local.

With reference to the title of this chapter, it is my conviction that in this new century the truly catholic Church will no longer set locality and catholicity over or against one another. Rather, the truly catholic, universal Church of Jesus Christ that is true to its nature is a glocal Church. The truly catholic Church is neither only local nor only global. Rather, it is both local-global simultaneously: it is glocal.

This will mean that the glocal Church's task of critical theologizing involves a dialectical tension: the gospel can only be known within cultural frameworks, yet the gospel is always distinct from, sometimes affirming of, and often prophetically critical of, all human cultures. These dialectical tensions call for us to begin our critical theologizing from an epistemological framework rather than a communicational one.

Thus, in order to do theology in a globalizing world we could begin from the following presuppositions:

- that ALL cultures are sinful and fallen and cloud ALL human understanding of God's revelation;
- that ALL cultures have some degree of general revelation or prevenient grace whereby certain aspects of God's revelation in Jesus Christ may be clearly understood;
- that ALL Christian revelation must necessarily be incarnated into a culture in order for it to be understood (it is to be "infinitely translatable"—Lamin Sanneh);
- that ALL understanding of the gospel in ALL cultures is partial (we "see only a reflection as in a mirror"—1 Cor 13:12);
- that no one Christian understanding of the gospel has a complete grasp of the "essence" God's revelation in Jesus Christ; that "contextualization" (or inculturation) is not a goal but rather an epistemological process of seeking to know God in context.

This will also mean that a truly catholic local group of believers is in fact the local manifestation of the universal glocal Church. It implies that, like my desktop PC that is an integral part of the Internet, a local group of disciples of Jesus by their very nature are part of the global Church. This glocal group of believers—no matter where they are in the world—are, therefore, commissioned to be "witnesses in Jerusalem, *and* Judaea, *and* Samaria, *and* the ends of the earth, simultaneously.

Thus a healthy glocal group of believers in this new century must be involved, at the same time, in God's mission locally *and* globally: that is, glocally.

This glocal missional perspective goes beyond the "purpose driven" church of Rick Warren. It is broader, deeper, and more organic than the rather mechanistic approach of "natural church development" (NCD) of Christian A. Schwarz. And a glocal perspective of the Church's missional calling is beyond the cell-based and "emerging Church" approaches. The glocal Church involves a group of believers being who they are: glocal in every aspect of their discipleship—and in every aspect of their mission theology.

This also means that church multiplication is transformed. Mission and evangelism as church multiplication is no longer mere geographic expansion of the mission agency. It is no longer merely the opening of new branch offices of the denomination. Church multiplication is no longer merely local. Rather, church multiplication becomes an invitation to those who do not yet know Jesus Christ to become disciples of Jesus, ambassadors of the kingdom of God, and members of the glocal Church: brothers and sisters with 1.5 billion others who profess a similar faith.

May we all learn to become who we are: one glocal Church of Jesus Christ sent in mission to the entire world, so loved by God.

PART II

THE MEANING OF MISSION THEOLOGY

CHAPTER 4
MISSION DEFINED AND DESCRIBED

Adapted from "'Mission' Defined and Described" in David Hesselgrave and
Ed Stetzer, editors. *Missionshift: Global Mission Issues in the Third Millennium.*
Nashville: B & H Publishing, 2010, 7–29. Used by permission

THESIS

The purpose of this chapter is to offer a brief historical overview of some ways in which the Christian Church has defined "mission" down through the centuries, and to demonstrate how the various definitions have influenced the thought and practice of the Christian Church's ministries in the world.

INTRODUCTION

It was Sunday noon and I was invited to eat lunch with the members of the "global outreach task force" of a local church. Earlier that morning, we had all been inspired by the wonderfully uplifting and celebrative worship at the church's three Sunday morning worship events at which I had been asked to preach. It was their "Global Outreach Weekend." Toward the end of our lunch I turned to Gloria,[83] the task force's chair person, and remarked,

"I am very impressed with the Task Force's organization and creative approach to this missions weekend. The Friday evening dinner was so well done, including the interviews of members of your church involved in ministries locally and globally. The mission fair had such a large number of display booths that highlighted all the mission activities and missionaries your church supports locally and globally. The international and local multicultural aspects of the music, the reports, and the visual presentations were so very well done! Thank you for inviting me to be a part of this celebration!"

---

83. Not her real name.

Gloria grinned and replied, "Thank you for your feedback. Your observations are important to us. But please notice that we did not call this our "missions weekend." If we had called it a "missions emphasis weekend," no one would have come. We know; we tried it before. The word "mission" turns everyone off. The members of our church do not want to be associated with anything called 'mission.' When we changed the name to "global outreach" everything changed. You see, Chuck, no one seems to know what mission is. But a majority of our members want to be involved in some kind of local and global ministries that will benefit those in need. They are especially interested in short-term projects and visits to different parts of the world. Now you see why when I invited you to preach I asked you not to use the word "mission" in your sermon.

I nodded thoughtfully as I listened to Gloria. During the last several years, I had often heard comments like hers. It would appear that "mission" and "missionaries" are two of the most misunderstood words in the vocabulary of North American churches today.

A.   The word "mission" as it is used today

Part of the confusion over the word "mission" may be the result of the way it is being overused today in numerous arenas. Out of curiosity, I did a Google search for the word "mission." I was offered 247,000,000 hits! By way of example, there are towns with the name "Mission." There are movies like "The Mission" and "Mission Impossible II." When NASA sends up a shuttle to dock with the international space station, that trip is called a "mission." The word is especially prominent in the business world because of the emphasis on corporations drawing up their "mission statement" as a way of articulating the most fundamental purpose for which the corporation exists. Although seemingly these uses of the word would have little to do with the Christian Church, yet each in fact describes a small portion of what the word can mean for Christian mission. The *Merriam-Webster's Collegiate Dictionary* offers a range of definitions, including its meaning with reference to Christian missionary activity.[84]

---

84. **mis•sion** \'mi-shən\ *noun*

[New Latin, Medieval Latin, and Latin; New Latin*mission-, missio* religious mission, from Medieval Latin, task assigned, from Latin, act of sending, from *mittere* to send]

obsolete : the act or an instance of sending

  a : a ministry commissioned by a religious organization to propagate its faith or carry on humanitarian work

  b : assignment to or work in a field of missionary enterprise

It is especially important that the Christian Church wrestle with its "mission" in the sense of articulating the reason and purpose for which it exists. Local congregations have been encouraged to write their "mission statement" as a means of focusing their various ministries. Denominations have developed their "vision and mission" statements, a process I was involved in with my denomination, the Reformed Church in America, whose "mission and vision" statement guided the denominational priorities for more than ten years. During the past fifteen years we have also become familiar with modified form of the word as in "missional church."[85]

---

c (1) : a mission establishment

(2) : a local church or parish dependent on a larger religious organization for direction or financial support

d : *plural* : organized missionary work

e : a course of sermons and services given to convert the unchurched or quicken Christian faith

(3) : a body of persons sent to perform a service or carry on an activity: as

a : a group sent to a foreign country to conduct diplomatic or political negotiations

b : a permanent embassy or legation

c : a team of specialists or cultural leaders sent to a foreign country

(4) a : a specific task with which a person or a group is charged

b (1) : a definite military, naval, or aerospace task, a bombing *mission*, a space *mission*,

(2) : a flight operation of an aircraft or spacecraft in the performance of a mission, a *mission* to Mars Merriam-Webster (1996). *Merriam-Webster's Collegiate Dictionary*, Springfield, Mass., Merriam-Webster,

85. In the early 1990s George Hunsberger, Darrell Guder, Inagrace Dietterich, Lois Barrett, Alan Roxburgh, Craig Van Gelder, and others founded "The Gospel and Our Culture Network" to develop the implications for North America of Lesslie Newbigin's challenge regarding the re-evangelization of the West, following the lead of "The Gospel and Culture" movement in England of the 1980s, spearheaded by Wilbert Shenk. The early conversations, reflection, and publications of "The Gospel and Our Culture Network" contributed to the creation of the concept of the "missional church." The term has now been used in so many ways as to become almost meaningless. A Google search for the term offered 933,000 hits! A quick overview demonstrates that the term now stands for any kind of new life, vision, vitality, and direction of the Church—often with little or no theological or missiological reflection. Foundational literature for this movement would include Hunsberger, George R. and Craig Van Gelder, eds., , *The Church between Gospel and Culture: the Emerging Mission in North America.* Grand Rapids: Eerdmans Publ. Co., 1996; Guder, Darrell L., ed., Inagrace T. Dietterich, Lois Barrett, George R. Hunsberger, Alan Roxburgh and Craig Van Gelder, *Missional Church: A Vision for the Sending of the Church in North America.* Grand Rapids: Eerdmans Publ. Co., 1998; Barrett, Lois, ed., Dale A. Ziemer, Darrell L. Guder, George R. Hunsberger, Walter Hobbs,

Down through the centuries, the Christian Church has defined its "mission" in a wide variety of ways. Sidney Rooy has highlighted the differences.

> There does not exist, nor has there ever existed, only one defini-
> tion of the mission of the Church; nor (one interpretation) as to
> what are the biblical foundations of that mission. If, like David
> Bosch, we define mission as missio Dei (the mission of God),
> we can say that this signifies the revelation of God as the One
> who loves the world God has created, who is concerned for this
> world, and who has formed the church to be an (active) subject
> called to participate in the historical project of establishing the
> kingdom of God. . . . Our understanding of this missio Dei has
> been subjected to many interpretations down through history.
> . . . Each definition and all understandings of the biblical bases
> of that mission are tentative and are subject to new evaluation
> and change. Truly, each generation must define mission anew.
> (Rooy 1998, 3–4; translation from the Spanish by Charles Van
> Engen.)

B.   The original biblical meaning of the word "mission"

Because our most foundational grounding is in the Bible, we begin to build our definition of "mission" by considering the biblical perspectives. The word "mission"
is rare in both the Hebrew Old Testament and the Greek New Testament. What
is emphasized regularly is the concept of being "sent," with an emphasis on the
authority and purpose of the sender. The New Testament uses *"apostello"* and
"pempo" somewhat interchangeably. The *Theological Dictionary of the New Testament*
tells us that,

Lynn Stutzman, Jeff Van Cooten, *Treasure in Clay Jars: Patterns in Missional Faithfulness,* Grand
Rapids: Eerdmans, 2003.

Some recent works that may be of interest to the reader are Earl Creps and Dan Kimball,
Off-Road Disciplines: Spiritual Adventures of Missional Leaders; Alan Roxburgh and Fred Romanuk,
The Missional Leader: Equipping Your Church to Reach a Changing World; Eddie Gibbs, *ChurchNext:
Quantum Changes in How We Do Ministry*; Michael Frost and Alan Hirsh, *The Shaping of Things
to Come: Innovation and Mission for the 21st-Century Church*; Neil Cole, *Organic Church: Growing Faith
Where Life Happens*; Ed Stetzer and David Putnam, *Breaking the Code: Your Church Can Become a
Missionary in Your Community*.

Apostéllō occurs some 135 times in the NT, mostly in the Gospels and Acts. *pémpō* occurs some 80 times, 33 in John, five in Revelation, 22 in Luke/Acts, only four in Matthew, and one in Mark. Apart from the special use of *pémpō* in John, the Lucan material predominates; . . . The religious character of the NT material explains the general predominance of *apostéllō*, and in the NT as a whole *pémpō* seems to be used when the stress is on the sending, *apostéllō* when it is on the commission, and especially (in the Synoptists) when it is God who sends.

In John, Jesus uses *apostéllō* to denote his full authority, i.e., to ground his mission in God as the One who is responsible for his words and works. But he uses *pémpō*, e.g., in the phrase "the Father sent me," so as to state God's participation in his work by the act of sending. . . . The mission of Jesus acquires its significance and force from the fact that he is the Son, not from its description in terms of *apostéllō*.

In the NT *apostéllō* certainly begins to be a theological word for "sending forth to serve God with God's own authority," but only in context and not with any radical departure from its normal sense. . . . [86]

In relation to the general use of *apostellō* in the NT we must say finally that the word does begin to become a theological term meaning "to send forth to service in the kingdom of God with full authority (grounded in God)."[87]

Jesus sends the twelve in Luke 9 and the seventy in Luke 10 on their mission to the Jews and to the world. After the resurrection, Jesus commissions his followers as ones being sent. Jesus said, "Peace be with you! As the Father has sent (*apestalken*) me, I am sending (*pémpo*) you" (John 20:21). Paul uses the term in its noun form (*apóstolos*) to refer to himself, his calling, his commission, and his authority derived from his being sent by Jesus the Messiah. Paul does this at the beginning of his

---

86. Gerhard Kittel, Gerhard Friedrich, and Geoffrey William Bromiley, *Theological Dictionary of the New Testament*. Grand Rapids, Mich: W. B. Eerdmans, 1995, c1985, S. 68. (Author's note: For ease of reading, I changed the Greek text words in the original to English transliteration, CVE).

87. Kittel, Bromiley, and Friedrich, *Theological Dictionary of the New Testament*, electronic ed. Grand Rapids, MI : Eerdmans, 1964–c1976, S. 1:406.

letters to the Romans, Corinthians, Galatians, Ephesians, Colossians, Timothy, and Titus. The writers of 1 and 2 Peter do the same.

So the first element of a definition of "mission" should be based on the concept of "sending." The Church is sent by its Lord. All through the Bible it is clear that the covenant people of God are sent by God to the "nations" who are not yet part of the people of God.[88] In Luke 4, Jesus refers to himself as one who is sent. "I must proclaim the good news of the kingdom of God to the other towns also, because that is why I was sent (*apestalên*)" (Luke 4:43). Like Jesus, his followers are also sent to proclaim the coming of the kingdom of God, to invite all peoples to become disciples of Jesus and responsible members of Christ's Church (Matt 28:18–20). This understanding of the word "mission" is most basic and should never be lost or eclipsed by subsequent discussions and refinements.

The church in the twenty-first century needs to keep the "sending" element of Christian mission in the foreground. Biblical mission is God's mission. Mission is participation in the mission of Jesus Christ, the Lord of the Church, in the power of the Holy Spirit. Mission is not merely church extension, nor is it merely doing good works of compassion. Mission is not to be determined by a mission agency's particular bias or agenda. Today there are as many cross-cultural missionaries sent and supported by churches and mission agencies in Asia, Africa and Latin America, as the total sent from Europe and North America. Yet, in the final analysis, the "senders" are not the denomination, not the mission agency, not the megachurch or its senior pastor, not a non-governmental relief agency. The authority of the mission enterprise is not that of the denomination, mission agency, self-proclaimed apostle, large relief agency, or a more advanced culture. The sender is Jesus Christ, whose authority defines, circumscribes, limits, and propels Christian mission.

C. The Constantinian redefinition of "mission"

For almost three centuries after the coming of the Holy Spirit at Pentecost, the Christian Church understood "mission" as outlined above. But with the changes effected by the emperor Constantine (306–337CE), the definition of mission changed dramatically. Sidney Rooy has given us an excellent summary of the impact that the Constantinian era had on the Church's understanding of mission. Rooy explains,

---

88. See, for example, Glasser, Arthur F. with Charles E. Van Engen, Dean S. Gilliland, and Shawn B. Redford, *Announcing the Kingdom: The Story of God's Mission in the Bible*, Grand Rapids: Baker Book House, 2003.

With the recognition of Christianity as an officially permitted religion based on the Decree of Milan in 313 AD, the context in which Christians exercised their mission changed dramatically. After that first large step, the next came in rapid succession: in 325 [Christianity] became the favored religion, in 380 it became the official religion, and by 392 it was the only tolerated religion [in the Holy Roman Empire]. That is, in the brief span of eighty years, Christianity went from being a persecuted religion to the persecuting religion. . . . During the Middle Ages, in the West, the king was considered the vicar of Christ and of God. . . .

Thus, in addition to the church, the [nation-state] became an agent of mission represented by the persons designated by the emperor. The method by which the church was extended included the imposition of the faith by [forcibly] destroying the pagan religions and the institution of the new religion. It is true that at times the gospel was extended through the work of missionaries, . . . but most of Europe was Christianized by conquest, the mass baptism of the pagans, and the construction of churches, monasteries and schools with the direct support of the political powers [of the day].

In the Constantinian [model of mission], the dominant motivation was the temporal and spiritual extension of [what was then considered to be] the "kingdom of God" [embodied in the emperor]. Without a doubt, there was confusion regarding the two kingdoms: the state and the church. Together with the huge masses that entered the church, many [popular] beliefs and customs were also accepted. Popular [or folk] religion, which has always existed, took on new directions that affected not only the doctrines and ceremonies of the church, but also influenced the way mission was understood. (Rooy 1998, 10–12; trans. by Charles Van Engen. See also, e.g., Bevans 2004, 173–74.)[89]

Forms of this model continued into the colonial era of the eighteenth and nineteenth centuries. Christian missions at times looked quite similar to the

---

89. Padilla, ed., *Bases Bíblicas de la Misión: Perspectivas Latinoamericanas*, Buenos Aires/ Grand Rapids: Nueva Creación/Eerdmans Publ. Co., 1998.

medieval model sketched above. "Whether we like it or not," Stephen Neill wrote, "it is the historic fact that the great expansion of Christianity has coincided in time with the worldwide and explosive expansion of Europe that followed the Renaissance; that the colonizing powers have been the Christian powers; that a whole variety of compromising relationships have existed between missionaries and governments; and that in the main Christianity has been carried forward on the wave of western prestige and power." (Neill 1964, 450; cited in Bosch 1980, 116).

Living in the twenty-first century, we should not be too hard in our judgment of the medieval and colonial models of mission. During the past one hundred and fifty years, Protestant mission endeavors from the North and West of the globe to the South and East at times implanted a cultural Protestantism that was too often more interested in propagating a particular form of civilization than in helping women and men come to faith in Jesus Christ. Culture, civilization, education, and technology too often replaced the emperor in eclipsing the gospel of faith in Jesus Christ. In today's mission activities, when denominations, mission organizations, or megachurches set out to "plant" new churches that are essentially identical branch offices of the sending organization, the parallels to the medieval view of mission are quite troubling.[90]

D. William Carey's Great Commission definition of mission

In the late 1700s, William Carey (1761–1834) suggested a different way of understanding mission. Carey "preached that the church's primary responsibility was foreign missions" (Reapsome 2000, 162). In his groundbreaking work, *An Enquiry into the Obligation of Christians to Use Means for the Conversion of the Heathens,* Carey based his view of mission on Matthew 28:18–20, a passage that eventually would be known throughout the Christian Church, particularly among Protestants, as the "Great Commission."[91] During the nineteenth and early twentieth centuries, the "Great Commission" (with Mark 16:15–16, Luke 24:46–49, John 20:21,

---

90. For discussion of this from a Latin American perspective, see Charles E. Van Engen, "¿Por Qué Sembrar Iglesias Saludables? Bases Bíblicas y Misionológicas" in J. Wagenveld, ed., *Sembremos Iglesias Saludables.* Miami: FLET, 2004, 43–96. The English version of this chapter was published as Charles Van Engen, "Why Multiply Healthy Churches," in Gary Teja and John Wagenfeld, ed., *Planting Healthy Churches.* Chicago: Multiplication Network Ministries, 2015, 23–60.

91. See, e.g, David Hesselgrave (2000). "Great Commission," in A. Scott Moreau, Harold Netland, and Charles Van Engen, *Evangelical Dictionary of World Missions.* Grand Rapids: Baker Book House: 412–14.

and Acts 1:8 alongside the Matthew passage) "came to play an extremely important role in missions and missiology" (Hesselgrave 2000, 414).

The Matthean version of the "Great Commission" drew from, and contributed to, a particular view of mission. Matthew's "Great Commission" was a primary component of the biblical foundation for the "Watchword" of the Student Volunteer Movement of the late 1800s that was later popularized by John R. Mott (1865–1955) as a motto for the great missionary conference held at Edinburgh in 1910: "the evangelization of the world in this generation."[92] We have space here to mention only a few of the related assumptions.

For about 150 years, up until the 1960s, Protestants who used the "Great Commission" as their foundation for mission assumed the following:
- That salvation was individualistic;
- That salvation had to do primarily with a spiritual and personal relationship with Jesus Christ;
- That the primary calling of the church's mission was geographic: Christians were called to "go";
- That the "going" was primarily from the West and North of the globe to the East and South;
- That the "make disciples" portion of the "Great Commission" was more important than the "baptizing and teaching" portions;
- That new converts should be gathered into churches resembling— and often belonging to—the sending churches and missions;
- And (especially during the last half of the nineteenth century) that new individual converts should be extracted from their non-Christian contexts, gathered into Christian mission stations, and taught the culture and civilization of the missionaries.

In 1955 Donald McGavran published *The Bridges of God: A Study in the Strategy of Missions*, in which he affirmed but radically reinterpreted the "Great Commission" missiology of Matthew 28:18–20 (McGavran 1955).[93] McGavran questioned the "mission station" approach. He suggested that the word "nations" (*ethne*) meant people groups rather than individuals. He affirmed that the imperative, the mandate, was to "disciple" people and not the geographically defined "going" as emphasized by earlier mission thought. He then suggested that the result of such

---

92. For a brief biographical sketch of this great missionary statesman, see, e.g., Douglas, "Mott, John Raleigh" in Ibid., 664

93. Ibid.

disciple-making activity should be measured in terms of the numbers of persons who were gathered in ethnically cohesive groups and became members of Christ's church. Founded by Donald McGavran in 1965, the Church Growth Movement built upon the basic tenets of the missiology of *Bridges of God*. By the 1970s and 1980s in some Protestant evangelical circles, the *ethne* had come to be understood as being "unreached people groups," a view that combined some geographic and individualistic assumptions with certain cultural and group-oriented emphases. But there was never a clear or precise theological or missiological comprehension of what "unreached" or "resistant" meant. (See Chapter 10 of this volume.)

E. "Mission" and the indigenous church model

The Great Commission understanding of mission emphasized the evangelization of those who were not yet followers of Jesus. Parallel to this view was a more institutionalized perspective advocated by Henry Venn (1796–1873) in England and Rufus Anderson (1796–1880) in the United States. These two mission administrators stressed that the goal of mission was the birth, nurture, and development of "self-supporting, self-governing, and self-propagating churches." James Scherer describes this view as follows.

> The new church-centered view [of mission], prominent around the middle of the nineteenth century through the work of Henry Venn and Rufus Anderson, . . . set forth the view that "church planting"—especially the planting of local "three-self" churches with their own autonomy and indigeneity—should be considered alongside personal conversion, an important goal of missions. The acknowledged "father" of mission science, Gustav Warneck could declare that mission activity was "the road from (existing) church to church (in the mission field)" (Scherer 1993, 82; Scherer is citing Duerr 1947).[94]

---

94. Roger Bassham wrote, "Evangelical mission thought (in the 1930s and 1940s) revolved essentially around evangelism, often understood in terms of individual conversions, with the implied aim of gathering believers into self-supporting, self-governing, and self-propagating churches on the basis of a closely defined basis of faith." Roger Bassham, *Mission Theology: 1948–1975, Years of Worldwide Creative Tension, Ecumenical, Evangelical and Roman Catholic.* Pasadena: William Carey Library, 1979

Though they may not have intended it so, the goal of mission advocated by Venn and Anderson as a principle of mission administration became a virtual definition of mission that dominated mission theology and practice among almost all older denominations and mission agencies for a hundred years, beginning in the mid-nineteenth century.[95] Many of those who followed Venn and Anderson tried to soften the institutional aspects of their view of mission. John Nevius (1829–1893), Roland Allen (1868–1947), Melvin Hodges (1909–1986) and Alan Tippett (1911–1988) offered refinements to the "three-self" formula that sought to stress the development of the spiritual, organic, theological, relational, social, cultural, and contextual aspects of missionary congregations. Yet the original "three-selves" have continued to dominate in Africa, Asia, and Latin America to such an extent that one can find "three-self" churches originally established by Western European and North American mission endeavors that today exhibit another kind of "self": they tend to be self-centered and selfish.

During 1970s and 1980s, many denominations in the United States adopted a form of the "three-self" formula as the administrative philosophy for planting new churches in the suburbs of North American cities, with very mixed results. Vestiges of this movement remain in some denominational church planting endeavors in the United States.[96]

More recently, the "emerging church" movement appears to be searching for ways to birth, nurture, and develop congregations that are "indigenous" to the center cities of the U.S. This new movement shows striking parallels to the search by the baby boomer generation to form kingdom-oriented, transformational faith

---

95. For an excellent summary discussion about "indigenous churches" and mission, see John Mark Terry, "Indigenous Churches" in A. Scott Moreau, Harold Netland, and Charles Van Engen, editors, 2000.

Evangelical Dictionary of World Missions 2000, 483–85. I grew up in the National Presbyterian Church of Mexico in which the "three-self" formula was the dominant mission perspective advocated by missionaries and national leaders alike. With over one million members, that denomination is one of the largest single denominations in Mexico. Yet it is in its infancy in both local and global missionsending. I believe the "three-self" formula is one of the major reasons for that denomination's lack of missionary vision and practice.

96. In China, beginning with the Marxist Cultural Revolution led by Mao Tse-Tung (1893–1976) in the late 1940s, a number of Christian denominations and their congregations were officially recognized by the Marxist government as "Three-Self Patriotic Movement" churches. This use of the term is unique and distinctive. An exploration of that history is beyond the scope of this book.

communities in the cities of the U.S. during the 1960s. Those who are leading these contemporary efforts could learn much from what their predecessors experienced in local and global mission in terms of birthing, nurturing, and developing indigenous churches around the world.

F.   "Mission" in the 1960s

Following the Second World War, many Western European missiologists and theologians, along with some of their counterparts in the older mainline denominations in North America, began to formulate a new view of mission. Having seen the disastrous consequences of the church's silence and irrelevance in the crisis of Western Europe during the 1930s and early 1940s, and following the inspiration of Dietrich Bonheoffer, among others, the churches associated with the fledgling World Council of Churches (founded in 1948) began to search for what they considered to be a more "relevant" missiology. They wanted to mobilize the churches to become involved with what God was doing in the world. This new view of mission crystallized around the phrase *missio Dei*, the mission of God, and represented a radical secularization of mission.

Missiologists like J. C. Hoekendijk demonstrated a deep pessimism about the church as a viable agent of God's mission. In fact Hoekendijk suggested that the best thing the church could do was to turn itself "inside out" and essentially cease to exist (Hoekendijk 1966). This led to an emphasis on God's mission oriented toward, and centered in, the kingdom of God and in the world rather than in the church.

James Scherer summarized this development as follows:

> The latter half of the nineteenth century and the first half of the twentieth were largely dominated by the church-centered concept as the practical goal for what were then called "foreign missions." Church-centrism replaced earlier individualistic mission theories derived from pietism and evangelical revivalism that focused on personal conversion [conversio gentilium] and "soul saving." . . .
>
> From 1860 to 1960 the church-centered goal of mission served a very useful purpose in replacing the earlier missionary pattern of individual conversions, in that it clearly defined the necessary steps toward planting churches among all nations.

But as the task of church planting advanced in all six continents, it was rapidly becoming obsolete as a missionary goal. . . .

After [the meeting of the International Missionary Council at] Willingen [in 1952], the church-centered mission framework . . . was no longer adequate for dealing with the problems facing churches engaged in mission in, from and to all six continents in the postcolonial era. Those problems required a missio Dei [mission of God] response, with a clearer understanding of the Trinitarian basis and nature of the church's mission, and an openness and sensitivity to the eschatological character of the kingdom, and the church's subordinate relationship to it.

[But] in the decade of the 1960s, missio Dei[97] was to become the play thing of armchair theologians with little more than an academic interest in the practical mission of the church but with a considerable penchant for theological speculation and mischief making. . . .

God was seen to be working out the divine purpose in the midst of the world through immanent, intra-mundane historical forces, above all secularization. The Trinitarian missio Dei view was replaced by a theory about the transformation of the world and of history not through evangelization and church-planting but by means of a divinely guided immanent historical process, somewhat analogous to deistic views of the Enlightenment. This secular view of God's mission made the empirical church virtu-ally dispensable as an agent of divine mission, and in some cases even a hindrance . . . The world set the agenda for the church, and the real locus of God's mission was no longer the church but the world.

Accordingly, the church must now receive its marching orders from the world . . . Humanization was the new keyword. . . . (Scherer 1993, 82–86).

---

97.   H. H. Rosin states that "Georg F. Vicedom's book, *Missio Dei, Einfurung in eine Theologie der Mission* (published in German in) 1958, . . . played a decisive part in the spreading of the term 'missio Dei," appeared in 1965 in the USA in an English translation entitled *The Mission of God: An Introduction to a Theology of Mission*, St. Louis: Concordia, 1965. (Cf. H. H. Rosin 1972, 24).

This radical redefinition of mission, with its strong impetus toward secularizing Christian mission became a reason for concern among many of the most loyal participants in the World Council of Churches. Stephen Neill, for example, warned that "When everything is mission, nothing is mission" (Neill 1959, 81; see also Blauw 1962, 109; 121–122). Neill felt it necessary to emphasize that, "The one central purpose for which the Church has been called into existence is that . . . it should preach the gospel to every creature. Everything else—ministry, sacraments, doctrine, worship—is ancillary to this." (Neill 1959, 112). Bevans and Schroeder comment, "It is important to heed Stephen Neill's warning that if everything is mission, then nothing is mission. Nevertheless, we need also to pay attention to David Bosch's warning to 'beware of any attempt at delineating mission too sharply'" (Bevans 2004, 9; Bevans and Schroeder cite Bosch 1991, 512).

In the twenty-first century, evangelical mission agencies are becoming increasingly committed and involved in humanitarian and compassion ministries through agriculture, education, medicine, AIDS-related ministries, "children at risk" movements, and so on. Given these new emphases in evangelical mission activism, it behooves us to consider carefully how evangelical views of mission today may be tempted to repeat the same errors made when mission was redefined and eventually lost in the World Council of Churches between the 1960s and the 1990s.

G. Evangelical reaction, redefinition, and reconstruction of mission from the 1980s to 2000

The 1960s was a time of great ferment around the globe. "In 1960 alone, seventeen new African nations were born."[98] In Latin America, dictatorships were rising and falling. Western Europe was regaining its strength. The cold war was in full bloom, along with the war in Vietnam. The Roman Catholic world was in an uproar after the Second Vatican Council. The baby boomers were changing the face of North America. Older churches and mission agencies were in a deep crisis as to their identity, purpose, direction, and priorities for mission action, while a host of new sodality mission agencies born after the Second World War were beginning to dominate the scene. In its April 1969 issue, what had been known as *The International Review of Missions*, the oldest missiological journal in the world,

---

98. Van Engen 1990, 212; citing Charles Forman, *The Nation and the Kingdom: Christian Mission in the New Nations*. New York, Friendship, 1964, 17.

dropped the "s" to become *The International Review of Mission*.[99] Many older denominations in the US abandoned the words "mission" and "missionary" and adopted the vocabulary of "fraternal workers" and "ecumenical sharing of resources."

The departure from a church-centric view that included the idea of individual conversion to faith in Jesus Christ was so drastic that Donald McGavran accused the World Council of Churches of "betraying the two billion." (McGavran 1972, 16–18). In *Crucial Issues in Missions Tomorrow*, published in 1972, McGavran wrote, "The [air]plane of missions has been hijacked . . . Helping older churches as well as helping younger churches is to be considered mission. From this new angle, mission ceases being gospel proclamation to non-Christians and becomes interchurch aid or good work done anywhere." (McGavran 1972, 190; see also Van Engen 1981, 20 and Van Engen 1990, 212–13)

The "integration" of the International Missionary Council (IMC) into the World Council of Churches impacted the evangelical mission theology of the 1960s.[100] Reacting against the mission thinking of the World Council outlined in the section above, a significant number of important evangelical leaders came together in two major mission conferences in 1966, inspired by the Billy Graham Association: the Congress on the Church's World Mission at Wheaton and the

---

99. In the editorial for that issue, William Crane wrote, "Missions in the plural have a certain justification in the diplomatic, political, and economic spheres of international relations where their nature, scope, and authority are defined by the interests of both those who initiate and those who receive them, but the mission of the Church is singular in that it issues from the One Triune God and His intention for the salvation of all men. His commission to the Church is one, even though the ministries given to the Church for this mission, and the given responses of particular churches in particular situations to the commission, are manifold. . . . The various studies and programmes initiated by the Division of World Mission and Evangelism in the past few years since integration into the life of the World Council of Churches, also reflect this concern for the one mission of the Church in six continents rather than the traditional concern for missions from three continents to the other three. W. H. Crane, "Editorial," *International Review of Mission* 58: 1969, 141–44.

100. In 1966, the Congress on the Church's Worldwide Mission was convened, representing a large crosssection of evangelical mission leaders. The delegates stated, "The birth of the World Council of Churches and the pressures to integrate the (IMC) into the framework of that organization brought to the forefront the problem of conservative theological missionary cooperation." Harold Lindsell, *The Church's Worldwide Mission*, 1966, 2. See also Charles Van Engen, "A Broadening Vision: Forty Years of Evangelical Theology of Mission, 1946–1986" in Joel A. S. Carpenter, Wilbert Shenk, eds., *Earthen Vessels: American Evangelicals and Foreign Missions, 1880–1980*, 1990, 203–32.

World Congress on Evangelism in Berlin. These gatherings would flow into the large world mission congresses at Lausanne (1974), Pattaya (1980), Manila (1989), Cape Town (2010), among others (see Van Engen 1990).

Out of this great ferment in evangelical mission thinking came a new evangelical synthesis and new definitions of mission for the twenty-first century. During the 1980s and 1990s evangelicals called for mission among "unreached people groups," groups that they considered lacked the presence of a viable church. This motivated evangelicals to form "Co-Mission," organized to mobilize the sending of a multitude of missionaries to the former Soviet bloc countries after the dismantling of the USSR.[101] This view of mission also led to an emphasis on mission in the "10–40 window," the area between 10 and 40 degrees north of the equator, spanning from the eastern edge of Western Europe to the north Pacific. It is considered to be the least evangelized area of the world where the greatest number of poor people are also to be found (Love 2000, 983).

Ralph Winter sparked a movement for "Frontier Missions," mission among those who have no natural contacts with Christians. After the Lausanne II congress in Manila, the AD 2000 and Beyond movement was born to mobilize Christians around the world for world evangelization, following a vision very similar to that of Edinburgh 1910.

Along with these initiatives, one can observe evangelicals struggling to bring together evangelism and social action once again. In their extreme reaction to the WCC emphases of the 1960s, evangelicals ended up splitting word and deed, speaking and doing, verbal proclamation and social transformation. Through a series of consultations, they sought to bring the two closer without necessarily giving one a priority place over the other. In 2010, the Lausanne Movement gathered for its third major congress in Cape Town, South Africa. The extensive documentation emanating from that gathering demonstrates the effort on the part of the leaders of the Lausanne Movement to articulate a mission theology that seeks the transformation of the whole person in relation with others, personally and socially.[102]

---

101. Sadly, many of these evangelical mission organizations and their missionaries tended to ignore the fact that the Christian Church had already been present there for more than a thousand years in the forms of Orthodox Christianity.

102. See, for example, "The Cape Town Commitment:" www.lausanne.org/content/ctc /ctcommitment—website inactive.

Today, at the beginning of a new century, evangelical mission is searching for new, appropriate, creative, and motivating definitions of mission. Increasingly, evangelical missiologists have adopted the biblical notion of God's mission (*missio Dei*) as pointing toward a more holistic view of mission. Orlando Costas, Samuel Escobar, René Padilla, and others called for a much stronger emphasis on the kingdom of God as a helpful paradigm of holistic and transformational mission action.[103] Evangelicals today would probably agree with James Scherer's observation.

> Abandoning the church-centered framework in no way implies forsaking the church's mission, but rather a revisioning of that mission from a fresh biblical, missiological, and above all, eschatological point of view. This remains a priority task for the theology of Christian mission today. (Scherer 1993, 85)

Evangelical missiology has been searching for a new cohesive synthesis. In 1999, Vinay Samuel and Chris Sugden compiled a collection of essays to which they gave the title, *Mission as Transformation* (Samuel 1999). The kingdom of God framework for mission is very strong in this volume. In 2000, evangelical theologians of mission gathered in Iguassu, Brazil to dialogue regarding the church's mission. A rapid scan of the topics shows an inclusive view of mission that sought to address many different missional agendas.[104] At a large evangelical mission congress in Thailand in 2004, the concept of "transformation" was suggested. In their desire to develop a holistic understanding of mission, evangelicals probably need to heed Stephen Neill's warning: when everything is mission, nothing

---

103. See, e.g., Orlando Costas, *The Church and its Mission: A Shattering Critique from the Third World*, 1974; Orlando Costas, *Theology of the Crossroads in Contemporary Latin America*, 1976; Orlando Costas, "The whole world for the whole gospel," *Missiology* 8 (Oct 1980): 395–405; Orlando Costas, *Christ Outside the Gate: Mission Beyond Christendom*: 1982; Samuel Escobar, "Beyond liberation theology: evangelical missiology in Latin America" *IBMR* 6 (July 1982): 108–44; C. René Padilla, *Mission Between the Times: Essays on the Kingdom*, 1985; C. René Padilla, *Misión Integral: Ensayos sobre el Reino y la Iglesia*, 1986; Orlando Costas, *Liberating News: A Theology of Contextual Evangelization, 1989*; Samuel Escobar, *De la Misión a la Teología*, 1998; Samuel Escobar, *Tiempo de Misión: América Latina y la Misión Cristiana Hoy*, 1999; Samuel Escobar, *The New Global Mission: The Gospel From Everywhere to Everyone, 2003.*

104. See Taylor, William D., ed., (2000) *Global Missiology for the 21st Century: The Iguassu Dialogue*, 2000. This work was published in Portuguese as *Missiologia Global para o século XXI: A consulta de Foz de Iguaçu*, William D. Taylor, ed., Londrina: Descoberta Ed., 2001.

is mission.[105] A cohesive, consistent, focused, theologically deep, missiologically broad, and contextually appropriate evangelical missiology has not yet emerged for this new century.[106]

H. Defining "missional" and "mission": a suggestion

A possible way forward in defining "mission" for the twenty-first century might involve an attempt to describe what a "missional" church would look like. Let me suggest one way to go about that. Here is my shorthand, abbreviated attempt at a definition of "missional."

With the term "missional," I emphasize the essential nature and vocation of the church as God's called and sent people. A missional ecclesiology is biblical, historical, contextual, praxeological (it is translated into practice which in turn critiques and reshapes theory), and eschatological. "Missional," with reference to the church, sees the church as the instrument of God's mission in God's world. Following Lesslie Newbigin and others, a church that is missional understands that God's mission calls and sends the church of Jesus Christ, locally and globally, in the power of the Holy Spirit, to be a missionary church in its own society,

---

105. The present trend for evangelical schools of world mission to change their name to "school of intercultural studies" is missiologically disturbing. "Intercultural studies" is not mission. When evangelical mission thought and actions in mission are reduced to "intercultural studies," the heart and soul of a biblical perspective of mission has been lost. As Johannes Verkuyl affirmed, "Missiology may never become a substitute for action and participation. God calls for participants and volunteers in his mission. . . . If study does not lead to participation, whether at home or abroad, missiology has lost her humble calling." (Johannes Verkuyl 1978, 6.)

106. In *Transforming Mission*, David Bosch offered the following definition of mission: "Mission (is) understood as being derived from the very nature of God. It (is) thus put in the context of the doctrine of the Trinity, not of ecclesiology or soteriology. The classical doctrine of the missio Dei as God the Father sending the Son, and God the Father and the Son sending the Spirit (is) expanded to include yet another "movement": Father, Son and Holy Spirit sending the church into the world. . . . Our mission has no life of its own: only in the hands of the sending God can it truly be called mission, not least since the missionary initiative comes from God alone. . . . To participate in mission is to participate in the movement of God's love toward people, since God is (the) fountain of sending love. . . . In its mission, the church witnesses to the fullness of the promise of God's reign and participates in the ongoing struggle between that reign and the powers of darkness and evil." David Bosch 1991, 390–91. (Quoted also in part in Darrell L. Guder, ed., *Missional Church: A Vision for the Sending of the Church in North America*, 1998, 5.)

in the cultures in which it finds itself, and globally among all peoples who do not yet confess Jesus as Lord. Mission is the result of God's initiative, rooted in God's purposes to restore and heal creation and call people into a reconciled covenantal relationship with God. "Mission" means "sending," and it is the central biblical theme describing the purpose of God's action in human history, with God's people, now the church, being the primary agent of God's missionary action.[107]

Thus, a church that is "missional," will be:

- **contextual:** A missional church understands itself as part of a larger context of a lost and broken world so loved by God.
- **intentional:** A missional church understands itself as existing for the purpose of following Christ in mission.
- **proclaiming:** A missional church understands itself as intentionally sent by God in mission to its context to announce in word and deed the coming of the kingdom of God in Christ.
- **reconciling:** A missional church understands itself to be a reconnecting and healing presence in its contexts—locally, and globally.
- **sanctifying:** A missional church understands itself as a special faith community gathered around the Word preached, celebrated and lived out together that brings a purifying influence to society.
- **unifying:** A missional church understands itself as an embracing, enfolding, gathering community of faith, anxious to receive persons into its fellowship.
- **transforming:** A missional church is "the salt of the earth" (Matthew 5–8), a transforming presence as the Body of Christ in mission (*koinonia, kerygma, diakonia, marturia*—Prophet, Priest, King, Liberator, Healer, Sage).[108]

Such a conception of a "missional" church would need to take into consideration the interrelationship of what Bosch has called the church's "mission intention" and the church's "mission dimension."[109]

---

107. This definition is based on Darrell Guder, ed., *Missional Church: A Vision for the Sending of the Church in North America*, 1998, 11–12, 4–5; see also David Bosch, *Transforming Mission: Paradigm Shifts in Theology of Mission*, 1991, 390.

108. The definition offered above is drawn from Charles Van Engen, *God's Missionary People*, 65–70; and Darrell Guder, editor, 1998, 254–64.

109. See David Bosch 1980, *in loco.*

CONCLUSION

So, what should I have told Gloria and her "Global Outreach Task Force"? She is also aware that the ways in which we define "mission" influences our motivations, the agents, the means, the goals, and the way we measure the results of our lives, ministries, and actions as Christians in the world. Maybe I could have helped Gloria and the members of her church begin to gain a biblical view of "mission" centered in Jesus Christ and shaped by the gospel of the kingdom of God. James Scherer suggested that.

> One of the crucial missiological problems of the second half of the twentieth century has been how to accomplish a successful transition from an earlier church-centered theology of mission to a kingdom-oriented one without loss of missionary vision or betrayal of biblical content. It can scarcely be denied that we are in the midst of such a transition. It is equally clear that we have not yet fully grasped the meaning of a move toward the kingdom orientation, which closely correlates with the Trinitarian missio Dei. . . . The fuller implications of this changeover for our missionary practice still lie in the future (Scherer 1993, 82).[110]

In 1986, I wrote, "A Broadening Vision: Forty Years of Evangelical Theology of Mission, 1946–1986." Although evangelical missiology has undergone some development in relation to the observations I made then, I will leave it to the reader to examine the extent to which evangelical definitions of mission have changed during these intervening years.[111]

---

110. In *Constants in Context*, Stephen Bevans and Roger Schroeder suggested a definition of mission for this new century. "Mission happens wherever the church is; it is how the church exists. Mission is the church preaching Christ for the first time; it is the act of the Christians struggling against injustice and oppression; it is the binding of wounds in reconciliation; it is the church learning from other religious ways and being challenged by the world's cultures. . . . Mission is the local church focusing not on its own, internal problems, but on other human beings, focusing elsewhere, in a world that calls and challenges it." Bevans and Schroeder 2004, 9; Bevans and Schroeder cite L. Legrand, *Unity and Plurality: Mission in the Bible*, 990, xii.

111. Twenty years ago, I wrote,

"Where to from here? Evangelicals have the possibility of exciting new developments ahead. They will probably find one of these to involve the theology of the Kingdom of God. . . .

Toward the end of my Sunday lunch with Gloria and her "Task Force," they consider thinking, sharing insights, and working together to write their own definition of "mission." Once they had crafted their definition of "mission" as a task force, they could use the word again, teaching and promoting it in their church in order to further mobilize their congregation to participate in God's mission in God's world. They found the idea intriguing and challenging. Then, as I was getting ready to leave for the airport, with a twinkle in her eye, Gloria asked me, "So, how do you define mission?"

"Gloria," I answered, "I've been working on that for about forty years now. Thus far in my own search for a definition, I have arrived at the following tentative attempt. 'God's mission (*missio Dei*) works primarily through Jesus Christ's sending the people of God to all peoples of the world and from faith to the absence of faith in settings of nominal Christianity to proclaim by word and deed the coming of the kingdom of God in Jesus Christ through the Church's participation in God's mission of reconciling people to God, to themselves, to each other, and to the world and gathering them into the Church, through repentance and faith in Jesus Christ, by the work of the Holy Spirit, with a view to the transformation of the world, as a sign of the coming of the kingdom in Jesus Christ.'"

May the Holy Spirit teach us how to be and to become more authentically God's missionary people (Van Engen 1991) in this new century, sent to a lost and hurting world so loved by God.

"First, this motif could provide a vehicle for greater breadth of vision, including wiser and more careful use of technology, more sensitive understanding of other Christians, and increased cooperation between churches.

"Second, evangelicals have yet to understand thoroughly and incorporate the pneumatological developments of the "Third Force in Missions" of the Pentecostal and charismatic movements . . ." (See, e.g., Paul Pomerville 1985; and Gary B. McGee 1986, 166–70.)

"Third, the relationship of evangelism and social action as goals of holistic mission has not yet been resolved. Evangelicals have the possibility of developing a new concept of evangelism for the whole person that combines a deep spirituality with a concern for each individual's total welfare . . .

"The motif that keeps emerging through all forty years as the principal driving force behind evangelical theology of mission is the 'spirit of Edinburgh 1910.' The 'Watchword' still captures the imagination of the evangelicals. They still consider themselves compelled to proclaim the gospel to the billions of people who have not yet believed in Jesus Christ. So, while some things about evangelicals' mission theology have changed a great deal, this theme endures. Without it, evangelicals would not be evangelical." (Van Engen 1990, 203–32.)

CHAPTER 5
CRITICAL THEOLOGIZING
IN MISSION THEOLOGY

"Critical Theologizing: Knowing God in Multiple Global/Local Contexts," in James R. Krabill, Walter Sawatsky, and Charles Van Engen, editors. *Evangelical, Ecumenical and Anabaptist Missiologies in Conversation*. Maryknoll: Orbis 2006, 88–97. Used by permission.

THESIS

In this chapter I suggest that we need to go beyond the initial emphases of contextualization as communication to develop ways in which we may recontextualize the gospel in always new local and global contexts. In order to do this we need to engage in critical contextualization (à la Hiebert 1984), in critical hermeneutics (à la Bosch 1991) and in critical theologizing in a global/local process of knowing God in context. In pursuit of this question, I will suggest three seemingly contradictory, dialectical couplets that demonstrate the need to do critical contextual theologizing: both one Church and many churches; both theology and theologies; both contextualization and recontextualization.

INTRODUCTION

My cousin David is a tall six-foot-six, lanky slow-speaking Dutch pastor, a man of few words. I remember the astounding transformation I saw in David after more than thirty years in pastoral ministry. For many years, David had been pastoring a struggling center-city church on the East Coast of the United States. Trying not to be discouraged, my cousin worked very hard to be a faithful shepherd of his flock. Toward the end of his long pastoral career I began to notice that he was less than enthusiastic about his calling.

For several years I did not see David until one day he invited me to his home for lunch. When I saw him I could hardly believe it was the same person. He was almost bouncing as he walked, he talked nearly nonstop in the car on the way to his home, and his enthusiasm and energy levels were contagious. I was amazed. Over lunch I popped the question.

"David, what has happened to you," I asked him. "You don't seem to be the same person I knew some years ago!"

David's wife was grinning, "He isn't the same. Tell him, David."

David smiled down at me and said, "After more than thirty years in the ministry, I have finally discovered what I am supposed to be doing in ministry."

I could hardly wait for what would come next.

"Chuck," David said, "I have discovered that as a pastor I am supposed to help people know God: nothing more, nothing less."

"Chuck, for years I have been working hard to meet budgets, maintain buildings, administrate programs, prepare and preach sermons, call on the sick and elderly, attend our denominational gatherings, and supervise staff. I have just discovered that these are not the essence of what I am supposed to be doing as a pastor. As a pastor, I am supposed to help people know God. And since I discovered this, I can hardly wait to wake up each morning and begin a new day helping my people know God!"

After making this discovery, David enrolled in an extensive course in Christian spirituality. He rearranged his daily schedule to include several hours of meditation, Bible study, and prayer. By the time I saw him he was teaching courses on spirituality at a local seminary. And subsequent to my conversation with him, David became the prayer coordinator for his denomination. The transformation was astounding to see. David had discovered the essence of his ministry: he was supposed to help people know God.

THE MISFIT OF THE GOSPEL
WITH HUMAN CULTURES

The misfit of the gospel with human cultures has been a perennial problem faced by the church in its mission. The apostle Paul referred to God's hidden self-disclosure both in terms of the created order and in relation to God's special revelation in Jesus Christ (Rom 1:20; 11:33–34). Revealed hiddenness—this is the paradox of divine self-disclosure in human consciousness and the most difficult part of contextualization theory.[112] The very fact that we know God only through

---

112. Karl Barth, *Church Dogmatics*, vol II, 1 (Edinburgh: T & T Clark, 1957) 184. Barth devotes an entire paragraph (Par. 27,179–254) of this volume to the discussion of the knowledge of God. Barth divides this in two parts: the "terminus a quo" (from which our knowledge proceeds by the grace of God's self-revelation to us) and the "terminus ad quem" (to which

faith should tell us that we do not know all there is to know about God. We see only as through a mirror, darkly (1 Cor 13:12). Texts like Job 36:26; Psalm 139:6; Acts 14:16–17; Romans 11:25, 33–36; 1 Corinthains 2:7; Ephesians 3:3; Colossians 1:15, 26; 1 Timothy 1:17; 3:16; and Revelation 10:7 emphasize the mystery and unknowability of God. Many theologians have affirmed this basic characteristic of God's revelation.[113] So the first step in contextualizing gospel communication involves the mystery of God's self-revelation in human cultures (Van Engen 1996, 71–72. See also Shaw and Van Engen 2003).

A second aspect of the misfit of the gospel with human cultures is the mismatch that came as a result of the Christian missionary movement.[114] As churches were born in multiple contexts over several centuries, the older faith assertions of western Christendom did not seem to fit the new cultures encountered with the gospel. A progression of attempted solutions were suggested, with an accompanying succession of words like "persuasion," "Christianization," "*compellere*," "accommodation," "adaptation," "fulfillment," "syncretism," "indigenization," "transformation," "enculturation," and "dialogue."[115]

---

our knowledge conduces to faith in the hidden God). It is important to compare this section of Barth's *Dogmatics* with Vols. I, 2 Par. 17; IV, 1, 483ff; and IV, 3, 135–65.

113. See, e.g., Louis Berkhof, *Reformed Dogmatics*. (Grand Rapids: Eerdmans, 1932) Part I, Section I, Chapter II; G. C. Berkouwer, *General Revelation* (Grand Rapids: Eerdmans, 1955, 285–32); Emil Brunner, *The Christian Doctrine of God* (Phil: Westminster, 1949, 117–36); Hendrikus Berkhof, *Christian Faith* (Grand Rapids: Eerdmans, 1979, 41–56 and 61–65); Wayne Grudem, *Systematic Theology* (1994, 149–55); Stanley Grenz, *Theology for the Community of God*, 1994, 62–67; Paul Jewett, *God, Creation & Revelation*, 1991, 38–43.

114. Charles Kraft examines this in depth in *Christianity in Culture* (1979, reprinted 2005). See also Mortimer Arias 2001; Kwame Bediako 1995; Stephen Bevans 1992, reprinted in 2002; Mark Branson and René Padilla, eds., 1984; Harvie Conn 1984; John De Gruchy and Charles Villa-Vicencio, ed., 1994; Bruce Fleming 1980; Dean Gilliland 1989a; David Hesselgrave and Edward Rommen 1989; Paul Hiebert 1985, 1991; Andrew Kirk 1997; Charles Kraft and Tom Wisely, eds., 1979; Eugene Nida 1960; Lamin Sanneh 1993; Wilber Shenk, ed., 1993; Wilbert Shenk 1999; Max Stackhouse 1988; Sunand Sumithra and F. Hrangkuma, edits 1995; Tite Tiénou 1993; F.J. Verstraelen, A Camps, L. A . Hoedemaker and M. R. Spindler, eds., 1995; Andrew Walls 2002; and Darrell Whiteman 2003.

115. Each of these words represents a particular approach to relating the Gospel to a new culture. Each also entails a particular understanding of God's self-disclosure in the midst of human cultures and the ability or inability of those cultures to "know" God in the context of their own cultural forms. I have summarized the various approaches to this matter in five perspectives: communication, indigenization, translatability, local theologizing, and epistemology. I will explain this in more detail in Chapter 7 of this book.

A rather recent word, "contextualization" involves theological issues like incarnation, revelation, truth, divine-human interaction, and the shape of corporate religious experience. Contextualization takes seriously the difference between gospel and culture, and accepts the fact that "the gospel always stands in divine judgment on human culture" (Hiebert 1979, 63). In *Constants in Context*, Stephen Bevans and Roger Schroeder suggest six "constants" evident in the church's missional theologizing down through the centuries: Christology, ecclesiology, eschatology, soteriology, anthropology, and dialogue with human culture. I believe there is a seventh constant that flows alongside those six affecting and being affected by them: "critical contextual theologizing."

Mission theology needs to rediscover the Church's fundamental calling: to help people know God in context. One way to frame the question might be the following. How do we remain faithful to God's complete and final revelation in the Bible and also be proclamationally relevant and missiologically appropriate in our understanding and communication of God's intended meaning in multiple cultures around the globe today? In pursuit of this question, I will suggest three seemingly contradictory, dialectical couplets that demonstrate the need to do critical contextual theologizing: both one Church and many churches; both theology and theologies; both contextualization and recontextualization. My interest in critical contextual theologizing derives from a realization that theology is not merely a list of propositions, confessional statements, or dogmas. Today more than ever doing theology in context involves a dynamic global/local process of knowing God in multiple contexts. This was mentioned earlier in Chapter 1.

BOTH ONE CHURCH AND MANY CHURCHES

We live in a new world. Acts 1:8 is now a reality. The disciples of Jesus Christ, numbering more than 1.5 billion are now literally witnesses of Jesus Christ everywhere in their Jerusalems, Judeas, Samarias, and their ends of the earth. As David Barrett alerted us more than thirty years ago (Barrett ed., 1982), the center of gravity of the Christian Church has shifted from North to South, from West to East. Today, nearly seventy percent of all world Christianity is found in Africa, Asia, and Latin America.[116] This shift does not only impact the number of Chris-

---

116. Years later, the importance of this shift was popularized by Philip Jenkins in *The Next Christendom: The Coming of Global Christianity* (2002). The title of Jenkins' work is unfortunate and misleading, since what is least desired by, and desirable for, the churches of Africa,

tians in the world, the languages they speak, and the locations where they may be found. It also means that the presence of the churches and the nature of mission sending is no longer centered in Europe and North America, but rather is now polycentric: cross-cultural missions send their missionaries from everywhere to everywhere, as Wilbert Shenk pointed out in *Changing Frontiers of Mission* (1999). It is estimated that a larger number of cross-cultural missionaries are being sent and supported today by the churches and missions in Africa, Asia, and Latin America than the total of those sent and supported from Europe and North America.

This shift also means that the center of gravity of doing theology has moved. Doing theology is no longer the monocentric and mostly monocultural enterprise of the Christian Church in Western Europe or North America. The Christian Church of the twenty-first century registers a monumental change with regard to the contextually appropriate agendas, categories, agents, methodologies, worldview assumptions, types of rationality, perspectives, and modes of articulation that influence the doing of mission theology around the globe. Critical theologizing is now a global/local activity.

As Christians, we all read the same Bible. My personal starting point is the assumption that the Bible is God's final and complete revelation, the Christian Church's only rule of faith and practice. And I believe the essence of the gospel is to confess with the mouth and believe in the heart, a proclamation in word and deed, that "Jesus Christ is Lord" (Rom 10:9–13; 1 John 4:1–3).

How, then, shall we do critical, contextual mission theology that grounds our reflection in the reading of the same Bible and yet also interfaces appropriately with a multiplicity of radically different contexts locally and globally? We are one church. In Ephesians, Paul writes, "There is one body and one Spirit, as there is also one hope held out in God's call to you; one Lord, one faith, one baptism; one God and Father of all, who is over all and through all and in all" (Eph 4:4–6).

The Christian Church does not confess "holy catholic church*es*," or "famil*ies* of God" or "bod*ies* of Christ" or "New Israel*s*." In the biblical view of the church the plural only refers to geographical location of churches, not the existential being of the Church. In its essence there is only one Church. In Ephesians *ekklesia* appears only in the singular (Van Engen 1991, 49).[117]

Asia and Latin America would be "a new Christendom." A recognition of the phenomenal contextually appropriate diversity of the churches who now form part of the one Church is quite the opposite of a "new Christendom."

117. Cf. Karl Barth 1958, 675.

Yet we are also many diverse churches. Paul affirms the Church's oneness as a preamble to describing the pluriformity of the gifts of the Spirit that are each a part of the one Body. "But to each one of us grace has been given as Christ apportioned it. . . . So Christ himself gave the apostles, the prophets, the evangelists, the pastors and teachers, to equip his people for works of service (*eis ergon diakonias*), so that the body of Christ may be built up until we all reach unity in the faith and in the knowledge of the Son of God and become mature, attaining to the whole measure of the fullness of Christ" (Eph 4:7–13). The pluriformity and polycentricity of the one Church whose life is expressed concretely in the multiform lives of many churches necessitates our learning to do critical contextual theologizing that is simultaneously local and global. The new global/local multiform oneness of the Church expressed in many churches calls for a new way of doing mission theology.

BOTH THEOLOGY AND THEOLOGIES

Doing mission theology in a globalizing world will necessarily entail theologizing that affirms both the unity of the Church's faith and the multiplicity of ways in which that faith is expressed in the global/local Body of Christ. We will be led astray if we affirm only one or the other of these twin truths. Unfortunately, down through the centuries the Church has in fact accepted only one or the other of them. Since Constantine, the Christian Church has tended to do theology from a predominantly monocentric and monocultural, mostly Western and Eurocentric perspective. The Medieval Synthesis consisted mainly of an articulation of a set of theological dogmas that were assumed to be universally true for everyone, everywhere, always. This produced the concept of "theology" as a singular noun understood to be the systematic aggregate of a set of unchanging propositions.

This monocentric view of doing theology dominated not only the Roman and Eastern churches, but also the various branches of Protestantism after the Reformation. And this perspective also permeated Protestant missions in their theologizing for over 150 years during the time of colonial missions that Paul Hiebert called, "The Era of Noncontextualization" in his article, "Critical Contextualization" (Hiebert 1994, 76–81).

In reaction to the hegemony of the Western church over the doing of theology, theologians from Africa, Asia, and Latin America have affirmed a polycentric perspective of theologizing. This view provided the impetus for the first Protestant use of the concept of "contextualization." The multiform and polycentric nature of the process of doing theology was emphasized by Shoki Coe and stressed through the publication in 1972 of *Ministry in Context* on the part of the Theological Education Fund of the World Council of Churches in particular. (See, for example, Coe 1976; Thomas, ed., 1995, 175–76; Bevans 2002, 153 nn 45 and 46; and Gilliland 2002.) Tite Tiénou has described it thus.

> The word "contextualization" was . . . chosen with the specific purpose of conveying the idea that theology can never be permanently developed. Everywhere and in every culture Christians must be engaged in an ongoing process of relating the gospel to cultures that are constantly changing. As long as the world endures, this process continues. For many people contextualization, not indigenization, is the term that best describes this never-ending process. (Tiénou 1993, 247; See, e.g., Kirk 1999, 91; and Van Engen 1989, 97 nn 18, 19)

The perspective of contextualization as local theologizing represents a constantly changing reciprocal interaction between church and context. It is a process of local reflection that begins with an analysis of the historical situation, proceeds to a rereading of Scripture, which in turn leads to interactive theological reflection concerning m the context. It involves an act of theologizing that propels the Christian to active engagement with the cultural, socioeconomic, and political issues extant in the context. Within this view of contextualization as local theologizing there is a wide spectrum of diverse viewpoints from a nearly total secularization of the process at one end of the spectrum to a heavy emphasis on the transformation of the church at the other end.

Some Roman Catholic theologians and missiologists have called this a process of "inculturation," an effort in "constructing local theologies." Nearly twenty years ago, in *Constructing Local Theologies* (1985) Robert Schreiter surveyed the contributions of what he called the "Translation Models," the "Adaptation Models" and the "Contextual Models" for such an effort. Schreiter's thinking on the subject has been furthered by the work of his colleague at the Catholic Theological Union in Chicago, Stephen Bevans, in *Models of Contextual Theology* (1992, rev. 2002). In the 2002 edition, Bevans presented six models of contextual theology, what he called the Translation, Anthropological, Praxis, Synthetic, Transcendental, and Countercultural models.[118]

Recently Clemens Sedmak of the University of Salzburg, Austria, in *Doing Local Theology: A Guide for Artisans of a New Humanity*, affirmed that,

> Theology is done locally. In order to be honest to the local circumstances theology has to be done as local theology, as theology that takes the particular situation seriously. . . . Theologies are developed in response to and within a particular social situation. Understanding the social situation is a necessary condition for understanding the genesis and validity of particular theologies. . . . The social, historical, cultural, and political context has an impact on the role of the theologian and his or her place in the context. (Sedmak 2002, 8, 95–96)

Dirkie Smit, professor of systematic theology at the Universities of Western Cape and Stellenbosch, points out that, "Contextual theologies. . . . have underlined the fact that all theology, all thinking and speaking about God, is contextual, is influenced by the contexts in which the believers live, including the so-called traditional theology of Western Christianity in all its forms" (Smit 1994, 44; see also Arias 2001, 64).

From a Protestant evangelical standpoint, Stanley Grenz writes,

> The commitment to contextualization entails an implicit rejection of the older evangelical conception of theology as the construction of truth on the basis of the Bible alone. No longer can the theologian focus merely on Scripture as the one complete theological norm. Instead, the process of contextualization requires a movement between two poles—the Bible as the source of truth and the culture as the source of the categories through which the theologian expresses biblical truth. . . . Contextualization demands that the theologian take seriously the thought-forms and mindset of the culture in which theologizing

---

118. Steve Bevans and Roger Schroeder have done us all a wonderful service in compiling many of the biblical, historical and theological issues the Church has faced as it has sought to preserve the *Constants in Context* in the midst of tremendous changes during the past twenty centuries. See Bevans and Schroeder 2004.

transpires, in order to explicate the eternal truths of the Scriptures in language that is understandable to contemporary people. (Grenz 1993, 90; see Wilbert Shenk 1999, 77)

Locating the theological task in the local context implies an epistemological approach to critical theologizing: it questions what we do and do not know about God in the local situation.[119] David Bosch highlighted the importance of this epistemological element in contextualization.

> Contextual theologies claim that they constitute an epistemological break when compared with traditional theologies. Whereas, at least since the time of Constantine, theology was conducted *from above* as an elitist enterprise . . . its main source was *philosophy*, and its main interlocutor the *educated non-believer*, contextual theology is theology *from below*, "from the underside of history," its main source (apart from Scripture and tradition) is the *social sciences*, and its main interlocutor the *poor* or the *culturally marginalized*. . . . Equally important in the new epistemology is the emphasis on the priority of praxis. (Bosch 1991, 423)

Bosch cautioned regarding the "ambiguities of contextualization," a discomfort which I share. Bosch affirmed,

> There can be no doubt that the contextualization project is essentially legitimate, given the situation in which many contextual theologians find themselves. . . . Still, some ambiguities remain, particularly insofar as there is a tendency in contextual theology to overreact [and] to make a clean break with the past and deny continuity with one's theological and ecclesial ancestry. (Bosch 1991, 425–26)

---

119. This epistemological perspective of contextual theology received added impetus after 1976 when "twenty-two theologians from Africa, Asia, Latin America and representatives of minority groups in North America founded the Ecumenical Association of Third World Theologians (EATWOT) in Dar es Salaam, Tanzania . . . By 2002 EATWOT's membership had grown to over 700 members . . . (John Mbiti 2003, 91). The conferences, papers and published books flowing from EATWOT during the past twenty-five years have provided strong support for an epistemological approach to doing contextually appropriate theology, especially in and from the two-thirds world." (See Inus Daneel, Charles Van Engen, and Henk Vroom, eds., 2003.)

"It goes without saying," Bosch remarked, "that not every manifestation of contextual theology is guilty of any or all of the overreaction discussed above. Still, [such ambiguities]. . . . remain a constant danger to every [legitimate] attempt at allowing the context to determine the nature and content of theology for that context" (Bosch 1991, 432).[120]

To view the doing of theology as the construction of one monolithic "theology" superimposed on all Christians everywhere violates the truth that God's revelation took place "at many times and in various ways" (Heb 1:1) and has always been received within the categories of specific cultural contexts. Thus David Bosch advocated an approach he called "critical hermeneutics" (Bosch 1991, 23–24). Bosch said, "Interpreting a text is not only a literary exercise; it is also a social, economic, and political exercise. Our entire context comes into play when we interpret a biblical text. One therefore has to concede that all theology [or sociology, political theory, etc.] is, by its very nature, contextual" (1991, 428).

However, at the other extreme, the atomization of a plurality of local "theologies" violates the oneness of the Church, the unity of the Holy Spirit, the singularity of the gospel, and the unity of all Christians who read the same Bible (see Bosch 1991, 427). Thus, neither monolithic uniformity nor atomized pluriformity are satisfactory approaches to doing theology in a globalizing world today. So the challenge before us in the twenty-first century is to find a way to know God in context, that is, we must learn to do critical theologizing globally/locally through reading the same Bible in the midst of multiple cultures. This in turn will involve us in both the initial contextualization of the gospel and the recontextualization of the gospel over time.

BOTH CONTEXTUALIZATION AND RECONTEXTUALIZATION

The global shift in the center of gravity of the global/local Christian Church calls for a third dialectical couplet that profoundly impacts the way we do theology in

---

120. "Contextualization," wrote J. Andrew Kirk, "recognizes the reciprocal influence of culture and socioeconomic life. In relating Gospel to culture, therefore, it tends to take a more critical (or prophetic) stance toward culture. The concept . . . is intended to be taken seriously as a theological method which entails particular ideological commitments to transform situations of social injustice, political alienation and the abuse of human rights" (Kirk 1999, 91). Kirk quotes from Miguez Bonino 1971, 405–7; cited also in Norman Thomas 1995, 174 and David Bosch 1991, 425. See also David Bosch 1991, 423.

the twenty-first century. As the one Church expressed in many churches seeks to reconcile one theology expressed in many theologies, there will be a need to recontextualize the gospel of Jesus Christ among multiple generations of believers, in differing contexts. Our new situation in this century entails a new understanding of contextualization itself. As noted above, at first, contextualization referred to the doing of theology in local contexts, bringing all the various cultural and contextual issues to bear upon the process of contextualization. However, by the late 1970s and 1980s Protestant evangelicals had redirected the term to point to a way of communicating the gospel meaningfully so that it would make sense to the receptor. We began to understand that it is the receptor who ascribes meaning to any communication (cf. Kraft 1983, 1991; and 1999b).

Thus in 1989 David Hesselgrave and Edward Rommen defined contextualization this way.

> Christian contextualization can be thought of as the attempt to communicate the message of the person, works, Word, and will of God in a way that is faithful to God's revelation, especially as it is put forth in the teachings of Holy Scripture, and that is meaningful to respondents in their respective cultural and existential contexts. (Hesselgrave and Rommen 1989, 200)[121]

The Western Protestant evangelical approach to contextualization, then, was to put contextualization at the service of gospel communication. Various communicational approaches to contextualization assumed that the gospel message being communicated was known and understood by the Christian communicators and that they were offering it to non-Christians who did not know the gospel. This was a simple one-way communication process. Communicational models of contextualization have dominated the Western Protestant evangelical view of cross-cultural missionary enterprise for the past several decades. And there are many places in the world where communicational models of contextualization

---

121. I don't have space here to mention the various ways in which folks have attempted to categorize the various "models" of contextualization. See, e.g., Steve Bevans 2002; David Bosch 1991, 420–32; Ashish Chrispal 1995; Bruce Fleming 1980; Dean Gilliland 1989a; 2002; Krikor Haleblian 1983; Donald Jacobs 1993, 235–44; Jan Jongeneel 1997: 6–9; 130–34; Andrew Kirk 1999; Bruce Nicholls 1979; Robert Schreiter 1985; Clemens Sedmak 2002; Max Stackhouse 1988; Charles Taber 1983; Tite Tiénou 1993, 235–52; Charles Van Engen 1989; 2004a; and Darrell Whiteman 1997.

continue to be needed (cf., e.g., Don Richardson 2000). We will examine these issues more completely in a later chapter of this book.

The world of this new century has undergone radical changes that significantly alter our approach to contextualization, changes that call for an epistemological approach of critical contextual theologizing that entails a recontextualization of the gospel everywhere the Church has existed for more than one generation. A first factor to consider that calls for an epistemological approach to contextualization is the fact that one quarter of the earth's population claims to be Christian in some fashion, and two-thirds of that Christian population is to be found in the South and East of the globe. This fact means that the process of contextualization must include a new epistemological effort. That is, contextualization now involves some Christian churches sharing with other Christian churches the way they, in their context, read the Bible and understand the gospel (cf., e.g., Phan 2003). Christians everywhere need to share with other Christians everywhere how they are coming to know God in context. Each step forward, each "translation" (cf. Sanneh 1993, 31; Walls 2002, 72–81) of the gospel offers the possibility of discovering something about God as revealed in the Bible that no one had previously seen. "As the gospel continues to take root in new cultures, and God's people grow in their covenantal relationship to God in those contexts, a broader, fuller, and deeper understanding of God's revelation will be given to the world church" (Van Engen 1996, 88–89).

This is what Andrew Walls has called "the Ephesian moment," drawing from a historical and cross-cultural reading of Ephesians.

> The Ephesian moment, then, brings a church [to be] more culturally diverse than it has ever been before; potentially, therefore, nearer to that "full stature of Christ" [Eph 4:13] that belongs to his summing up of humanity. The Ephesian moment also announces a church of the poor . . . The Ephesian question at the Ephesian moment is whether or not the church in all its diversity will demonstrate its unity by the interactive participation of all its culture-specific segments, the interactive participation that is to be expected in a functioning body. (Walls 2002, 81)

Tite Tiénou suggests that

> Accepting difference [in contextual theological formulations] raises [an] important issue related to the formation of indigenous

theologies, namely the polycentric nature of Christianity. If we believe that Christians from other cultures can enrich our faith or help us correct our mistakes, we are in effect saying that Christianity is not permanently wedded to any human culture. Put another way, the acceptance of difference means that the Christian faith can be at home in any culture. Consequently Christianity has as many centers as the number of cultures of its adherents. (Tiénou 1993, 248–59)

This deepening, broadening, enriching of our understanding of God's revelation in the Bible is only possible if there is an ongoing conversation between the local churches and the global church in mutually enriching process of critical theologizing.

A second factor calling for an epistemological approach to contextualization in this new situation of ecclesial diversity has to do with the second, third and fourth generations of believers in each location. In most of the cases where contextualization was seen as a communicational process the intent was for Christians to communicate their understanding of the gospel in culturally appropriate ways to those who were not yet Christian. This involved an initial contextualization or indigenization of the gospel message.

But the world has changed. Now one can go to almost any country in the world and find the children, grandchildren and great grandchildren of the first Christian believers. In other words, in addition to considering the meaning of the gospel for the first-generation converts, it is also imperative that we reflect on the meaning of the gospel for their children and grandchildren. This involves a recontextualization of the gospel, a rereading of Scripture in the midst of a new and changed reality being faced by the second, third and fourth generations of Christians. Without such an intentional recontextualization, without a careful rereading of the gospel in a changed context, without a process of critical theologizing in that context, it is highly probable that the children and grandchildren of the church will become Christian in name only (Gibbs 1994, 17–38) and eventually either mix pre-Christian concepts with their inherited Christian ideas, or become post-Christian nonbelievers. This was precisely the challenge for the churches in Western Europe that Lesslie Newbigin articulated in the final years of his life, to which Wilbert Shenk responded in spearheading the Gospel and Culture Initiative in England and Western Europe. The present search by many in the West to articulate the faith in a fashion that will be understandable and acceptable to post moderns is an example of this kind of recontextualization. Wilbert Shenk has been at the forefront of this initiative as well.

This matter is even more poignant in churches whose members are immigrants. We know that there are more human beings moving around the globe now than ever before in the history of the earth. And the fashion in which the first generation of immigrants knows God will differ from the way the second, third and fourth generations of those families may know God. The language, culture, worldview, values, perspectives of each generation is significantly different from that of the previous generation. This is a complex matter that is beyond the scope of this work. But we need to recognize this dynamic when we consider the issues facing us in doing mission theology in our new world.

CONCLUSION

So the task of critical theologizing involves at least the three dialectical couplets we have examined in this chapter: one Church/many churches; one theology/many theologies; and both contextualization and recontextualization of the gospel.[122] To know God in context is to know God always within specific cultural frameworks; yet the gospel is always distinct from, sometimes affirming of, and often prophetically critical of, all human cultures.

David Bosch offered six affirmations that may help us link contextualization with theology and mission.

---

122. In order to do theology in a globalizing world, the world Church needs to begin from at least the following presuppositions:

- That all cultures are sinful and fallen and cloud all human understanding of God's revelation;
- That all cultures have some degree of General Revelation or Prevenient Grace whereby certain aspects of God's revelation in Jesus Christ may be clearly understood;
- That all Christian revelation must necessarily be incarnated into a culture in order for it to be understood (it is to be "infinitely translatable"—Lamin Sanneh);
- That all understanding of the Gospel in all cultures is partial (we "see as through a glass darkly" 1 Cor 13);
- And that no one Christian understanding of the Gospel has a complete grasp of the essence of God's revelation in Jesus Christ; and thus that contextualization is not in itself a goal but rather an epistemological process of seeking to know God in context.

1. Mission as contextualization is an affirmation that God has turned toward the world . . . (It is not necessary to dichotomize our Godward faith relationship from our commitment and involvement in the world. [Van Engen].)

2. Mission as contextualization involves the construction of a variety of "local theologies . . ." (But a too expansive multiplication—or atomization—of "theologies" has profoundly negative implications for relativizing the oneness of the Christian Church's faith in the same gospel.)

3. There is not only the danger of relativism, where each context forges its own theology, tailor-made for that specific context, but also the danger of absolutism, of contextualism. . . .

4. We have to look at this entire issue from yet another angle, that of "reading the signs of the times"; an expression that has invaded contemporary ecclesiastical language. . . .

5. In spite of the undeniably crucial nature and role of the context, then, it is not to be taken as the sole and basic authority for theological reflection. . . .

6. Stackhouse has argued that we are distorting the entire contextualization debate if we interpret it only as a problem of the relationship between praxis and theory.

    The best models of contextual theology succeed in holding together in creative tension theoria, praxis and poiesis—or, if one wishes, faith, hope and love. This is another way of defining the missionary nature of the Christian faith, which seeks to combine the three dimensions. (Bosch 1991, 426)

I am beginning to think that my cousin David had it right not only for his pastoral ministry but also for doing theology in a globalizing world. Maybe in the final analysis our job as critical contextual theologians is basically to help people know God in their context: nothing more, nothing less.

CHAPTER 6
A MISSIOLOGY OF TRANSFORMATION IN MISSION THEOLOGY

This chapter was originally written with a North American evangelical readership in mind. It was first published as "Toward a Missiology of Transformation," in *Transformation: A Unifying Vision of the Church's Mission*, edited by Luis K. Bush, for the Thailand gathering of the Forum on World Evangelization, in September 2004, 93–117. Reprinted with permission as "Toward a Missiology of Transformation," in Doug Priest and Nicole Cesare, editors. *Get Your Hands Dirty: Mission in Action*, Knoxville: Mission Services, 2008, 77–90. Used by permission.

THESIS

My thesis is that an evangelical missiology of transformation builds on classical concepts of mission developed over the last 100 years, overcomes the dichotomies between evangelism and social action that arose 50 years ago, and recreates itself in a trinitarian mission theology of transformation appropriate to the global/local challenges, and opportunities of church and world in this new century.

INTRODUCTION

When my son, Andrew, was four and five years old he had several toys called "transformers." They were large plastic figures of a soldier or a *samurai* warrior. When one began turning the various components around and refashioning the object, it would turn out to be a jet airplane or an armored vehicle: it would "transform." It was still the same toy, but its various shapes were quite different.

When I think of mission theology today I think of my son's transformers. Mission praxis and missiological analysis in the twenty-first century must undergo a similar radical transformation. It needs to be always the same mission, God's mission, *missio Dei*. Yet we are today in a very different mission situation than we were, say, 100 years ago.

HISTORICAL LOCATION: SETTING THE STAGE

For us to understand where we are going in the future in articulating a mission theology of transformation, it is important to remind ourselves of our past. Let me briefly summarize where we have been in our missiological reflection one hundred years ago and fifty years ago. Such a summary may offer us lenses with which to see the future.

In *Post-Capitalist Society*, Peter Drucker said this:

> Every few hundred years in [human] history there occurs a sharp transformation. We cross what . . . I have called a "divide." Within a few short decades, [a] society rearranges itself—its worldview, its basic values, its social and political structures, its arts, its key institutions.
>
> Fifty years later, there is a new world. And the people born then cannot even imagine the world in which their grandparents lived and into which their own parents were born. We are currently living through just such a transformation. (Drucker 1993, 1)

A hundred years ago, global mission was Western mission, a mostly one-way street from the West and North to everywhere else on the globe. At that time the dominant perspectives had to do with how Western missions could cooperate among themselves, how pioneer areas and peoples could be reached for the first time with the gospel, and how the fledgling churches in Africa, Asia, and Latin America could be helped to become self-governing, self-propagating and self-supporting.

At the beginning of the twentieth century there was great optimism about Western culture of modernity and Western civilization. It was assumed that other religions would soon decrease in influence or die out altogether. Mission was predominantly directed to rural areas and medicine, education, and agriculture were often seen as means to the evangelization of those who were not yet Christians. Missions activities were carried out predominantly by denominational mission organizations, with some notable exceptions like the China Inland Mission, the London Missionary Society, the Bible Societies, and others.

In a video lecture series in 1984 on "How My Mind has Changed about Mission," Stephen Neill observed that at the time of the great mission congress of Edinburgh, 1910, there were "nine grounds for sober optimism." I summarize them below.

- The geographical exploration of the planet was nearly complete.
- There was increased safety of human life in the world—wars had ceased.
- The health of missionaries was much better.
- Conduits had been won to every major religion, everywhere; every social system had yielded some converts.
- Major languages had been learned.
- The Bible was available in the most widely spoken languages.
- The churches themselves had become engaged in missionary work overseas.
- The gigantic Student Christian Movement was in place.
- Third World churches were already becoming missionary churches in their own right.

Neill concluded that lecture by observing that there were "three great changes of which we were unaware" in mission at the beginning of the twentieth century.

- That many lands would soon be closed to foreign missionary endeavor.
- That there would be a recovery and rise of the great non-Christian religions.
- That the decline of the church would be mainly in the West, and in the most firmly established churches.

Yet through it all, in the midst of all the changes, Neill affirmed that, "The aim of all our preaching is that our hearers get clear picture of Jesus Christ. We really want people to become Christians. If we have seen Christ and life in Him, we desire that all should see Him—this is mission" (Neill 1984).

A century ago Christian missions generally shared a consensus around a classical view of mission that did not split evangelism and social action. Missiologists generally saw the gospel as impacting all of life. They had a common definition of mission, articulated and popularized by the watchword of the Student Volunteer Movement (SVM): "The evangelization of the world in this generation." That "watchword" was later used by John R. Mott as the title of his most famous book and was also adopted as the motto of the great World Missionary Conference of Edinburgh, 1910. The SVM's watchword assumed a somewhat holistic view of mission, even though we must recognize that such a view was too often encased in a Eurocentric goal of Christianization and civilization. Yet even that goal assumed a conversion component.

That view of mission also involved a great deal of tension. We must recognize that the Venn-Anderson three-self formula that dominated the scene was heavily ecclesiocentric (mostly introverted and rather static), and lacked a commitment to transform the culture or change the political and socioeconomic realities of the day.[123] The emphasis on social service of a hundred years ago in terms of agriculture, medicine, and education were not seen as activities over against verbal proclamation and personal faith conversion. They were seen as integral aspects of proclamation of a gospel that called for conversion. After the Second World War this changed in North American thinking about mission and a great gulf was created between those who advocated socioeconomic and political change over against those who affirmed verbal proclamation as being central to mission.

MIDCENTURY REACTIONS: OVERCOMING DICHOTOMIES

Then came the world wars; the French, Mexican, Bolshevik, and Maoist revolutions; the Korean War; the birth of the World Council of Churches; and the search to reconstruct Europe and Japan, among other events. The globe began to shrink due to the rise of airplane travel, radio, telephones, and television. And the churches in Asia, Africa, and Latin America began to grow, mature, and rise in global influence. The perspectives of mission changed radically, producing profound dichotomies.

Fifty years ago new nations arose around the globe. The "moratorium" debate[124] brought to the foreground of mission consciousness the development, growth, and mission role of those who were first called "younger" and later "national" churches

---

123. I believe one of the greatest obstacles to world evangelization today is the persistent hangover of the "three-self formula." The desire for churches to be "indigenous" is laudable and should be encouraged. But holding too tightly to that introverted and institutionally ossified formula as the goal of missions activities has tended to created churches all over the world that exhibit two other characteristics: self-centered and selfish. In the 1980s, Chuck Kraft, Paul Hiebert and others called for the churches everywhere in the world to become "self-theologizing." That challenge was on the right track, and this book is a small attempt to contribute toward that goal. An example of someone who has caught Hiebert's vision of broadening and deepening the indigeneity of the church in the context of North America is Jervis David Payne, *Discovering Church Planting: An Introduction to the Whats, Whys, and Hows of Global Church Planting*, Colorado Springs: Paternoster, 2009, 18–24.

124. For a summary treatment of this view, see Van Engen 2000 and Van Engen 2001.

in Africa, Asia, and Latin America.[125] Some Western Protestant churches and missions were talking about the end of the so-called "missionary era," and advocating it be replaced by an "ecumenical era" of church-to-church cooperation, and the global sharing of resources.[126] Global ecumenicity became a major agenda, coupled with a strong emphasis on sociopolitical change in Africa, Asia, and Latin America.

Reacting to this direction in ecumenical mission theology, the evangelical Protestants, especially in the United States, formed new coalitions to emphasize verbal proclamation and personal conversion over against sociopolitical, economic, and humanitarian goals in mission. Seemingly, evangelical Protestants were no longer bothered by an "uneasy conscience" (Henry 1947) with regard to the social dimensions of the gospel. New cooperative ventures for world evangelization arose in the meetings in Wheaton 1966 and Berlin 1966 that eventuated in the Church Growth Movement, the Lausanne Movement,[127] the AD2000 Movement and other Western-based initiatives that saw mission in more traditional terms of finding missiologically effective means where by "men and women may become disciples of Jesus Christ and responsible members of Christ's Church" (McGavran 1970, 35; Wagner 1989, 16).[128]

We might summarize the mission perspective of the 1950s and 1960s as follows:

- National churches began to mature throughout Asia, Africa, Latin America, and Oceania.
- New nations were born, particularly throughout Africa, and a strong anticolonial critique of mission arose among older churches.
- Sodality faith missions increased in number and significance, particularly in North America.
- The moratorium debate grew.

---

125. This development began with the 1938 meeting of the International Missionary Council in Tambaram, India (International Missionary Council 1938). See Van Engen 1996, 148–49.

126. For a look at some of the developments in this way of thinking, see Van Engen 1996, 145-58

127. Documents emanating from these gatherings can be accessed on the Lausanne website.

128. For a summary treatment of these developments in evangelical Protestant mission theology, see Van Engen 1990.

- A two-way traffic of conversation regarding world mission arose with an increasingly strident critique coming from the younger national churches.
- The Commission on World Mission and Evangelism (CWME) met in Mexico City in 1962, with the theme: "Mission in Six Continents."
- A strong ecumenical movement took shape in the WCC.
- The Vatican Council II transformed the Roman Catholic Church.
- The Protestant split between evangelism and social action worsened.
- Evangelical/ecumenical debates arose and became more heated, paralleling two different readings of the Bible (a traditional view and a more sociopolitically and economically-oriented view).[129]
- Global evangelical coalitions and cooperative structures were created—most notably the Lausanne Movement.
- Two-thirds world theologians began to raise their voices offering new perspectives on the mission of the church.

After World War II there was a rather severe split between differing views of Christian mission. Heavily impacted by a guilty conscience about the Holocaust and the Third Reich, and following the lead of J. C. Hoekendijk, the World Council of Churches folks stressed a theology of relevance with heavy sociopolitical agendas, over against personal faith.

In reaction to that, and especially disillusioned by the integration of the IMC into the WCC,[130] evangelically-minded folks in Europe and North America stressed verbal proclamation that would seek personal conversion to Jesus Christ, over against sociopolitical agendas (see Van Engen 1996, 128–36). The Civil Rights movement in the U.S. and liberation theology movements in Latin America, the Philippines, South Korea, India, and elsewhere simply exacerbated the split. Donald McGavran's writings, as polemical as they were, though pointing in what I would consider to be the right direction, too often encouraged a widening of the gap between these opposing views of mission.

---

129. See, e.g., Donald McGavran 1977.

130. It is hard to underestimate the impact that the move to integrate the IMC into the WCC at the New Delhi conference of the IMC in 1961 had on evangelical mission theology. See Van Engen 1996, 132–33, particularly footnotes 19–22 and 1996, 150, footnote 14.

Fifty years later, we find ourselves still challenged by Harold Lindsell's words offered in 1962.

> It is regrettable that fifty years after Edinburgh [1910] there cannot be a world congress for mission that transcends some of the unimportant differences dividing those of similar missionary aims. . . . Perhaps the faith missions may be able to enlarge this vision and provide a creative and dynamic leadership for a new age of missionary advance. (Lindsell 1962, 230)

The historical development of theology of mission I have outlined above should give evangelicals pause in the way we use certain phrases. For example, "The Whole Church taking the Whole Gospel to the Whole World" was not the creation of the Lausanne movement at the Lausanne II meeting in Manila in 1989 where evangelicals began using the phrase and continued to use it extensively until the Laussane III in Cape Town. It was first used by the Central Committee of the World Council of Churches meeting in Rolle, Switzerland in 1951.[131]

"Mission on Six Continents" or some such phraseology that emphasized the multiple directions of global mission from everywhere to everywhere was first used at the Commission on World Mission and Evangelism (CWME) gathering in Mexico City in1963. (See Orchard, *Witness in Six Continents* 1964.)

In volume 4 of his *Church Dogmatics*, along with other writings, Karl Barth stressed that mission derives from the triune God's mission. He stated that mission does not belong to the church, nor is the church the one to decide what her mission is. Rather, mission is grounded in God's purposes, God's methods, God's goals. During earlier centuries the church, especially in Roman Catholic circles, understood that God the Father sent the Son, Jesus Christ, and the Father and the Son sent the Holy Spirit. But Barth added a new element. Barth stated that God's mission is directed to the world, and God sends the Church to the world as a participant in God's mission. This viewpoint soon came to be known as *missio Dei*, the "mission of God"

Lately, the concept of *missio Dei* appears to be used with regularity among evangelicals. But it is not a new concept. David Bosch and others affirm that it was

---

131. See, e.g., John A . Mackay 1963, 13; J. C. Hoekendijk 1966, 108; Charles Van Engen 1981, 382; and Charles Van Engen 1996, 150.

first articulated by Karl Barth in 1932[132] and, following Barth, by Karl Hartenstein in 1952. It was associated with a trinitarian view of mission at the IMC conference in Willingen, 1952. The concept was popularized by Georg Vicedomin 1958 and became rather common currency in the ecumenical movement after Mexico City, 1963 (see Henry Van Dusen 1961; Georg Vicedom 1965). Georg Vicedom's understanding of *missio Dei* is close to what I have described above as Karl Barth's viewpoint. And at that moment Vicedom was suggesting the term as a way to (1) free mission from its ecclesiocentric prison and (2) offer an understanding of mission that no longer split evangelism and social action. However, during the next fifteen years or so, it was filled with many additional agendas. For example, the term was used as the conceptual foundation for the WCC and NCC discussion about "the missionary structures of the congregation" in 1963 (cf. Colin Williams 1963, 1964 and World Council of Churches 1968), a short-lived endeavor with little or no actual missionary outreach to the world. Many additional agendas—especially sociopolitical and economic issues—were loaded into the concept. As James Scherer pointed out, in conciliar theology of mission the ship of *missio Dei* was eventually loaded with so much baggage it nearly sank.[133]

As I sought to demonstrate in *Mission on the Way*, when church and mission are confused and fused, and when the *missio Dei* is made to stand for any and all activities that the church may want to carry out in the world—then Stephen Neill's

---

132. Cf. David Bosch 1980, 167. In my reading of Barth, I do not believe we can ascribe to Barth the full-blown concept of *"missio Dei'* as a model for the church's mission in the world, the way it was developed in the World Council of Churches after 1952 and is now used extensively by the evangelical movement. I read Barth as simply stating that mission to the world is grounded in, derives from, is defined by the trinitarian God's mission. Mission is God's mission and is not to be owned or controlled by the church or by the needs of the world. After 1952 the concept was filled with a host of other agendas beyond Barth's perspective.

133. See, e.g., H.H. Rosin, *Missio Dei: An Examination of the Origin, Content and Function of the Term in Protestant Missiological Discussion*, 1972; James Scherer 1987, 93–125; James Scherer, "Church, Kingdom, and Missio Dei: Lutheran and Orthodox Correctives to Recent Ecumenical Mission Theology 1993, 82–88; Johannes Verkuyl, 1978, 328–31; 197–204; David Bosch 1980, 242–48; 1991, 389–93; Van Engen 1981, 277–79, 305–323; 1991, 108; 1996, 150–53; Andrew Kirk 1999, 229; Jan Jongeneel and Jan van Engelen 1995, 447–48; Jan Jongeneel 1997, 59–61; D.T. Niles. 1962; George Vicedom "Missio Dei" in Stephen Neill, Gerald H. Anderson and John Goodwin, eds., 1971, 387; John McIntosh, "Missio Dei" in Moreau, Netland and Van Engen, eds., *Evangelical Dictionary of World Missions* 2000, 631–33; Lesslie Newbigin *The Open Secret* 1978, 20–31; Roger Bassham 1979, 67–71.

dictum seems to prove out: "When everything is mission, nothing is mission."[134] In the World Council of Churches the term eventually referred to a change of order in the concept of mission. The classical mission perspective begins with God who works primarily through the Church to reach and transform the world (God-Church-world). But J. C. Hoekendijk's deep pessimism about the church motivated him to suggest in *The Church Inside Out* (1966) that a new order was called for, an order that became an essential part of the WCC's understanding of *missio Dei* after its Fourth Assembly in Uppsala in 1968. After 1968, following Hoekendijk's lead, *missio Dei* was used in WCC circles to emphasize that God was at work in the world and the best thing the church could do was to join the movements of what God was doing in the world (God-world-church). This secularizing change of order had profound and far-reaching effect on the mission theology of the folks associated with the World Council of Churches. Given the history of the term, I believe evangelical missiologists must be careful to articulate clearly what they mean—and what they do not mean—when they speak of *missio Dei*.

I do not believe anyone was really satisfied with the dichotomy between verbal proclamation and social action. The 1970s and 1980s involved multiple attempts to narrow the gap. The Lausanne Movement birthed a number of consultations, papers, and gatherings seeking to rethink the matter of the "priority of evangelism" as it had been articulated by John Stott in the Lausanne Covenant. In the 1970s, though still using the language of the "evangelistic mandate" as paralleling the "cultural mandate," Arthur Glasser began to draw from the works of Oscar Cullmann (1951), Hermann Ridderbos (1962) and George Ladd (1974) to develop the notion of the kingdom of God as a way of bringing evangelism and social action closer together. There is today a very substantial global consensus around the kingdom of God theme as a way of building a more wholistic view of mission (see, e.g., Van Engen 1991, 101–18). This motif has been prominent in the mission theology of René Padilla and his associates in the Latin American Theological Fraternity (LATF). Drawing from the kingdom of God theme they have developed the idea of "integral mission" as a conceptual framework that might bridge the gap between verbal proclamation and social action.[135]

---

134. Stephen Neill 1959, 81; quoted by Johannes Blauw 1962, 109.

135. The first major publication of the Latin American Theological Fraternity (LATF) was entitled, *El Reino de Dios y América Latina (The Kingdom of God and Latin America).* Since then the LATF has consistently emphasized what Padilla and others have called "integral mission." See, e.g., Orlando Costas 1974; 1982; Mortimer Arias 1980, 1984, 1998, 2003; René Padilla

The Evangelical Association of Third World Theologians (EATWOT) wrestled with the problem at the early stages of their conversations.[136] Members of the Asia Theological Association also sought to articulate a more wholistic understanding of mission that would bridge the old dichotomies, as evidenced in the writings of, for example, Ken Ghanaian (1989, 1992). In the World Council of Churches there arose a greater interest in matters of spirituality and spiritual formation. And Latin American Liberation Theologians like Gustavo Gutierrez began to explore matters of spirituality and spiritual formation as integral to liberation.

So in the 1980s and 1990s we see evangelical perspectives of mission beginning to be interested in a "wholistic" approach to mission. I believe an impetus for this may have been the fact that the predominantly North American-based sodality mission agencies, active for more than fifty years, saw themselves relating to second- and third-generation converts and maturing churches in Africa, Asia, and Latin America. These converts, fruit of the early evangelization of these Western evangelical mission sodalities, have begun to search for ways in which the gospel they accepted may impact the socioeconomic, cultural, and political realities in which they find themselves. These new generations of converts are now living in circumstances of oppression, persecution, disease, hunger, and abject poverty. And they are beginning to ask their brothers and sisters in the West what should be the impact of the gospel upon the reality they are now experiencing.

With the decline of the church in the West, and the center of gravity shifting so that two-thirds of all world Christianity is now in Asia, Africa, Latin America and Oceania, the Church of Jesus Christ is increasingly a church of the poor and oppressed. So at the beginning of this new century, Christians around the globe suffer all the same oppression, want, and need as the non-Christians in their contexts. David Barrett signaled this development already in an article published in the October, 1983, issue of the *International Bulletin of Missionary Research,* "Silver and Gold Have I None: Church of the Poor and Church of the Rich?" (David Barrett 1983, 146–51).

Thus the global "Enquiry" movement that Luis Bush spearheaded was very important. It had the potential of spawning a reconceptualization of the nature of mission that flows from the fountainhead of the majority church in the majority

---

1986; Samuel Escobar 1998; 1999; 2002; Timothy Carriker 1992; and Valdir Steuernagel 1991, 1992

136. Cf., e.g., John Mbiti 2003. (I mentioned this more at length in a footnote in an earlier chapter.)

world, articulated by majority Christians spread now on all six continents. One might say that for the first time since Constantine, over 1600 years ago, the world church has the potential of constructing its understanding of mission with the building blocks drawn from the experience, life, vitality, and vision of churches and missions in the south and east of the globe as well as the north and the west. All this leads to a desire to rethink and reconceptualize the nature of mission at the beginning of this new century.

THE PRESENT SITUATION: RECOVERING BELIEVABILITY

When I was young, growing up in San Cristobal de Las Casas, Chiapas, in Southern Mexico, the word "transformer" referred to those large round containers hanging on electrical poles that transformed high-voltage electricity into a form usable in a domestic home. With some regularity they would blow up, leaving us all in the dark. The genius of those transformers was that they converted the energy from the high-tension power lines—energy that was not useful and was in fact harmful for our homes—and transformed it into voltage, wattage, and cycles that were appropriate for use in our homes. It adapted the electricity to the context of our homes.

At the beginning of this new century, I believe we are in just such a situation in our reconceptualization of global/local mission of the Church. With two-thirds of world Christianity located now in the South and East, I believe that one of the most significant issues of global/local mission on, from, and to six continents in today's world will involve the *believability* of the Church and its mission. From the perspective of those who are not yet Christians, amidst the marketplace of competing religious affiliations, in a global climate of profound spiritual hunger and curiosity, is the Church and its mission believable? It would appear that earlier attempts to articulate a relevant mission theology have fallen short. In what follows I will mention several integrating ideas that have been suggested in the past to focus our mission endeavors and I will point out why I believe they are not sufficient for our mission in our world today.

- As I have pointed out, the three-self formula is not good enough: it is too ecclesiocentric and introverted. It looks at the church through a predominantly institutional lens and is easily blinded to the issues facing those living in the contexts outside the church.

- The "priority of evangelism" language is not contextually appropriate enough for most situations. It seems more concerned with forming *apriori* propositionally-framed definitions of evangelism than it is to respond to the needs, aspirations, concerns, and dreams of the persons in the surrounding context who yet do not know Jesus Christ. The balance of word and deed in our evangelism should be receptor-oriented and contextually informed.

- The kingdom of God language is helpful, but has taken on a host of different meanings and forms in actual practice—and it seems to be too easily narrowed to predominantly vertical perceptions of the gospel, with a loss of the horizontal issues at hand. I am beginning to see that, to be true to the Bible's picture of God and God's mission, I must permeate the kingdom language with language about relationship, about covenant, about love of God and neighbor. Though such a framework may be assumed by those who speak about the "kingdom of God," it is not always apparent nor often emphasized.

- As mentioned in the discussion above, the *missio Dei* language, though potentially useful, needs major clarification today because of the multiple, confusing, and sometimes contradictory baggage the term carries. How are we to distinguish that which is part of the *missio Dei* and that which is not?

- We must be careful not to make everything mission—and lose mission in the process.[137]

- The language of "wholistic mission," "integral mission," or "incarnational mission" may also have something to offer, but at times these terms seem to draw from perspectives that continue to

---

137. One way that I have attempted to do this is to borrow from Stephen Neill's definition of mission "the intentional crossing of barriers from Church to nonchurch in word and deed for the sake of the proclamation of the Gospel" (Neill 1984, video). I define mission as follows: God's mission works primarily through the people of God intentionally crossing barriers to all peoples of the world and from faith to the absence of faith in settings of nominal Christianity, to proclaim by word and deed the coming of the Kingdom of God in Jesus Christ through the Church's participation in God's mission of reconciling people to God, to themselves, to each other, and to the world and gathering them into the Church through repentance and faith in Jesus Christ by the work of the Holy Spirit with a view to the transformation of the world as a sign of the coming of the Kingdom in Jesus Christ.

labor with a dichotomy between mission as verbal and personal proclamation and mission that seeks sociocultural and structural change. At other times "incarnational mission" seems so culture affirming that the prophetic scandal of the cross and the challenge of the gospel to transform all of life may be eclipsed by the desire to identify with the receptors.

All in all, it is as if we as evangelicals have begun to realize that if mission were looked at as a coin, we must take seriously both the "heads" and the "tails" side of the coin. But we seem to continue our quest to keep the "heads" and "tails" separate yet together, rather than recognize that the coin, for example, is a "quarter." (This illustration has to do with a coin of 25 cents in the U.S. or Canada.) I would suggest that a missiology of transformation might help us to speak of mission as the "quarter" rather than as "heads" and "tails."

TOWARD A MISSION THEOLOGY OF TRANSFORMATION

David Bosch gave his *magnum opus* the title, "Transforming Mission." And in doing so, he meant to offer a play on three meanings:

- In the New Testament and over time, the concept of mission was transformed in such a way that a variety of "paradigms" of self-understanding took shape related to the Church's conceptualization of mission.
- Over time, the activities of mission transform the Church as it participates in God's mission.
- Bosch's readers—and the Church at large—need to allow the Holy Spirit to transform their idea of mission to include at least the thirteen "elements of an emerging ecumenical mission paradigm" that Bosch outlines in the last chapter of his book.

I would suggest that Bosch's use of the concept of "transformation" did not go far enough. In Romans 12:2, the Apostle Paul admonishes his hearers, "Do not conform to the pattern of this world but be transformed by the renewing of your mind. Then you will be able to test and approve what the will of God is—his good, pleasing and perfect will." Paul here calls for *metamorphosis!*[138] A missiology of

---

138. Interestingly, all the English language translations I checked translated this with "be transformed." The New English translated the verse as, "Adapt yourselves no longer to

metamorphosis would entail the kind of mission that we see in the transformation of the woman of Sychar—and of the village of Sychar—in John 4.

Metamorphosis is the word used to describe the phenomenal transformation that happens when a chrysalis becomes a butterfly! I believe a biblical missiology of transformation envisions just such a change in persons, social structures, and nations of our world because of the gospel of the kingdom and the work of the Holy Spirit.

Such a missiology of metamorphosis would involve the kind of radical change we see in Paul after meeting Jesus on the Damascus road. This is God's mission that seeks to rescue (people) "from the dominion of darkness and [bring them] into the kingdom of the Son he loves, in whom we have redemption, the forgiveness of sins." (Col 1:13–14) This is such profound, all-pervasive transformation that Paul would end up saying, "I have been crucified with Christ and I no longer live, but Christ lives in me. The life I now live in the body, I live by faith in the Son of God, who loved me and gave himself for me" (Gal 2:20).

This is a missiology that seeks to turn the world upside down. Because the Church's mission is to participate in Jesus' mission—and Jesus' mission sets the parameters of the Church's mission, the Christian Church in mission that intends to "proclaim good news to the poor . . . to proclaim freedom for the prisoners and recovery of sight for the blind, to set the oppressed free, to proclaim the year of the Lord's favor" (Luke 4:18–19). At the end of a chapter discussing "the goal and purpose of mission," Johannes Verkuyl pointed to a missiology of metamorphosis by emphasizing "the kingdom of God as the goal of the *Missio Dei.*" Here are some excerpts of his thought.

> The kingdom to which the Bible testifies involves a proclamation and a realization of a total salvation, which covers the whole range of human needs and destroys every pocket of evil and grief affecting [hu]mankind. Kingdom in the New Testament has a breadth and a scope, which is unsurpassed; it embraces heaven as well as earth, world history as well as the whole cosmos.
>
> The kingdom of God is that new order of affairs begun in Christ which, when finally completed by him, will involve

the pattern of this present world, but let your minds be remade and your whole nature thus transformed. Then you will be able to discern the will of God, and to know what is good, acceptable and perfect."

a proper restoration not only of [hu]man's relationship to God but also of those between sexes, generations, races, and even between [humans] and nature. . . .

When we inquire into the practical consequences of viewing mission from the perspective of the kingdom and its structures, one of the first things to mention is our God-given call to invite human beings to come to know Jesus as the Messiah of the kingdom. . . . Two things are necessary in order to lead people to the Messiah and to invite them to confess him in word and deed. In the first place, they must come to know what the New Testament says about him. . . . The second thing necessary as we lead people to the Messiah is for each of us to recall that the living Lord is actually present. . . . Therefore every generation discovers fresh aspects about him and confesses him in a new manner. . . .

Precisely because we have accepted the kingdom as the frame of reference and point of orientation for our missionary task, we must go on to claim that a call to conversion must necessarily follow our proclamation. . . . Within the framework of the kingdom, conversion has been viewed properly as one of the inclusive goals of mission. . . .

According to the New Testament, proclaiming the messianic message must always be accompanied by gathering, preserving and adding to the people of God. . . . Missiology must always save a spot for ecclesiology and for the study of churches in their own environments. . . .

Viewing our missionary task within the wider perspective of the kingdom will lead us to still another insight: participation in the fight against every vestige of evil plaguing [hu]mankind is an intrinsic part of our calling. According to the Bible the kingdom does not belong to the future. It is a present reality, which, though not yet fully revealed, does nevertheless show definite signs of being underway. . . .

It is gratifying to be able to note at the end of this study of the goal of the *missio Dei* and our concomitant mission that missiology is more and more coming to see the kingdom of God as the hub around which all of mission work revolves. . . .

The churches on all six continents need to be alert to changing needs and set their priorities accordingly. But even so they must present the entire message of the kingdom and not reduce it to just one point. We would be most inhuman if we should treat only the most acute and pressing needs of people and deprive them of the full range of God's promises by failing to mention the Messiah himself. . . . At the same time, it would be a sign of sinful sloth and indolence if we were not to attempt in faith, together with the children of the kingdom throughout the world, to erecting the midst of the wide range of human burdens and evils signs and signals of that which is coming. He who prays, 'Thy kingdom come, thy will be done' is thereby called to aid in spreading the kingdom of God over the length and breadth of the earth." (1978, 197–204)

Verkuyl's trinitarian, kingdom-oriented emphasis echoed Lesslie Newbigin's view expressed in *The Open Secret*. "The Christian mission," he affirmed, "is an acting out of a fundamental belief and, at the same time, a process in which this belief is being constantly reconsidered in the light of the experience of acting it out in every sector of human affairs and in dialogue with every other pattern of thought by which men and women seek to make sense of their lives. [This] fundamental belief disembodied in the affirmation that God has revealed himself as Father, Son, and Spirit. I shall therefore [look] . . . at the Christian mission in three ways—as the proclaiming of the kingdom of the Father, as sharing in the life of the Son, and as bearing the witness of the Spirit" (1978, 31).

A MISSIOLOGY OF TRANSFORMATION: RECREATION IN A NEW CENTURY

How, then, may we go about constructing a trinitarian, kingdom-based missiology of transformation? It seems to me that a first step would be to affirm that mission is not fundamentally ours: it does not belong to the church, it is not the property of mission agencies, it is not owned by the Christian NGO's (nongovernmental organizations). It is not for us to determine the content or parameters of our mission. Rather, following the emphasis first articulated by Vicedom, mission is most fundamentally God's mission: it is *missio* Dei. This being true, it is essential that we construct a theological foundation on which to build the rest of the superstructure of a missiology of transformation. Such a foundation cannot be essentially anthropological or strategic, demographic or linguistic, political or economic, sociological, psychological or political. It is also not determined by the needs, demands, or aspirations of our target audiences. The pilings driven into the soft earth of our various contexts, pilings that will support the structure of a missiology of transformation must be theological truths drawn from Scripture and from the Church's understanding of God learned throughout twenty centuries of the Church's experience and reflection about God. This is a tall order and is far beyond the limits of this book. However, in the final section of this chapter I want to describe in broad strokes, in the form of a set of summary statements, what I believe could be the content of a trinitarian, kingdom-based missiology of transformation. We begin, then, as does the Bible, with affirmations about God the Father Almighty, creator of heaven and earth.

GOD THE FATHER

Christians care for creation not because it is "mother earth" (New Age paganism), nor because its care guarantees the survival of the human race (secular humanism), but rather because it is the creation of, and is cared for and supported by our heavenly Father in Jesus Christ (Psalm 8, John 1, Col 1, and Eph 1). We know that there is a link between the salvation of humans and the salvation of the earth. "For the creation waits in eager expectation for the children of God to be revealed . . . in hope that the creation itself will be liberated from its bondage to decay and brought into the freedom and glory of the children of God" (Rom 8:19–21). And we know that the status of creation is intimately connected with the relationship of humans with God. When humans rebelled against God in the Garden of Eden, creation itself fell. And now "We know that the whole creation has been groaning as in the pains of childbirth right up to the present time . . . (because) the creation waits in eager expectation for the (children) of God to be revealed" (Rom 8:22,19). God is always, at all times, actively involved in the preservation and re-creation of all that is. Thus a missiology of transformation that participates in the *missio Dei* involves Christians in the care, preservation, and re-creation of all the created order.

All humans are members of the same human family (we are all cousins, as it were) created by the same God (Gen 1–3, John 1). And all human life is intrinsically valuable because, though fallen, it is created by God, in God's image. Thus, as children of the Creator God, Christians are inherently against all that dehumanizes and destroys life. A missiology of transformation will involve a profound commitment to affirming all that values, cares for, and enhances human life. The God of the Bible loves all humans equally (cf. the Tables of Nations of Gen 10 and Acts 2). "For God so loved the world" (John 3:16) includes all humanity, including all those who are not yet Christian. So a missiology of transformation will seek by all legitimate means to call all peoples to a living faith relationship with their Creator in Jesus Christ by grace through faith, granted us by the Holy Spirit.

Because God the Creator of all has placed humans as stewards over God's creation, a missiology of transformation is a missiology of stewardship. This stewardship is not merely the careful and wise use of what you and I have. Rather, it is the careful, purposeful and loving care of all that belongs to God. And all that we have belongs to God. Christians understand that it is their God-given responsibility and calling to be stewards of all that God has created (Gen 1–3, Ps 8, Heb 2:6–9).

The God of the Bible is a compassionate God, slow to anger and abounding in mercy (see, e.g., Ex 34:6; 2 Chr 30:9; Ps 86:15) who would not have any to perish but rather desires that everyone should come to repentance (2 Peter 3:9). Thus we as Christians love all other human beings because God first loved them and gave his life for them—in that while we all were yet sinners, Christ died for us and for them (Rom 5:8). Our motivation for mission derives from God's creation, God's love, God's mission, and God's desire. To be "children of God" (John 1:12) entails participating in God's mission. We are, therefore, eager to preach the gospel to all peoples because we are in fact "obligated both to Greeks and non-Greeks, both to the wise and foolish" (Rom 1:14). We participate in our Father's calling all people to himself, for "Anyone who believes in him will never be put to shame. For there is no difference between Jew and Gentile—the same Lord is Lord of all and richly blesses all who call on him, for 'Everyone who calls on the name of the Lord will be saved'" (Rom 10:11–13).

GOD THE SON: JESUS THE CHRIST

Christians in conversation with people of other faiths confess that there is salvation in no one else: only through faith in Jesus Christ (Acts 4:12). A missiology of transformation will acknowledge the general revelation or prevenient grace that

God has shown in the midst of other faiths, but will affirm as well that only in Jesus Christ is God's complete revelation—and only in Jesus Christ is there salvation.

The Incarnation shows us that salvation involves the creation of a completely new person, for "if anyone is in Christ, the new creation has come: the old has gone, the new is here" (2 Cor 5:17). Thus a missiology of transformation will be involved in the creation and re-creation of persons, seeking for them to become fully complete, fully human in Jesus Christ.

Incarnational contextuality points us to receptor-oriented communication and contextualization. Jesus adapted his mission not only to humans, but also to specific humans: e.g., compare his mission with Nicodemus to his mission with the woman of Sychar (John 3 and 4).

The content of the Church's mission is defined and circumscribed by Jesus' mission. In Luke 4, Jesus describes and declares the essence of his mission. Drawing from the way the New Testament describes Jesus' messianic mission, as the Body of Christ, the Church's mission involves at least *Koinonia, Kerygma, Diakonia,* and *Marturia* by being for the world a community of prophets, priests, kings, healers, liberators, and sages as the loving community of the King (see Van Engen, *God's Missionary People,* 87–132).

A Christological foundation of a missiology of transformation will also involve discipleship in two senses. First, our Great Commission calling is to make disciples—to call, invite, and gather those who will become disciples of Jesus Christ. Secondly, Christ's disciples are to "offer (their) bodies as a living sacrifice" with a view to being continually transformed in order to "test and approve what God's will is—his good, pleasing and perfect will" (Rom 12:2). As disciples of Jesus we are by nature missionary disciples and "Christ's love compels us" to be ambassadors of reconciliation in a hurting, troubled and conflicted world (2 Cor 5:14–21).

Christ's lordship is lordship over all humans. One day, "every knee will bow" to his lordship (Phil 2). Our privilege, right, and duty are to proclaim the gospel of the kingdom that "Jesus is Lord" in every corner of the globe, among every people group, to every person. Christ's lordship is also over the principalities and powers of this world, including global economic, political, social, and structural centers of power.

GOD THE HOLY SPIRIT

The Holy Spirit transforms all of life—every aspect and all facets of one's life. Thus a pneumatologically-grounded missiology of transformation will seek the creation and re-creation of the whole person, permeating all relationships and human structures relative to that person's life.

The Holy Spirit convicts "the world to be wrong about sin and righteousness and judgment" (John 16:8). The Holy Spirit converts (transforms) persons, giving them grace and faith to believe in Jesus Christ. The Holy Spirit is the agent of transformation of persons from inside out. Conversion is not possible except by the work of the Holy Spirit. Thus missiology of transformation can only happen through the work of the Holy Spirit. A missiology of transformation will seek, in the power of the Holy Spirit, to create and re-create the spiritual life of persons along with the physical, social, emotional and intellectual aspects of their being. A corollary of this is to recognize that a pneumatological missiology of transformation will by its very nature involve a variety of forms of spiritual warfare.

A pneumatologically-grounded missiology of transformation entails the realization that only the Holy Spirit creates the Church—and only the Holy Spirit empowers and directs the Church's mission (Boer 1961). The Holy Spirit forms, transforms and re-forms the Church to be, know, do, serve, and relate in ways depicted by a host of biblical metaphors of the church in mission like salt of the earth, light of the world, earthen vessels filled with the pearls of the gospel, Body of Christ, a new humanity, ambassadors of reconciliation, the family of God, among many others. The spirituality of Christians, of churches, and of mission agencies must be transformed through the ministry of the Holy Spirit and directed in mission to a lost and hurting world so loved by God.

The gifts of the Holy Spirit are given to the Church for mission in the world. And the fruit of the Holy Spirit are the Spirit's gift to the world through the presence of the community of faith that embodies that fruit. Our world is in desperate need of the fruit of the Holy Spirit: love, joy, peace, patience, kindness, goodness, faithfulness, gentleness, and self-control (Gal 5:22). And this fruit is based on people living out the Decalogue in love of God and neighbor. Such fruit, in the power of the Holy Spirit will radically transform—it will fundamentally alter—the realities in which we live today.

Jesus Christ rules in the kingdom through the ministry of the Holy Spirit. We cannot have a kingdom missiology unless we have an equally broad, deep, high, and wide pneumatological conception and praxis in mission.

As the down payment of eternal life (Eph 1:14), the Holy Spirit creates hope for the coming of the kingdom in Jesus Christ (see Chapter 12 in this book). A pneumatologically-grounded missiology of transformation will eagerly await the final day when Christ returns and the final, full transformation will occur in a new heaven and a new earth. Then transformed Christians in a transformed reality will gather around the throne of the Lamb and sing, "Worthy is the Lamb who was slain to receive power and wealth and wisdom and strength and honor and glory and praise!" (Rev 5:12).

The summary statements offered above are but an outline of what I believe is involved in articulating the theological underpinnings of a missiology of transformation. At the heart of this vision is a commitment to radical change.

CONCLUSION

During the 1970s and 1980s I served as a missionary in Tapachula, a tropical city on the Mexican border with Guatemala. There, a "transformer" was a small box into which we plugged our appliances to regulate the electricity coming to them. That "transformer" would raise the voltage to acceptable levels and would cushion electrical surges. These devices were invaluable for the extended life of our electrical appliances.

In like fashion, global/local mission in the twenty-first century must be contextually and culturally appropriate to the needs, aspirations, worldviews, and agendas of the persons in each context. In order to meet such demands, a missiology of transformation will need to be based on a trinitarian view of mission that is in continuity with what we have learned about mission during the past one hundred years and also in rather significant discontinuity with mission praxis as that has been carried out during the past one hundred years. Continuity and discontinuity. That would seem to be the essence of the concept of "*trans-formation*." A missiology of transformation involves *trans*—and—*formation:* discontinuity and change coupled with continuity and re-creation.

TRANS–(discontinuity)

A missiology of transformation calls for movement, for metamorphosis, for change, for conversion, for a change of heart. Without a change of heart, a change of self, of being, nothing will change. Merely a change of religious affiliation, merely an individual, vertical conversion will not change the persons, structures, systems, and cultures of this world. To be believable the church and Christians must be good for something—they must be able to demonstrate to the people of their contexts and nations that they have something concrete, measurable, visible, positive, constructive, and helpful to offer their contexts and nations. This calls for radical conversion as much of the church and of Christians to their mission of being Christ's transforming presence in the world—just as much as conversion of non-Christians to faith in Jesus Christ.

–FORMATION (continuity)

A missiology of transformation also calls for incarnational contextuality, for wrestling with the relationship of gospel and culture in thousands of different contexts worldwide. This transformation is not merely a change of religious affiliation, not merely a matter of new church membership. This is not merely civilization or education, or a change of ethical behavior; it is not merely socioeconomic and political betterment. Rather, a missiology of transformation entails the *new formation*, the *re-creation* of whole persons—of all and every aspect of their lives, each in their particular context in terms of knowing, being, doing, serving, and relating to one other: it has simultaneously personal, social, structural and national implications. It involves reconciliation with God, self, creation, others, and the sociocultural economic and political structures.

John ends his gospel by saying, "Jesus performed many other signs in the presence of his disciples which are not recorded in this book. But these are written that you may believe that Jesus is the Messiah, the Son of God, and that by believing you may have life in his name" (John 20:30–31). That you may have life. Like a sponge is permeated with water, so our mission is to offer new life to the women and men of our world of the twenty-first century in which all of their life, every aspect of life, all arenas of life are permeated with the presence of God the Father, Son, and Holy Spirit. And the rich and powerful of this world need to be transformed, they need to be converted, just as much as the poor and the weak.

This is a time of massive social change in Africa, Asia, Eastern Europe, the Middle East, and Latin America—as well as the cities of Western Europe, Australia, and North America. And the Church of Jesus Christ is there to proclaim the gospel and contribute to the building of new nations and the rebuilding of old ones. The Church of Jesus Christ stands for love, joy, peace, reconciliation, and the value of human life.

Our mission is a mission of transformation. I think Gisbertus Voetius (1589–1676) had it right—but, because of his Christendom perspective, he was incomplete in his view of the goal of the God's mission. Voetius stated that the goal of mission is three-fold: the conversion of people to Jesus Christ, the planting and development of the church, and the glory of God. (J. H. Bavinck 1977, 155; Bosch 1980, 126–27; Verkuyl 1978, 21; Moreau, Netland, Van Engen 2000, 1002)

I believe that in the twenty-first century we must add a fourth goal, inserted between "planting and development of the church" and "the glory of God," as seen below. We know that today about one-quarter of the earth's population in some fashion professes their faith in Jesus Christ. Those Christians are spread now around the globe in every nation on earth, speak more languages, and have more ease of communication and travel than ever before in the history of the Church. For the first time in human history the Church of Jesus Christ can present the gospel in an understandable form to every human being on the face of the planet. But that means that the Church also has the opportunity, duty, and calling to be a transforming presence in every corner of the globe. Thus, I believe we should add a fourth goal of mission, as follows:

- the conversion of people to Jesus Christ;
- the planting and development of the church;
- the *transformation* of the Church and, through the Church's ministries, the *transformation* of the contexts and nations in which the churches are to be found; and
- the glory of God.

Orlando Costas was right when he affirmed that the Church can only be a penultimate goal of mission, not the final goal. Socioeconomic and political change is also merely a penultimate goal of mission. A trinitarian, kingdom-oriented missiology of transformation will hold to only one goal: the glory of God (see, e.g., Eph 1:6, 12, 14). One day we will all stand together with all those from every language, family, tribe and nation who have washed the robes in the blood of the Lamb. We will all stand around the throne of the Lamb and sing, "Worthy is the Lamb who was slain . . ." (Rev 5:12).

Our mission is to participate in Jesus' mission whose mission it was to do God's mission in the power of the Holy Spirit: no more, no less. This is a mission of radical transformation—a mission of metamorphosis. What shape must this take in the interim between the "already" and the "not yet" of the coming of the kingdom of God? I believe Lesslie Newbigin captured it well when he challenged us all to give concrete presence, life, and expression to our mission (our mission as transformation) in and through the life of local congregations spread around the globe. He said it this way.

> The primary reality of which we have to take account in seeking
> for a Christian impact on public life is the Christian congrega-
> tion. . . . The only hermeneutic of the gospel is a congregation of
> men and women who believe it and live by it. . . . This commu-
> nity will have, I think, the following six characteristics:
>
> - It will be a community of praise.
> - It will be a community of truth.
> - It will be a community that does not live for itself.
> - It will be a community . . . sustained in the exercise of the
>   priesthood in the world.
> - It will be a community of mutual responsibility.
> - It will be a community of hope.[139]

Whether it is a toy in the hands of my son, Andrew, a large container hanging
from a pole, or a small electrical box in southern Mexico, the three images tell
us one thing: they were meant to be always the same yet always changing into
something different. So it is with our mission in this new century. Our mission is
to proclaim in word and deed always the same gospel that is always taking on new
forms: it is always transformed and always transforming.

---

139. Lesslie Newbigin 1989, 222–33.

PART III
THE METHODS
OF MISSION
THEOLOGY

CHAPTER 7
FIVE PERSPECTIVES OF APPROPRIATE MISSION THEOLOGY

This chapter was originally published in "Five Perspectives of Appropriate Mission Theology," in Charles Kraft, ed., *Appropriate Christianity*, Pasadena: William Carey Library, 2005, 183–202. Used by permission.

THESIS

The search for an "appropriate Christianity" involves the development of a contextually appropriate mission theology that includes elements of at least five different perspectives of contextualization: communication, indigenization, translatability, local theologizing, and epistemology.

INTRODUCTION

Some years ago, Charles Kraft challenged us to search for "appropriate Christianity," by which he meant, "a Christianity that is appropriate to the Scriptures, on the one hand and appropriate to the people in a given culture, on the other."[140] Although such a desire is not new, the recent convergence of a number of perspectives and tools of contextualization offers us a series of steps which may further our search for "appropriate Christianity" in specific contexts. In this chapter, I will summarize five paradigms of contextualization that have developed over the past several centuries of missionary activity. I have called them communication, indigenization, translatability, local theologies, and epistemology.

---

140. Charles Kraft, ed., 2005, 5.

APPROPRIATE CONTEXTUALIZATION
AS COMMUNICATION[141]

Attempts to construct a contextual theology appropriate to both the Scriptures and to a new receptor culture can be traced as far back as the work of Orthodox missionaries to the Slavic peoples, Cyril (826–869) and Methodius (815–885), and early Roman Catholic missionaries like the Jesuits Robert de Nobili (1577–1656) in India and Matteo Ricci (1552–1620) in China (See Moreau 2000, 694, 834). Beginning with William Carey (1761–1834) whenever Protestant missionaries have encountered a new culture and a new language, like their Orthodox and Roman Catholic counterparts, they have been concerned with communicating the message of the gospel to their receptors in languages and forms acceptable and understandable to the new receptors.

David Hesselgrave and Edward Rommen emphasized the communication aspect of contextualization.

> From this point of view [drawing from Eugene Nida's three-culture model (Nida 1960)], Christian contextualization can be thought of as the attempt to communicate the message of the person, works, Word, and will of God in a way that is faithful to God's revelation, especially as it is put forth in the teachings of Holy Scripture, and that is meaningful to respondents in their respective cultural and existential contexts. Contextualization is both verbal and nonverbal and has to do with theologizing; Bible translation, interpretation, and application; incarnational lifestyle; evangelism; Christian instruction; church planting and growth; church organization; and worship style. . . . with all of those activities involved in carrying out the Great Commission. (Hesselgrave and Rommen 1989, 200).

Even today contextualization as communication continues to be important. It means that the gospel communicator must not only learn the language and culture of the receptor but must also become so steeped in the thought patterns and deep-level meanings of the receptor as to begin to think and reflect within the

---

141. Names associated with this paradigm would include William Carey, Eugene Nida, David Hesselgrave, Charles Kraft, Marvin K. Mayers, and Sherwood Lingenfelter, among many others.

receptor's worldview. Thus the Christian missionary who wishes to communicate cross-culturally must learn to do what Charles Kraft has termed "receptor-oriented communication" (Kraft 1983, 1991) which also means "communicating Jesus' way" (Kraft 1999). We must never lose sight nor underestimate the importance of this most fundamental aspect of contextualization. As the Christian cross-cultural missionary communicates the gospel, faithfulness to the message is paramount.

What I have called a "communication" paradigm Stephen Bevans has termed the "translation model" of contextual theology. Bevans writes,

> Of the six models we will be considering in this book, the translation model of contextual theology is probably the most commonly employed and usually the one that most people think of when they think of doing theology in context. . . . Practitioners of the translation model also point out that it is possibly the oldest way to take the context of theologizing seriously and that it is found within the Bible itself. . . . In many ways, every model of contextual theology is a model of translation. There is always a content to be adapted or accommodated to a particular culture. What makes this particular model specifically a translation model, however, is its insistence on the message of the gospel as an unchanging message. . . . If there is a key presupposition of the translation model, it is that the essential message of Christianity is supracultural or supracontextual. Practitioners of this model speak of a "gospel core" (Haleblian 1983, 101–102). . . . In any case, what is very clear in the minds of people who employ the translation model is that an essential, supracultural message can be separated from a contextually bound mode of expression . . . Another presupposition of the translation model [is] that of the ancillary or subordinate role of context in the contextualization process. Experience, culture, social location, and social change, of course, are acknowledged as important, but they are never as important as the supracultural, "never changing" gospel message (Bevans 2002, 37–41).[142]

---

142. Names associated with the communication paradigm are William Carey, Eugene Nida, David Hesselgrave, and Charles Kraft, among many others.

The view of contextualization as communication (or accommodation, or adaptation—whatever word or model one chooses to work with) has had at least one significant weakness. The common assumption has been that the Christian missionary or group of Christians in mission know and understand all that needs to be known and understood about the gospel they are wanting to communicate. In this perspective, the gospel communicators do not need to concern themselves about the extent to which their own culture has syncretized, obscured and possibly contradicted the gospel. The gospel communicators do not believe that they themselves need to learn anything new about the gospel. Rather, the major methodological task involves a movement from Christians of one cultural context communicating a culturally appropriate gospel to persons in a new context who have not yet heard or no longer can hear the message of the Bible.

Paul Hiebert rightly pointed out that in the past this perspective was mixed with an attitude of superiority on the part of Western culture (especially during the era of colonialism) and became essentially a "noncontextual" approach. "This stance," Hiebert wrote, "was essentially monocultural and monoreligious. Truth was seen as supracultural. Everything had to be seen from the perspective of Western civilization and Christianity, which had shown themselves to be technologically, historically and intellectually superior to other cultures; and so those [receptor] cultures could be discounted as 'uncivilized.' The missionary's culture was 'good,' 'advanced,' and 'normative.' Other cultures were 'bad,' 'backward,' and 'distorted.' Christianity was true, other religions were false" (Hiebert 1984, 290–291). Communication was deemed to be important, but the content of the message being communicated went unexamined because the missionary communicators assumed they knew and understood all there was to know and understand about the gospel they were communicating.

As converts were won throughout the world, new Christians speaking a host of new languages were gathered into churches. This led to a second important perspective on contextualization: indigenization.

APPROPRIATE CONTEXTUALIZATION AS INDIGENIZATION

Wilbert Shenk considers the concept of the indigenous church to be "the great theoretical breakthrough of the nineteenth century."

From its earliest days the modern missionary movement was marked by multiple perspectives. On the one hand, mission promoters frequently depicted the task to be done as a fairly simple process of presenting the Christian message in a straight-forward manner to peoples sunk in darkness and despair, peoples who consequently would respond gladly and quickly. On the other side was the growing group of missionaries in the field who knew firsthand how complicated the process was. As foreigners they had to master a strange language—often before it was written—and try to understand a highly intricate culture with quite another worldview. Learning the new language and culture were requisite to any effective communication of the Christian message. As the complexity of the task became more apparent, mission theorists moved through several stages as they sought to conceptualize the task.

The great theoretical breakthrough in missions thought in the nineteenth century was identification of the indigenous church as the goal of mission. Other theoretical and policy developments were largely embroidering on this basic theme. (Shenk 1999, 75)[143]

In his article in the *Evangelical Dictionary of World Mission,* John Mark Terry said, "The term 'indigenous' comes from biology and indicates a plant or animal native to an area. Missiologists adopted the word and used it to refer to churches that reflect the cultural distinctives of their ethnolinguistic group. The missionary effort to establish indigenous churches is an effort to plant churches that fit natu-rally into their environment and to avoid planting churches that replicate Western patterns" (Moreau, Netland, and Van Engen, eds., 2000, 483).

In *God's Missionary People* I summarized what I called then the "Seven Stages of Emerging within Missionary Congregations."

[When we study mission history, we see] at least seven stages in the emerging of a local and national missionary church—stages that have been repeated time and again in church-planting

---

143. Names associated with the indigenization paradigm of contextualization would include, among others, Henry Venn, Rufus Anderson ("three-self"), John Nevius, Roland Allen, Mel Hodges, Donald McGavran, Alan Tippett, and Don Richardson.

situations. We might summarize the development of the church in a given context in this way:

1. Pioneer evangelism leads to the conversion of a number of people.

2. Initial church gatherings are led by elders and deacons, along with preachers from outside the infant body.

3. Leadership training programs [select], train, and commission indigenous pastors, supervisors, and other ministry leaders.

4. Regional organizations of Christian groups develop structures, committees, youth programs, women's societies, and regional assemblies.

5. National organization, supervision of regions, and relationships with other national churches begin to form.

6. Specialized ministries grow inside and outside the church, with boards, budgets, plans, finances, buildings, and programs.

7. Indigenous missionaries are sent by the daughter church for local, national, and international mission in the world, beginning the pattern all over again. (Van Engen 1999, 43–44)

These seven steps reflect the development of a new group of disciples of Jesus Christ toward becoming an indigenous church that naturally fits and reflects its local context. As mission churches (1910s and 1920s) became known as younger churches (1930s and 1940s) and then as national churches (1950s and 1960s), the concept of the indigenous church underwent significant development. British Henry Venn (1796–1873) and American Rufus Anderson (1796–1880) used the word to stress the sustainability of a new group of believers in a new culture. In the late nineteenth century, indigeneity was predominantly used as an administrative and organizational concept. For a new church to sustain itself apart from external missionary assistance, it needed to become self-supporting financially, self-governing organizationally, and self-propagating evangelistically. Fifty years later John Nevius (1829–1893) and Roland Allen (1868–1947) expanded and deepened the concept of indigeneity of the new churches, stressing issues of Bible study, leadership formation, the spontaneous work of the Holy Spirit, the ministry of the members through the exercise of their spiritual gifts, and the creation of church structures that could sustain themselves without outside dependence. Building on all four of these, Mel Hodges (1909–1986), American missionary administrator with the Assemblies of God, called for the planting and growth of *The Indigenous Church* (1953), an emphasis that became one of the cornerstones of McGavran's mission theory and of the Church Growth Movement.

Indigeneity had to do with the fit between the forms and life of a church and its surrounding context. In *Verdict Theology in Missionary Theory* (1969), Alan Tippett (1911–1988) expanded the concept of indigeneity to include self-image, self-functioning, self-determining, self-supporting, self-propagating and self-giving. This was further expanded and deepened by Charles Kraft in *Christianity in Culture* (1979) to include the concept of "dynamic equivalence churchness" (Kraft 1979, chapters 13–17). As the churches in Asia, Africa, Latin America, and Oceania grew and matured, the concept of indigeneity led to a third perspective of contextualization: translatability.

APPROPRIATE CONTEXTUALIZATION AS TRANSLATABILITY

A third perspective of contextualization emphasizes the incarnational nature of the gospel as being infinitely translatable into any and all human cultures—a faith relationship with God that can be woven into the fabric of any and all worldviews. The gospel of Jesus Christ can be incarnated, given shape, lived out, in any cultural context—it is infinitely universalizable.[144]

The perspective of appropriate contextualization as translatability draws heavily from the concept of the incarnation so dominant in the Gospel of John. John tells us that "The Word became flesh and made his dwelling (tabernacled) among us. We have seen his glory, the glory of the One and Only, who came from the Father, full of grace and truth" (John 1:14).

In *Christianity in Africa*, Kwame Bediako discusses the "translatability" of the faith. "Andrew Walls," Bediako writes, "has taught us to recognize the Christian religion as "culturally infinitely translatable" (Walls 1981, 39). "Translatability is

---

144. Names associated with this paradigm would include, among others, Lamin Sanneh, Kwame Bediako, John Mbiti, Rene Padilla, and Andrew Walls.

also another way of saying universality. Hence the translatability of the Christian religion signifies its fundamental relevance and accessibility to persons in any culture within which the Christian faith is transmitted and assimilated" (Bediako 1995, 109).

The "translatability" of the Christian gospel and Christian Church entails something broader, deeper and more pervasive than communication of a message. This paradigm stresses the fact that the gospel can take on new forms and shapes as it is born in new contexts. Gospel and Church are not foreign plants that have been slightly modified to be able to grow in foreign soil. Rather, this gospel is a new hybrid seed with new and different characteristics that allow it to sprout, grow and flourish in a new climate. Marc Spindler, along with other Roman Catholic missiologists, has called this "inculturation."

> (Inculturation) implies that in Latin America, Africa, Asia, and other places the new churches can and should understand and express the Christian faith in terms of their respective cultures. Even more, it means that the gospel itself receives its shape in the total culture of the people among whom the church is planted and in the nation of which the church is essentially an integral part.
>
> Successful inculturation may be said to occur when the gospel and the church no longer seem to be foreign imports but are claimed in general as the property of the people. (Spindler 1995, 139–40)

Lamin Sanneh speaks of "mission as translation," a process that creates what Sanneh terms the "vernacular credibility" of the gospel as it takes new shapes in new cultural settings. It is important to listen to Sanneh at this point.

> Mission as translation makes the bold, fundamental assertion that the recipient culture is the authentic destination of God's salvific promise and, as a consequence, has an honored place under "the kindness of God," with the attendant safeguards against cultural absolutism. . . . Mission as translation affirms the *missio Dei* as the hidden force for its work. It is the *missio Dei* that allowed translation to enlarge the boundaries of the proclamation.

Needless to say, Christian mission did not adhere consistently to the rule of translation, but translation in itself implies far-reaching implications that are worth considering, whatever may be the position of particular missions toward it. . . . Translation is profoundly related to the original conception of the gospel: God, who has no linguistic favorites, has determined that we should all hear the Good News "in our own native tongue." Mission as cultural diffusion conflicts with the gospel in this regard, and historically we can document the problems, challenges, and prospects that attended Christian expansion across cultures under the consistent rule of translation. . . .

Where mission failed to achieve a vernacular credibility it has called forth and deserved every criticism it received, then or in retrospect. Ethnographers and other scholars who have criticized mission for its foreign nature have in a backhanded way conceded the principle that Christianity and vernacular credibility are related. . . .

Vernacular translation begins with the effort to equip the gospel with terms of familiarity, and that process brings the missionary enterprise into the context of field experience. . . . There is a radical pluralism implied in vernacular translation wherein all languages and cultures are, in principle, equal in expressing the word of God . . . Two general ideas stem from this analysis. First is the inclusive principle whereby no culture is excluded from the Christian dispensation or even judged solely or ultimately by Western cultural criteria.

Second is the ethical principle of change as a check to cultural self-absolutization. . . . This introduces in mission the *logos* concept wherein any and all languages may confidently be adopted for God's word. (Sanneh 1993, 31, 174–75, 208–9)[145]

In 1985, René Padilla offered three important observations concerning this incarnational view of intercultural communication.

---

145. See also Kwame Bediako's reflection on Sanneh's proposal in Bediako 1995, 119–23.

The consciousness of the critical role that culture plays in communication is of special importance for the intercultural communication of the gospel. There are at least three reasons for this.

> The incarnation is a basic element in the gospel. Since the Word became man, the only possible communication of the gospel is that in which the gospel becomes incarnate in culture in order to put itself within the reach of (humans) as . . . cultural being(s) . . .
>
> Without a translation that goes beyond the words to break into the raw material of life in the receiving culture, the gospel is a fantasy. The gospel involves the proclamation of Jesus Christ as Lord of the totality of the universe and of human existence. If this proclamation is not directed to specified needs and problems of the hearers, how can they experience the Lordship of Christ in their concrete situation? To contextualize the gospel is so to translate it that the Lordship of Jesus Christ is not an abstract principle or a mere doctrine but the determining factor of life in all its dimensions and the basic criterion in relation to which all the cultural values that form the very substance of human life are evaluated. . . .
>
> In order for the gospel to receive an intelligent response, either positive or negative, there must be effective communication, communication that takes into consideration the point of contact between the message and the culture of the hearers. There can be no true evangelization unless the gospel confronts cultural values and thought patterns. (Padilla 1985, 2–93)

This element of "translatability" or "universalizability" that Bediako, Walls, Sanneh, Padilla, and others have emphasized means that there is a deepening, widening, filling, and enriching of the way Christians live out the gospel in their context. Ever since Luke listed his "table of nations" in Acts 2, mentioning those who "heard their own language being spoken" (Acts 2:6 cf,8.11), the truth of the universally-appropriate nature of the incarnation has been evident throughout mission history. The gospel is by its very nature native to every culture on earth. All humans were created by the same God, Creator of heaven and earth, the God of Abraham, Isaac, and Jacob.

Whether one speaks of natural theology, general revelation, common grace, prevenient grace, "redemptive analogies" (Richardson 2000, 812–13), or the lights of God's revelation dispersed amidst all cultures (Barth), the implication is the same (though recognizing the profound theological differences between these concepts in many other respects). Together they point to a most fundamental fact: all humans are created by the same God; all are addressed equally by Jesus Christ, the Word made flesh; and the Holy Spirit enables all to hear the gospel in their own language. "For God so loved the [entire] world . . ." (John 3:16). God speaks and understands all languages. Listen again to Lamin Sanneh.

> Christian life is indelibly marked with the stamp of culture, and faithful stewardship includes uttering the prophetic word in culture, and sometimes even against it. . . . in [the apostle Paul's] view God's purposes are mediated through particular cultural streams.
>
> The mission of the church applied this insight by recognizing all cultures, and the languages in which they were embodied, as lawful in God's eyes, making it possible to render God's word into other languages. Even if in practice Christians wished to stop the translation process, claiming their form of it as final and exclusive, they have not been able to suppress it for all time. It is this phenomenon that the concept of translatability tries to represent. . . . Translatability ensures that the challenge at the heart of the Christian enterprise is . . . kept alive in all cultural contexts. . . . (Sanneh 1993, 47–48)

This being so, Christians must grapple with the profound implications of the fact that the Christian faith is internally compatible, consistent and coherent with—and can be fully and naturally expressed in—every culture. A realization of the translatability of the gospel moves contextual mission theology beyond indigenization to incarnation. The example of the Church in Africa may be helpful at this point. Together with other two-thirds world theologians, Kwame Bediako and John Mbiti described the struggle to deepen and broaden the African understanding of the gospel. Bediako's summary of Mbiti's views are instructive.

Mbiti was early in his observation of the lack of sufficient and positive engagement by Western missions with African cultural and religious values. He saw the result of this in an African church which had "come of age *evangelistically*, but not *theologically:*" "a church without theology, without theologians and without theological concern" as he was writing in 1967 and 1969.

Mbiti, however, soon came to make a distinction between "Christianity" which "results from the encounter of the gospel with any given local society" and so is always indigenous and culture-bound, on the one hand, and the gospel, which is "God-given, eternal, and does not change" on the other. In 1970 he wrote: "We can add nothing to the gospel, for this is an eternal gift of God; but Christianity is always a beggar seeking food and drink, cover and shelter from the cultures it encounters in its never-ending journeys and wanderings" (Bediako is quoting Mbiti 1970, 438).

Mbiti rejected the notion of indigenizing Christianity as such on African soil. Bediako cites Mbiti as saying, "To speak of 'indigenizing Christianity' is to give the impression that Christianity is a ready-made commodity which has to be transplanted to a local area. Of course, this has been the assumption followed by many missionaries and local theologians. I do not accept it any more" (Mbiti 1979, 68).

In contrast, the gospel is to be seen as "translatable," taking on fully African deep-level meanings in addition to surface-level cultural forms. "For Mbiti therefore," Bediako writes,

> The gospel is genuinely at home in Africa, is capable of being apprehended by Africans at the specific level of their religious experience, and in fact has been so received through the missionary transmission of it. . . . The theological principle we see operating in Mbiti's thought is that of translatability—the capacity of the essential impulses of the Christian religion to be transmitted and assimilated in a different culture so that these impulses create dynamically equivalent responses in the course of such a transmission. Given this principle, it is possible to say that the earlier concern to seek an 'indigenization' of Christianity in Africa, as though one were dealing with an essentially 'Western' and 'foreign' religion was, in effect, misguided because the task was conceived as the correlation of two entities thought to be unrelated. . . . The achievement meant here is not to be measured in terms of Western missionary transmission, but rather by African assimilation of the Faith. . . . It was therefore misguided to assume that African converts to Christianity

assimilated the missionary message in Western terms rather than in terms of their own African religious understanding and background. (Bediako 1995, 118–19)

APPROPRIATE CONTEXTUALIZATION AS LOCAL THEOLOGIZING

Thus far we have surveyed three paradigms of contextualization broadly conceived: communication, indigenization, and translatability. Together these three deal generally with a one-way movement of gospel proclamation in word and deed: a movement from those who know God and believe they understand the gospel to those who do not know, have never heard, or no longer can hear of God's love for them. We have looked at appropriate contextualization in a broad and general sense as involving the search for what Charles Kraft has termed, "appropriate Christianity: a Christian expression of the faith that is appropriate to the Scriptures, on the one hand, and appropriate to the people in a given culture, on the other" (Kraft, ed., 2005, 5).

In his dictionary article in the *Evangelical Dictionary of World Missions*, Dean Gilliland discussed how one might define contextualization understood broadly.

> There is no single or broadly accepted definition of contextualization. The goal of contextualization perhaps best defines what it is. That goal is to enable, insofar as it is humanly possible, an understanding of what it means that Jesus Christ the Word, is authentically experienced in each and every human situation. . . . Contextualization in mission is an effort made by a particular church to experience the gospel for its own life in light of the Word of God. (2000, 225)[146]

In the rest of this chapter I will survey two additional paradigms of appropriate contextualization that have arisen in missiological reflection during the past forty years: local theologizing and epistemology. In contrast to the previous three

---

146. To the best of my knowledge, Dean Gilliland was the first—and maybe has been the only professor—to be in a faculty position that included "contextualization" in the name. After serving as a cross-cultural missionary and theological educator in Nigeria, he taught for many years in the School of World Mission of Fuller Theological Seminary.

paradigms we have examined, these last two involve an intentional two-way conversation between church and gospel on the one hand and the contextual reality, on the other.

I have entitled this section "local theologizing" as a way to cut through today's confusion surrounding the term contextualization. In this section I am dealing with what many have called contextualization in a narrow sense: that is, as having to do with humanization, with the impact of sociopolitical, economic, cultural, and other forces in a given context, with the task of doing theology in a particular context.[147]

Contextualization as the development of local theologies was originally catalyzed by the publication, in 1972, of *Ministry in Context* on the part of the Theological Education Fund of the World Council of Churches and is associated with the writings of Shoki Coe in particular (See, e.g., Coe 1976; Norman Thomas, ed., 1995, 175–76; and Stephen Bevans 2002, 153 nn 45 and 46.)

Ashish Chrispal of Union Biblical Seminary in Pune, India, explains his view of contextualization (conceived as doing theology in context).

> The historical world situation is not merely an exterior condition for the church's mission: rather it ought to be incorporated as a constitutive element into her understanding of mission, her aims and objectives. Like her Lord, the church-in-mission must take sides *for* life and *against* death; *for* justice and *against* oppression. Thus mission as contextualization is an affirmation that God had turned toward the world. . . . Contextualization implies all that is involved in the familiar term indigenization which relates to traditional cultural values, but goes beyond it to take into account very seriously the contemporary factors in cultural change. It deals with the contemporary socioeconomic, political issues of class-caste struggles, power politics, riches and poverty, bribery and corruption, privileges and oppression—all factors that constitute society and the relationship between one community and another. (Chrispal 1995, 1,3)

---

147. Names associated with this paradigm would include, among others, Shoki Coe, Robert Schreiter, Dean Gilliland, Clemens Sedmak, Stephen Bevans, Ashish Chrispal, Tite Tienou, and Andrew Kirk.

Contextualization in this more technical sense of the word involves theologizing as an action rather than theology as a received composite of affirmations: thus the use of the word theologizing as a verbal form rather than theology as a noun. Tite Tiénou explains.

> The term "contextualization" entered missiological literature in 1972 through the report of the Third Mandate of the Theological Education Fund. . . . At that time, Shoki Coe was director of the Theological Education Fund, an agency sponsored by the World Council of Churches and administered under the auspices of the Commission on World Mission and Evangelism. According to Coe, indigenization is a static concept since it "tends to be used in the sense of responding to the gospel in terms of traditional culture" whereas contextualization is "more dynamic. . . . open to change and . . . future-oriented. (Coe 1976, 20, 21)
>
> The word "contextualization" was therefore chosen with the specific purpose of conveying the idea that theology can never be permanently developed. Everywhere and in every culture Christians must be engaged in an ongoing process of relating the gospel to cultures that are constantly changing. As long as the world endues, this process continues. For many people contextualization, not indigenization, is the term that best describes this never-ending process. (Tiénou 1993, 247)

This dynamic process called contextualization (narrowly understood) draws from all aspects of human experience in a local context and fosters a conversation between the reality of the context and the church's understanding of the gospel. "Contextualization," writes Andrew Kirk, " recognizes the reciprocal influence of culture and socioeconomic life. In relating gospel to culture, therefore, it tends to take a more critical (or prophetic) stance towards culture" (Kirk 1999, 91; see Van Engen 1989, 97 nn 18, 19.).

The perspective of contextualization as local theologizing represents a constantly changing reciprocal interaction between church and context. It is a process of local reflection that begins with an analysis of the historical situation, proceeds to a rereading of Scripture which in turn leads to interactive theological reflection concerning the context: an act of theologizing that propels the Christian to active engagement with the cultural, socioeconomic, and political issues extant in the context. Within this view of contextualization as local theologizing there is a wide spectrum of diverse viewpoints from a nearly total secularization of the process at one end to an emphasis on the transformation of the church at the other end.

Contextualization in this narrow and more technical sense involves not only theologizing as an active process, but also expands the scope of the sources of one's theological reflection to include all appropriate aspects of human experience. This dynamic process of interaction with all aspects of the context was highlighted by R. Yesurathnam, professor of Systematic Theology in the Church of South India.

> The term contextualization includes all that is implied in indig-
> enization or inculturation, but seeks also to include the realities
> of contemporary, secularity, technology, and the struggle for
> human justice. . . . Contextualization both extends and corrects
> the older terminology. While indigenization tends to focus on
> the purely cultural dimension of human experience, contex-
> tualization broadens the understanding of culture to include
> social, political, and economic questions. In this way, culture
> is understood in more dynamic and flexible ways, and is seen
> not as closed and self-contained, but as open and able to be
> enriched by an encounter with other cultures and movements.
> (Yesurathnam 2000, 53)

Stephen Bevans highlighted the countercultural and dialogical aspects of local engagement in contextualization. "Contextualization points to the fact that theology needs to interact and dialogue not only with traditional cultural value, but with social change, new ethnic identities, and the conflicts that are present as the contemporary phenomenon of globalization encounters the various peoples of the world. . . . Contextualization, then, [is] the preferred term to describe the theology that takes human experience, social location, culture, and cultural change seriously" (Bevans 2002, 27).

> Contextual theology's addition of culture and social change to
> the traditional *loci* of scripture and tradition already marks a
> revolution in theological method over against traditional ways
> of doing theology. . . . Both poles—human experience and the
> Christian tradition—are to be read together dialectically. In
> addition to this basic shift in theological method, a number of

other methodological issues have emerged. When human experience, world events, culture, and cultural change are taken as *loci theologici*, one can ask whether theology is always to be done formally or discursively. What, in other words, is the *form* that theology should take? As theology becomes more of a reflection on ordinary human life in the light of the Christian tradition, one might ask whether ordinary men and women might not, after all, be the best people to theologize. (Bevans 2002, 16–17)

Clemens Sedmak of the University of Salzburg, Austria brought together many of the emphases that Schreiter's call for *Constructing Local Theologies* had in common with Bevans' challenge to effectively utilize *Models of Contextual Theology*. In *Doing Local Theology: A Guide for Artisans of a New Humanity*, Sedmak offered a number of theses. Among them, he affirmed that,

Theology is done locally. In order to be honest to the local circumstances theology has to be done as local theology, as theology that takes the particular situation seriously. Local theology can be done with basic theological means. It can be done by the people, and it is done with the people . . . Local theologies recognize that theology takes shape within a particular context. Theologies are developed in response to and within a particular social situation.

Understanding the social situation is a necessary condition for understanding the genesis and validity of particular theologies. . . . Theology that tries to do justice to its place in culture and history is contextual. Contextualization literally means, 'weaving together.' . . . Theology is always done within a concrete local social structure that provides rich resources for constructing local theologies and for developing a local identity as a theologian. The social, historical, cultural, and political context has an impact on the role of the theologian and his or her place in the context. (Sedmak 2002, 8, 95–96).

Dirkie Smit, Professor of Systematic Theology at the Universities of Western Cape and Stellenbosch, pointed out that, "Contextual theologies. . . . have underlined the fact that all theology, all thinking and speaking about God, is contextual, is influenced by the contexts in which the believers live, including the so-called traditional theology of Western Christianity in all its forms" (Smit 1994, 44; see also Arias 2001, 64.)

From a Protestant evangelical standpoint, Stanley Grenz echoes the importance of correlating (he draws the term from Paul Tillich here) the existential human questions posed by the context and the revelatory answers found in the Bible. "The commitment to contextualization . . . ," Grenz writes,

> entails an implicit rejection of the older evangelical conception of theology as the construction of truth on the basis of the Bible alone. No longer can the theologian focus merely on Scripture as the one complete theological norm. Instead, the process of contextualization requires a movement between two poles—the Bible as the source of truth and the culture as the source of the categories through which the theologian expresses biblical truth. . . . Contextualization demands that the theologian take seriously the thought-forms and mindset of the culture in which theologizing transpires, in order to explicate the eternal truths of the Scriptures in language that is understandable to contemporary people (Grenz 1993, 90; see also Shenk 1999, 77).

APPROPRIATE CONTEXTUALIZATION AS AN EPISTEMOLOGICAL PROCESS

A fifth paradigm of contextualization has to do with an epistemological process of hermeneutical examination and critique of the context and its implications for a missional understanding of the gospel in that specific context. In the 2002 revised and expanded edition of *Models of Contextual Theology*, Stephen Bevans added a model he called the "countercultural model" of contextualization.

> What this model examines more than any other model is how some contexts are simply antithetical to the gospel and need to be challenged by the gospel's liberating and healing power . . . The countercultural model draws on rich and ample sources in scripture and tradition. . . . More than any other model, . . . it recognizes that the gospel represents an all-encompassing, radically alternate worldview that differs profoundly from human experiences of the world and the culture that humans create.

> Particularly in contexts that exude a "culture of death," in con-
> texts in which the gospel seems irrelevant or easily ignored, or in
> those in which the gospel has become "a stained glass version"
> of a particular worldview, this model can prove to be a powerful
> way by which the gospel is able to be communicated with new
> freshness and genuine engagement. (2002, 118)[148]

Appropriate contextualization as an epistemological approach emphasizes the sense that in each new context, in each new cultural setting, followers of Jesus Christ have an opportunity to learn something about God they had not previously known. Christian knowledge about God is seen as cumulative, enhanced, deepened, broadened and expanded as the gospel takes new shape in each new culture. This was my thesis in "The New Covenant: Knowing God in Context" (1989, reprinted in 1996, 71–89).

In 1979, Bruce Nicholls suggested a distinction between what he called existential contextualization (the type common to World Council of Churches circles) and dogmatic contextualization (one that begins with the biblical text as ultimately the only rule of faith and practice). (See Nicholls 1979, 24; Stults 1989, 151; and Chrispal 1995, 5.) When contextualization is viewed as an epistemological endeavor in numerous contexts, as a process that searches for a deepening and broadening understanding of God in particular contexts, it does not fit easily into either of Nicholl's categories. Appropriate contextualization as epistemology accepts the contextual (and existential) reality as itself a significant component of its theological (and dogmatic) reflection in which Christians broaden and deepen their understanding and participation in God's mission in a given context.

In his dictionary entry on "Contextualization," Dean Gilliland summarized six models of contextualization: the Critical, Semiotic, Synthetic, Transcendental and Translation models. Gilliland affirmed that,

> The strength of contextualization is that if properly carried out,
> it brings ordinary Christian believers into what is often called
> the theological process. . . . The objective of contextualization
> is to bring data from the whole of life to real people and search
> the Scriptures for a meaningful application of the Word (who)

---

148. Bevans is quoting from Douglas John Hall, "Ecclesia Crucis: The Theologic of Christian Awkwardness," in George R. Hunsberger and Craig van Gelder, eds., *The Church Between Gospel and Culture: The Emerging Mission in North America*. G. R.: Eerdmans, 1996, 199.

"dwelt among us" (John 1:14). The missiological significance for contextualization is that all nations must understand the Word as clearly and as accurately as did Jesus' own people in his day (Gilliland 2002, 227).

A dozen years earlier, Gilliland had suggested four questions that are of paramount consideration in the task of constructing a contextually appropriate theology:

- What is the (culture-specific, contextual) general background?
- What are the presenting problems or issues?
- What theological questions arise?
- What appropriate directions should the theology (and missiology) take? (Gilliland 1989b, 52)

Theologians and missiologists the world over are now more than ever aware that Christianity is no longer a Western religion. This should not surprise us, since the Christian Church did not begin as a Western religion: it began as a Middle Eastern, North African and central Asian religious expression of faith in Jesus Christ. Today there are Christian believers in every political nation and among every major culture, though there yet remain many unreached people groups.

"Contextualization," wrote J. Andrew Kirk, "recognizes the reciprocal influence of culture and socioeconomic life. In relating gospel to culture, therefore, it tends to take a more critical (or prophetic) stance toward culture. The concept. . . . is intended to be taken seriously as a theological method which entails particular ideological commitments to transform situations of social injustice, political alienation and the abuse of human rights. José Miguez Bonino speaks of 'raising up the historical situation to the theological level' and of 'theological reflection in the concrete praxis. . . . The inflexible will to act from the historical situation, analyzed by means of sociopolitical instruments and adopted in a theological option, identifies. . . . the starting point of the theological task'" (Kirk 1999, 91). [149]

David Bosch highlighted the importance of this epistemological element in contextualization.

> Contextual theologies claim that they constitute an epistemological break when compared with traditional theologies. Whereas, at least since the time of Constantine, theology was

---

149. Kirk is quoting from Miguez Bonino 1971, 405–407; cited also in Norman Thomas 1995: 174 and David Bosch 1991, 425.

conducted *from above* as an elitist enterprise . . . its main source
was *philosophy*, and its main interlocutor the *educated non-believe*,
contextual theology is theology *from below*, "from the underside
of history," its main source (apart from Scripture and tradition)
is the *social sciences*, and its main interlocutor the *poor* or the *culturally marginalized*. . . . Equally important in the new epistemology
is the emphasis on the priority of praxis. (1991, 423)

Bosch goes on to mention five characteristics of this epistemological approach
to contextualization:

- First, there is a profound suspicion that not only Western science
  and Western philosophy, but also Western theology. . . . were actually designed to serve the interests of the West, more particularly
  to legitimize "the world as it now exists.." . . .
- Second, the new epistemology refuses to endorse the idea of the
  world as a static object which only has to be *explained*. . . .
- Third, (there is) an emphasis on *commitment* as "the first act of theology" (quoting Torres and Fabella 1978, 269). . . .
- Fourth, in this paradigm the theologian can no longer be "a lonely
  bird on the rooftop (K. Barth 1933, 40), who surveys and evaluates
  this world and its agony; he or she can only theologize credibly if
  it is done *with* those who suffer.
- Fifth, then, the emphasis is on *doing* theology. The universal claim
  of the hermeneutic of language has been challenged by a hermeneutic of the deed, since doing is more important than knowing
  or speaking. . . . From praxis or experience the hermeneutical
  circulation proceeds to reflection as a second . . . act of theology.
  The traditional sequence, in which *theoria* is elevated over *praxis*, is
  here turned upside down. This does not, of course, imply a rejection of *theoria*. Ideally, there should be a dialectical relationship
  between theory and praxis. . . ."Orthopraxis and orthodoxy need
  one another, and each is adversely affected when sight is lost of
  the other" (Bosch 1991, 424–25; Bosch is quoting Gutierrez 1988,
  xxxiv).

Bosch cautioned us regarding the "ambiguities of contextualization," a discomfort which I share. He registers his concerns by offering six affirmations that
serve to link contextualization with theology and mission:

- Mission as contextualization is an affirmation that God has turned toward the world. [150]
- Mission as contextualization involves the construction of a variety of "local theologies . . ."[151]
- There is not only the danger of relativism, where each context forges its own theology, tailor-made for that specific context, but also the danger of absolutism of contextualism. . . .
- We have to look at this entire issue from yet another angle, that of "reading the signs of the times"; an expression that has invaded contemporary ecclesiastical language. . . .
- In spite of the undeniably crucial nature and role of the context, then, it is not to be taken as the sole and basic authority for theological reflection. . . . [152]
- The best models of contextual theology succeed in holding together in creative tension *theoria, praxis* and *poiesis*—or, if one wishes, faith, hope and love. This is another way of defining the missionary nature of the Christian faith, which seeks to combine the three dimensions (Bosch 199, 426–32).

With the center of gravity having shifted from the North to the South, from the West to the East, mission in the twenty-first century will be from everywhere to everywhere. And all aspects of the reality of each particular context will—and must—have an impact on the content and the method of mission theology in each place. As Andrew Kirk has pointed out, true theology will be—must be—missiological.

> My thesis is that it is impossible to conceive of theology apart from mission. All true theology is, by definition, missionary theology, for it has as its object the study of the way of a God who is by nature missionary and a foundation text written by

150. Bosch affirms that it is not necessary to dichotomize our Godward faith relationship from our commitment and involvement in the world.

151. But a too-expansive multiplication—or atomization—of "theologies" has profoundly negative implications for relativizing the oneness of the Christian Church's faith in the same Gospel.

152. Bosch observes here that Stackhouse has argued that we are distorting the entire contextualization debate if we interpret it only as a problem of the relationship between praxis and theory. Bosch cites Max Stackhouse 1988, 85.

and for missionaries. . . . Theology should not be pursued as a set of isolated disciplines. It assumes a model of cross-cultural communication, for its subject matter both stands over against culture and relates closely to it. Therefore, it must be interdisciplinary and interactive. (Kirk 1997, 50–51)

There can be no theology without mission—or, to put it another way, no theology which is not missionary. (Kirk 1999, 11)

In the words of David Bosch,

Just as the church ceases to be church if it is not missionary, theology ceases to be theology if it loses its missionary character. The crucial question, then, is not simply or only or largely what church is or what mission is; it is also what theology is and is about. We are in need of a missiological agenda for theology rather than just a theological agenda for mission; for theology, rightly understood, has not reason to exist other than critically to accompany the *mission Dei*. So mission should be "the theme of all theology" (Gensichen 1971, 250). . . . It is not a case of theology occupying itself with the missionary enterprise as and when it seems to it appropriate to do so; it is rather a case of mission being that subject with which theology is to deal. For theology it is a matter of life and death that it should be in direct contact with mission and the missionary enterprise" (Bosch 1991, 494).

Although he probably would not share the economic and political viewpoints of some of the authors mentioned above, the epistemological slant of the methodology being suggested appears similar to the concept of "critical contextualization" developed by Paul Hiebert (Hiebert 1984). Hiebert called for a "critical contextualization" that involved an interactive process that takes the Bible seriously and also interacts constructively with the context.

Critical contextualization does not operate from a monocultural perspective. Nor is it premised upon the pluralism of incommensurable cultures. It seeks to find metacultural and metatheological frameworks that enable people in one culture to understand messages and ritual practices from another culture with a minimum of distortion. It is based on a critical realist epistemology that sees all human knowledge as a combination of objective and subjective elements, and as partial but increasingly closer approximations of truth. It takes both historical and cultural contexts seriously. And it sees the relationship between form and meaning in symbols such as words and rituals, ranging all the way from an equation of the two to simply arbitrary associations between them. Finally, it sees contextualization as an ongoing process in which the church must constantly engage itself, a process that can lead us to a better understanding of what the Lordship of Christ and the kingdom of God on earth are about (Paul Hiebert 1984, 295).

CONCLUSION

So what is the next step? I believe the next step involves a search for a methodology in contextual mission theology that simultaneously affirms the universality of the gospel and the particularity of its incarnation in specific times and places. We need a methodology in mission theology that takes the Scriptures and the Church's historical reflection on them seriously—and at the same time locates it in the environment of the context and the faith pilgrimage of the persons in that context. This is a methodology that involves the whole church who with the Bible in one hand and a newspaper in the other, asks over and over again Gilliland's four questions we mentioned earlier—and then proceeds to discover what God's mission entails in that place at that particular time.

Dan Shaw and I began to explore a way forward to create such a methodology by means of the concept of hermeneutical horizons that we learned from Hans Georg Gadamer, Grant Osborne, and others. In the fusion of horizons of meaning, subjectivity, objectivity, and all aspects of the context itself are understood as being merged. Mission theology, then, involves an understanding of, and an examination of, the interrelationship between multiple horizons of meaning: biblical and contemporary. But this matter is beyond the scope of this book.[153]

---

153. The reader interested in this topic can see Dan Shaw and Charles Van Engen, 2003.

CHAPTER 8
CONTEXTUALLY APPROPRIATE MISSION THEOLOGY

This chapter is adapted from Van Engen, "Toward a Contextually Appropriate Methodology in Mission Theology," in Charles Kraft, ed., *Appropriate Christianity*, Pasadena: William Carey Library, 2005, 203–26. Used by permission.

THESIS

In order to give rise to an "appropriate Christianity" in a given context, Christians in that context need to construct a method of mission theologizing such that the method itself is appropriate to Scripture, to the people of that context, and in relation to the world Church, yielding over time a contextually appropriate understanding of God's revelation to which the people of that culture may respond and by which they may be transformed (in truth, allegiance and power). This contextually appropriate methodology will need to be integrational, local, incarnational, praxeological and dialogical.

INTRODUCTION

In the previous chapter, I summarized five paradigms of contextually appropriate mission theology that build on each other: communication, indigenization, translatability, local theologies, and epistemology. Drawing a variety of insights from these five paradigms, in this chapter I will offer an outline of a method of mission theologizing whereby the method itself may be constructed to be appropriate both to Scripture and to the people of a context. The method I will outline below involves five steps that give rise to five characteristics of a contextually appropriate mission theology that is:

- Integrational: Understanding the gospel of Jesus Christ
- Local: Approaching a new context anew
- Incarnational: Preparing for new action
- Praxeological: Living out the gospel in appropriate action
- Dialogical: Reshaping our understanding of the gospel

The method outlined below involves an action of hermeneutical spiraling that weaves a tapestry of interaction between gospel and culture, between Church and context, between what Christians know and understand about God and what Christians experience in living out their faith in the world. As illustrated in Figure 4 below, this involves a dynamic interactive spiraling over time of theology from above with theology from below, seeking a deepening wisdom regarding the Church's understanding of God. In chapter four of *Communicating God's Word in a Complex World* (Shaw and Van Engen 2003), I drew from the work of Anthony Thiselton (1980) and Grant Osborne (1991), among others, to describe this theologizing activity as a dynamic, ongoing interaction of four horizons.

The methodology that I will describe below involves just such spiraling. I will describe one revolution of the spiral only. The reader needs to understand that what is being described in the following five steps is a theological and missiological process that needs to be repeated again and again by the people of God in a given context in order for them to discover a contextually appropriate mission theology in their particular situation. The first step, then, involves integration.

The Hermeneutical Spiral

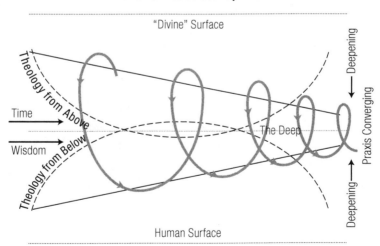

FIGURE 4: The Hermeneutical Spiral
(Read from top left to bottom right.)

INTEGRATIONAL: UNDERSTANDING THE GOSPEL OF JESUS CHRIST

The first step in the construction of a contextually appropriate mission theology involves a careful and intentional fusing of four sources of data from which the mission theologian draws understanding: Bible, context, church, and personal pilgrimage. Over the past three decades, there has been a significant consensus in mission theology on the need to integrate at least three domains of our knowledge in a dynamic, interrelated whole: *Word* (the primacy of the Bible in all contextual theologizing), *world* (the impact of culture, socioeconomics, political realities, and all other arenas of human life in the reality of a given context) and *church* (the primary agent of God's mission in the world). As we saw in an earlier chapter, these three (word, world, church) constitute the basic framework of missiology. Some would call this the interaction of text, context and faith community.[154]

Some years ago, I began to understand that I was missing a fourth arena that is very important for constructing a contextually appropriate mission theology. I had neglected to include the arena of personal pilgrimage of the followers of Jesus as agents of God's mission. This first step of the process in constructing a mission theology involves self-examination on the part of the mission theologian and the missional church. In this first step we examine our own knowledge and understanding of God and God's mission as it is informed and shaped by four domains. See Chapter 2, Part 2 of this volume for an explanation of this four-domain construction of mission theology. The reader will want to go back to Chapter 2 of this book and review the explanation of the four domains of missiology. An understanding of the interrelationship and the integration of those four domains is at the heart of this first step in the process of constructing a mission theology.

Having examined ourselves concerning the domains of knowledge that have informed and shaped our mission theology at a given time and context, we are prepared to take the second step in seeking a contextually appropriate mission theology: we approach anew the local context where our mission action will take place.

---

154. In *Mission on the Way* I described the way these three sources of missiological data impact the development of mission theology (Van Engen 1996, 22–26). I also adapted this tripartite understanding of theologizing in mission in *God So Loves the City* as it applies to developing a theology of mission in the city (Van Engen and Tiersma 1994, 271–85).

LOCAL: APPROACHING A NEW CONTEXT ANEW

The mission theologian is now ready to approach a context in a new way. This context may be a completely different cultural and contextual setting than the mission theologian's own. Or it may be the same culture and same geographic location as that where the mission theologian has been all along. The method we are considering in this chapter is intentionally designed to be useful for constructing an appropriate mission theology in one's particular context. After the reflection has been carried out in step one as outlined above, mission theologians will encounter their own context with new understanding and will see it with new eyes.

The second step in seeking a contextually appropriate mission theology involves an analysis both of the past and the present. Around the globe, 1.5 billion persons claim allegiance to Jesus Christ in some way. Over two-thirds of all world Christianity is now in Asia, Africa, Latin America and Oceania. Christians may now be found in every country, in every city, in every region of the globe. There are still thousands of unreached people groups, but there are no untouched people groups. Even unreached people groups have been impacted by the history of the interaction of the churches and missions with their culture in their context at some point in the recent or distant past. This means that the mission theologian never approaches a context *de novo*. There is no so-called *tabula raza* situation left in the world. Thus, when mission theologians approach their context of mission they will begin by asking historical questions concerning the past interaction of churches and missions with the context—and the impact the context has had on the churches and missions to which it has been related.

Such analysis of the local context must therefore be trinitarian. It must first begin with prayer and a recognition of the work of the Holy Spirit. In the Book of Acts, Luke provides us with the historical and theological foundation of our mission theology. We know that Christ's mission is carried out by the work and "in the power of the [Holy] Spirit" (Moltmann 1977). This leads us to ask two questions. (1) What has the Holy Spirit been doing in this context in the distant and recent past? (2) What does the Holy Spirit want to do today and tomorrow in this context? Mission is not ours. It does not belong to the churches or the mission agencies. Churches and missions participate in God's mission (*missio Dei*) guided, propelled, corrected and empowered by the Holy Spirit.[155] Mission in the way of

---

155. See, e.g., Rosin, 1972; Scherer 1987, 106–25; Scherer 1993, 82–88; John McIntosh 2000 631–33; Verkuyl 1978, 197–204; and in "Christ's Way," in CWME Conference in San

Jesus is always carried out in an atmosphere of the fruit of the Holy Spirit. And the gifts of the Holy Spirit are given for mission (Eph 4:11–16).

From Pentecost forward, mission is the action of the Holy Spirit through the agency of the church. All theory and action of mission need to be saturated by the guidance of the Holy Spirit and prayer. Like a river, the Holy Spirit's empowerment and direction flows from Jesus Christ to the world.

Having recognized the role of the Holy Spirit and prayer in the development of an appropriate mission theology, the mission theologian can proceed to examine three historical aspects that have to do with church and mission in the particular context: (1) the history of mission action by churches and missions in the context (who did what, when); (2) the history of mission theory exhibited by the churches and missions active in the context (their motivations, theoretical constructs, goals, and rationale for the methods chosen); and (3) the story of the dynamic two-way interaction of the churches and missions with the people of the context—and the impact of the context on the churches and missions involved.

Everywhere you and I go, there exists a history of the church's interaction with that context. There are both direct and indirect historical factors. The history of mission action in a specific context has too often been ignored especially by mission activists in the construction of their missiology. Throughout history people have tended to first go and do mission, and only later have they realized that they needed more complete and intimate knowledge of the history of mission action in that context.

No one should develop mission theology in a local context without first doing their homework concerning the history of mission activity, mission theory, and missional interaction between the Christian Church and the people in a particular context. Whether one thinks of China, Ghana, Russia, Brazil, Japan, Australia, Saudi Arabia, Thailand, South Africa, Korea, Kenya, Mexico, Germany, the United States, Guatemala, or England, for example, in each place churches and missions—and the local people's view of the churches and missions—have been shaped uniquely in each place by historical factors.

There is also a mission theory associated with the historic missional action, and this history of mission theory will help to guide the mission theologian. The particular theological traditions (Roman Catholic, orthodox, ecumenical, evangelical, Pentecostal/charismatic) have influenced the theoretical framework that has informed mission action in each place at particular times.

Antonio, Texas in 1989, in F. Wilson, edit 1990.

INCARNATION: PREPARING FOR NEW ACTION

The third step in developing a contextually appropriate mission theology moves us from analysis of the past to consideration of the present, on the way to the future. Our examination of the four domains was present tense. The second step was past tense. Now we move to considering what an appropriate mission theology should look like in the context where we find ourselves. To stop our reflection at this point yields mission studies but does not lead to active participation in appropriate mission action. This is not satisfactory. As Johannes Verkuyl has said,

> Missiology is the study of the salvation activities of the Father, Son, and Holy Spirit throughout the world geared toward bringing the kingdom of God into existence. Seen in this perspective missiology is the study of the worldwide church's divine mandate to be ready to serve this God who is aiming his saving acts toward this world. In dependence on the Holy Spirit and by word and deed the church is to communicate the total gospel and the total divine law to all (humanity). Missiology's task in every age is to investigate scientifically and critically the presuppositions, motives, structures, methods, patterns of cooperation, and leadership which the churches bring to their mandate. In addition missiology must examine every other type of human activity which combats the various evils to see if it fits the criteria and goals of God's kingdom which has both already come and is yet coming. . . . Missiology may never become a substitute for action and participation. God calls for participants and volunteers in his mission. In part, missiology's goal is to become a 'service station' along the way. If study does not lead to participation, whether at home or abroad, missiology has lost her humble calling (Verkuyl 1978, 5–6).

This is the point where we move from the past to the future. This is a critical integrative step. It begins to organize all of the thinking done so far. It transforms and focuses our missiological reflection into the construction of specific plans for mission action. As I mentioned earlier in Chapter 2 and as can be seen in Figure 5 below, I have sought to represent in a diagrammatic form the interaction of the various theological categories of mission theory with several illustrative aspects of missional action.

Foundational Categories of Mission Theory	Missio Dei	Missio Hominum	Missiones Ecclesiarum	Missio Politica Oecumenica	Missio Christi	Missio Espiritu Sancti	Missio Futurum / Adventus
God's Missional Action	*The Mission of God*	*Missional Use of Human Agents*	*Missions Through the Corporate People of God*	*Missional Action in Global Civilization*	*Messianic Mission Through Jesus Christ*	*Mission Through the Holy Spirit*	*Kingdom Mission in the Predictable Future and Surprising Advent*
The Context of Mission							
The Agents of Mission							
The Motives of Mission							
The Means of Mission							
The Methods of Mission							
The Goals of Mission							
The Results of Mission							
Hope/Utopia of Mission							
Prayer in Mission							
Spiritual Power in Mission							
Structures for Mission							
Partnerships in Mission							
Presence, Proclamation, Persuasion, Incorporation							

FIGURE 5: A Working Grid of Mission Theology

The interfacing of the mission categories (placed along the horizontal axis) with the aspects of missional action (placed along the vertical axis) yields a host of new questions for mission theology. Each square in the grid constitutes a specific question for appropriate mission theology in a local context. This is the move from description to prescription. The vertical aspects of God's mission (*missio Dei, mission hominum, missiones ecclesiarum, mission politica oecumenica, mission Cristi, missio Spiritu Sancti,* and *mission futurm / adventus*) interface with the horizontal categories of human mission action (Motivation, Means, Agents, Goals, etc.) in a complex interweaving of divine and human interaction. Each square of the grid constitutes a specific missiological question with a particular emphasis.

In this third step of the process, the mission theologian begins to translate the theory, history and reflection into concrete plans of action. Over the years, I have found this process very helpful in my own missionary career. It is essentially a simplified form of strategic planning. Thus, in this third step the mission theologian begins to address the question, "So what?" What should we be doing in mission in our context, at this time? Drawing from what we learned in steps 1 and 2, what do we sense the Holy Spirit leading us to do? Who should be the agents? What should be the means and methods? What are specific goals that we may seek to achieve?

PRAXEOLOGICAL: LIVING OUT THE GOSPEL IN APPROPRIATE ACTION

The fourth step in developing an appropriate mission theology has to do with translating the reflection into concrete action. David Bosch, among others, have made a case for the fact that the mission of the Church involves aspects of both missional dimension and missional intention (Bosch 1991, 494–96). There are dimensions of the impact of the presence of the disciples of Jesus in a particular context. Their very presence at times may have significant impact on the contextual reality. The dimensions of the presence of the gospel and of the Church should not be minimized. However, the dimensional aspect is not enough. The Church is also called to active participation in God's mission. The Church is sent into the world by Jesus Christ its head to carry out concrete and specific missional action in each context. This involves the aspect of missional intention. In a given context, what do the churches and missions intend to do? What intentional action steps are called for as the fruit of the reflection carried out in the previous three steps?

Once Christians commit themselves to being involved in missional action, they need to ask careful, sensitive and wise questions that will help to clarify the nature of the task, the action to be taken, the transformation sought, and the results that should be observable as fruit of the action. Each of these questions needs to be appropriate to the context.

Based on the integration offered by the grid, the contextual mission theologian begins to inquire regarding the interrelation of church and context in a specific time and place. In this new "here and now" there are specific issues of the church's missional dimension and missional intention vis-à-vis the context. How is the church already engaged in mission in its context? What resources does the church have to carry out mission? What constitutes action that is appropriate both to the mission theory and to the nature of the context?

In Chapter 2, I defined mission as follows.

> God's mission works primarily through the people of God intentionally crossing barriers from the people of God to all peoples of the world and from faith to the absence of faith in settings of nominal Christianity, to proclaim by word and deed the coming of the kingdom of God in Jesus Christ through the Church's participation in God's mission of reconciling people to God, to themselves, to each other, and to the world and gathering them into the Church through repentance and faith in Jesus Christ by the work of the Holy Spirit with a view to the transformation of the world as a sign of the coming of the kingdom in Jesus Christ.

As churches and missions engage in missional action it is important that they understand the impact of the action itself on their mission theology. Just as the Jerusalem Council in Acts 15 based its mission decisions on what the Holy Spirit had done in Acts 10, so the churches and missions gain new insight into what is appropriate mission theology in a context precisely through the action of mission itself. The action is itself theological.[156]

At this point the contextual mission theologian will translate the reflection into mission action in a particular context, at a specific time, through and with particular people, with specific missional goals in mind. Reflection leads to action which in turn transforms and informs our new reflection, which then leads to new missional action. This dynamic theological interaction of action-reflection-action has been a significant gift that Latin American scholars have offered the world church.

---

156. For a discussion of how this praxeological method of theologizing plays out in narrative theology, see Van Engen 1996, 44–68.

Though the notion of praxis is not an exclusively Latin American idea, during the past thirty years Latin Americans have been the dominant voice calling for this approach to doing theology in context.[157]

The missional action should be consistent with the foregoing theory (developed in steps 1 to 4 above). In Hiebert's centered-set perspective, churches may be moving towards Christ and at the same time carrying out mission in the church's context. The one cannot exist without the other. Churches moving away from Christ are not participating in Christ's mission.

A praxeological approach to contextually appropriate mission theology is made possible when one's theological method is built on what Paul Hiebert has called a "centered-set" approach. In this form of theologizing, the primary concern of the mission theologian is that reflection and action—praxis—be centered and moving toward Jesus Christ in whose mission we participate. In *Anthropological Reflections on Missiological Issues*, Hiebert develops the "characteristics of centered sets." It is instructive for us to listen to Hiebert at this point.

"First," Hiebert says, "a centered set is created be defining the center or reference point and the relationship of things to that center. Things related to the center belong to the set, and those not related to the center do not. . . ." This and the quotations that immediately follow are taken from Hiebert 1994, 123–31.

---

157. The following citations may aid the student of contextually appropriate mission theology to understand the meaning and significance of "praxis." Robert McAfee Brown, *Theology in a New Key*, 1978, 50–51. José Míguez Bonino, *Christians and Marxists*, 1976, 91–102. José Míguez-Bonino. "Hermeneutics, Truth and Praxis," in Míguez-Bonino, *Doing Theology in a Revolutionary Situation*. Phil.: Fortress, 1975, 86–105. Clodovis Boff, *Theology and Praxis*, 1987, xxi–xxx. Leonardo Boff, *Liberating Grace*, 1979, 3. Leonardo and Clodovis Boff, *Introducing Liberation Theology*, 1987, 8–9. Robert McAfee Brown, *Unexpected News*, 1984. Ernesto Cardenal, *Flights of Victory*, 1985, 11–12, 23–25. Rebecca Cho, *The Praxis of Suffering*, 1986, 36–37, 115–17, 120–21. Orlando Costas, *Theology at the Crossroads*, 1976, 8–9. Severino Croatto, *Liberación y Libertad: Pautas Hermeneúticas*, Buenos Aires: Ediciones Mundo Nuevo, 1973. Gustavo Gutierrez, "Liberation Praxis and Christian Faith," in: Gibellini, *Frontiers*, 1975, 1–33. Deane Ferm, *Third World Theologies: An Introduction*, 1986, 15. Gustavo Gutierrez. *We Drink From Our Own Wells*. 1984a, 19–32. Gustavo Gutierrez. *The Power of the Poor in History*, 1984b, vii–viii, 50–60. Gustavo Gutierrez, *Theology of Liberation*, 1988, 6–19. Roger Haight, *An Alternative Vision*, 1985, 44–48. Rene Padilla, *Mission Between the Times*, 1983, 83. Robert Schreiter, *Constructing Local Theologies*, 17, 91–93. Waldron Scott, *Bring Forth Justice*, 1980, xv. Spykman, Cook, et al., *Let My People Live*, 1988, xiv, 226–231. Raul Vidales, "Methodological Issues in Liberation Theology," in: Gibellini, *Frontiers*, 1975, 34–57.

"Second, while centered sets are not created by drawing boundaries, *they do have sharp boundaries* that separate things inside the set from those outside it—between things related to or moving toward the center and those that are not. Centered sets are well-formed, just like bounded sets. They are formed by defining the center and any relationships to it. The boundary then emerges automatically. Things related to the center naturally separate themselves from things that are not. . . ."

"Third, there are two variables intrinsic to centered sets. The first is membership. All members of a set are full members and share fully in its functions. There are not second-class members. The second variable is distance from the center. Some things are far from the center and others near to it, but all are moving toward it. . . ."

"Fourth, centered sets have two types of change inherent in their structure. The first has to with entry into or exit from the set. Things headed away from the center can turn and move toward it. . . . The second type of change has to do with movement toward or away from the center. Distant members can move toward the center, and those near can slide back while still hearded toward it."

Hiebert goes on to demonstrate that Hebrew culture was structured as a centered set, based on relationships, especially in terms of a covenantal relationship of the People of Israel to the God of Abraham, Isaac, and Jacob.

Hiebert then asks, "What happens to our concept of Christian if we define it in centered-set terms? First, Christians would be defined as followers of the Jesus Christ of the Bible, as those who make him the center or Lord of their lives. . . . Second, there would be a clear separation between Christians and non-Christians, between those who are followers of Jesus and those who are not. The emphasis, however, would be on exhorting people to follow Christ, rather than on excluding others to preserve the purity of the set. . . . Third, there would be a recognition of variation among Christians. . . . Fourth, two important types of change would be recognized in centered-set thought. First, there is conversion, entering or leaving the set. . . . The second change is movement toward the center, or growth in a relationship. A Christian is not a finished product the moment he or she is converted. Conversion, therefore, is a definite event followed by an ongoing process. Sanctification is not a separate activity, but a process of justification continued throughout life."

Hiebert then proceeds to look at the Church as a centered set and missions as a centered set, following the four characteristics he mentioned earlier.

Paul Hiebert's idea of a "centered-set" theological methodology outlined above is an especially important guide in developing contextually appropriate mission theology. It provides a means by which we can be firmly and tightly anchored in truth in Jesus Christ, yet simultaneously open to differing worldviews, see through different cultural lenses as we read the Scriptures, and interact creatively with differing contexts—all within the same world Church comprised of the disciples of the one Center, Jesus Christ.

DIALOGICAL: RESHAPING OUR UNDERSTANDING OF THE GOSPEL: PRAXIS

In the fifth step of a search for a contextually appropriate mission theology, the mission theologian analyzes how the missional action of step four is brought to bear upon the four domains that were examined in the first step of this process.

For the past forty years, Latin Americans have been at the forefront of a particular method in contextual theology having to do with the "hermeneutical circle" as it was articulated and interpreted by people like Juan-Luis Segundo (1976), among others.[158] The hermeneutical circle of Latin American Liberation Theology spearheaded an intentional process whereby one's contextual hermeneutic moved toward a commitment to the preferential option for the poor, which in turn opened one's eyes to reread the meaning of Scripture for today's situation (a hermeneutics of significance). This provided new lenses through which one could reread the context of ministry.

Segundo began with the context of a people's reality and developed four decisive steps: (1) a people's plausibility structure (to use Peter Berger's term) leads to a particular agenda or question; (2) a people's agenda, question, or existential concern provides an approach to the biblical text; (3) understanding the text from the point of view of the people's agenda provides a particular application back to the context; and (4) that application leads to a new agenda or question that can be implemented in the context, which starts the cycle all over again. This process

---

158. See, for example, Clodovis Boff (1987, 63–66; 132–53); Leonardo Boff and Clodovis Boff (1987, 32–35); Guillermo Cook (1985, 104–126); Samuel Escobar (1987, 172–79); Dean Ferm (1986, 25–26); Gustavo Gutierrez (1988, 13); Roger Haight (1985, 46–59); Jose Miguez Bonino (1975, 90–104); C Rene Padilla (1985, 83–91); Robert Schreiter (1985, 75–94); Juan Luis Segundo (1976, 7–38); Gordon Spykman et al (1988, 228–30); Jon Sobrino (1984, 1–38); and Raul Vidales (1979, 48–51).

leads to a circular movement whereby the present context informs the meaning of the text and maintains the entire circular flow, hence the term "hermeneutical circle."

In Segundo's methodology, certain ideas (Segundo calls them "ideologies") emerge out of a particular context examined by an interpreter with eyes that involve a 'hermeneutics of suspicion."[159] These concepts are, then, a reflection of the mission theologian's perspective, a hermeneutic of that situation that forces questions about the perspectives of the people in those circumstances. Based on the new insights into the context gained in such a reexamination, the mission theologians should then reread the Scriptures. As the mission theologians reread the Scriptures, they see things they did not see before because they are asking new questions that reflect a new understanding derived from the new context. Drawing from the new insights the mission theologians have gained from Scripture, they encounter anew their context with new insight derived from their new reading of Scripture. Below is a diagram of this process.

---

159. In Segundo's thought there are four decisive moments or factors influencing the hermeneutical circle:

There is our way of experiencing reality that leads us to ideological suspicion. (Mannheim's three elements are involved in Segundo's understanding of this first stage: (a) a concrete evaluational experience of theology; (b) an act of the will on the part of the theologian with respect to his/her theology; (c) a direction in treating new problems that derives from this act of the will.

There is the application of our ideological suspicion to the whole ideological superstructure in general and to theology in particular.

There comes a new way of experiencing theological reality that leds us to exegetical suspicion, that is, the suspicion that the prevailing interpretation of the Bible has not taken important pieces of data into account.

We have our new hermeneutic, that is, our new way of interpreting the fountainhead of our faith (i.e., Scripture) with the new elements at our disposal (Segundo 1976, 7–38).

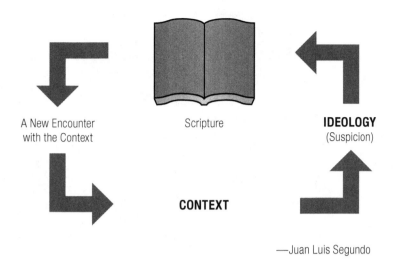

Read counterclockwise beginning with the "context"

FIGURE 6: Segundo's Hermeneutical Circle

Following this structure, some theologians have used the term "exegeting the context." to signify a particular perception of reality. This process is extremely important for the development of a contextually appropriate mission theology. The hermeneutical circle seeks to build a dynamic interactivity between the contemporary context and the missiological theory and perspectives of the mission theologian.[160] The hermeneutical circle provides a way to reflect on the missional action of step four.

Reflection, reexamination, rethinking, and reconceptualizing are needed. Reflection should take place addressing the consistency between the action taken and the initial conceptualization found in the integrating idea. Where there are anomalies, inconsistencies, and contradictions between the understanding of the integrating idea and the action taken, we must look more carefully. The place of the anomalies is the place where the reconceptualization begins all over again. This creates a process of action/reflection molded through time. Having taken the five steps, the process begins again.

---

160. This explanation of the hermeneutical circle as developed by Juan Luis Segundo is an adaptation of a similar section in chapter four of Dan Shaw and Charles Van Engen 2003.

This brings us back to an awareness of the spiraling process of deepening our knowledge of God and understanding of God's mission (see Figure 7). As was said at the beginning of this chapter, the process outlined here is not complete with only one cycle. This process needs to be repeated countless times over many years for the mission theologian to begin to grasp "how wide and long and high and deep is the love of Christ." (Eph 3:18)

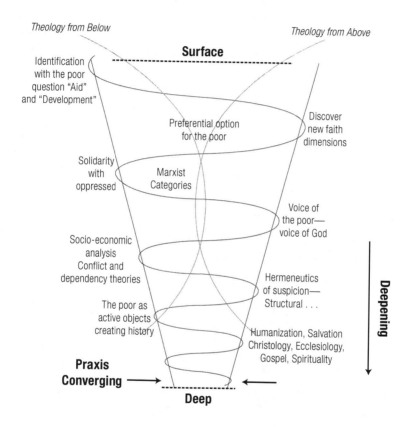

FIGURE 7: The Hermeneutical Spiral

Looking at the process in its entirety, the reader can visualize the integrating idea flowing through the steps outlined above that transform the integrating idea from theory into action. In this process, it is evaluated, examined, enhanced, energized, enacted, and finally reintegrated with the four original domains so that reconceptualization can take place leading toward a refinement of mission.

Over time, therefore, this becomes an iterative process that is constantly making adjustments in mission theory and practice.

CONCLUSION

In this chapter I have outlined a method whereby mission theologians might discover a contextually appropriate mission theology for their time and in their context. Our task is as simple as saying to our neighbor in word and deed: "Jesus loves you, this I know for the Bible tells me so." Yet God's mission is also an extremely complex endeavor filled with a host of issues which we have only begun to understand. We perceive "the depth of the riches of the wisdom and knowledge of God" (Rom 11:33) in merely fragmentary ways because we "see but a poor reflection, as in a mirror" (1 Cor 13: 12).

In doing mission theology we need to be aware that content and method are intimately intertwined. The content of our missional reflection influences (I would almost say, determines) the methodologies that we use to think about that content. And the methodologies we use in such reflection influence the way we understand, perceive, examine, and integrate the content of our mission theology. This means that mission theology is always transforming us, and our missiological reflection is always in the process of transforming our mission theology.

CHAPTER 9
SPECIALIZATION AND INTEGRATION IN MISSION THEOLOGY

This chapter was originally written as a reflection on missiological education as that was taking place in the School of World Mission/Institute of Church Growth of Fuller Theological Seminary and published as "Specialization/Integration in Mission Education" in Dudley Woodberry, Charles Van Engen and Edgar J. Elliston, eds., *Missiological Education for the 21st Century: the Book, the Circle and the Sandals*, Maryknoll: Orbis, 1996, 208–31. Used by permission. I have broadened the treatment here to deal more generally with the matter, since it impacts all of us everywhere in the world when we wrestle with the place and role of missiology (especially mission theology) in theological education.

THESIS

This chapter examines the role and place of missiological formation in theological education as a microcosm or case in point of mission theology and suggests the need for a delicate balance between specialization and integration in a four-arena approach to missiology.

INTRODUCTION

The purpose, shape, styles and delivery systems of missiological education cannot be determined in a vacuum. Rather, to be a faithful servant of the Church, missiological education for the twenty-first century must derive from the changing nature of mission itself. Our definition of mission then influences our perspectives of the nature and purpose of missiology, which in turn shapes missiological education. And, due to the multidisciplinary nature of missiology, the heart of the discussion is found in the tension between specialization for a task and integration for understanding.

This means a difficult search for a balance between specialization and integration, between having institutes or training programs that foster the growth of churches, and having schools that develop new missiological theory and encourage new insight concerning the world mission of the churches. In what follows I will discuss the tension between specialization and integration in missiological education from five perspectives: (a) the location of missiology in theology education, (b) the definition of missiology, (c) the ICG/SWM as a case in point, (d) a four-arena approach to missiology, and (e) a pyramidal model for finding a dialectical synthesis between specialization and integration in our understanding of mission theology and missiology. Finally, I will list what appear to be the minimal components of a missiological education that bridges the specialization/integration dialectic.

SPECIALIZATION/INTEGRATION AND THE LOCATION OF MISSION EDUCATION

The shape of missiological education depends on the place it is given in the larger curriculum of formation for ministry and mission in church and world. The place of missiology (and thus missiological education) in the larger theological curriculum has been a subject of much discussion for the past hundred years and is an issue not yet resolved, as Johannes Verkuyl pointed out. Verkuyl offered an excellent overview of this, mentioning Friedrich Schleiermacher, Abraham Kuyper, J. H. Bavinck, Karl Graul, Gustav Warneck, Walter Freytag, J. C. Hoekendijk, Charles Forman, Creighton Lacy, and William Richey Hogg.[161]

Olav G. Myklebust and James Scherer, among others, concentrated on the question of the relation of missiology as a discipline to the rest of traditional theological education, asking whether missiology should remain independent from theological education, or should somehow be incorporated as part of it.[162] James Scherer summarized this issue in 1987.

---

161. J. Verkuyl 1978, 6ff. The background perspectives for the discussion in this chapter is drawn from what I learned from Johannes Verkuyl's thought concerning the place and role of missiology in theological education. Although dated, this portion of Verkuyl's *magnum opus* is an unequaled treasure-trove of information about the discipline of missiology. Though we do not have room to deal with it in this chapter, another way of looking at the specialization/ integration issue is to examine the people who have been involved in doing missiological teaching, reflection, adminsitration, and praxis. Verkuyl's chapter on "The History of Missiology during the Nineteenth and Twentieth Centuries" is an excellent survey in this regard, unparalleled in the field. See *Contemporary Missiology* 1978, 26–88.

162. Notice that the matter of independence of missiological education versus incorporation into the regular theological curriculum is a disciplinary variation of the specialization (thus independence) over against integration (thus incorporation) question.

As Myklebust's studies have shown, early continental missiology was set up largely on the "independent model," designed to give status and recognition to the autonomy and worth of the then unproved discipline alongside the more venerable and recognized fields of theological instruction (Myklebust 1955).[163] Recent continental missiology, by contrast, has taken a decidedly more integrative and interdisciplinary approach. Missiology in the United Kingdom, to the extent that it was done, showed a preference for complete integration into the field of church historical studies (Myklebust 1959), the assumption being that ecclesiology properly understood would generate missiological reflection. Here the discipline was never really established at the university level, and only in training colleges such as those at Selly Oak is missiology taken seriously. Missiological reflection in the U.K. was mainly done in mission executive offices by able administrators such as Max Warren and John V. Taylor . . . In our view, missiology needs freedom from a too tight embrace by ecclesiastical structures so as to be unimpeded in fulfilling its primary task of permeating the entire world with the knowledge of God's saving acts. (J. Scherer 1987a, 520)

A. Universities

The upshot of this was that during the last several decades, missiological education followed four general models in its struggle to find a place in the sun. In the first place, much missiological education became resident in university faculties (the Netherlands, Germany, and Scandinavia), as a "science of missions" or as "mission studies." Whatever it may be called, in the university setting missiological education emphasized the integrational perspective, rather than task-oriented specialization for mission action. Specialization happened only as a secondary matter, primarily through the particular directions that individuals chose for their

---

163. One must remember that the predominant model of doing mission in Western Europe and (to a slightly lesser degree) in North America at the turn of the century was through mission agencies loosely associated with the churches, not through ecclesiastical structures as such. It would be natural, then, to assume that mission studies would also be carried out apart from the regular traditional track of theological education.

doctoral studies. These, however, were located more generally in an integrational perspective of missiological reflection.

B. Seminaries

A second model placed missiology within theological seminaries that trained professional clergy for church ministries in the United States and Canada. This pattern is being followed in many places in Africa, Asia, and Latin America, as well. But here, too, missiology struggles to know in which department or division it belongs, and how it may fit within the larger curriculum of standard theological education.[164]

Twenty years ago, in North America a new type of relation of missiology with traditional theological education developed around the interest in "globalization," sparked by the Association of Theological Schools (ATS).[165] (See, e.g., Norman Thomas 1989, 103–7.)[166] Even so, missiological education remained subsumed under the larger agendas of general theological education. And although many

---

164. See, e.g. O. G. Myklebust 1959; Josef Glazik 1968; Ralph Winter 1969, 1979; Charles Forman 1974; R. Pierce Beaver 1976; David Hesselgrave, ed., 1978, 1979; Ross Kinsler 1983, 1985; William Richey Hogg 1987; Addison Soltau 1988; Harvie Conn 1983; David Bosch 1982. One of the most helpful collections of essays along this line was the product of a miniconsultation on "Missions in Theological Education," sponsored by the World Evangelical Fellowship, March 17–20, 1980 at High Leigh Conference Centre. Gathered from a number of journals, the essays appeared together in Harvie Conn and Samuel Rowen, eds., 1984.

In 1987 James Scherer gave an excellent overview of "Missiology as a Discipline and What it Includes" at the Annual Meeting of the Association of Professors of Mission, subsequently published in *Missiology* XIII:4 (Oct, 1987) 445–60. In that presentation he reminded folks about previous efforts to define the nature and scope of missiology. These include Myklebust (1955, 1957, 1961), Wilbert Shenk (1987) Alan R. Tippett (1973, 1974), along with Scherer's own earlier presentations on the subject (1971, 1985). One of the most recent discussions of this can be found in David Bosch: 1991, 489–498. See also "Inleiding: Wat Verstaan Wij Onder Missiologie" in: F. J. Verstraelen 1988, 17–23.

165. Norman Thomas offered an excellent presentation on this issue to the Association of Professors of Mission (APM) in Chicago, June, 1989, on "Globalization and the Teaching of Mission," subsequently published in *Missiology* XVIII:1 (Jan, 1990) 13–23. See also Alan Neely 1993.

166. Please note in what follows that some missiologists work on defining "mission," and then derive what they mean by the discipline of missiology, while others define "missiology" and then derive what they mean by "mission." I do not have space here to evaluate the implications of either choice. Rather, I will assume that the missiologists in question are wanting to be

persons who graduated from these programs went into full-time cross-cultural ministries, their preparation was by and large oriented to the agendas and forms of traditional theological education, not toward specialization for cross-cultural mission action. Thus these programs usually provided a minimum of familiarity with missiology from an integrational point of view, with little formation for mission in terms of specific task-oriented specialization.

C. Bible schools

A third model found in Europe and North America involved the Bible school movement that offered grassroots, practical biblical training for Christian ministry and mission. During the last hundred years, Bible colleges, Bible institutes and Bible schools arose all over the world, specifically oriented toward equipping people for the tasks of ministry and mission. Ken Mulholland spoke about this phenomenon—a development that radically changed the face of ministry formation, of mission education, and of mission praxis.[167]

The Bible school movement was strongly oriented to the practice of ministry and mission. So it is no surprise to find that in the movement's approach to missiological education there arose a host of specializations in mission, for the varying tasks of missions. Although biblical studies were considered foundational, and these provided a degree of integration in mission education—yet the final purpose was praxeological and activist. Reflection was considered important, yet right action was essential.

All three of these models can be found today in Africa, Asia, Latin America, and elsewhere. And all three models were represented by speakers at the conference in 1995 which became Woodberry's book. It is beyond my scope here to delineate the resulting differences they represent in terms of their understanding of mission, their perspective of missiology, and the pros and cons of their respective modes of missiological education.

D. Schools of world mission

Of more recent vintage, a fourth model has arisen. During the last half-century or so we have seen the birth of schools of world mission or centers for mission studies. Although these have depended on, and interacted with the three models we saw

---

consistent, and that, in the final analysis, the two issues are too closely connected to make a difference in terms of our purpose here.

167. Woodberry 1996, 43–56.

above, they created something new that differed from all of them. Rather than opting for either specialization or integration, this fourth model is a dialectical one that is oriented in both directions. Structurally semi-independent from the regular channels of theological education, these schools of mission pursue research, reflection, historical recording, or data-gathering mission and, simultaneously, they seek to advance the training of professional missionaries for doing mission more effectively. These schools of world mission have tended to gather a group of highly specialized scholars who contribute their individual expertise both to further the missiological insights of their students and to train those who practice mission.

But the school of mission paradigm contains a built-in dialectical tension between specialization and integration—a tension that has gone mostly unexamined and unresolved. As an activist school with specific agendas, Fuller's ICG/SWM where I taught for twenty-seven years belongs to this fourth type. This has to do with the relationship of specialization to integration in missiology.

Before we go on to examine the ICG/SWM, however, we need to examine the way we define mission and missiology. Because the way one defines mission (and thus missiology) influences the emphasis one adopts in terms of the specialization/integration continuum, which in turn affects the way one carries out missiological education. This continuum can be appreciated better by examining three sample definitions of mission and/or missiology.

SPECIALIZATION/INTEGRATION AND THE DEFINITION OF MISSION OR MISSIOLOGY

There is an intimate relationship between the issue of specialization versus integration, and the way mission is defined. In this section I will first explain how I see the continuum between specialization and integration as this influences missiology. Then I will give three examples of definitions of mission (or missiology) that differ markedly in their relation to the continuum. That will prepare us for the next section, where we will examine how the inherent tensions in the continuum affect mission education and, by extension, mission theology.

As I see it, missiology struggles to live between two radically different ends of a continuum that looks like the following:

← SPECIALIZATION	INTEGRATION →
Action	Reflection
Mission defined by action/goals	Mission defined by concepts
Results	New insights
Task-oriented	Understanding-oriented
Present/Future-oriented	Past/Present-oriented
"Strategies/Methods"	"Mission studies"
"Institute of . . ."	"School of . . ."

At one end are those missiologists who are interested in asking about the assumptions behind concepts of mission. They are committed to discovering new insights about mission and missiology. They are dedicated to profound reflection about mission and to listening to those who have been involved in, and reflected upon, the mission enterprise. Research at this end of the continuum involves predominantly the recent or distant past: who did what, what they did, why they did it, and how they articulated the vision that shaped their mission. The search at this end is for understanding and deeper wisdom. Mission is defined in terms of a consistent, coherent, appropriate and clear relation to various concepts, perspectives and assumptions as to what mission ought to be.

At the other end of the continuum one finds the activist missiologists. For the sake of clarity, I will describe them over against the other end of the continuum. Viewed thus, the activists appear concerned about the doing of mission. They are committed to discovering new methods and strategies for mission and missiology. They are dedicated to more effective evangelization, and want to mobilize the churches for mission. Research at this end of the continuum involves predominantly an examination of the results of mission action: did the methods bring about the desired missional goals. This missiology is predominantly future-oriented, interested in past and present primarily as it points to new, more effective action. The search at this end is for increased transformation, brought about by effective missional action. How one defines mission is of concern not so much in terms of the idea of mission but in relation to the actions and resulting effects of mission.

Now, of course, this is a continuum. Missiologists at the "integration-reflection" end would want me to clarify that they are interested in action; and those at the "specialization for action" end would want me to state that they are interested in right action that is based on appropriate reflection. And yet, the approach to mission and missiology differs markedly in terms of the two extremes of the continuum.

The tension between integration and specialization in missiology is closely related to the way one defines mission or missiology. David Bosch and James Scherer have written about the difficulty of such definition. In 1987, James Scherer stated that,

> The quest for an agreed definition of *missiology* remains elusive, and neither the ASM (American Society of Missiology), nor the teaching fraternity represented by the APM, has been able to come up with one. The reasons, I would suggest, are partly attributable to *internal* differences in aims and viewpoints between those who teach the discipline, and partly to *external* factors such as unresolved relationships between missiology and the goals of theological education in general, as well as profound changes in theological trends and attitudes in the past 25 years which have had their impact on thinking about both mission and missiology. Indeed, the most serious for missiology. . , is current indecision, or at least divergence of opinion, about what mission fundamentally is.[168]

Earlier, David Bosch sounded a similar note when he wrote, " In many circles, there is a great deal of uncertainty about what mission really is . . . The picture is one of change and complexity, tension and urgency, and no small measure of the confusion exists over the very nature of mission itself. Our task is to enter the contemporary debate and seek answers that are consonant with the will of God and relevant to the situation in which we find ourselves" (1980, 8–9).[169]

Here let me highlight three definitions that, although they do not contradict each other, differ markedly in their perspectives. I have chosen these three because, in spite of their differences, all three definitions have impacted, and will continue

---

168. In this same article, Scherer quotes O. G. Myklebust as saying, "As I see it, the question, primarily and fundamentally, is not 'what missiology is,' but 'what mission is.' The present uncertainty is in no small degree accounted for by the failure of many missiologists to make the TEXT rather than the CONTEXT the point of orientation. Far too much attention, to mention just one example, is paid to religious pluralism and far too little to God's revelation and saving acts in Jesus as recorded in Holy Scripture" (Myklebust 1987).

169. Also quoted in Scherer 1987, 519.

to influence, the nature of missiological education. The samples I have chosen are not extreme. It would be inaccurate to place any one of these definitions at one extreme or the other of the continuum. However, by laying them side by side, we may gain a clearer sense as to how they tend to emphasize one end or the other.

SPECIALIZATION   INTEGRATION

(Mission action)   (Mission studies)
McGavran   Tippett   Verkuyl[170]

A. Johannes Verkuyl

Standing on the "mission studies" end of the continuum, Johannes Verkuyl's definition demonstrates a "from above" perspective that tends to be more reflective, although it is still oriented toward missional participation.[171]

> Missiology is the study of the salvation activities of the Father, Son, and Holy Spirit throughout the world geared toward bringing the Kingdom of God into existence. Missiology's task in every age is to investigate scientifically and critically the presuppositions made of structures, methods, patterns of cooperation, and leadership which the churches bring to their mandate. In addition, missiology must examine every other type of human activity which combats the various evils to see if it fits the criteria and goals of God's kingdom which has both already come and is yet coming . . . Missiology may never become a substitute for action and participation . . . If study does not lead

---

170. It is important to note the difference between these three in terms of the titles of their major works. Johannes Verkuyl's work is entitled *Contemporary Missiology: An Introduction*; Alan Tippett's is called, *Introduction to Missiology*; but Donald McGavran's is *Understanding Church Growth*. A comparison of the three will show that they differ markedly in their approaches—primarily in relation to the specialization/integration dynamic. Interestingly, David Bosch's work is entitled, *Transforming Mission*—and one is hard pressed to find a concise definition of either mission or missiology in its 534 pages.

171. Notice that I have not included in this discussion other definitions offered in the field that reduce missiology to purely descriptive research, data gathering, limited history writing, and theoretical reflection. Although these ways of defining missiology are clearly valid, they are beyond the scope of the discussion in this chapter.

to participation, whether at home or abroad, missiology has lost her humble calling (Verkuyl 1978, 5–6).

B. Alan Tippett

Verkuyl's approach to missiology and mission might be characterized as reflection that leads to action. In contrast, Alan Tippett's definition has the marks of a researcher who is interested in researching and reflectively analyzing the actions and events of missionary practice, especially as they are impacted by (and impact) the cultures in which they occur. So Tippet says,

> Missiology is defined as the academic discipline or science which researches, records and applies data relating to the biblical origin, the history (including the use of documentary materials), the anthropological principles and techniques and the theological base of the Christian mission. The theory, methodology and data bank are particularly directed towards:
> 1. the processes by which the Christian message is communicated;
> 2. the encounters brought about by its proclamation to non-Christians;
> 3. the planting of the Church and organization of congregations, the incorporation of converts into those congregations, and the growth and relevance of their structures and fellowship, internally to maturity, externally in outreach as the Body of Christ in local situations and beyond, in a variety of culture patterns (Tippett 1987, XIII).

Tippett's definition lies slightly further toward the activist end of the continuum than Verkuyl's. But Tippett does not go as far in the activist direction as Donald McGavran. Notice in the following that, although Verkuyl and Tippett offered definitions of "missiology," Donald McGavran's is a definition of "mission."[172] Nowhere have I been able to find Donald McGavran defining "missiology" as such.

---

172. It is interesting to note here that a book published in Spanish that is essentially a development of Donald McGavran's and Peter Wagner's church growth theory was given

C. Donald McGavran

Donald McGavran's definition of mission (the basis for what we could assume to be his view of missiology) is similar to, but differs in important ways from, both of the above. Although McGavran begins his thinking "from above," with regard to God's desires and plans, the heart of his perspective is "from below" in the sense of being most thoroughly concerned with the results of the action of the missiology in question.

> To many, mission is widely defined as, "God's total program for humans," and we have considered the alternatives arising from that definition. Mission may now be defined much more narrowly. Since God as revealed in the Bible has assigned the highest priority to bringing men and women into living rela-tionshipo to Jesus Christ, we may define mission narrowly as *an enterprise devoted to proclaiming the good news of Jesus Christ, and to per-suading men and women to become his disciples and responsible members of his church.* (McGavran 1990, 23–24)

Donald McGavran's definition of mission is thoroughly activist. His concern is with effective missional strategy and action that yields specific results. The reason to research and reflect is for the sake of mobilization and action.

The interplay of the three definitions offered above provides a good spring-board for considering the dialectical tension between specialization and integration that impacts the missiology of Fuller's ICG/SWM, as a case in point of the issue I am focusing on in this chapter.

SPECIALIZATION/INTEGRATION IN DYNAMIC TENSION IN THE ICG/SWM

When Donald McGavran moved from Eugene, Oregon, to Pasadena, Califor-nia, he founded an institute devoted to fostering the growth of churches. In a soul-searching article about "Church Growth at Fuller,"[173] Arthur Glasser reminds his hearers that McGavran's book *The Bridges of God* was published in 1955, and

---

the title, Misionología (missiology), a matter that presented no apparent objection from either McGavran or Wagner. Cf. Larry Pate 1987.

173. This article was first presented verbally by Arthur Glasser to the American Society of Missiology in Chicago, June, 1986.

was said by some to be "the most read missionary book in 1956." Still, Glasser says, "In my judgment the church growth movement actually began in January, 1961, when McGavran founded what he called the *Institute of Church Growth* (ICG) in an unused corner of the library of a small Christian college in remote Eugene, Oregon." (Glasser 1987, 403)[174]

A. Specialization

McGavran's founding of a specialized Institute of Church Growth placed him at the "specialization-activist" end of our continuum. It was quite clear in those early years that research, writing, speaking and thinking were to be devoted to mobilizing people for church growth.[175] Church growth defined the integrating center and determined the outer limits of the Institute's missiology. Those who cared about the same missional activity could come and join McGavran in researching church growth. Mission, mission education and missiology were all seen through the lens of church growth principles that were to foster the numerically verifiable growth of churches. McGavran's publication from the mid-1960s to the early 1970s were clear, focused, and insistent on this point. Here there was no tension, no dialectic. Integration was only relevant as it incorporates various cognate disciplines that fostered the main agenda: church growth. Such a specific focus was necessary, if one was to gain a hearing by the larger mission community, not be ignored, and start a movement. And McGavran had all the right stuff to do just that.

Yet this was not the whole picture. To see McGavran and his associates in the ICG exclusively as church growth enthusiasts is an inaccurate caricature. McGavran's founding of a specialized institute of church growth did not thereby exempt him from the integrative nature of missiology.[176]

---

174. For a history of the church growth movement, see, e.g., Charles Van Engen 1981, 325–34; Thom S. Rainer 1993, 19–72; Gary McIntosh 2015; Gary McIntosh 2016, 19–27; among others.

175. See my *The Growth of the True Church* (1981), chapter six for an overview of this. During the late 1960s and 1970s, McGavran debated not only with the folks at the World Council of Churches, but also with the evangelicals in North America, as well as with mission administrators and practitioners worldwide. In terms of church growth, he had a profound influence on the Southern Baptists and the Pentecostals, among others.

176. One thing that comes clear in Middleton's definitive biography of McGavran is this larger picture of McGavran as a missiologist of breadth, depth, insight and integrational instincts. See Vernon J. Middleton. *The Development of a Missiologist: The Life and Thought of*

B. Integration

To see McGavran as an integrational missiologist, we must look to the antecedents from which he drew his missiology. We have space here for only a few related examples. We could go all the way back to Gisbertus Voetius, the Dutch missiologist. Voetius (1589–1676) spoke of the threefold goal of mission as being the conversion of the "heathen," the planting of the church, and the glorification and manifestation of divine grace.[177] I believe that Donald McGavran was aware of Voetius, though nowhere can I find McGavran quoting Voetius. But in a real sense McGavran's missiology was a restatement of Voetius, 375 years later, in a way that represented the best of a historic and biblical understanding of mission. Yet even Voetius, in the combination of those three goals, was involved in a tension between specialization of means and integration of goals.

Donald McGavran's well-known dependence on the Great Commission of Matthew 28 placed him as an heir of William Carey.[178] Even though Carey went to India to work toward the conversion of those who did not know Jesus Christ, in fact Carey became more of an integrative missiologist than a specialist: a farmer, a merchant, a linguist and translator, a trainer of leaders, and so forth.

The German missiologist, Gustav Warneck (1834–1919), considered by many to be the father of missiology, was very influential in the European scene. Although he may have exerted little direct influence on Donald McGavran, echoes of Warneck's concern for the integration of missiology can be seen in McGavran's writings. This is especially so as these are then mediated through the administrative missiology of Henry Venn and Rufus Anderson. Their strong emphasis on what later would be known as the "indigenous churches"[179] shows the influence on McGavran of Venn and Anderson's "three-self" concept, strengthening the ecclesial emphases of McGavran's approach. But this too involved McGavran and his friends in a tension between the integration of all that it meant for their

---

Donald Anderson McGavran, 1897–1965. Pasadena, School of World Mission PhD Dissertation, 1990. See also Gary McIntosh 2015.

177. See J. H. Bavinck 1977, 155.

178. McGavran's missionary career in India, along with the impact of the Indian context on his missiology, also links him closely with Carey.

179. One of McGavran's early symposium volumes (1965) with contributions from his many friends contains a chapter written by Melvin Hodges on "Developing Basic Units of Indigenous Churches."

churches to be "indigenous," and specialization of methodologies to produce the desired results.

Then came the Student Volunteer Movement and John R. Mott, along with Roland Allen, both of whom deeply influenced McGavran.[180] We could go on to mention Hendrick Kraemer and John Mackay, along with J. H. Bavinck, Arthur Brown, and many others whose influence on McGavran can be traced in his writings. In each case, McGavran the integrative missiologist stands in tension with McGavran the "Father of Church Growth."[181]

When McGavran started the Institute of Church Growth, he immediately brought in Alan Tippett, an anthropologist by trade—but also a reflective missiologist, as we saw earlier in his definition of missiology. Then the school began to add faculty: Peter Wagner, Ralph Winter, Charles Kraft, Arthur Glasser, J. Edwin Orr, and so forth. The "School of World Mission" side, multidisciplinary, more reflective, and more integrational, was developing. It appears that McGavran was able to keep the two sides (action/specialist and reflection/integrationist) functioning in a mutually supportive manner. Even so, McGavran's dominance in the ICG/SWM meant that the bottom-line was that mission was to foster the numerical growth of churches. In the final analysis, McGavran was an activist.

By 1973, the two sides of the school could be seen delicately balanced in the volume that Alan Tippett edited in honor of Donald McGavran, *God, Man and Church Growth* (Tippett 1973). This volume, with all the ICG/SWM faculty contributing, was an interesting representation of the two sides of the continuum, showing how carefully folks struggled to preserve a dynamic tension between the two perspectives of missiology. Yet, clearly, church growth activism was central.

Another example of this tension was the Lausanne Covenant. The strong influence of the ICG/SWM on the Congress on Evangelism in Lausanne, 1974, is well known, and the activist, results-oriented emphasis on church growth is clearly at the center of the Covenant. What some may miss, however, is the tension evident in the documents of the conference between specialization for a task and integration for understanding. I believe this tension is a direct result of the impact that the faculty of the ICG/SWM had on Lausanne and the subsequent movement.

---

180. William Burkhalter wrote a doctoral dissertation ably demonstrating the close affinity of McGavran's missiology with that of Roland Allen. See Burkhalter 1984.

181. Cf. Tim Stafford, "The Father of Church Growth," *Christianity Today* (Feb 21, 1986) 19–23; reprinted in *Mission Frontiers* (VIII:1, Jan. 1986), 5–13.

When Arthur Glasser read a paper on "Church Growth at Fuller" at the 1986 meeting of the American Society of Missiology, he spoke of the relationship of the Institute of Church Growth to the School of World Mission. It was only a couple of years later that David Bosch was invited to make an oral presentation to the ICG/SWM faculty and highlighted similar issues.[182] In both cases, the foundational issue had to do with the balance of the ICG church growth activist side and the SWM integrational side of the school's missiology. A comparison of these two papers is very interesting. Art Glasser was concerned that the church growth focus not get lost, a concern I shared at the time. David Bosch's concern was that church growth activism (which he supported) not skew the perceptions and valuations by which the school's missiology was being integrated.

C. Creative tension

Clearly this is an important continuum, and mission theology must hold together both ends. So the matter of balance is crucial. During the late 1970s and 1980's, as other faculty and programs were added, Fuller's ICG/SWM continued to multiply its arenas of investigation and specialization. Eventually, "church growth" as a subject of inquiry began to appear as one part of a larger missiological whole. By 1993, the ICG/SWM counted at least eighteen different specializations, known as "concentrations," structured in a number of masters' and doctoral programs. [183] This might be seen as bringing about a reduction in the activist church growth side of the continuum, resulting in a lowering of the creative and dynamic tension between the two sides of the continuum.

The creative tension between "institute of" and "school of world mission" may be one of the most powerful forces that propels missiology. The tension itself may give rise to the creativity. If missiology were to lose the tension, if it went in either direction, it might lose its creative, innovative edge. Curricular considerations, the mode of integration, and the deepest values do in fact differ between the two perspectives. The "institute of" has as its most basic issue the doing of

---

182. Cf. D. Bosch 1988.

183. By 1996, the ICG/SWM was offering the following concentrations, listed in alphabetical order: Anthropology, Chinese Studies, Church Growth, Communications, Contextualization, Family in Mission, General Missiology, International Development, Islamic Studies, Jewish Studies, Korean Studies, Leadership, Research in Missiology, Spirituality and Power Ministry, Theology of Mission, Translation, Urban Mission. After 2000, a number of other concentrations were added.

mission and measures its success in terms of tangible results. The "school of world mission" perspective, on the other hand, has as its bottom line the doing of appropriate mission, and measures its success by its insight, understanding, and biblical/theological fidelity.

Is there a way to affirm the whole of the continuum? Is there a way whereby mission theology, specifically, can serve mission agencies who want professional training for their personnel within their own individual agendas and missional tasks, and at the same time serve the world church that needs teachers of reflective missiological integration, related to the larger missiological academy, and participating in global missiological theorizing?

SPECIALIZATION/INTEGRATION IN A FOUR ARENA APPROACH TO MISSION EDUCATION

One way to begin to address the inherent tensions between specialization and integration is to look at the four arenas of missiological investigation (word, world, church, and personal pilgrimage) that we examined in earlier chapters of this book and consider what they include and how they interface with each other. In so doing, we can affirm all three definitions of missiology given above, without losing their individual emphases. Together, the four-arena integration can show us how both the specialist-activist and the reflective-integrationist viewpoints of missiology may come together in a creative synthesis.

A full-fledged missiology needs to eventually emanate in biblically informed and contextually appropriate missional action. If it does not emanate in informed action, we are merely a "resounding gong or clanging cymbal" (1 Cor 13:1). The intimate connection of reflection with action is absolutely essential for missiology and, specifically, for mission theology. At the same time, if our missiological action does not itself transform our reflection, we have held great ideas—but they may be irrelevant or useless, sometimes destructive or counterproductive—and even our commitments to "acts of faithfulness" may come to naught because they derive from uninformed reflection.[184]

The foregoing discussion led us at the ICG/SWM at Fuller Theological Seminary in the late 1990's to experiment with taking the four-arena perspective one

---

184. This concept was at the center of the missiology of the 1989 meeting of the Commission on World Mission and Evangelism (CWME) at San Antonio, Texas. See, e.g., World Council of Churches 1989; Wilson 1990; David Bosch 1992.

step further to perceive a unified whole that is at once integrational and activist. We have found that a pyramid seems to represent most clearly the way we can bring together the four arenas of missiology, tie them to specific specializations, and integrate it all within our overall purpose in mission.

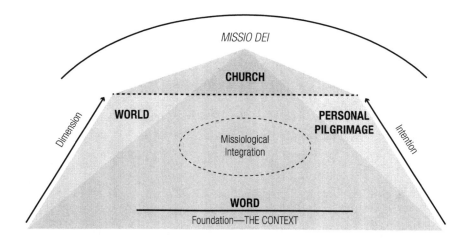

**School of World Mission Model of
Missiological Integration—original 1998**

FIGURE 8: Seeing Missiology as a Pyramid

In Figure 8 above, the pyramid has four faces and a base in a three-dimensional relationship that draws three things together: the four faces of an integrational Missiology, the particular specialization of the mission practitioner, and the foundation placed in the context. In this way, specializations in mission are grounded on a broader base of integrational missiology, directed toward specific goals of mission, and affirmed in their specific tasks in mission. By the same token, the four-arena structure of mission needs to be expressed in concrete action (usually through specifically specialized tasks), for the sake of mission. The integrating idea of a mission practitioner's central mission purpose becomes the central core that integrates the entire pyramid, draws the edges together toward the center, and offers the bottom-line motivations and goals of the practitioner's particular missiology. The dynamic interrelation of these various aspects can be more clearly understood if we look at the pyramid as being at once praxis, integration and paradigm formation.

A. Praxeological

First, as reflected in the above pyramid, missiology is *praxeological*. One of the most helpful ways to interface reflection and action is by way of the process known as "praxis." Although there have been a number of different meanings described to this idea, [185] I believe that Orlando Costas' formulation is one of the most constructive.

"Missiology," Costas says,

> is fundamentally a praxeological phenomenon. It is a critical reflection that takes place in the praxis of mission . . . [It occurs] in the concrete missionary situation, as part of the church's missionary obedience to and participation in God's mission, and is itself actualized in that situation . . . Its object is always the world, . . . men and women in their multiple life situations . . . In reference to this witnessing action saturated and led by the sovereign, redemptive action of the Holy Spirit, . . . the concept of missionary praxis is used. Missiology arises as part of a witnessing engagement to the gospel in the multiple situations of life. (Costas 1976, 8)

The concept of "praxis" helps us understand that not only the reflection, but profoundly the action as well are part a "Missiology on the way" that seeks to discover how the church may participate in God's mission in God's world. Just as in Scripture word and deed are coupled together in the narrative of God's revelation to humans, so missional action is seen as itself being theological, and serves to inform the reflection, which in turn interprets, evaluates, critiques, and projects new understanding in transformed action. Thus the interweaving of reflection and action in a constantly spiraling pilgrimage offer a transformation of all aspects

185. See, e.g. Robert McAfee Brown 1978, 50–51; Raul Vidales 1975, 34–57; Spykman et al 1988, xiv, 226–231; Robert Schreiter 1985, 17, 91–93; Orlando Costas 1976, 8–9; Leonardo and Clodovis Boff 1987, 8–9; Waldron Scott 1980: xv; Leonardo Boff 1979: 3; Deane Ferm 1986, 15; René Padilla 1985, 83; Rebecca Chop 1986, 36–37, 115–117, 120–121; Gustavo Gutierrez 1984a, 19–32; Clodovis Boff 1987, xxi–xxx; and Gustavo Gutierrez 1984b, vii–viii, 50–60.

of our missiological engagement with our various contexts. I described this in a previous chapter.

B. Integrative

Secondly, missiology is *integrative*. What is increasingly forcing itself on our attention is the way in which the several faces of the pyramid *in their difference* must be brought together *in their integration*, for transformational missiology to work. Bible, Church, and World (or text, community and context) cannot be affirmed integratively and simultaneously unless we become very clear about how we define the integrating theme that holds the whole together. The various corners of the pyramid are drawn together by means of an integrating theme.[186] Because of the complexity of the inter- and multidisciplinary task of missiology, missiologists have found it helpful to focus on a specific integrating idea that would serve as the hub around which one may approach a rereading of Scripture. This integrating theme is selected on the basis of being contextually appropriate and significant, biblically relevant and fruitful, and missionally active and transformational. As I discussed in an earlier chapter in this book, a host of different integrative themes are possible, yet all must be held together in terms of their proximity to Jesus Christ, the Head of the Body, the Church.

Clearly we are trying to avoid bringing our own agendas to the Scriptures and superimposing them on Scripture. This was the mistake made by liberation theologians, from which they did not recover. Rather, what is being sought is a way to bring a new set of questions to the text, questions that might help us see in the Scriptures what we had missed before. This new approach to Scripture is what David Bosch called, "critical hermeneutics."[187]

As we reread Scripture, we are faced with new insights, new values, and new priorities that call us to reexamine the motivations, means, agents, and goals of our missiology. This, in turn will call for rethinking each one of the traditional theological loci. Thus we will find ourselves involved in a contextual rereading of Scripture to discover anew what it means to know God in context. Robert McAfee Brown called this type of reflection, "Theology in a New Key" (1978) and "Unexpected News" (1984).

---

186. Cf. Van Engen 1987 and 1991, 59–71; H. Berkhof 1979, 14–15, 409; and Van Engen 1981, 237–39.

187. See David Bosch 1991, 20–24.

In Latin America, for example, this missiological and praxeological process has especially focused on issues of Christology and ecclesiology.[188] In today's missiological enterprise, it appears that we need to allow our rereading to offer us new insights into the scope and content of our missiology, derived from a profound rethinking of all the traditional theological loci.[189]

In 1987, the Association of Professors of Mission discussed at length what missiology is, and how it does its reflection.[190] In the subsection dealing with theology of mission, it was said that,

> The mission theologian does biblical and systematic theology differently from the biblical scholar or dogmatician in that the mission theologian is in search of the "habitus," the way of perceiving, the intellectual understanding coupled with spiritual insight and wisdom, which leads to seeing the signs of the presence and movement of God in history, and through his church in such a way as to be affected spiritually and motivationally and thus be committed to personal participation in that movement . . .
>
> Such a search for the "why" of mission forces the mission theologian to seek to articulate the vital integrative center of mission today . . . Each formulation of the "center" has radical implications for each of the cognate disciplines of the social sciences, the study of religions, and church history in the way they are corrected and shaped theologically. Each formulation supports or calls into question different aspects of all the other disciplines . . . The center, therefore, serves as both theological content and theological process as a disciplined reflection on God's mission in human contexts. The role of the theologian of mission is therefore to articulate and "guard" the center, while at the same time to spell out integratively the implications of the

---

188. Harvie Conn has given us a summary form of just this sort of thing in 1993a, 102–3.

189. Orlando Costas was one of the most creative, integrative, and biblically focused praxeological missiologists in this regard. His concept of "integral church growth" has yet to permeate missiological and theological education as deeply as it needs to. See Costas 1974, 90–91; 1975, 68–70; 1979, 37–60; and 1992, 116–122.

190. Cf. Van Engen 1987, 523–25.

center for all the other cognate disciplines. (Van Engen 1987, 524–52)

When we look at the central core of the pyramid, we see the "integrating idea" or "habitus," of missiology as an interdisciplinary discipline. David Bosch used the term, "elements" in a similar vein, to describe (in *Transforming Mission*) the component parts of an "emerging ecumenical missionary paradigm." [191] I believe one way to view thirteen different "elements" is to see them as thirteen interrelated but differing "integrating ideas," each seeking in its own unique way to apply the three general arenas to a particular context in time and space. We could, then, see each one of them as if they were differing elliptical orbits, tracing each in their own way a unique path around the Center, Jesus Christ. But all of them are also in some way related to each other.[192]

As Bosch said it,

> The elements discussed below should by no means be seen as so many distinct and isolated components of a new model; they are all intimately interrelated. This means that in discussing a specific element each other element is always somewhere in the background. The emphasis throughout should therefore be on the wholeness and indivisibility of the paradigm, rather than on its separate ingredients. As we focus our torchlight on one element at a time, all the other elements will also be present and visible just outside the center of the beam of light. (1991, 369)

Might this not offer a way whereby missiology with its many specializations could be held together, integrated, as each specific agenda of missional action draws its own elliptical orbit around the pyramid of Word, World and Church, and Personal Pilgrimages?

Possibly one of the sources of our confusion in defining missiology, and thus missiological education—and a reason why such definition is so elusive—is that missiologists have too easily spoken past each other, against each other, and opposite each other in terms of the "integrating ideas" that hold their particular

---

191. Bosch 1991, 368ff.

192. What Karl Barth asked about the church must also be asked about our missiology. "How far does (the Church) correspond to its name? How far does it exist in a practical expression of its essence? How far is it in fact what it appears to be? How far does it fulfill the claim which it makes and the expectation which it arouses?" (1958, 641).

missiologies together. In actual fact, whether our missional goals be numerical church growth or Bible translation, socioeconomic liberation or interreligious dialogue, cross-cultural proclamation evangelism or international relief and development—each missiological agenda can be seen to represent a different orbit around the Center of the pyramid. The question, then, becomes one of proximity or distance of that orbit from Jesus Christ.

C. Paradigm forming

Thirdly, missiology involves *paradigm formation*. The central integrating idea that draws together the corners of the pyramid is that which serves to *focus* our missiology. However, we must also be concerned with the *limits* of our missiology, so that we may prevent our missiological education from getting so broad that it becomes meaningless. The integrating idea asks, "What is our bottom-line agenda?" But we must still work to avoid the pitfall Stephen Neill highlighted so well when he said, "If everything is mission, nothing is mission."[193] This involves something that philosophy of science has called "paradigm construction" or "paradigm shift."

We know that paradigm shift is normally understood (especially in philosophy of science) as a corporate phenomenon that occurs over a rather long period of time and involves the reflective community interacting with reference to a particular issue. However, David Bosch has initiated many of us into seeing paradigm formation as a powerful way of helping us reconceptualize our mission with reference to specific communities, in specific contexts.

A paradigm becomes "a conceptual tool used to perceive reality and order that perception in an understandable, explainable, and somewhat predictable pattern" (Van Engen 1992b, 53). It is, "an entire constellation of beliefs, values, and techniques . . . . shared by the members of a given community" (Küng and Tracy, eds., 1989, 441–42). Thus a paradigm consists of "the total composite set of values, worldview, priorities, and knowledge which makes a person, a group of persons, or a culture look at reality in a certain way. A paradigm is a tool of observation, understanding and explanation" (Van Engen 1992b, 53).

Thus a trinitarian missiological paradigm, shaped by a biblical understanding of the kingdom of God, would flow from the fact that the Church's mission derives its motivation, means, agency, and goals from the "*missio Dei*," from God's trinitarian mission, through human agency, primarily by means of the Church,

---

193. This well-known phrase can be found in many places. See, e.g., Stephen Neill 1959, 81; Johannes Blauw 1962, 109. See also Van Engen 1993b

directed toward the whole inhabited earth. This larger viewpoint might help us understand the breadth of all the various issues that influence our missiological paradigm construction and color our hermeneutic of text, community, context and personal pilgrimage—but it would also help us comprehend the limits of our praxis, the periphery beyond which we are no longer in touch with Jesus Christ, and therefore no longer participating in God's mission.

D. Limited

So, fourthly, missiology is *limited*. The pyramid, taken as a whole, represents the boundary beyond which our missiological education gets so broad that it becomes meaningless. We know that missiology deals with a host of cognate disciplines. But we also are now aware that not everything in all those disciplines is missiology. To "give an answer to everyone who asks . . . for the hope that (we) have" (1 Pet 3:15) is mission. To study the phenomena of human religions is not. To use linguistics for the translation of the Scriptures and witness of our faith is mission. To only study languages is not. To seek to improve the way we do our accounting, business practices, administration and management in our mission organizations is related to missiology. But not all administrative and management theory is missiological. To seek new ways in which the Church can be God's people in the cities of our world is mission. But not all sociology of urbanization is mission.

However, even here various mission theorists and practitioners will differ. Some will hold to a paradigm that is much wider than others. On the one hand the scope of God's mission is as broad as we could possibly draw it. But on the other hand, the limits are more circumspectly defined by that which calls for conversion and new relationship to Jesus Christ. In the final analysis, Jesus Christ wants to "draw all (people) to him," (John 12:32); and does not "wish than any should perish" (2 Pet 3:9). That is at once the breadth and the limit of that which constitutes mission.

If we were to study Luke 4, for example, as a paradigmatic description of Jesus' mission from this point of view, we might find some hints as to how our missiological pyramid is both integrated and limited. Although Jesus' mission is as broad and large as Luke 4:18–19, yet it is circumscribed by that which is found in Luke 4:1–13. Jesus' mission will not include only feeding the hungry, or only political power, or only spectacle. There are limits beyond which Jesus, and therefore the Church cannot go. Yet within these limits, the community needs to be as creative as possible in its reading of the text, to bring to its context the full length and breadth, height and depth of the love of God in Jesus Christ (Eph 3).[194] And these three take on concreteness in the missional action of the agents of mission.

And so, the tension persists and the process continues, in the power of the Holy Spirit.

---

194. For further reflection on the topic of this chapter, the reader may want to consult Charles Van Engen, "Biblical Theology of Mission's Research Method," in Edgar Elliston, eds., with Pablo Deiros, Viggo Søgaard and Charles Van Engen; *Introducing Missiological Research Design*, Pasadena: WCL, 2011, 113–18.

PART IV

THE GOALS OF MISSION THEOLOGY

CHAPTER 10

MISSION THEOLOGY
REGARDING THE RESISTANT

Taken from "Reflecting Theologically about the Resistant," in J. Dudley
Woodberry, ed., *Reaching the Resistant: Barriers and Bridges for Mission*,
Pasadena: William Carey Library, 1998, 22–75. Used by permission

THESIS

A missiological and theological understanding of "resistance" or "resistant people" must be grounded biblically in a recognition of human sinfulness that reflects the way humanity spiritually and relationally rejects God's loving self-disclosure to humankind. This would imply that a missiological discussion of "receptivity/resistance" should deal primarily with issues of spirituality, theology, and reconciliation with God, self, others and the world—and secondarily with matters of worldview, sociology, contextualization, or strategy.

INTRODUCTION

When my daughters were twelve and fourteen, my wife, Jean, and I moved from Michigan to California. At that time, I sat them both down (and I did this later with my son as well) and very seriously I informed the girls,

"Look, I want you to know that for the next ten years or so your Dad is going to get more and more stupid. Each year you will be surprised at how much dumber your Dad will be getting.

The girls, with big, wide eyes responded, "Really, Dad, what's wrong? Is it a tumor?"

"No, don't worry," I said, " I can't explain it all to you now. I just want you to know that this is going to happen—and don't worry too much about it. Because you will discover that from the time you are about 23 or so until you are 35 years old, each year I will begin to get smarter! So in about 25 years I will be as smart as I am now—so don't worry too much about it."

Now the reader may wonder what this has to do with the topic of this chapter. Well, anyone who has had teenaged children will be able to explain. Once each of my three children hit twelve or thirteen, they became *resistant*. Although I played basketball for over a quarter of a century, suddenly I could not coach them, I could not teach them—and I seemed to know nothing about basketball. And although I played varsity soccer in high school and college and had coached my son for a number of years, once my son was thirteen, Dad did not seem to know anything about soccer—actually, Dad did not seem to know anything about anything, including girls! Similarly, I have found that, although I have served as consultant to churches, presbyteries, and mission agencies, I clearly know absolutely nothing about relationships, organizations, how my children's friends are coping, or anything having to do with human relations. My children became a *resistant people group*!

So, having learned from them, I have come to realize that I cannot do a "Theology of the Resistant"—because I don't know anything about it! You would have to ask the "resistant!" But maybe I can offer some thoughts on the subject that the reader may find helpful.

THE NEED FOR THEOLOGICAL REFLECTION WITH REGARD TO THE RESISTANT

This chapter is divided in two main sections. In the first section, I review the development of the concepts of resistance and receptivity in evangelical missiology. This is important if we are to understand the missiological framework of the concept about which we are doing theological reflection. This clarification must include the fact that one cannot consider the concept of "resistant peoples" apart from its association with the idea of "receptive" peoples. In the second section I will offer an outline of the theological reflections that would seem to be appropriate with regard to these concepts.

The origin of the concepts "responsive" and "resistant" are to be found in church growth theory that was predominantly based on sociology and strategy. The concept of "resistant peoples" was first popularized by Donald McGavran. In the late 1930s and 40s, together with J. Waskom Pickett, McGavran began to ask questions about why churches in India seemed to grow among some people groups and not among others.

A. The concept of group

First, although it is beyond the scope of this chapter to deal with McGavran's concepts of "people," "people group," "group conversion," and "multi-individual conversion," yet it is important to note that the concept "resistant" was used very early by Donald McGavran as a term modifying "people." McGavran grew up and was a lifelong cross-cultural missionary in India, the context in which he developed his mission theology. There is development in McGavran's writings in the way he defined the term, yet throughout, the concept of groupness, corporateness, and social cohesion remained constant. One must remember that for McGavran this issue was absolutely basic, influencing even his hermeneutic of Matthew 28:18, where he read "*matheteusate panta ta ethne*" as "disciple the peoples" of the world. Here are some samples of the way McGavran defined a "people."

> In the West Christianization is an extremely individualistic process . . . Peoples were thought of as aggregates of individuals whose conversion was achieved one by one. The social factor in the conversion of peoples passed unnoticed because peoples were not identified as separate entities.
>
> However, a people is not an aggregate of individuals. In a true people intermarriage and the intimate details of social intercourse take place within the society. In a true people group individuals are bound together not merely by common social practices and religious beliefs but by common blood. A true people is a social organism which, by virtue of the fact that its members intermarry largely within its own confines, becomes a separate race in their minds. Since the human family, except in the individualistic West, is largely made up of such castes, clans and peoples, the Christianization of each nation involves the prior Christianization of its various peoples as peoples. . . . (McGavran 1955, 8–10)
>
> A nation is usually a conglomerate of peoples, sometimes bound together by language, religion and culture and sometimes divided by just these factors. (McGavran 1959, 41)
>
> (People) meet the Church not only as isolated individuals but as multitudinous societies, each made up of interrelated individuals

who are often of one blood, language, dialect, or section of the country . . . Among the many aspects of human society none is more important to church growth than these homogeneous units of [hu]mankind. . . . The general population may be compared to a mosaic. Each piece of the mosaic is a society, a homogeneous unit. It has its own way of life, its own standards, and degree of education, self-image, and places of residence. . . .

This sociological viewpoint is factual and reasonable. (Humans) do live in societies. . . . What is commonly called group conversion is really *multi-individual conversion*. It is many individuals believing on the Lord at the same time in shared knowledge of the joint action and mutual dependence on each other. Such multi-individual action has very different marginal meanings and results from lone individual action taken in the teeth of group disapproval.

Recognizing homogeneous units and claiming them for Christ emphasizes the biblical goal of discipling the tribes. (McGavran 1965, 69, 71–73)

Thus, essentially, the starting point for reflection on "resistant peoples" must be the concept of "peoples," from which we can then move on to make the observation that a particular people group may be "resistant." The concept of "resistant" was one that sought to describe something about a corporate group, namely, the way that group responded to mission actions carried out in, and with, the group (McGavran 1974, 2–5, 38–40; 1977, 74–76).

B. The concept of "responsive" groups

Secondly, we should be aware of the fact that originally McGavran's and Alan Tippett's emphasis did not fall on "resistant," but rather on "responsive" peoples. In *Bridges of God*, McGavran said,

As we search for light as to how *peoples* become Christian, the story of the early Church has a great contribution to make. . . . Perhaps most important of all, we see how the intentional missionary labors of the early Church, headed by Paul, were devoted in large measure deliberately to following responsive peoples and to expanding existing impulses to Christ in the hearts of people. (McGavran 1955, 36; see also McGavran 1959, 52)

Fifteen years later, in his *magnum opus*, McGavran developed this concept further.

The receptivity or responsiveness of individuals waxes and wanes. No person is equally ready at all times to follow "the Way. . . ." This variability of persons is so well known that it needs no further exposition.

Peoples and societies also vary in responsiveness. Whole segments of (hu)mankind resist the gospel for periods—often very long periods—and then ripen to the Good News. In resistant populations, single congregations only, and those small, can be created and kept alive, whereas in responsive ones many congregations which freely reproduce others can be established. (McGavran 1970, 216; see also McGavran and Hunter III 1980, 30–31, 112)

Earlier, in 1972, Alan Tippett had written a chapter entitled, "The Holy Spirit and Responsive Populations," emphasizing that the concept of a "people" is helpful as it allows the missiologist to take the next step and ask about responsiveness.

When we speak of "responsive populations" we are thinking of large homogeneous units of people who, once they have made their decision, act in unison. . . . Not all populations are responsive. Fields *come* ripe unto harvest. The harvest time has to be recognized, and harvesters have to be sent in at the correct season. . . . Responsive populations should mean many people movements and great numerical church growth. Identifiable groups are waiting to be won for Christ. When the group responds, a congregation has to be created, preferably with the same structure as the group itself. . . . Those responsible, as the stewards of the ingathering, need common sense, humility, anthropological understanding, and a strong personal faith to be good stewards; but, above all, they need obedient submission to the Holy Spirit, without whose power and blessing there could be no mission at all. (Tippett 1972, 77–78, 97–98)

So the early emphasis of McGavran and his associates was positive, seeking to identify those people groups that were more responsive—and having identified them, to respond appropriately in terms of mission strategy and action. That brings us to the third major step in the process of theoretical construction (see McGavran 1973, 47–48).

C. Selective targeting of responsive groups

Thirdly, McGavran, proceeded to affirm a rule of thumb of mission strategy: that missions should invest much among groups that have been deemed responsive, and "inhabit lightly" the areas where peoples were not responsive [McGavran even used the term "irresponsive" (McGavran 1955, 120)—did he mean "unresponsive?"]. C. Peter Wagner and others followed that thinking to the next seemingly logical step, stressing that once the responsive populations have been identified, missions should learn the art of selectively targeting those people groups that were identified as receptive.

Eddie Gibbs warns us about this which he calls an "axiom" of church growth theory.

> It is an axiom of church growth thinking that highest priority must be given to presenting the gospel to the receptive rather than wasting effort in futile attempts to convince the resistant. To help the evangelist and church planter identify receptive soil there are a number of indicators, most of which point to people in transition or trauma. But unless due regard is given to the work of the Spirit, this church growth principle is liable to be unscrupulously exploited rather than conscientiously applied. . . . What is clear is that there needs to be a caring, articulate Christian presence at such times (of transition or trauma) to be available to the Spirit in presenting the riches and claims of Christ. (Gibbs 1986, 192)

Over time this idea as an "axiom" of mission practice has been critiqued and rightfully discredited in missiological circles. However, we also know that humans tend to group themselves with others of similar worldview and culture, and we know that humans tend to do their deepest-level reflection and thinking (including loving God with their minds) in their "heart" (first) language. So it is important to consider carefully the matter of groupness when thinking about receptor-oriented communication of the gospel.

D. Recognizing the mosaic of varying receptivity

Fourthly, we are indebted to McGavran, Tippett, Wagner and others in helping us see that in any given nation, and especially in any specific city or area there may in fact be a rather complex mosaic of various people groups, and that the receptivity or resistance may vary from group to group—and the factors that contribute to their receptivity or resistance also may differ markedly. Thus, McGavran affirmed,

> Unless churchmen (sic) are on the lookout for changes in receptivity of homogeneous units within the general population, and are prepared to seek and bring persons and groups *belonging to these units* into the fold, they will not even discern what needs to be done in mission. They will continue generalized "church and mission work" which, shrouded in fog as to the chief end of mission, cannot fit mission to increasing receptivity. An essential task is to discern receptivity and—when this is seen—to adjust methods, institutions, and personnel until the receptive are becoming Christians and reaching out to win (others) to eternal life. (McGavran 1970, 232)

Later, McGavran wrote, "In almost every land some pieces of the mosaic are receptive to the gospel. Church growth (folks) keep pointing out that we live in a responsive world" (McGavran in Priest 1984, 252–53). The inevitable conclusion drawn from this observation was selective targeting. Mission strategists should direct most of their efforts to the receptive mosaics and "occupy lightly" the people groups or parts of the mosaic that are yet resistant (McGavran 1970, 229–30).[195]

As Delos Miles said in *Church Growth: A Mighty River,*

> Priority in church growth should be given to those who are most receptive to the gospel. We should put our greatest resources where they will provide the largest harvest now. McGavran calls

---

195. It is beyond the scope of this chapter to evaluate the swarming of mission agencies into certain parts of the world and into specific contexts that this concept produced with, in some cases, rather disastrous results. The history of such swarming into Indonesia and into the former Soviet Union are examples.

this "Winning the winnable while they are winnable." George
Hunter is convinced that the "Church Growth movement's
greatest contribution to this generation's world evangelization
will be its stress upon receptivity.

Hence, church growth presents us with a priority of priorities! Top priority is to be given to evangelism. Within that
priority foremost attention is to be given to winning the winnable. Gospel acceptors are to have priority over gospel rejectors.
(Miles 1981, 90–91; Miles is quoting from McGavran 1970, 256
and Hunter III 1979, 104).

C. Peter Wagner explained it this way:

Virtually every discussion about the principle of the harvest or
resistance and receptivity raises the concern about the resistant.
Missionaries have been working among specific people groups
for years with little or no harvest. Nor do they anticipate a
harvest in the near future. Are these missionaries out of the will
of God? Should we abandon people such as Muslims? Do we
bypass the unresponsive? These excellent questions need to be
brought out into the open. It is at this very point that some have
rejected not only the harvest principle, but the entire Church
Growth Movement as well.

No church growth advocate I know has ever suggested that
we bypass the resistant. The Great Commission says that we are
to preach the gospel to all creatures. Donald McGavran from
the beginning has taught that we should "occupy fields of low
receptivity lightly" (Donald McGavran 1980, 176–78). In many
cases Christian workers can do nothing more than establish a
friendly presence and quietly sow the seed. God continues to
call many of his servants to do just that, and I am one who
supports and encourages them." (Wagner 1987, 88–89).

Here Wagner is echoing McGavran's strong stance on this issue. McGavran
categorically stated, "No one should conclude that if receptivity is low, the Church
should withdraw mission" (McGavran 1970, 229).

E. Biblical support for selective targeting: the Parable of the Sower

Selective targeting was supported by appealing to the Parable of the Sower (Matt 13:1–23). As far as I have been able to find, this parable was first mentioned in a contemporary missiological context by Ralph Winter, followed by Peter Wagner and others. Subsequently, the Parable of the Sower became known in church growth literature as the Parable of the Soils, with a hermeneutical approach that concluded that the parable provided a biblical support for selectively targeting the people groups and contexts in which one chose to do mission activity.

As early as 1971, Ralph Winter affirmed, "The ultimate missionary significance of (the Parable of the Soils) emerges with crystal clarity: this parable is the stoutest biblical basis for seeking receptive peoples and investing our time with those who will reproduce" (Winter 1971, 146). This was echoed in that same year by Peter Wagner. "Sowing the seed is necessary, but the parable (of the Soils) refines the concept and teaches that *intelligent* sowing is necessary if the proper harvest is to come as a result. The obvious principle for missionary strategy is that, before sowing the seed of the Word, we will do well to test the soil. . . . As much as possible, responsible missionary strategists should strive to eliminate careless and broadcast sowing" (Wagner 1971, 42).

In 1987, C. Peter Wagner affirmed that,

> The parable says that the seed which fell on good ground produced fruit thirty-, sixty- and one hundredfold. The fertility of the soil, then, is the most important independent variable. This "soil," according to the interpretation, is people who have been so prepared that they hear the word and understand it (see Matt 13:23).
>
> So one way to increase the effectiveness of evangelistic strategy planning is to determine ahead of time which individuals or groups of individuals have hearts prepared by the Holy Spirit to receive the Word. . . . Careless sowing of the gospel message is not usually the most effective evangelistic procedure. To the degree possible . . . we should test the evangelistic soil. Once we test the soil, we can use the energy and time and other resources

available for our evangelistic task in a much more productive
way. (Wagner 1987, 61–62)[196]

In evangelical missiology, this parable has been a standard proof text for
selective targeting. See, e.g., J. Robertson McQuilkin 1973, 24–32; George Peters
1981, 68–71; Donald McGavran 1970, 215ff; 1980, 245ff; 1990, 179ff; C. Peter
Wagner 1987, 61–62; and Thom Rainer 1993, 250.

I will return to a further consideration of the Parable of the Sower later in
this chapter.

F. Defining "Receptivity"

At this point we need to backtrack and ask how "receptivity" was first determined.
On what basis was one to judge that a particular group was "receptive?" The
answer appears obvious and harmless: In church growth literature, the predominant basis for judging a people to be "receptive" seemed to have been based on
the fact that in the midst of a particular group *some churches were growing rapidly.* For
McGavran, this meant that someone had been able to see the beginning of a people
movement. For McGavran and Wagner, it meant that when one did a comparative
statistical church growth analysis of the various denominations, congregations or
missions laboring among a particular people, one found that the churches (or at
least some of them) were growing rapidly. As Wagner said it,

> Years of research has shown that, among many others, three
> major indicators of resistance-receptivity stand out and ought
> to be considered whenever determining where to plot a given
> people group on the axis. They are (1) where churches are
> already growing, (2) where people are changing, and (3) among
> the masses. . . . It sounds almost too elementary to say that recep-
> tivity can be expected where churches are already growing. But
> it needs to be highlighted because many evangelistic planners
> develop their strategy on the opposite consideration. They
> determine, on principle, to evangelize in places where churches
> have not been growing. For those who have a view to the

---

196. See also J. Robertson McQuilkin 1973, 24–32; George Peters 1981, 68–71; Donald A.
McGavran 1970, 215ff; 1980, 245ff; 1990, 179ff; and Thom Rainer 1993, 250.

harvest, such may not be the most efficient approach. (Wagner 1987, 78)[197]

G. The Resistance-Receptivity Axis

This foundational definition ("receptive" peoples are those among whom many churches are growing rapidly) proceeded to give rise to the development by McGavran, Dayton, Wagner, and others of the "Resistance-Receptivity Axis,." shown below. In *Evangelism and Church Growth: A Practical Encyclopedia*, Elmer Towns defines this axis as, "A measurement scale by which people are designated according to their openness to the gospel" (Towns 1995, 340).

Highly Resistant to the Gospel							Highly Receptive to the Gospel			
-5	-4	-3	-2	-1	0	+1	+2	+3	+4	+5
Strongly Opposed		Somewhat Opposed		Indifferent			Somewhat Favorable		Strongly Favorable	

FIGURE 9: The Resistance-Receptivity Axis[198]

As we will see later, the "resistance-receptivity axis" fuels the question as *to what* the group may be receptive or resistant? In answer, various persons in the church growth movement developed a rather sophisticated analysis of various factors which might contribute to resistance or to receptivity. Working especially with matters of local contextual, local institutional, national contextual and national institutional factors, one can quite helpfully sort out various issues that may be contributing to a group's place on the scale at a particular time and in a particular context. In my opinion, this analysis of factors that enhance or inhibit growth has been one of the most creative, constructive, and helpful elements of church growth theory.

---

197. In this volume Wagner then went on to elaborate on his understanding of these three major indicators of where a particular people group would fall on the resistance-receptivity axis. See Wagner 1987, 78–88.

198. Edward R. Dayton 1980, 47; reproduced in C. Peter Wagner 1987, 78. (See also McGavran 1970, 228; C. Peter Wagner 1971, 150–51; R. Daniel Reeves and Ronald Jenson: 1984, 69; C. Wayne Zunkel 1987, 158; Edward Dayton and David A. Fraser 1990, 129–30.)

H. "Resistance/receptivity" as second-level terms.

Exactly what are we saying if the basis of our calling a group of people "receptive" is due to the fact that we can find churches growing rapidly among them? I would suggest that in using such terms, the church growth movement was actually not saying anything specific about the group itself. I do not believe the terms told us anything about a group's worldview, its cultural or religious systems, its faith issues, its spiritual openness, or its psychoemotional willingness to receive new ideas. Rather, the terms are, in my opinion, second-level derivative observations. The logic would go something like this.

- Based on the fact that some churches are growing rapidly, and
- based on the assumption that churches grow most rapidly among people whom we have termed "receptive,"
- therefore we conclude that these people are receptive.

An associated concept that serves to demonstrate the above has to do with recent efforts in the church growth movement directed toward spiritual issues during the 1990s. Beginning in mid-1990s, some folks like Wagner and others, worked in areas of "strategic level spiritual warfare" and seemed to be saying that "receptive" or "resistant" may be terms that should be understood to speak about the unseen cosmic-level spiritual forces operating on and in a people. In this case, again, the terms would tell us little about the people themselves. Instead, they could be understood to refer to the spiritual forces or spiritual environment operative among, and on, that people group at that particular time.

Thus, I would suggest that, viewed theologically, the early use of "responsive" or "receptive" as used by McGavran, was predominantly descriptive of the churches and their growth—not about anything inherent or intrinsic to the group itself. I'm beginning to see that "receptive" and "resistant" have been essentially sociological terms, descriptive of an observable phenomenon (the numerical growth of congregations), not theological terms speaking about the spiritual state of a people group.

I. Missiological developments

Three major, powerful and influential developments in evangelical missiology flowed from the theoretical framework of resistant/receptive people groups.

Hidden/Unreached Peoples

The first major missiological implication that flowed from the theoretical frame-work I have outlined above has to do with the concept of "hidden peoples" and then "unreached peoples" which Ralph Winter highlighted. These became very important in evangelical missiology, first at Lausanne, 1974 (Douglas, ed., 1975), then at Pattaya, 1980 (Douglas 1980, 43–44; Scott 1981, 57–75; Coggins 1980, 225–32; Winter 1980, 79–85), then at the World Consultation on Frontier Missions held in Edinburgh, 1980 (Starling, edit 1981), and most recently in the "Adopt-A-People" movement and the AD2000 Movement's stress on the 10–40 Window. All of these derived in some way from the theoretical framework outlined above. One could also include here the MARC research (Dayton and Wagner, et al) on unreached peoples, and specific assumptions behind some of David Barrett's research which also drew from this theoretical complex. No matter that one (and I do) may strongly support the missionally activist initiatives represented by these movements in evangelical missiology. That is not my point here. Rather, I wish for us to see that we have left unanswered one of the most significant and foundational theological and missiological questions: what are we saying when we say "recep-tive" or "resistant?"

Contextualization

A second missiological development that flowed from this theoretical complex was the desire for careful contextualization of the gospel in such a way that resistance could be avoided or at least lessened. As Donald McGavran suggested, "Each population, therefore, must have its own formula. . . . The essentials of the gospel, the authoritative Bible, and the unchanging Christ remain the same for all pop-ulations. But the accompaniments can and must be changed freely to suit each particular case." (McGavran 1970, 231)

> Hard, bold plans for proclaiming Christ and persuading (people) to become His disciples and responsible members of His Church are a *sine qua non* of Christian mission. Their boldness will be enhanced by their sympathetic approach to the bewildering multitudes of every nation. They are essential to right strategy.
>
> Right strategy will divide the world into cultural units— those where Christian mission is correctly seed-sowing and those where it is correctly harvesting. Both kinds of culture are found, and there is no clear line between them. Wrong strategy

fails to note the difference between responsive and resistant segments of society. Right strategy not only notes the difference, but
constantly explores to discover ways of identifying each variety
of population and of fitting the missionary effort of each church
correctly to each variety. (McGavran 1972a, 105–6)

So in creating the School of World Mission/Institute of Church Growth at
Fuller Theological Seminary, Donald McGavran brought in Alan Tippett, then
Charles Kraft, to be joined later by Dean Gilliland and Dan Shaw—all experts
in cultural anthropology and contextualization theory. (e.g., Dean Gilliland, ed.,
1989) Their assumption was that effective mission action must be based on deep-
level cultural understanding of the receptors.[199]

Homogeneous Unit Church Planting

Although this is beyond the scope of this chapter, it is important to note here
that a third missiological development became a strong emphasis in the American Church Growth movement on planting homogeneous unit principle (HUP)
churches. I have space only to mention some of the sample publications produced
by Donald McGavran, Win Arn, Peter Wagner, and others that explained,
strongly supported, and contextualized for North America the concept of planting
HUP churches in North America, a stream of missiological thought flowing from
the conceptual fountain of measuring and responding to the resistance/receptivity
of a particular people group. Here are some samples:

1971 C. Peter Wagner, *Frontiers of Mission Strategy*;

1973 Donald McGavran and Win Arn, *How to Grow a Church*;

1976 C. Peter Wagner, *Your Church Can Grow: Seven Vital Signs of a Healthy
Church*;

1977 Donald McGavran and Win Arn, *Ten Steps for Church Growth*;

1979 C. Peter Wagner, *Our Kind of People*;

1980 Donald McGavran and George Hunter, *Church Growth Strategies
that Work*;

1981 Donald McGavran, "Why Some American Churches are
Growing and Some are Not," (in Elmer Towns, John N. Vaughan
and David J. Seifert, eds., 1981, 285–294);

---

199. See, e.g., Charles Van Engen, Darrell Whiteman, and J. Dudley Woodberry, eds.,
2008, 3–46.

1981 Donald McGavran, *Back To Basics in Church Growth*;

1981 C. Peter Wagner, *Church Growth and the Whole Gospel*;

1984 Donald McGavran, *Momentous Decisions in Mission Today*;

1984 C. Peter Wagner, *Leading Your Church To Growth*;

1986 C. Peter Wagner, "A Vision for Evangelizing the Real America;"

1987 C. Peter Wagner, *Strategies for Church Growth*;

1990 C. Peter Wagner, *Church Planting for a Greater Harvest*;

1996 C. Peter Wagner, *The Healthy Church*; and

1996 Thom Rainer, *The Book of Church Growth*.

We might draw two observations from surveying the above titles. First, the matter of "resistance/receptivity" has been very influential in evangelical missiology during the last thirty years, and cries for careful thought, examination, and critique. Secondly, the concepts themselves are quite unclear in terms of that to which they refer, especially with reference to spiritual and theological understanding. The terms have referred mostly to the fact that among a particular people group churches may be observed to be growing, and therefore the group should be targeted, and therefore specific cultural issues should be considered in missiological strategies directed towards it. But the lack of theological clarity is especially glaring when one focuses on the "resistant" part of the formula. Because, qualifiers and explanations notwithstanding, we might assume that for the "resistant," we would conclude the opposite of all the assertions previously made about the "responsive." Namely, that among the resistant we should carry out very little mission endeavor, that we should be especially careful about the contextualization of the gospel, and that we should not be too concerned about targeting resistant groups until such time as they become "receptive."

Yet, significantly, and in contradiction to the earlier perspective, in recent emphases in the AD2000 Movement, in Wagner's and others' ministries, and in many mission initiatives dealing with the "10–40 Window" one finds mission leaders calling for intentional and aggressive mission to be carried out precisely among some of the most resistant peoples of the world.

All of this is to say that we are in need of a thorough rethinking of the theological meaning of the term, "resistant." This, then, is the substance of the next part.

AN OUTLINE OF THEOLOGICAL
REFLECTION ABOUT THE RESISTANT

In what follows I would like to develop in a kind of outline form a progression of theological and biblical affirmations that may help us clarify the issue at hand. And the starting point, as I see it, must be positive (following early McGavran), not negative. So the progression of ideas is as follows:

A. All humans are loved always by God.

God recognizes and values all peoples in their cultural and ethnic diversity. Within their particularity of ethnicity God loves all peoples and invites all to faith in Jesus Christ, each in their own special cultural and ethnic makeup. Whether they respond or not, God still loves all peoples. "For God so loved the world that he gave his one and only Son that whoever believes in him shall not perish but have eternal life" (John 3:16).

So the first affirmation that the Bible calls us to make has to do with a complementarity between cultural particularity and God's missional universality. Throughout the Scriptures, we find the people of God stressing God's careful sensitivity to particular cultural differences, recognizing the existence of different peoples and people groups. The "nations" are not just an amorphous amalgam of individuals caught in various webs of political dominance. Rather, they are "families, tribes, languages," each special in their particularity. However, at the same time, we find affirmed time and again that God loves *all* peoples—that God desires to be in covenant with, and extend an invitation to, all peoples. So all the peoples will be blessed in and through Abraham. Here, then, we can recognize McGavran's insistence on people groups—but we must also see here a profound redefinition of "receptivity" and "resistance."

The words of Jesus to Nicodemus focus the biblical narrative of God's universality of love for all peoples—and God's particularity of loving a plurality of specific and different peoples. One need only trace the theme through Scripture to see how very important it is in understanding God's mission. Risking belaboring the point, I will simply point out a few illustrative biblical references that may help us see God's mission as the outworking of the universality of God's love of all peoples in their cultural and historical particularity.

Genesis

Three times in the first eleven chapters of Genesis we are told that God is the creator and judge of all peoples. All people are created in Adam and Eve; all people descend from Noah; all people have their languages confused and are then spread out over the entire earth after the Babel episode. In each case, there is a recognition of the particularity and difference of various peoples—as is signaled by the inclusion of the Table of Nations in Genesis 10—yet in each case this multiplicity of peoples are collectively and unitedly said to be the object of God's concern.

Abraham

When God calls Abram, his call involves being a blessing to a plurality of nations—but through the particularity of one clan whose origins are traced back to Nahor and Terah from the Ur of the Chaldeans. They are particular instruments of God's mission, chosen with the intention of being a blessing to many particular peoples within the universality of God's concern, care, love, and judgment of all peoples.

Deuteronomy and II Chronicles

God's love of all peoples is repeated in Deuteronomy and, for example, also in 2 Chronicles. 1 Peter 2 draws from Deuteronomy 10:14–22. The creator Lord God (to whom "belong the heavens, even the highest heavens, the earth and everything in it") chose Israel out of all the nations, and now calls Israel to exhibit compassion and care for the fatherless, the widow, and the aliens who represent the plurality of particular nations. Thus many years later, even at Solomon's dedication of the Temple, the symbol of the most centralized form of Israel's faith, even here, Solomon prays, when "the foreigner who does not belong to your people Israel but has come from a distant land because of your great name. . . . come and pray toward this temple, then hear from heaven. . . . Do whatever the foreigner asks of you, so that all the peoples of the earth may know your name and fear you . . ." (2 Chron 6:32–33).

Jesus and Isaiah

So it is no accident that Jesus, the Messiah of Israel, would use Isaiah's language in speaking of Herod's Temple as "a house of prayer for all nations" (Isa 56:7; Mark 11:17). In fact, the complementarity of universality and particularity is very strong in Jesus' ministry. Jesus at one point sends his disciples "to the lost sheep of Israel" (Matt 10:6). Yet this is the same Jesus and the same gospel of Matthew that will very strongly emphasize that the disciples are to meet him in the cosmopolitan, multicultural setting of Galilee. There he will say, "all authority in heaven and on earth has been given to me. Therefore go and make disciples *ta ethnē*"—of all nations (Matt 28:18–19).[200] The gospels strongly support the vision articulated by Simeon at the time of Jesus' dedication in the temple: Jesus is the Lord of lords and the Messiah of Israel and he is "(God's) salvation, which you have prepared in the sight of all nations: a light for revelation to the Gentiles, and the glory of your people Israel" (Luke 2:30–32). Later, when Jesus describes his own mission, drawing from Isaiah 35, 49, and 61, he will proclaim his mission in Nazareth, speaking of it as a mission of preaching good news to the poor, freedom to the prisoners, recovery of sight for the blind, to release the oppressed and to proclaim the year of the Lord's favor in global, universal terms that have specific, local contextual significance in Galilee (Luke 4:18–19; 7:22–23).

Paul

Paul emphasized God's love of all peoples. Even in the oft-cited universal passages like Galatians 3:28 ("There is neither Jew nor Gentile, neither slave nor free, nor is there male and female. . . .") and Colossians 3:11 ("Here there is no Greek or Jew, circumcised or uncircumcised, barbarian, Scythian, slave or free. . . ."), the cultural distinctives are not erased. The particularity of ethnicity, sexuality, and socioeconomics is not ignored. Yet, in the midst of such specific forms of homogeneity, there is a universality of union (not uniformity of culture)—a universality of oneness in Jesus Christ: "you are all one in Christ Jesus" (Gal 3:28); "but Christ is all, and is in all" (Col 3:11). Thus in Ephesians, Paul's ecclesiology recognizes the distinctive differences of being Gentile or Jewish ("This mystery is that through the gospel the Gentiles are heirs together with Israel, members together of one body, and sharers together in the promise in Christ Jesus" [Eph 3:6]). Yet Paul also affirms that they are brought together into one new family in Jesus Christ (Eph 3:15). This does not mean that Jews must live like Gentiles, neither must Gentiles live like Jews. Paul follows the dictum of the Jerusalem Council in Acts 15 in affirming the cultural differences, yet creating a new oneness in Jesus Christ. In Acts 21, Paul participates in a Jewish rite of purification in the temple in Jerusalem,

---

200. This combination of universality and particularity, with special emphasis on the Gospel of Matthew was the subject of Paul Hertig's PhD dissertation done at the School of World Mission at Fuller Seminary (Matthew's Narrative Use of Galilee in the Multicultural and Missiological Journeys of Jesus. Lewiston, NY: Edwin Mellon Press, 1998).

knowing he will be arrested, but making a public statement that Jews who are now believers in the Messiah may still follow Jewish custom. Thus, even though "there is no difference between Jew and Gentile—the same Lord is Lord of all" (Rom 10:12), yet the proclamation of the gospel, according to Paul, is "first to the Jew, then to the Gentile" (Rom 1:16). In this regard, I have offered an outline of Paul's missiology in Romans in "The Effect of Universalism on mission theology" in *Mission on the Way.*[201]

John in Revelation

In Revelation, John echoes the same kind of complementarity of particularity and universality. Peppered all through the Revelation, John keeps emphasizing the fact that Christ is bringing together people "from every tribe and language and people and nation" (Rev 5:9; 7:9). In Revelation 21, in the vision of the New Jerusalem which is a picture of the Church, there is a plurality of "nations" that will "wake Luke by its light, and the kings of the earth will bring their splendor into it. . . . The glory and honor of the nations will be brought into it . . ." (Rev 21:24–26). Thus, there is a recognition and celebration of the differences and distinctives of a plurality of different peoples and cultures—yet a oneness in their coming into the same New Jerusalem, to be in the presence of the one Lamb of God who takes away the sin of the world. In *Mission on the Way* I spoke of this as a missiology that is "faith-particularist" (in Jesus Christ), "culturally pluralist" (dealing with all the various peoples of the earth) and "ecclesiologically inclusivist" (all peoples are invited to the marriage supper of the Lamb).[202]

This brief review of the complementarity of universality and particularity may seem unnecessary and perhaps even redundant to some readers. However, I believe it is of utmost importance that this biblical orientation strongly influence the rest of our reflection concerning resistance and receptivity. The way we understand God's love of all peoples will influence our missiological orientation to the issues facing us today in mission around the world, among peoples, some of whom are responsive, and some that are resistant. Too strong an emphasis on universality will drive us toward uniformity and blind us to cultural distinctives—and the differences in the particular response/resistance represented by a particular people group. Too strong an emphasis on particularity will push us to narrow our

---

201. Van Engen, *Mission on the Way: Issues in Mission Theology,* Grand Rapids: Baker, 1996, 159–68.

202. Ibid., 183–84.

mission endeavor to only certain groups of people whom we have tagged "receptive," ignoring or neglecting others. Either option has serious consequences for following Christ in mission.

As I read Scripture, I see God affirming cultural distinctives. I see Babel as judgment, yes, but also as grace. The beauty of resplendent creativity shines forth in the wonderful multiplication of families, tribes, tongues and peoples of humanity. Rather than destroy humanity (which in the Noahic covenant God had promised not to do), God chooses to confuse the languages. This confusion, although an act of judgment, mercifully preserves all humanity in its cultural and ethnic distinctives, differences so significant that we are given a Table of Nations to enumerate the civilizations known to the compilers of the Pentateuch. These differences are so significant that when the Holy Spirit comes at Pentecost one of the first extraordinary acts of the Holy Spirit is to enable people of many different languages to hear the proclamation of the gospel *in their own language*. Yet these distinctive features of multiple cultures are not allowed to divide humanity's relation to YHWH, nor to support the concept of a national or ethnic plurality of gods. There is one God, creator and sustainer of *all peoples*. Oneness in plurality, plurality in oneness. Particular universality, universal particularity. How can we give concrete, lived out shape to this biblical view of reality as God sees it? Should this theology of humanity not be normative for us as we consider the meaning of the concept of "resistant peoples?" I believe it should.

We could compile a long list of valid theological, missiological and strategic motivations for mission among specific "responsive" peoples, and why it is legitimate to "occupy lightly" areas where "resistant peoples" live. However, I would suggest that the most basic and pervasive of all our missional motivations must derive from the universal scope of God's mission as depicted in Scripture and spoken by a particular Messiah (Jesus) to a particular Jewish teacher of the law (Nicodemus): "For God so loved the world (of many peoples, tribes, tongues and nations) that he gave his one and only Son. . . ." (John 3:16). God loves all peoples and wants to develop a covenantal relationship with all peoples.

B. All humans are receptive: they have a profound spiritual hunger to know God.

The affirmation that God loves all peoples has a complementary side in the spiritual hunger evident in all humans. As the continued multiplication of religious systems and forms over the centuries and in every culture attests, human beings are incurably religious. Even in the face of materialistic atheism like that which was prevalent for so long in the former Soviet Union, (or in post-Christian atheistic secularism in the West, or the cultural revolution in China), even in these environments one can see evidences of profound spiritual hunger that eventually stimulates major social upheaval. Whether we relate this to general revelation or to prevenient grace or to common grace, this is something very basic in affirming that all peoples are receptive in their desire and need for an encounter with the divine.

What I have in mind here is not Roman Catholic natural theology in the train of Thomas Aquinas. I do not mean, either, a vague human construction of religion as an expression of the highest value of culture. Nor do I mean the European nineteenth century Protestant version of natural theology against which Karl Barth spoke so forcefully. Nor do I mean a pluralist approach either through comparative religions, phenomenology of religion, religious psychology, or a theo-centric pluralism all of which draw in some way from the assumption of a common thread of humanity's interest in the nouminous. Neither do I mean exactly the "point of contact" between reason and revelation that Emil Brunner advocated when he spoke of "humanity (having) within itself 'a capacity for revelation' or 'a possibility of . . . being addressed,' which enables a person to apprehend and receive God's revelation.[203] Nor do I mean a too easy, revelatory approach to general revelation about which John Calvin, Hendrik Kraemer, Karl Barth, G. C. Berkouwer, Hendrikus Berkhof, Donald Bloesch, Millard Erickson, Stanley Grenz and Alistair McGrath, among others, have expressed anxiety and discomfort. [204]

---

203. Emil Brunner 1946; quoted in Donald Bloesch 1992, 153.

204. Donald Bloesch has given us a helpful overview of this discussion in Bloesch 1992, 161–65. Donald Bloesch was probably on the right track when he wrote,

"Revelation as I conceive it yields real knowledge of God, but knowledge that is personal and concrete, not speculative and abstract. I agree, moreover, that revelation, even understood as occurring exclusively in Christ, does not necessarily entail the acceptance of salvation, but what it does bring us is the reality of salvation. . . . I am coming to agree with Hendrikus Berkhof that "general revelation" is a term that should probably now be abandoned because of its ambiguity and imprecision. [Bloesch is referring here to Hendrikus Berkhof 1979, 74–77.] If revelation is essentially a personal encounter, general revelation would seem to contradict this essential dimension of revelation. If revelation is defined as God's effectual communication of his will and purpose to humanity, then we have no revelation in nature that can be positively conjoined with the biblical meanings of "unveiling" (apokalypsis) and "manifestation" (from

Rather, what I am speaking of is, in Alvin Plantinga's words, that "God has implanted in us all an innate tendency . . . or disposition to believe in God" (Plantinga 1992, 67). John Calvin referred to this disposition as a "*sensus divinitatis*" or a "*semen religionis*" whereby, in Calvin's words, "There is within the human mind, and indeed by natural instinct, an awareness of divinity . . . God himself has implanted in all (persons) a certain understanding of his divine majesty. . . . As experience shows, God has sown a seed of religion in all [people].[205] Or as G. C. Berkouwer expressed it,

---

phanerow). . . . It is probably better to regard this general working of God as an exhibition or display of his power and goodness than as a revelation that effectively unveils or conveys his plan and purpose for our lives. Through his general working in nature and conscience, we are exposed to the mercy of God as well as to his wrath and judgment, but God's light and truth are disclosed to us only in the encounter with Jesus Christ as presented in Holy Scripture.

"It is appropriate to speak of a general presence of God in nature and history, but this general presence does not become a revelation of his grace and mercy until it is perceived in the light of Jesus Christ. Only in the light of Christ, Karl Barth contended on the basis of Psalm 39:9, can we properly discern God's general light in nature. Yet the light in nature is a reflected or derivative light. It is not a source of the light of Christ but a witness to it, a witness recognizable only to the eyes of faith . . . In short, while the wonders of nature manifest God's deity and power, because of human sin they fail to give us real knowledge. They do bring us a deep-seated awareness of God—sufficient, however, to condemn us, not to save us" (Bloesch 1992, 164–65).

These considerations led Bloesch to disagree with prevailing conservative Protestant views of natural theology as exemplified by Bruce Demarest when Demarest says, "Only when one sees himself as a sinner before the God of Creation does the offer of reconciliation in the gospel make sense. If intuitional and inferential knowledge of God were not present, God's gracious communication to man in the form of special revelation would remain a meaningless abstraction. Special revelation, then, begins at the point where man's natural knowledge of God ends. Natural theology is properly the vestibule of revealed theology. . . . Special revelation completes, not negates, the disclosure of God in nature, providence, and conscience." (Bloesch is quoting here from Bruce Demarest 1982, 250–51.)

Donald Bloesch rejoins, "Against Demarest I contend that to posit prior human receptivity to the gospel is to make salvation contingent on the human will as well as on divine grace. And to suggest that we can see ourselves as sinners before we are awakened to the truth of God's reconciliation for us in Christ is to attribute to human beings power that is simply not countenanced by the biblical witness or by the witness of the Reformation. I also disagree that special revelation completes the knowledge of God derived from nature and conscience, for this conveys the misleading impression that the two kinds of knowledge are of the same nature and therefore can be joined together" (Bloesch 1992, 162).

205. Jean Calvin 1960, 43, 47. See also Alvin Plantinga 1992, 67–68.

The *sensus divinitatis* is not an organ of the knowledge of God which transcends the corruption of human nature; it is an unavoidable impression left on [humans] by the prevailing power of God. . . . All [people] have a sense of religion, and there is "no nation so barbarous, no race so savage as not to be firmly persuaded of the being of God." (Berkouwer 1955, 152)[206]

Further, Berkouwer says,

The *semen religionis* is preserved by God in the human heart. This does not relieve the darkness, but it does help explain how it is that religions still arise in a fallen world and how it is possible that these false religions bear a marked resemblance of order. (Berkouwer 1955, 169)

Psalm 19 and Romans 1 are commonly mentioned passages in Scripture understood to speak of this disposition to believe in God. Psalm 19:1–4 says,

The heavens declare the glory of God; the skies proclaim the work of his hands. Day after day they pour forth speech; night after night they display knowledge. There is no speech or language where their voice is not heard. Their voice goes out into all the earth, their words to the ends of the world.

Paul stated in Romans 1:19–20,

What may be known about God is plain to [humans]. For since the creation of the world God's invisible qualities—his eternal power and divine nature—have been clearly seen, being understood from what has been made . . .

Paul articulated this concept even more thoroughly in his well-known sermon at the Areopagus in Athens, applying it to the Athenian worship of "The Unknown God," one whom Paul claims to know and to proclaim.

Thus Donald Bloesch, with his deep discomfort regarding general revelation, spoke of this

general working of God as an exhibition or display of his power and goodness. . . . Through his general working in nature and

---

206. Berkouwer is quoting here from Calvin 1960, 44.

conscience, we are exposed to the mercy of God as well as to his wrath and judgment. . . . It is appropriate to speak of a general presence of God in nature and history. (1992, 164)

Stanley Grenz says

> We share a common dependency on something external to, or beyond any shape that we can give to our 'world.' The God-shaped vacuum within us, to which this dependency bears silent witness, is a testimony in the human heart to the reality of God. . . . By virtue of the fact that we are created beings, God had directed each of us to a common human destiny. Just as our common human dependency bears witness to the reality of God, so also the residue of the divine image within us is a dimension of (what he calls) general revelation. Our awareness that we are directed beyond the present stands as a silent witness to the reality of God for whom we are created. (1994, 179)

In McGrath's words,

> God has endowed human beings with some inbuilt sense or presentiment of the divine existence. It is as if something about God has been engraved in the heart of every human being. Calvin identifies three consequences of this inbuilt awareness of divinity: the universality of religion (which, if uninformed by the Christian revelation, degenerates into idolatry), a troubled conscience, and a servile fear of God. (1994, 160)

Hendrikus Berkhof speaks of this innate disposition.

> The first thing we will then have to say is that man (sic)[207] is apparently a being who is made to encounter God, to respond to his Word. Man is a responding creature. . . . I want to describe man as a 'respondable' being. . . . From the point of view of theology it must be said that man had only become fully man when he became aware of God's presence and learned to pray.

---

207. I have chosen not to rewrite Hendrikus Berkhof's writing into inclusive language. Where he uses "man," he means "humanity."

By describing man as "respondable" we delimit him from the outset in his maturity and autonomy. The first word does not come from him. He is made man by an initiative from the outside and from above. His creativity is based on re-creativity. And no less important is that with this description we have found that man's essence lies in a relationship, namely the relationship with God. From the standpoint of the Christian faith it is out of the question to regard man as a self-contained being who later happens to enter into relationships with other beings. Man is that creature who is made to live with God. . . .

Meanwhile, by labelling man "respondable" we have given only a formal description. He is made to respond to the Word of God. But the content of that Word is the holy love with which God beneficially turns to his human creatures. Man is not made just for responding as such, but for responding to this Word, that is, to God love. Love can only be responded to with reciprocal love. Man is made for *love*. He cannot do without that nurturing love from the outside, nor without responding to that love. . . . In this relation of receiving and giving live, man heeds his most central calling and actualizes his true essence. In love, man becomes himself. (1979, 181–85)[208]

The importance of this innate disposition cannot be underestimated in its influence as a working assumption in much of our evangelical missiology. Let me briefly mention four related missiological arenas where this assumption seems to be operative. First, Donald McGavran's theories of group conversion, indigenous church forms and cultural appropriateness assumes this innate disposition. McGavran's axiom was, "[Women and] men like to become Christians without crossing unnecessary racial, linguistic and class barriers" (McGavran 1970, 198).[209] Based on this assumption, McGavran developed an extensive analysis of what he called the *Bridges of God* (1955) advocating the intentional use of natural relational, cultural and social networks for gospel proclamation.

---

208. See also Robert K. Johnston. *God's Wider Presence: Reconsidering General Revelation*. Grand Rapids: Baker, 2014.

209. See also George Hunter III 1979, 121; Eddie Gibbs 1981, 117; Donald McGavran 1984, 100; Wayne Zunkle 1987, 100; Thom Rainer 1993, 254.

> The faith spreads most naturally and contagiously along the
> lines of the social network of living Christians, especially new
> Christians, . . . Receptive undiscipled men and women usually
> receive the possibility (of faith in Jesus Christ) when the invi-
> tation is extended to them from credible Christian friends,
> relatives, neighbors, and fellow workers from within their social
> web. (McGavran and Hunter 1980, 30)

The assumption behind McGavran's axiom is that once we can get beyond social, cultural, and relational barriers, people will be disposed to receive the gospel. Their innate hunger for God will come into play.

Secondly, the assumption of this innate disposition toward God is also built into theories of indigenization, contextualization and communication in evangelical missiology. As Charles Kraft pointed out in *Communication Theory for Christian Witness*, (1983, 1991) meaning in communication is ascribed by the hearer, not by the speaker. "The key participant (is) the receptor" (1991, chapter 6). Thus, if we can learn the art of listening well, and can begin to develop receptor-oriented communication, the innate desire for God will move the receptor to being open to a relationship with God in Jesus Christ. "To love communicationally," says Kraft, "is to put oneself to whatever inconvenience necessary to assure that the receptors understand" (1991, 15).

It is beyond the scope of this chapter to delineate the various models and approaches to contextualization by Protestant evangelicals like David Hesselgrave (1978), David Hesselgrave and Edward Rommen (1989); Harvie Conn (1977, 1978, 1984), Paul Hiebert (1978, 1985, 1987, 1989, 1994), Charles Taber (1979a, 1979b, 1979c) Charles Kraft (1979, 1983), Dean Gilliland (1989), Krikor Haleblian (1982a 1982b, 1983), Daniel Shaw (1988, 1989), and others. Contexualization theory follows this path, assuming that if one can present the gospel in a way (and with a biblical content) that is culturally appropriate to a people group—that the members of the group will then be free to respond positively to the message, given their innate desire for God.[210] This foundational assumption may be found in contextualization theory, no matter whether the model is one of communication, cultural relevance, liberation, interfaith dialogue or knowing God in context (Van Engen 1996, 74–75).

---

210. See, e.g., David Hesselgrave and Edward Rommen 1989, 211.

Thirdly, people's innate disposition toward God is also presupposed in the search for the various factors of receptivity and resistance as these have been developed in evangelical missiology (particularly in church growth theory). Here it is assumed that certain experiences will bring people to be more responsive to the their innate desire and need for God. C. Wayne Zunkel, for example, lists 191 "stress-causing situations in life" that may be times of greater receptiveness to the gospel (Zunkel 1987, 149–56). We will return to this when we ask *to what* certain people may be resistant or receptive.

Fourthly, the commonly used language in evangelical missiology concerning "redemptive analogies" to be found in a receptor culture also seems to assume that there are present in all cultures what Karl Barth called "lights" that witness to God's existence, power and provision. The assumption that one can find such analogies in a given cultural context and then use them as "contact points" or communicational bridges for gospel proclamation presupposes a desire on the part of the persons in that culture to know and be related to God.

So, given this innate predisposition, with reference to both the resistant and the receptive, we find a need to affirm that all humans are receptive. However, this immediately pushes us to a third major affirmation about resistance-receptivity: all humans are resistant.

C. Because of sin and the fall, all humans are resistant to God all the time.

It is a mistake to think that general revelation provides a natural knowledge of God apart from the work of the Holy Spirit by grace through faith in Jesus Christ. Paul's point in Romans 1 was not that there is revelatory knowledge of God apart from Jesus Christ—but rather that humanity is condemned and without excuse because of its rejection of the greatness and goodness of God that can be seen in creation. Thus general revelation is a reason for judgment and a proof of the sinfulness of humanity, not a basis for inclusivist or pluralist approaches to theology of religion, contra Clark Pinnock, John Sanders and others.[211] As I have demonstrated elsewhere,[212] Paul's foundational point in Romans 1–3 is that, although the Jews separated the world into two kinds of people (Jews and Gentiles), in the final analysis, "all have sinned and fall short of the glory of God" (Rom 3:23). Thus a new universality and a new particularity is constructed by Paul in the first eight

---

211. See Van Engen 1996, 169–90.
212. See Van Engen 1991b, 191–194 and 1996, 159–68.

chapters of Romans, based not on ethnicity but on faith in Jesus Christ. In other words, the innate disposition toward belief in God which we saw above is very weak and limited precisely because of the pervasiveness of sin and the fall. So John Calvin rightly distinguished between knowledge of God as creator and knowledge of God as redeemer.

As Stanley Grenz says,

> Although the concept of general revelation is valid and helpful, it is also limited. It is restricted in scope. What God has made available to all persons through general revelation does not provide the complete self-disclosure of God. On the contrary, general revelation functions only as a testimony to the presence of the God who is the reality standing both behind and within the world. . . .
>
> The limited use of the concept is evident in the Bible itself. Paul's main purpose is not to set forth the thesis that creation testifies to the reality of God. Rather, his point is that sinful humans suppress even the testimony heralded by the natural creation. Because of human sin, people do not in fact give ear to this available testimony . . . All humans stand justly condemned before a holy God." (Grenz 1994, 180–81)

"A natural knowledge of God," says McGrath, "serves to deprive humanity of any excuse for ignoring the divine will; nevertheless, it is inadequate as the basis for a full-fledged portrayal of the nature, character, and purposes of God. . . . Knowledge of God the redeemer—which for Calvin is a distinctively *Christian* knowledge of God—may only be had by the Christian revelation, in Christ and through Scripture" (McGrath 1994, 161).

Donald Bloesch comments. "While the wonders of nature manifest God's deity and power, because of human sin they fail to give us real knowledge. They do bring us to deep-seated awareness of God—sufficient, however, to condemn us, not to save us" (Bloesch 1992, 165).

G. C. Berkouwer emphasized Karl Barth's perspective at this point. Barth drew a very sharp distinction between revelation and religion. Berkouwer explains.

> [Karl Barth] has reacted violently against almost every theory of psychology of religion and religious historicism. His reason is that they all seriously impugn the absoluteness of revelation. Far

from paying honor to human religion, Barth speaks of religion as unbelief. Revelation is the abolition of religion. . . . "Religion is . . . an affair, yea rather, *the* affair of the godless man." All religion is cut off sharply from faith. Religion is nothing but the attempt to know God by way of man's own abilities, an attempt that is unmasked by revelation as resistance to revelation and grace. It forms an enterprise of man by which he encroaches with his own means and power upon what God wills to do and does in his revelation. . . . Since natural religion is the religion of fallen man, it accounts for the normalcy of unbelief, of resistance to revelation and grace. (Berkouwer 1955, 158–59)[213]

As Berkouwer demonstrates, one need not necessarily accept Barth's radical differentiation between religion and revelation to still understand that human beings have and do continue to rebel and reject the light that God offers. In the words of John, "He came to that which was his own, but his own did not receive him" (John 1:11). So John Calvin affirmed that human beings "do not . . . apprehend God as he offers himself, but imagine him as they have fashioned him in their own presumption" (Calvin 1960, 47).[214]

There are several very important implications that can be drawn from this third major reflection about "resistance." First, any theology of conversion in evangelical missiology must begin by speaking of the miraculous work of the Holy Spirit by grace through faith in Jesus Christ. No amount of effectiveness in relation to contextualization can promise that humans will say *yes* to God. Quite the contrary. Even if—or precisely *when*—humans come to understand the gospel being offered to them—even if they understand it in very appropriate cultural, relational and social forms—humans will still say *no* to God, apart from the working of the Holy Spirit. Thus, we must listen carefully to those who have been emphasizing the matter of spiritual issues in church growth and missiology, for

---

213. Berkouwer is quoting from Karl Barth *Kirchliche Dogmatik* I,2, 327. Berkouwer also quotes from Barth, *The Epistle to the Romans*, London: Oxford U. Press, 1933, 246 as saying, "Through religion we perceive that men have rebelled against God and that their rebellion is a rebellion of slaves."

214. Calvin follows this with a series of comments on Psalms 14:1 and 53:21 to the effect that human beings, "after they have become hardened in insolent and habitual sinning, furiously repel all remembrance of God. . . . But to render their madness more detestable, David represents them as flatly denying God's existence." (1960, 48)

conversion is not promised, much less guaranteed, simply on the basis of good contextual methodology.

Second, the fact that all humans are sinful and resistant should heighten our awareness and care in relation to some contemporary emphases on spiritual warfare. Just as we see the lie in the perspective of Enlightenment humanism that all humans are good and holy, so we also need to understand the inaccuracy of presenting humanity as a neutral battle ground on which opposing spiritual forces wage their warfare. If all humans choose against God, if all humans have sinned and fallen in Adam and Eve, then humanity is not neutral. Thus mission is not simply a matter of throwing our weight toward the right side of the conflict. Instead, our mission involves proclamation in word and deed that Jesus Christ is Lord, calling all humans to radical conversion and total transformation so that, in the words of John's Gospel, "all who did receive him, to those who believed in his name, he gave the right to become children of God—children born not of natural descent, . . . but born of God" (John 1:12). We are involved in spiritual warfare. But that warfare includes transforming the human heart from death to life (which only the Holy Spirit can do), from rebellion against God to loving faithful obedience to God (Rom 7).

Thirdly the fact that "all have sinned and fall short of the glory of God" means that a biblical understanding of "resistance" is no longer a sociological term simply referring to the fact that few churches have grown among a particular people. Rather, the term now takes on a biblical meaning that "resistance" entails saying *no* to God's covenantal initiative. This is a matter of faith. God is the "self-disclosing God," using Hendrikus Berkhof's term (Berkhof 1979, 105). God is the God of the covenant, a loving God who comes to all humans and says, "I will be your God and you will be my people" (Van Engen 1989, 1996). "Resistance" is refusing the invitation that God extends. If "resistance," then, represents a negative faith response to God's initiative, this points us to the next two reflections: (d) *some humans are resistant all the time* and (e) *some humans are resistant some of the time to some things.*

D. Some humans are resistant all the time, to all missional approaches.

If "resistance" is understood biblically and theologically as humans saying *"no"* to God's gracious invitation, then to understand "resistance" more deeply we need to reexamine the Parable of the Sower (Matt 13:1–23; parallels in Mark 4:1–12, Luke 8:4–10). This parable most specifically addressed the matter of varying responses to the Word of God. As we saw earlier, this parable has been used by some to support the concept of selective targeting in evangelization. I would suggest that the matter of selective targeting is not at all what the parable is about. But the parable *is* about recognizing that, given the same gracious invitation on the part of God, different persons will respond differently.

The Parable of the Sower appears in all three synoptic gospels. Without getting into the details of the particular redaction of each gospel writer and the place and emphasis which each gives to the parable, it is enough to note here that the context of the parable is strongly missiological. All three gospels mention that the parable is told by Jesus while surrounded by large crowds, the audience of Jesus' mission (Matt 13:2). Yet the explanation of the parable is addressed to the disciples (Matt 13:10). Now although a detailed exegetical treatment of the parable is beyond the scope of this chapter, let me suggest the basic emphases that I believe are to be found in this parable. [215]

Contrary to those who would use this parable as a foundation for selective targeting of mission endeavor (renaming it the "Parable of the Soils"), I would suggest that the Parable of the Sower is in fact about the Sower, about Jesus' mission, and by extension the mission of the disciples. And as such, it is actually an explanation by Jesus of why he speaks in mysterious parables and not plainly—and why some respond positively (are receptive) and why others respond negatively (are resistant). The parable speaks of the fact that Jesus presented his message *to everyone alike*, but that some were willing to hear and others were not. The difference in soils may have something to tell us about receptivity. But if this is so, it will *not* tell us to concentrate on the good soil. That may be good farming but it is totally extraneous to the text of the parable.

The parable of the sower speaks about those who are too blind to see, too deaf to hear, whose hearts are too dull to respond (see Matt 13:14–15 where Isaiah's prophecy is mentioned which echoes Deut 29:4, and can be found in Isa 42:19, 20; Jer 5:21; and Ezek 12:2). The problem which the parable addresses is this: in view of the people's blindness, deafness, and hardness of heart, why does Jesus speak in mysterious parables and not in plain language (Matt 13:10)? The different soils are the key to the answer given (Matt 13:11). What is being presented is the "mystery" of the kingdom of God which is to be perceived by faith (as did the prophets of old, including Isaiah), not by sight (Matt 13:17). Faith is recognized in the one who "hears the word and understands it. This is the one who produces a crop . . ." (Matt 13:23, NASB). So, given the word that is being

---

215. The following section is adapted from Van Engen 1981, 356.

proclaimed by Jesus to everyone, why do some receive that word, and why do some reject it?

Here we must at least take note of the sociocultural context of the parable. We can see it in our mind's eye. There is a field, surrounded by cactus (thorns) that serves as a fence around the outer perimeter of the field. There is a path that cuts through the field where people want Luke to get from one end to the other. Over in one part of the field there is a section that, although it looks excellent on the surface, has a ledge of flat rock just six inches or so below the surface of the tilled soil. And there is part of the field that has rich loam, deep and fertile. The farmer, in the method of that day, has plowed the field with a wooden plow that only tills a few inches of topsoil. Now the farmer takes his bag of seed, slings it over his shoulder, and begins to waLuke back and forth across the field. His sowing of the wheat seed is done by reaching into the bag and then broadcasting the seed out of his hand to let it fall where it will, all over the field. Jesus' teaching and ministry was like that. In Luke's words, Jesus went about the towns and villages, preaching the gospel of the kingdom and healing (e.g., Luke 4:43; 8:1).

Given this mental picture, it is clear that the parable does not have to do with selective sowing—but with differences in reaping. If anything, the parable is a command to universal, all-inclusive, indiscriminate proclamation, knowing that the "field" (the world, or possibly a particular people group in a particular context) contains many kinds of "soils" all mixed together. The farmer's assessment is that of a critical realist. He knows that some of the seed will "bear fruit" but others will not. The farmer in the parable does not restrict his sowing to the "good ground." The farmer in the parable may not know what is good ground (since his wooden plow cannot go deep enough to find the shallow rock bottom). The path where people walk through the field is an inevitable hard spot where the scattered seed which was not planted one at a time in that day, or with modern planters, will surely fall. For the farmer to try to restrict his sowing to only "good ground" would be not only difficult but absurd, for he would have to stay a long way away from the cactus hedge, he would have to try to avoid having seed fall on the path that cuts across the field, and he would have to spend a great deal of time digging deeply under the surface to know where the stone layer is located. In order to do all of that, he would end up also neglecting much good soil.

In other words, if something is crystal clear about this parable, it is the *indiscriminate* sowing of the seed, not the selective proclamation of the gospel.

But there are four other very important lessons that I believe Jesus wanted the disciples to learn. First, the farmer sows indiscriminately, *in spite of knowing that the responses will vary*. The farmer understands his field, and he knows (in fact he expects) differences in response. Secondly, the response of the seed is not to the sower, but rather consists in growing, developing, giving fruit—it is response to the Word, to the kingdom, and to God. Thirdly, notice in Jesus explanation of the parable (Matt 13:19–23), there are a variety of agents that create heightened resistance in addition to the conditions of the field. One thing is the condition of the field (the human heart), which itself contributes to a variety of responses. But there are others in this picture. The "evil one" is here. Trouble and persecution are here. And the worries of this life and the deceitfulness of wealth are here as well. In other words, the world, the flesh, and the devil all contribute to the lack of response (that is, to "resistance") on the part of the hearers. Fourth, there is a background to this parable that deals with the God's *providence*. Paul would later say, "I planted the seed, Apollos watered it, but God has been making it grow. So neither the one who plants nor the one who waters is anything, but only God who makes things grow" (1 Cor 3:6–7). In the providence of God (who, all through the Scriptures is the one who gives the harvest of grain) the seed that falls on good ground (and the one who hears the word and understands it) "produces a crop." It is not in the seed to become "hundred, sixty or thirty times" what was sown. Rather, God, in God's mysterious, providential, loving fashion makes it grow and multiply (like the "mustard seed" in the parable that follows this one in Matthew).

This matter of other agents that exacerbate the resistance—that is, that lower the receptivity—directs us naturally to our final proposition: *some humans are resistant some of the time to some things.*

But before we move on, let me add a caveat. Please don't misunderstand me here. Although I do not believe the Parable of the Sower can be used legitimately to support selective targeting of mission, this does not mean I am opposed to selective targeting. To direct our mission resources to a specific audience at a particular time in an intentional and concerted fashion is not only good mission planning, it also demonstrates a high degree of contextual and receptor-oriented sensitivity. But there are other ways to provide biblical support for selective targeting. Some possible texts might include: Matthew 9:37–38 (workers in the harvest); Matthew 10:11–14 ("shake the dust off your feet"); Matthew 10:6 ("go to the lost sheep of Israel"); Matthew 15:24 ("only to the lost sheep of Israel"—with reference to Jesus mission). Jesus' ministry is focused on specific people and places. In John 4 he "had to go through Samaria," for example. And Paul's mission is highly targeted and specific. Selective targeting is also important if one considers *to what* a particular group of persons is resistant or receptive.

E. Some humans are resistant some of the time to some things

With the story of Abraham in Genesis 12, we are informed of God's decision to use humans agents as instruments (*missio hominum*) for God's mission (*missio Dei*) of self-disclosing, covenantal love that reaches out to humanity to reestablish the broken relationship between humans and God. God chooses Abraham so that through him all the nations of the earth will be blessed. But *missio hominum* makes things fuzzy with regard to "resistance" and "receptivity." In choosing to use human agency, God has chosen to use sinful, fallible humans with their mixed motivations, mixed methods, mixed goals, and mixed authenticity to extend God's invitation. But precisely because of such human agency, the receptor's response to God's invitation (now extended through other humans) may be less a matter of saying *yes* or *no* to the divine initiative, and be more a matter of response to the particular human instrument. There may be times, therefore, when "resistance" to God's invitation is decreased or increased on account of the human agents, the messengers of God's invitation. So when we think of the "resistance" in relation to mission theology, we must consider it not only in terms of the receptor's response to the divine initiative—but also the receptor's response to the human instrument. And we must be careful not to confuse the two. Just because there is a negative response to my particular approach or message may not necessarily mean the receptor group is "resistant" in the sense of saying *no* to God. Their negative response to my instrumentality may, in fact, be more a commentary on my own ineffectiveness, sinfulness, foreignness, or inappropriateness as a bearer of the Good News. My church or agency and I may be bad news, rather than Good News. This issue forces us to ask, *to what* may humans be "resistant?"

Roy Pointer framed this issue in two complementary questions. "When there is no (favorable) response to the preaching of the gospel," he wrote, "there are two basic questions that need to be asked. 'Is the group resistant?' and 'Is the group receptive, but we are evangelizing them wrongly?'" (Pointer 1984, 159).

Referring positively to Pointer's work on this matter, C. Peter Wagner affirmed,

> Because of the crucial need to balance tests for correct methodology over against presumed resistance, it is helpful to

distinguish, as Roy Pointer, between emic resistance and etic resistance, (Pointer 1984, 159), or to use more familiar terms *Ho Ho* general resistance and specific resistance. General (or emic) resistance is caused by factors within the group or individual we are trying to reach. In many cases there is little or nothing we can do about such resistance. But specific (or etic) resistance has to do with the individual or group doing the evangelizing. It is here that we can exert some control by changing the evangelizers or by changing the methods. If wise adjustments are made, the resistance may dissolve. (Wagner 1987, 92.)[216]

It is beyond the scope of this chapter to review the multitude of factors that church growth theory has discovered over the past sixty years as contributing to a group's resistance or receptivity to gospel proclamation. The resistance/receptivity axis consists of many complex interwoven factors that impact a group's openness (or lack thereof) to God's invitation.

Because the matter of human instrumentality affects our theology of "resistance" so deeply, let me simply make mention of four major blocks of factors affecting a group's resistance/receptivity to the gospel and briefly comment on the theological issues they represent.

- factors found within the receptor group and its culture (emic, general, intrinsic to the group—includes national and local contextual factors)
- factors found within the church and mission agents (etic, specific, extrinsic to the group—includes national and local institutional factors)
- factors involved in the way the receptor group perceives the church's witness
- spiritual factors affecting both the missionary agent and receptor group.

Some groups are resistant because of contextual factors.

One of the most helpful products of church growth research during the last sixty years has been to identify the myriad contextual (both national and local) factors that impinge on the resistance/receptivity of a particular people group. These

---

216. This is part of a chapter entitled, "Testing the Soil."

include worldview, religious, socioeconomic, political, and historical factors. There are a number of changes that can occur in the historical development of a people group that will begin to make the members of the group receptive to hearing the gospel and willing to respond positively to that which they hear. And a developed theology of the "resistant" will be very sensitive to developing an appropriate hermeneutic of the context, reading carefully the signs of the times as they impact a particular people group, and then responding to the opportunity as it presents itself.

However, besides studying and understanding the contextual factors, we need further development of a theology of contextual analysis (I mean something different here than "contextualization"). Such a theological analysis of the context would include a theology of culture that opens itself to all the elements to be found in the group's worldview that may be consistent and coherent with biblical revelation. This involves a theology of culture that reexamines the contextual factors in light of the knowledge of God that God may have placed in the context and which provide bridges for incarnational proclamation. Secondly, such reflection on the context would call for a full-blown theology of providence, where one seeks to understand what God is doing in the world in terms of drawing a group through historical and creational means from resistance to receptivity. This, however, will call, thirdly, for a careful theology of suffering, for we must never excuse oppression and suffering by subsuming it to a utilitarian view that accepts suffering because it is producing greater openness to our mission endeavors. Fourthly, a theological hermeneutic of the context of resistance would also entail a profound reexamination of the ministry of the Holy Spirit and the presence of the Church as being agents through whom God, in God's providence, may be able to call a group from resistance toward receptivity. Fifth, there is a theology of intercessory prayer involved here that calls on God, in his Providence, in the midst of the already/not yet rule of Christ the King, through the operation of the Holy Spirit, to give a particular people group a "heart of flesh rather than a heart of stone" (Ezek 11:19; 36:26).[217]

---

217. Another approach to contextualization involves examining the interrelationship of a group of followers of Jesus vis-à-vis their cultural and religious context. John Travis created a spectrum from C1 to C6 that describes these complex relationships. Travis describes this spectrum as follows:

"The C1–C6 Spectrum compares and contrasts types of "Christ-centered communities" (groups of believers in Christ) found in the Muslim world. The six types in the spectrum are differentiated by language, culture, worship forms, degree of freedom to worship with

Some groups become resistant because of factors within the church.

A second group of issues has to do with the internal or intrinsic institutional factors inside the church. First is the issue of the spirituality of the church itself. Down through the centuries, I believe the nominalism and secularization of the church itself has been one of the greatest obstacles to world evangelization—and one of the factors that I believe has contributed greatly to resistance on the part of groups outside the church. This has been the case with state churches in Europe, old-line denominations in North America, the traditional Roman Catholic hierarchy in Latin America, and the colonially ghettoized churches in Africa, for example. When the church has nothing new or different to offer a particular group, or when the church is part of the problem in oppressive contexts, I believe resistance is increased on the part of the receptor groups.

Secondly, the churches in the context may have lost their missional intention. They may have turned inward to such a degree that they have no commitment to presenting a credible gospel to a particular people group, whether that is across the street or around the world. Again, older churches in Europe and North America exhibit this loss of commitment to an alarming degree. In that case, to label a particular group "resistant," is quite inaccurate. It may be more accurate to speak of their being "ignored," with particular reference to the church's intentionality, rather than to the receptivity of the receptor group. For example, the emphasis in North American Church Growth circles in the 1980s and 1990s to plant upper middle class, white, suburban churches tended to give the impression that groups of people in the center-cities of North America were "resistant" to the gospel. Nothing could have been further from the truth—they were simply being ignored by a movement whose primary focus was been the white, Anglo-Saxon, upper middle class suburban ghetto.

---

others, and religious identity. All worship Jesus as Lord and core elements of the gospel are the same from group to group. The spectrum attempts to address the enormous diversity which exists throughout the Muslim world in terms of ethnicity, history, traditions, language, culture, and, in some cases, theology. This diversity means that myriad approaches are needed to successfully share the gospel and plant Christ-centered communities among the world's one billion followers of Islam. The purpose of the spectrum is to assist church planters and Muslim background believers to ascertain which type of Christ-centered communities may draw the most people from the target group to Christ and best fit in a given context. All of these six types are presently found in some part of the Muslim world." *Evangelical Missions Quarterly* (October 1998): 407–408. See also https://www.thepeopleofthebook.org/about/strategy/c1-c6-spectrum/.

In situations of nominalism and loss of mission vision, renewal and reformation become important keys to issues of resistance and receptivity. This has been borne out in so many instances down through the history of the church. But this is also beyond the scope of this chapter. Suffice it to say that renewal and revitalization of the church internally might be one of the most significant factors in helping a particular people group be open to saying *yes* to God. This issue is a significant one everywhere in the world today.

Thirdly, our theology of conversion may itself create resistance. As McGavran and Pickett pointed out decades ago, typical Western expectation of a particular form of conversion may create unnecessary barriers. Such expectation of conversion may include a host of cultural issues that are not intrinsic to the gospel. Thus, McGavran's axiom comes into play: "(women and) men like to become Christians without crossing (unnecessary) racial, linguistic, or class barriers" (McGavran 1970, 198). This issue is central to the Gentile mission in the book of Acts. Too often modern churches and missions have insisted on superimposing a particular kind, style or form of conversion upon those who would say *yes* to God. We need much more careful missiological work in reflecting upon a theology of conversion: individual and/or multi-individual; punctiliar, process or series of transforming moments; only vertical in relation to God or also including reconciliation to self, others and the world; only rational/mental assent to a set of propositions, or including profound experiential, participatory events. These are but a few of the questions we must ask ourselves if we are to avoid creating unnecessary resistance. During the past several decades, studies of the conversion of millennials in North America and Europe have shown that in their case, participation often comes before commitment. Folks like Eddie Gibbs and Ryan Bolger have studied this phenomenon extensively.

Fourth, the relation of the church to its surrounding culture and political structures must be carefully studied if the church is not to increase resistance. A church that insists on being strongly counter-cultural may create resistance. An example of this has been the tense and sometimes conflictive discussion about worship styles in the churches of North America and Europe.

I suspect this has been part of our difficulty in the evangelization of Japan, for instance. The insistence of the older churches in Japan on basing their theological reflection and ministry formation on German theology, coupled with their heavy use of an educational model of being church, together with their strong avoidance to interacting theologically with issues of Shinto shrines, holy places, ancestor veneration, and the world of the unseen—all these have, it would seem, contributed to the sense of foreignness of the older churches in Japan, as seen through the eyes of the Japanese people. Thus, at a time of profound religious searching, especially on the part of Japanese young people, the older churches in Japan seem isolated and out of touch—possibly increasing resistance rather than aiding receptivity.

Another example in relation to Islam, may be the church's strong insistence over the centuries that our predominant theory of atonement must derive from a form of Anselmian satisfaction theory and a forensic understanding of justification by faith, based on legal assumptions. This theological construct on the part of churches and missions—evident in evangelical missiology as well—creates a built-in difficulty for muslims to accept the gospel. Yet as I study the words of Jesus and the preaching and teaching of Paul and the first century church, I find a rather wide range of ways to present God's covenantal invitation, "I will be your God and you will be my people;" presentations that do not necessarily need a satisfaction theory of atonement to be valid forms of conversion and reconciliation.

Thus "resistance" may in fact be the result of unexamined, unresolved, and unnecessary theological and cultural issues within the church itself. Notice I say "unnecessary." There is also the "scandal of the cross," a scandal which must never be ignored or downplayed in calling sinners to repentance. But let's make sure the difficult barriers to conversion have to do with the "scandal of the cross" and not unnecessary cultural, theological or historical walls of our own making. Mission vis-à-vis the resistant should begin by examining the beam in our own eye before we try to extract the sliver in the eye of the receptor.

Some groups become resistant because of the lack of cultural and spiritual interface between the church and the receptor group.

Increased resistance may also be the product of an inappropriate cultural or spiritual interface between the church and the receptor group. Here we are dealing with neither the group as such, nor with the church only. Rather, we must examine the issues that may raise the boundary between the church and the receptor group because of the lack of an appropriate interface between them. Such lack will create unnecessary resistance.

The first element we might point to in this missiological interface has to do with the particular history of the encounter of the church with a specific people group. Everywhere in the world today, wherever the church is involved in mission, there is a historical background (some immediate, some more remote) of the receptor group's encounter with the church. We ignore this historical data to our peril. I could list hundreds of illustrations here. Obvious cases in point might be the encounter of Islam with Christianity, the conquest by Spain of the pre-Colombian peoples of Latin America, the European colonial baggage surrounding the encounter of the peoples of Africa with European churches, the story of Aleut christianization by early Russian Orthodox missionaries (compared today with Aleut encounter with the government of the United States), and the encounter of the peoples of Hawaii with early Christians, missionaries and others, and more recently the place of christianity in western capitalism as that interfaces with peoples of Eastern Europe and China. We need much more careful, repentant, self-critical and prayerful reflection on these histories if we are to understand more deeply how "resistance" may involve not so much a particular people saying "*no*" to God, but rather rejecting the way Christians have interacted with them throughout the centuries.

This may also include issues of long historical and cultural animosities that need reconciliation and redemption before gospel proclamation may take place. Some years ago, for example, I was speaking with a Brazilian missionary who in the previous eleven years had planted four churches in Paris among French Parisians. When he told me about his successful church planting I expressed great surprise, since I have always assumed the French people to be rather "resistant" to the gospel. With a wide grin of joy, the Brazilian missionary remarked, "You Americans, Caucasians, and English-speakers can't do this, but we Brazilian Portuguese-speakers can." The Tower of Babel is always with us in one way or another.

A second element of this interface between the church and its context has to do with the church's own missional intentionality in relation to a particular people. As David Liao pointed out some years ago, it may be that a people is not so much "resistant" as "neglected." Too easily we are be tempted to label a group that does not respond to our form of evangelization as "resistant," when in fact it may be the church's lack of cultural and spiritual sensitivity that has increased resistance through neglect.

In 1972 David Liao studied the situation of the Hakka Chinese in Taiwan, a people whom some had labeled, "resistant." The product of Liao's study is a marvelous case study to show that those whom some would call "resistant," may in fact simply have been *neglected* by the church. "The thesis of this book," wrote Liao, "is: Many seemingly resistant peoples in the world, like the Hakkas, are really being neglected" (Liao 1972, 15). In his introduction to the book, Donald McGavran wrote,

As the church carries out the mandate of her Lord to disciple the nations, she continually meets unresponsive peoples. As missionaries carry the good news to the two billion who have yet to believe, they often encounter indifferent or resistant populations.

Sometimes unresponsiveness is due to hardness of heart, pride, or aloofness; but more often than we like to think, it is due to neglect. The gospel has been presented to an "unresponsive" ethnic unit in the trade language, not its mother tongue. The only church its members could join was one made up of people of a different culture. The only pastors its congregations could have were those from another ethnic unit or subculture. . . .

It is a great merit of David Liao's book, *The Unresponsive: Resistant or Neglected?* that it focuses attention on this church problem, commonly found in all six continents. . . . Mr. Liao is convinced that failure of the church to grow among the Hakkas is best explained by the fact that the Hakkas have been neglected, their language has not been learned, and they have had to join Minan- or Mandarin-speaking congregations. Consequently to them "becoming Christian" has come to mean "leaving our beloved Hakka people" (Liao 1972, 7).

Liao is most thought-provoking when he deals with the issue of ancestor worship in relation to the evangelization of the Hakka and of Chinese in general. A careful, culturally appropriate, biblically faithful, and missiologically intentional theology of ancestor veneration still cries for development. In many parts of Latin America, Africa, Asia, Oceania, and even North America (among Native Americans, especially), a theology of those who have gone before us, of the "living dead," of the ancestors (whatever we may call them) is desperately needed if we are going to address one very important element of gospel proclamation that the church has essentially neglected. It is too easy to label a group "resistant" when in fact its lack of response may be due more to the church having lost its missionary vision, its commitment to gospel proclamation, or its willingness to pay the price of self-examination, repentance, and transformation that may be called for in order to be appropriate agents of God's mission in a specific context.

Thirdly, the interface between the church and a particular people group may be strongly impacted by the authenticity of the church's witness as that is perceived by a receptor group. Lesslie Newbigin, writing from a context of the church's evangelization of the post-Christian and post-Christendom West, called this the church's role of being a "hermeneutic of the gospel" for the people in the surrounding context.

In this picture we have the receptor group looking in, into the life of the church. This is centripetal, "showcase" mission, as is strongly developed in parts of Scripture, for example in Deuteronomy and the Psalms. It is the kind of mission Jesus referred to when he said, "By this everyone will know that you are my disciples, if you love one another (John 13:35).

I believe the sinfulness of the church is one of the most powerful factors creating resistance among those who are not yet Christian in North America and Europe, as well as other parts of the world. The divisiveness, the shameful ways Christians too often treat one another in the church, and the lack of authenticity on the part of the church and its leaders contributes to those outside being resistant to hearing God's loving invitation extended in word and deed. Particularly in the West, I believe the church's lack of authentic witness may be too easily excused or ignored by simply labeling those outside the church as being "resistant." Matters of spiritual renewal, revitalization, reformation, and conversion of members and leaders in Christ's church must be reexamined carefully in order to see how they may or may not be contributing to the supposed "resistance" of a particular receptor group.

Fourthly, and finally, the cultural appropriateness of the church's identity, means, and message may also affect the resistance/receptivity of a target group. In Pointer's words,

> Etic resistance (or receptivity) is determined by factors introduced by the evangelising agent. In this case the group or individuals are or would be responsive to the gospel but the methods used fail to communicate it effectively, so that no disciples are made or churches planted. Cultural distance between the missionary or church and the unevangelised group is often the cause. In many British churches there is also the self-imposed exile of the church from the people. (Pointer 1984, 159)

What Pointer called "the self-imposed exile" of the church has been termed "the distant church" by folks in Denmark, for example. In fact the church has become so removed from those whom it would evangelize—culturally, socially, relationally, structurally, liturgically distant—that the chasm created by the church makes evangelization impossible. In such a case, it is too easy to label those outside the church as being "resistant," when in fact the difficulty lies in the gulf which the church itself has created. This, I believe is what Luke seeks to convey in the story of Peter's conversion in Acts 10. In terms of the mission of Israel of that day, it was far easier to label others "unclean" than to accept the commission of God's mission for Israel's witness among the peoples surrounding it. Yet the God of Abraham, Isaac, and Jacob, the God who is worshipped by Cornelius the centurion, says to Peter, "Do not call anything impure that God has made clean" (Acts 10:15).

This need for the church's own conversion is where I think prayer movements today have much to offer us. Movements like those led by Edgardo Silvoso and others that call for all the pastors in a city to begin to pray together on a regular basis, or for church members to participate in prayer marches—these movements affect not only the spiritual climate of the context but also the transformation and renewal of the church, as well as the dynamics of the interface between the church and the people groups in the context. Maybe the "resistant" are thus because we have not prayed in such a way that the Holy Spirit may convert us to be fit instruments of gospel proclamation.

Yet we must remember what we have said earlier in relation to the Parable of the Sower. After all is said and done, even when humans in a people group may understand completely the message brought to them by a spiritually authentic and appropriate agent of God's mission—even then, some humans may (and probably will) choose to say "*no*" to God's gracious invitation in Jesus Christ through the operation of the Holy Spirit.

CONCLUSION

I want to conclude with some good news. Some months ago my oldest daughter called me to ask my advice on some issues she was facing with maintenance on her house. As I was talking with her, she suddenly exclaimed, "Dad! It's happening!"

"What," I asked, surprised.

"You really are! You really are getting smarter! It's just like you said!"

Well, I want you to know that my problem is beginning to find a remedy. I am getting smarter—and my children are getting receptive. Some years ago, my sixteen-year-old son had grave doubts about my sanity! But his sisters reassured him that there was hope for me yet, and he now also believes that I'm getting smarter.

Theological reflection with regard to the resistant? All I know is that we need desperately to examine ourselves and call on the Holy Spirit to transform us in order to make us appropriate and useful agents of God's mission in the midst of God's providential invitation to all peoples. God does not want "anyone to perish, but everyone to come to repentance" (2 Pet 3:9). Maybe you and I can mostly stay out of the way, and as our Lord Jesus Christ's love compels us, may we be transformed by the Holy Spirit, new creations, ambassadors of reconciliation, calling to a fallen world, loved by God, "We implore you on Christ's behalf, Be reconciled to God" (2 Cor 5:20). Then we will see a miracle happen: the "resistant" become "receptive"—and they say "*yes*" to God's gracious invitation.

CHAPTER 11

MISSION THEOLOGY OF MISSION PARTNERSHIPS

Taken from "Working Together Theologically in the New Millennium: Opportunities and Challenges," in Gary Corwin and Kenneth Mulholland, eds., *Working Together With God to Shape the New Millennium*. Pasadena: WCL, 2000, 82–122. Edited, and adapted in "Toward a Theology of Mission Partnerships," *Missiology*, XXIX: 1 January, 2001, 11–44. Reprinted in "Toward a Theology of Mission Partnerships," in *Intercultural Ministry: Readings on a Global Task*, Jim Lo and Boyd Johnson, eds., Indianapolis: Precedent Press, 2006, 103–24. Used by permission

THESIS

Because our oneness is grounded in Jesus Christ (and not found in corporate, organizational, administrative, financial, structural or historical unity), we are called to partner together for world evangelization, serving one another in love and humility as we participate in Christ's mission, offering to one another the unique gifts given by the Holy Spirit to our various organizations and churches (regionally and globally), until we all together grow up into the measure of the stature of the fullness of Christ (Eph 4:1–5:2).

INTRODUCTION

Some years ago, my house in California needed to be painted on the outside. So, I contracted my son, Andrew, who was then sixteen, to work for me and together we began working our way around that two-story house with stucco walls. I remember that a couple of weeks into the project I was starting to climb a ladder to prime some eaves that my son had just scraped, when he came running to the foot of the ladder.

"Dad, Dad," he exclaimed. "I just thought of something I had never thought of before!"

"What's that?" I asked, trying not to fall off the ladder in the wake of his unexpected enthusiasm.

"Dad, when two people work well together, they can accomplish more than twice what they could do working alone!"

That discovery on the part of my son was worth the whole summer. And that fact is the heart of the issue facing us in missionary cooperation.

Why should we work together in the new millennium? Why should we work together? Is it not much easier to work separately than to work together? North American mission sending during the 1980s, 1990s, and early 2000s has seen the proliferation of what I call "mom-and-pop mission shops," small, independent, often family-owned, entrepreneurial Christian agencies, mission initiatives, and NGOs. We have lived through a time of decentralization, separation, and celebration of competition and difference. All over the world we have seen the phenomenon that when persons do not like the kind of church they are attending, they simply start another one more to their liking. If they disagree with the policies of their mission agency, they start another mission.

A person, couple, family, small group, or megachurch senses the call of God to initiate a mission thrust. They gather support wherever it may be found and off they go to do their "mission." Not much time wasted on psychological testing, little effort spent on organizational orientation, no need to convince a large mission organization or denomination concerning their vision. They are called and they go: clean, quick, efficient, focused.

Those of us associated with large mission agencies or denominational mission organizations may also ask, "Why should we work together?" We all have our turf to care for, our own fundraising needs to look after in order to pay our own bills and expenses. We have our own working principles and procedures that differ from those of other organizations. We have our own corporate identity to define, our own specialization in mission that provides the basis on which we present ourselves to our supporters. We work hard to create our own structures, to define our own purpose and mission, to protect our own interests and to direct our unique vision. Each of us is trained to emphasize our own special contribution to world mission. Each of us sees our mission endeavor, the Church, and the world through the colored glasses of our own agendas.

Moreover, we seem to find it easier to trust the people in our group than those who belong to other organizations. When I was young, my mother used to repeat an old Dutch proverb that reflected her own pioneering roots in Northwest Iowa: "The whole world is crazy except you and me, and sometimes I wonder about you!" Might it also be applicable to mission partnerships?

We all have our own special geographic, continental, confessional, cultural, national, linguistic, historical and relational biases that affect the way we cooperate with others. The history of the Church and its mission is replete with examples of theological and nontheological factors of immense influence in mission partnership and cooperation. Well-meaning people deeply committed to world evangelization have found it hard to work together. Ever since Paul and Barnabas could not agree on their assessment of John Mark, dedicated disciples of Jesus have often found it necessary each to go their own way in world evangelization.

Conversely, creating partnerships takes time and energy, is initially expensive, tends to slow the participants down, and does not always yield the focused mission activity first envisioned by the partners. It runs the risk of diffusing and redirecting everyone's energies, and sometimes yields less creative mission initiatives than the partners might have demonstrated by doing mission independently.

In the words of the 1996 Evangelical Manifesto of the NAE, "We confess that although we value unity and united evangelical action, we too often do more to build our own ministries than to cooperate at making it difficult for someone in our own neighborhoods to be lost for eternity."[218]

The question is even sharper when we consider that the center of gravity of world Christianity has now shifted to the East and the South. Earlier, we noted that two-thirds of world Christianity is now to be found in the majority world. Today more full-time cross-cultural missionaries are being sent and supported by churches in Asia, Africa and Latin America than the total sent from Europe and North America. So partnership and cooperation becomes even more complex as it begins to involve multiple cultures and global relationships. The shadows of paternalism, control, bitter experiences, and power struggles raise their ugly heads when we begin to search for new forms of cooperation between those who once were the senders (and may now be the receivers) and those who once were the receivers (and may now be the senders). Former senders and receivers alike must now work as equal partners in mission endeavors with other churches and missions. Partnership in mission in the twenty-first century will involve combinations of the following.

- Church-with-church cooperation;
- Mission-with-mission partnering;
- Sending mission with receiving church;

---

218. NAE 1996, 3. It is no easy thing to define what we mean by "evangelical." Some helpful sources may be found in Van Engen 1990, 205, footnote 4.

- Sending church and receiving mission;
- Formerly receiving church, now a mission, partnering to serve a new receiving church or mission;
- Multicultural teams that draw support from, and are accountable to, persons, churches or mission agencies all over the globe;
- Local congregations who send their own missionaries, cooperating with older or newer receiving churches or mission agencies; and
- Global, multilateral cooperative mission endeavors.

It will not be easy to work together in the twenty-first century. So why should we? In this chapter I would like to suggest four reasons why we need to partner together in world evangelization.

Why work together?

- Because together we belong to Jesus Christ.
- Because together we belong to each other as members of the global body of Jesus Christ.
- Because together we each exercise our spirit-given gifts in ministry as we participate in Christ's mission.
- Because we grow together as together we grow into the fullness of the stature of Jesus Christ.

Why work together? So that the world may believe that Jesus is the Christ (John 17: 21). Together we can evangelize the world in our generation.[219] I

---

219. The "Watchword" was popularized by John R. Mott and others in the Student Volunteer Movement toward the end of the nineteenth century. In 1900 John R. Mott published a book with the title, *The Evangelization of the World in This Generation.* Gerald Anderson quotes Mott's explanation of his understanding of the "watchword." "'The watchword,' [Mott] said, 'means the giving to all men an adequate opportunity of knowing Jesus Christ as their Saviour and of becoming His real disciples.' This is what Christ implied in the Great Commission. It means preaching the gospel to those who are now living; it does not mean the conversion of the world, according to Mott" (Anderson 1988, 382).

The "watchword" was still a strong motivational element of the missiology of Edinburgh, 1910, the springboard of much partnership and cooperation among churches and mission agencies during the 20th Century. See, e.g., Stephen Neill 1964, 332; William Richey Hogg 1952; and World Missionary Conference, 1910. 1910.

Neill comments, "The slogan was based on an unexceptional theological principle—that each generation of Christians bears responsibility for the contemporary generation of non-Christians in the world, and that it is the business of each such generation of Christians to see to it, as far as lies within its power, that the Gospel is clearly preached to every single non-Christian in the same generation. This is a universal and permanent obligation; it applies

have organized this chapter around four themes: *together, working, diversity,* and *theology.*[220] I want to draw our reflection from a rereading of Ephesians 4:1–5:2. In each section I will review a theme from Ephesians 4, then reflect on lessons learned during the twentieth century that could help us in the next millennium. We work together as we follow (and colabor with) Jesus Christ in mission in God's world in the power of the Holy Spirit. In the words of the Manila Manifesto: "Christ calls the whole church to take the whole gospel to the whole world."[221]

WE WORK TOGETHER BECAUSE TOGETHER WE BELONG TO JESUS CHRIST: THE MOTIVATION FOR MISSIONAL PARTNERSHIPS

Why should we partner together? *Because together we belong to Jesus Christ.* This is our most fundamental motivation for mission partnerships.

A.   The Biblical Text

An essential source for a biblical theology of the Church's mission is found in Paul's letter to the Ephesians. A careful study of Ephesians offers an overview of the missionary nature of the Church. Paul saw the Church as an organism that should continually grow in the missional expression of its essential nature. And, although I do not have space here to develop all the relevant missional themes found in Ephesians, I do want to bring out four of those found in Ephesians chapter 4. Although Paul uses at least fifteen different word pictures or images to portray the

---

to Christian witness both within what is commonly called Christendom and beyond it. If the principle is to be rejected, the New Testament must first be rewritten" (1964, 332).

220. There are many different meanings of "unity." The New Delhi Assembly of the World Council of Churches explored the possible meanings of unity. See *Evanston to New Delhi: 1954–1961* (Geneva: WCC, 1961); W.A . Visser 't Hooft, ed., *The New Delhi Report* (Geneva: WCC, 1961), 116–135. The Conciliar Movement's preoccupation with "visible" unity moved the discussion in the WCC in the wrong directions that overemphasized structural and organizational uniformity and eventually led to loosing both church and mission. See chapter 8, "Conciliar Mission Theology," 145-56 from Van Engen, *Mission on the Way*, 1996.

221. "Calling the Whole Church to take the Whole Gospel to the Whole World" was one of the two themes (together with "Proclaim Christ Until He Comes") of the Lausanne Movement's meeting in July, 1989, in Manila, Philippines. Three outstanding examples of statements that have encouraged and shaped evangelical approaches to cooperation and partnership are the 1974 Lausanne Covenant, the 1989 Manila Manifesto, and the 1996 NAE Evangelical Manifesto.

Church in Ephesians, yet the theme that grounds all others is the fact that when Paul speaks of the Church he uses only the singular—there is only *one Church*—no more!

The apostle Paul says, "There is one body and one Spirit, just as you were called to one hope when you were called; one Lord, one faith, one baptism; one God and Father of all, who is over all and through all and in all" (Eph 4:4–6). We do not confess "holy catholic church*es*," or "famil*ies* of God": or "peopl*es* of God" or "bod*ies* of Christ" or "New Israel*s.*" In the biblical view of the church the plural only refers to the geographic location of local congregations, not the essential being of the Church. In its essence there is only one Church. In Ephesians *ekklesia* appears only in the singular.[222]

So we must begin where Paul starts. Recognizing that we are all "prisoners for the Lord" who beg, beseech, urge (Παρακαλώ) churches and missions alike to "live a life worthy of the calling (we) have received."[223] Christ's calling, then, entails a life of a "new self, created to be like God" (Eph 4:24). This new missionary way of life includes understanding that we belong *together* in one Body under one Head, Jesus Christ.

This entails the cultivation of specific attitudes with which we perceive ourselves and others (*working*); includes the exercise of our gifts in mission and ministry (*diversity*), and seeks to grow as one Body into the stature of its Head, Jesus Christ (*theology*).

This calling is not one we predetermine or decide upon by ourselves. Rather, it is a calling extended to us by our Head, Jesus Christ. Our oneness in Jesus Christ (Eph 4:5,6,13) is not predicated on our being able to work easily together. Nor that we like each other—although, hopefully, we do! Nor does it depend upon our agreeing with one another in all perspectives, in all propositions, dotting every "i" and crossing every "t" in the same way.

Our oneness is drawn from the singleness of our one Savior and Lord. It is Christ's calling. There is no substitute for this foundational motivation for working together. We work together because we are servants of the same Lord who want to live a life worthy of the calling our Lord has extended to us all. There is an indispensable and irreplaceable link between our mission and our discipleship in Jesus

222. Van Engen 1991, 49. See also Karl Barth *Church Dogmatics* 4.1.

223. Or in the language of 2 Cor 5:14, Christ's love compels us to become ambassadors of reconciliation. As persons who have been transformed in and through the mission of Jesus Christ (2 Cor 5:11–21), we are "God's coworkers" (2 Cor 6:1).

Christ. This was the original concept expressed by Cyprian in the well-known phrase, *"extra ecclesiam nulla salus."* As Carl Braaten has said,

> The entire theme of ministry in the New Testament is bound to the person of Jesus Christ as the decisive eschatological event of God's reconciling Word. Christ alone is the unity in, with, and under the pluriformity of ministries that arose in primitive Christianity. Ministry is Christocentric in all the New Testament writings. . . . If there is any authority in the church, that authority can be none other than Jesus Christ, as the authority is mediated through those whom he commissioned to be his ambassadors.[224]

"The work of Jesus the Messiah," writes Wilbert Shenk, "embodies the *missio Dei*. This is normative for all mission and must determine the character, strategy, and stance of mission in our contemporary world. This allows for neither triumphalism nor defeatism. It calls for missionary witness that embraces the fullness of the gospel in response to the times in which we live."[225]

---

224. Braaten 1985, 123–24.

225. Wilbert Shenk 1993, "Contents," Chapter 1. Beginning at the Willingen (1952) conference of the IMC, affirmed at the Mexico City conference of the newly formed Commission on World Mission and Evangelism, and popularized by Georg Vicedom's 1965 book, *The Mission of God*, the concept of missio Dei has represented a mixed blessing. On the one hand, it has helped missiology to stress the fact that "mission is not primarily an activity of the church, but an attribute of God. God is a missionary God" (Bosch 1991, 390).

However, as Hoedemaker points out, "In the course of the years the flag missio Dei has been flown on ships carrying a broad range of cargoes . . ." (Hoedemaker 1995, 164). So James Scherer says, "In the decade of the 1960s missio Dei was to become the plaything of armchair theologians with little more than an academic interest in the practical mission of the church but with a considerable penchant for theological speculation and mischief making" (1993, 85). Given these cautions, however, Bosch still felt the concept could be helpful. "On the other hand, it cannot be denied that the missio Dei notion has helped to articulate the conviction that neither the church nor any other human agent can ever be considered the author or bearer of mission. Mission is, primarily and ultimately, the work of the Triune God, Creator, Redeemer and Sanctifier, for the sake of the world. Mission has its origin in the heart of God. God is the fountain of sending love. This is the deepest source of mission. It is impossible to penetrate deeper still; there is mission because God loves people" (1991, 392). See Georg Vicedom 1965; D. Bosch 1980, 239–44; Arthur Glasser 1983, 90–99; D. Bosch 1991, 370; 389–93; James Scherer 1993, 82–88; L. A . Hoedemaker 1995, 162–66.

So Paul begins by reminding us that the calling is the Lord's, in whose service and for whose sake he is willing even to be a prisoner. In the next breath Paul echoes the Christologies of John 1 and Colossians 1, and draws from the cosmic Christology in Ephesians chapter 1, whereby Christ is said to "fill everything in every way," (1:19–23). Paul affirms a trinitarian perspective of oneness: "There is one body and one Spirit—just as you were called to one hope when you were called—one Lord, one faith, one baptism; one God and Father of all, who is over all and through all and in all" (Eph 4:4–6).[226]

We are *together* because we are together *in Jesus Christ*. The biblical reality is this: it is

- Christ's world, not ours (context of mission);
- Christ's church, not ours (structures of mission);
- Christ's mission, not ours (motivation for mission);
- Christ's yoke and action, not ours (means of mission by the Holy Spirit);
- Christ's leading and direction, not ours (goals of mission);
- And Christ's calling and selection; we do so only secondarily (agents of mission).

We are not passive agents in all this—but neither do we determine, control, or circumscribe Christ's mission. We all know this, don't we? Why then do we so often act in our churches and mission agencies as if this were not so?

B. Missiological Concerns

Affirming the oneness of Church and mission in Jesus Christ creates as many questions as answers. In the second part of each of the four sections of my presentation, I want to draw briefly from an example in mission history during the twentieth century of what that point does *not* imply, then suggest what it *could mean* for mission partnerships in the next millennium.

What our oneness does not mean.

This oneness does not necessarily mean structural or organizational unity. Mission history demonstrates that affirming our oneness in Christ does not in itself necessarily signify that such unity must take structural or organizational form. A prime example of making this leap was the movement in 1961 at the New Delhi Assembly of the World Council of Churches (WCC), when the International Missionary Council (IMC) was integrated into the WCC. This was a

---

226. See also Carl Braaten 1990.

very controversial development, with strong passion on both sides of the issue. What Max Warren has called a "preoccupation with structures" ruled the day, and the IMC was integrated into the WCC because there were those who felt that they needed to demonstrate the unity of mission and church in a structural and organizational way. Warren observes,

> Structural changes may well be necessary because change is necessary, and some structures inhibit change. But there is no axiomatic increase in spiritual vitality simply because necessary changes have been defined by new structures.
>
> Some elementary awareness of this fact might serve to curb the contemporary passion for structural change which too easily becomes an escape from obedience to more urgent demands: as, for instance, actual obedience to the Missionary Commission.[227]

One of the results of the integration of the IMC into the WCC was that a significant number of evangelicals left the WCC and became active in the evangelical movement later represented by such major gatherings as Wheaton, 1966; Berlin, 1966; Lausanne, 1974; Pattaya, 1980; Manila, 1989; GCOWE in Seoul, 1994; and Capetown, 2010.

A second result of "Integration" took thirty years to become evident. The integration of the IMC into the WCC eventually led to the loss of a commitment to biblical mission on the part of the WCC and the near disappearance of the emphases formerly associated with the IMC.[228] Stephen Neill's dictum, "When everything is mission, nothing is mission," was borne out historically in the case of the integration of the IMC into the WCC.[229]

A third result of the enthusiasm regarding structural unity led to the euphoria in WCC and NCCC circles in the 1960s regarding the "Missionary Structures of

---

227. Warren 1978, 199.

228. See Van Engen, "Conciliar Mission Theology, 1930's–1990s," in Van Engen, *Mission on the Way*, 1996, 145–56. The "integration" of the IMC into the WCC provides a fascinating case study of structural unification—one that is very complex, and has a number of possible interpretations. See, e.g., Paul Pierson 2000, 300–303; C. Henry 1967, 86; Max Warren 1974, 156–58; 1978; David Bosch 1978, 55; 1980, 187–88; O. Costas 1982, 36; D. Bosch 1991, 457–61; Van Engen, *Mission on the Way*, 1996, 132–33.

229. See Stephen Neill. *Creative Tension*, London: Edinburgh House, 1959, 81 in Johannes Blauw, *The Missionary Nature of the Church*, Grand Rapids: Eerdmans, 1962, 109.

the Congregation."[230] The enthusiasm over structural unity in mission, however, was never translated into missional action that brought persons to new faith in Jesus Christ and new membership in Christ's church. Unfortunately, the "Missionary Structures of the Congregation" movement ended up following J. C. Hoekendijk's mistaken pessimism about the church and unwarranted optimism concerning *The Church Inside Out*, entailing a secularized ecclesial presence in the world. If the conciliar movement had followed Johannes Blauw's lead in *The Missionary Nature of the Church*, (a work he published around the same time as Hoekendijk's writings), the results would have been very different. In its early years "The Gospel and Our Culture" network in the U.S. began to repeat the same mistakes inherent in "the missionary structures of the congregation," though substantial correction and redirection was offered later by Darrell Guder.[231]

These issues and others stimulated cautions like the following from W. Harold Fuller.

> A church-centric position is usually accompanied by a strong church union attitude, which can overshadow evangelism. All Christians should be concerned about sectarianism and unnecessary divisions. Some see disunity as an obstacle to witness. However, if the goal of organizational union is put ahead of witness, it may be self-defeating. Union may demand compromise that hinders witness. Lack of church union can be used as an excuse for not witnessing. . . . The central force of missions for (conservative evangelicals) is not ecumenism but a personal witness of Jesus Christ as Savior and Lord."[232]

We need to be committed to giving visible expression to our oneness—but that does not necessarily entail structural or organizational unity. New structures may be needed to meet new challenges, but they do not of themselves bring transformation nor stimulate new mission endeavors. As Eddie Gibbs has said, "When denominations (and mission agencies) are in desperate need of renewal, they will restructure."[233]

---

230. See WCC 1968, 16ff, 69ff; Van Engen 1981, 300–23.

231. See Darrell Guder, ed., 1998, chapters 1, 8, 9. It is interesting to compare this with the earlier emphases in Hunsberger and Van Gelder, eds., 1996.

232. Fuller 1980, 74–75.

233. Personal conversation with the author. See Eddie Gibbs 1994, 101–9.

What this oneness could mean

Our oneness in Jesus Christ means that the gospel is for everyone. A Christological view of Church and mission implies the universality of the gospel. Because Jesus Christ is Lord of all, because Jesus Christ gave His life for all, the Good News of salvation in Jesus is for the whole inhabited earth. As Lamin Sanneh has said, the gospel is "infinitely translatable."[234] It is not the property or right of one group—it is an offer open to all. This does not suggest pluralism or inclusivism in terms of salvation. Rather, as I have shown in *Mission on the Way*, a biblical approach to mission among the religions of the world entails a perspective that is at once "faith-particularist, culturally pluralist, and ecclesiologically inclusivist."[235]

It means that the gospel is to be offered to all those who yet do not know Jesus Christ, to folks from every tribe, tongue, family, people and nation. This is the universality of the Church that by definition makes the Church *God's Missionary People*.[236] Thus, for Paul, it was not optional that he was called "to preach to the Gentiles the boundless riches of Christ, and to make plain to everyone the administration of this mystery" (Eph 3:8–9). When Christians and churches begin to lose their global mission commitment and involvement, they are on a path to becoming only shadows of themselves—they are no longer fully the Church that Jesus Christ intends them to be. Mission motivation derives from our discipleship in Jesus Christ. Thus the Apostle Paul said in 2 Corinthians 5:14, "Christ's love compels us"—that together we may be Christ's ambassadors of reconciliation.

The greatest harm to the gospel is when we say we obey the same Lord and believe the same gospel but we compete, contradict and conflict with one another in our witness to those who are not yet disciples of Jesus Christ. This brings us to our second word: "Working."

WE WORK TOGETHER BECAUSE TOGETHER WE MAKE UP THE BODY OF JESUS CHRIST: THE MEANS FOR MISSIONAL PARTNERSHIPS

We normally think of Ephesians 4 as one of the primary passages having to do with the gifts of the Holy Spirit, which it is. And we will consider that in the next part. But a closer examination of the chapter shows us that Paul gives even more

---

234. Sanneh 1989.

235. Van Engen, *Mission on the Way*, 1996, 169–87.

236. Van Engen, *God's Missionary People*, 1991.

emphasis to the attitudes with which Christians are to treat one another. The lists here echo the "fruit of the Spirit" as found in Galatians 5. Paul offers two other similar lists of virtues in 2 Corinthians 6:6 and Colossians 3:12–15. Applied to mission partnerships, these attitudes are profoundly practical suggestions on Paul's part as to how we may work together. They are the means by which we can partner with one another in mission. We've heard them all before. But listen to them again—this time, thinking about what it might be like to experience these in the context of mission partnerships. We are all "prisoners of the Lord." Therefore, we live a life worthy of our calling when we treat each other in this way.

C. The Biblical Text

Paul wrote the Ephesian letter probably with an assumption that the letter would be circulated to a number of other churches in the region. The second-person pronouns in this letter are all plural. In the southeastern part of the United States, we would say, "y'all." So he challenged all the believers with the following words.

> Be completely humble and gentle; be patient, bearing with one another in love. Make every effort to keep the unity of the Spirit through the bond of peace. . . .
>
> You must no longer live as the Gentiles do, in the futility of their thinking. . . . You were taught, with regard to your former way of life, to put off your old self, which is being corrupted by its deceitful desires; to be made new in the attitude of your minds; and to put on the new self, created to be like God in true righteousness and holiness. Therefore each of you must put off falsehood and speak truthfully to your neighbor, for we are all members of one body. In your anger do not sin. . . .
>
> Do not let any unwholesome talk come out of your mouths, but only what is helpful for building others up according to their needs, that it may benefit those who listen. And do not grieve the Holy Spirit of God, with whom you were sealed for the day of redemption. Get rid of all bitterness, rage and anger, brawling and slander, along with every form of malice. Be kind and compassionate to one another, forgiving each other, just as in Christ God forgave you.

> Follow God's example, therefore, as dearly loved children
> and live a life of love, just as Christ loved us and gave himself up
> for us as a fragrant offering and sacrifice to God. (Eph 4:2–5:2)

Let me make three brief observations. First, we are in fact not the ones who work in mission. The Holy Spirit works in mission—and works through us. Therefore, if we exhibit inappropriate attitudes and destructive interpersonal relationships, we "grieve the Holy Spirit" who is the One carrying out the work of mission. This pneumatological instrumentality of mission was recognized very early by the Jerusalem church, as we see in Acts 12 and Acts 15. Because Christ's mission is wrapped in the presence and power of the Holy Spirit, our interpersonal relationships have a profound effect on our spirituality—personally and corporately—and ultimately they affect our mission.

This is consistent with Jesus' words to his disciples when he cautioned them about their interpersonal relationships as they participated in his mission. "You know that the rulers of the Gentiles lord it over them, and their high officials exercise authority over them. Not so with you. Instead, whoever wants to become great among you must be your servant, and whoever wants to be first must be your slave—just as the Son of Man did not come to be served, but to serve and to give his life as a ransom for many." (Matt 20:25–28). In other words, we must exercise the gifts of the Holy Spirit only in an atmosphere permeated by the fruit of the Holy Spirit.

Secondly, although we customarily think of this passage in terms of a local congregation and its members, it is instructive to apply it to the corporate cultures of our mission organizations. What does this passage have to tell us when we let it become a beacon shining into the inner workings and relationships of our mission organizations and denominational mission structures? I believe Paul is signaling here that the internal life of our Christian organizations must be consistent with our missional goals. We cannot say we are a mission agency dedicated to compassion and love if internally our mission organization is not permeated by grace, love, forgiveness and compassion through the Holy Spirit. We cannot bring Good News if we ourselves are the bad news.

Thirdly, the Body of Christ is a global Body. Thus, the attitudes mentioned by Paul become imperatives (and tests of authenticity) for the way in which we should treat each other globally—between East and West, between North and South, between sending agency or church and receiving agency or church. The attitudes Paul emphasizes are the aroma that folks should smell, the taste they should get, when they become involved in our mission structures and partnerships. In our missionary cooperation we cannot afford to be only goal- and production-oriented. Our partnerships, our interpersonal and interorganizational relationships must be consistent with the stated goals of our mission cooperation. When this is not so, our entire mission enterprise is compromised both internally and spiritually as well as externally and proclamationally.

Our missional spirituality, then, seems to be affected more deeply by what comes from our hearts than from those among whom we carry out our mission. Like a duck that does not get wet in water, like an earthworm that does not get dirty in the mud, so our spirituality is not contaminated so much by what comes to us from outside, nor so much by those with whom we are associated. Rather, we are contaminated by what comes from our own hearts (the works of the flesh of Galatians 5). So Jesus could carry out his mission among sinners, yet be the sinless Son of God. This seems to be what Jesus was referring to when he said, "What goes into someone's mouth does not defile them, but what comes out of their mouth, that is what defiles them (Matt 15:11).

Similarly, at least in the context of Ephesians 4, separation, keeping our doctrine pure, does not seem to be as foundational or essential a virtue as is living "a way of love" (Eph 5:2). "Be completely humble and gentle; be patient, bearing with one another in love" (Eph 4:2). "Do not be yoked together with unbelievers" is used by Paul in 2 Cor 6:14 to refer to the relationships of Christians with those who are not Christian—the passage has little or nothing to do with our relationships between and among believers. And even this does not preclude our participation in Christ's mission among and to those who are not yet Christian. Otherwise, the proclamation of the gospel to the Gentiles would have been impossible for the early Christians. (See also Luke 6:45; Matt 12:34; Acts 10:14–15; James 3:6.)

D. Missiological Concerns

What implications might we draw, then, for working together in the new millennium? I will briefly mention what I believe it does not mean, and then what it could mean.

What these attitudes do not mean.

The attitudes of working together in mission partnerships which Paul called for in Ephesians 4 do not necessarily mean we create comity agreements in mission. One of the ways the missionary community attempted to cooperate in mission was through creating comity agreements. Especially prevalent around the turn of the century, American mission agencies (most mainline denominations) sought to divide up the territories of various two-thirds world countries so that Western missions would not be stumbling all over each other in their mission endeavors. These literally "gentlemen's agreements" (mostly created by men) were primarily motivated by a desire to display an appreciation for each other and a respect for each other's mission enterprises. Many comity agreements seem to have been well-intentioned attempts to avoid duplication and reduce the appearance of competition. However, in the long run they have had mixed results. The mission gathering of Panama 1916 is a good illustration of these dynamics. That is discussed elsewhere in this book.

An interesting case in point in Latin America was the situation created by the "Plan of Cincinnati" in relation to U.S. mainline Protestant missionary work in Mexico. In 1914, with folks still experiencing the euphoria of the great missionary conference of Edinburgh, 1910, eight denominations gathered in Cincinnati to work out a comity agreement with regard to their work in Mexico.[237] My impression from the documentation about this meeting is that there were no Mexican leaders present. The result of the meeting, the "Plan of Cincinnati," entailed moving almost all related missionary personnel from one area in Mexico to another, since one area would no longer be Presbyterian, for example, but would become Methodist, another would no longer be Congregational, but Presbyterian, and so forth. There was to be a united seminary and a united publishing house.

Even today, Mexican church leaders call this plan the "Plan of Assassination," playing on the Spanish words of "Cincinnati" and "Asesinato." The results of this plan were very detrimental for the evangelization of Mexico by mainline Protestant missions, destructive of interchurch relations particularly in Mexico, and to this day negatively impacting US-Mexico mission-church relations at least in the National Presbyterian Church.[238] The shadow of the "Plan of Cincinnati" was still very real in the late 1970s when I was personally involved in negotiating a new umbrella partnership document between my denomination, the Reformed

---

237. The Presbyterian Church (South), the Presbyterian Church (North), the Congregational Church, the Methodist Episcopal Church (South), the Methodist Episcopal Church (North), the Disciples of Christ, the Friends Church, and the Associated and Reformed Presbyterian Church.

238. See Saúl Tijerina Gonzalez, ed., *1872–1972 Centenario: Iglesia Nacional Presbiteriana de México.* Monterrey: Comité Pro-Centenario, 1973, 154–58.

Church in America, and leaders in the National Presbyterian Church of Mexico. Based on my experience, I do not believe "oneness" should necessarily entail comity agreements as we have known them in the past.

Comity agreements tended to create divisions and fragmentation of witness in Latin America, ended up legitimating tribal hatred and strife in Africa, and atomized the church throughout Asia. In Africa, comity agreements have resulted in the churches too often using denominational loyalties and ecclesiastical structures mostly to divide various groups from each other within their own countries rather than bringing them together as positive contributors to the wholeness of their nation.

At times, comity agreements have gone a step further and propelled churches to unite structurally and organizationally. This was the case, for example, in India and Japan. However, all over the world united churches seem to spend more time trying to hold themselves together organizationally and structurally in their internal life than witnessing together of the gospel to those who were not yet Christian in their midst.

History does not support the assumption that comity agreements or church unification increased the participation and innovation in mission on the part of the participants. Nor did it necessarily multiply the number of those who were presented with understandable and contextually appropriate communication of the gospel.

And yet, we must hasten to affirm another equally important fact. The cacophony of conflicting and competing claims on the part of divided churches and mission agencies is no longer a luxury the Church of Jesus Christ can afford in this millennium. So we need to keep looking for ways to encourage one another to exhibit the attitudes that Paul commends to us in our internal organizational life and out interorganizational partnerships. This points us to a brief suggestion of what "working together" might mean.

What these attitudes could mean.

As we face this new millennium, Paul's challenge in Ephesians 4 calls us to consider in "humility, gentleness and patience," that each of us as churches and organizations belong to each other as part of the universal, global, people of God. This means that we need to rethink how we participate together in the universality of the Church. What does it mean for the Church to be inherently "ecumenical?" Although some of us here might wish to avoid any use of the word "ecumenical,"

I would suggest that we might want to consider resurrecting the original sense of the word.

The original meaning was not because a conference or gathering represented various Christian traditions, much less that it represented different religious faiths, as it is sometimes used today. Although there are a number of uses of the term "ecumenical," the most basic has to do with "the whole inhabited earth," and with the Church's mission that is directed to the whole earth and the whole human race. Thus the Manila Manifesto stated, "We affirm that God is calling the whole church to take the whole gospel to the whole world" (Affirmation # 21). This was the original meaning of the term when it was used at the turn of the century. W. Richey Hogg wrote that the first time this was used in the official title of a conference was at the Ecumenical Missionary Conference held in New York in April–May, 1900. "'Ecumenical' was used . . . not because the conference represented every branch of the Christian church, but 'because the plan of campaign which it proposes covers the whole area of the inhabited globe.'"[239]

> [This use of the term ecumenical refers to a basic] notion of the Church-in-mission in the world. [It] refers to something which might be called the "worldwideness" of the scope of the "ecumenical" Church-in-mission. It is the worldwide scope of the universal Church-in-mission which calls upon all churches and Christians to be in relationship and cooperation for the sake of the task which is worldwide and too large for any one church. It is the worldwideness of the One Church which mandates the need for all churches to strive for visible, tangible unity. Kenneth Grubb spoke of this worldwide sense of "ecumenical." "But the true nature of the Church is supranatural and ecumenical," [Grubb said]. Its very existence is a rebuke to the overweening pretensions of exaggerated nationalism whether in East or in West. It should be the glory, rather than the reluctance, of a church to enter into relations of mutual aid with other churches, without reference to nationality as a finally determining factor.[240]

---

239. Hogg 1952, 45.

240. Van Engen 1981, 380. The quotation from Kenneth Grubb is taken from Roland Allen 1962, vii–viii.

This use of the term ecumenical is related to its original meaning in Hellenistic and then in New Testament thought. Gerard Kittel tells us that, "The word is fairly common in the New Testament. . . . *oikoumé* derives from current Hellenistic usage. . . . The reference is simply to the glad message which is for all nations and the whole earth (in reference to Mk. 13:10).[241]

John Mackay traced the early use of the word ecumenical in relation to the mission of the church. Mackay pointed out that the term

> originated as a geographic term, which in both Greek and Roman civilizations took on political and cultural significance. The Greek noun '*oikouméne*' means literally the 'inhabited earth.' The adjective '*oikoumenikos*,' from which 'ecumenical' is directly derived, means 'that which has to do, or is coextensive, with the inhabited earth.' . . . In the religious history of [humankind], the only force that has created the '*oikoumene*' which has been 'ecumenical' in a dynamic sense, has been the Gospel of Christ.[242]

After comparing the term's use in the "Ecumenical Missionary Conference" in 1900, Mackay offered a definition of the term that was adopted by the Central Committee of the WCC in 1951, after Mackay apparently objected to restricting the term to a sense of organic unity only. The definition reflects the same global perspective we mentioned above. "We would especially draw attention to the recent confusion in the use of the word 'ecumenical.' It is important to insist that the word, which comes from the Greek word for the whole inhabited earth, is properly used to describe everything that related to the whole task of the whole church to bring the Gospel to the whole world."[243]

This global view of "ecumenical" was supported by Hans Küng in his definitive volume on *The Church.* Küng related the catholicity of the Church to its sense of being essentially missionary, as "referring to the whole world; it was to serve the world through its proclamation of the Gospel, 'Go into all the world and preach the Gospel to the whole of creation' (Mark 16:15), to 'all nations' (Matt 28:19), as 'witnesses . . . to the end of the earth' (Acts 1:8), 'until the end of the world' (Matt 28:20) . . . We can see that from its very origins and by its very nature the Church is worldwide, thinking and acting with reference to the world, to the whole

---

241. Kittell and Friedrich, eds, 1964–1976, 158–59.

242. Mackay 1963, 8.

243. Mackay 1963, 16.

inhabited earth, the *oikoumene*. This universality can therefore be expressed in the word 'ecumenical,' concerning the whole inhabited earth."[244]

The term should be recaptured and used in its original meaning—to refer to the vision of the whole church carrying the whole gospel to the whole inhabited earth. If the term is used to refer to "the whole inhabited earth" and to the universality of the Church and its mission, then it fits naturally as an adjective modifying the "ecumenical" nature of the global evangelical movement, as David Bosch pointed out in 1980. Bosch spoke then about an evangelical theology and activity in mission that is "ecumenical" in the broader sense of the term, as having to do with the whole inhabited earth. He pointed to the Wheaton Declaration (1966), the Frankfurt Declaration (1970), the Berlin Declaration on True and False Ecumenicity (1974), and the International Congress on World Evangelization in Lausanne, Switzerland (1974) as illustrative of this global orientation.[245]

We could add, among a multitude of others, the Urbana mission conferences of the Foreign Missions Fellowship of InterVarsity Christian Fellowship; the Billy Graham evangelistic ministries and crusades; the Consultation on World Evangelization at Pattaya, Thailand in 1980; the Congress on Frontier Missions held in Edinburgh in 1980; the Lausanne II gathering in Manila in 1989; the Lausanne Movement itself; the AD 2000 and Beyond Movement; Lausanne III in Capetown in 2010; the World Evangelical Fellowship; the United Bible Societies; Wycliffe Bible Translators; the Overseas Missionary Fellowship; Youth With a Mission; Missionary Aviation Fellowship; World Vision; and the Third World Mission Association that met in Kyoto, Japan, in October, 1999. These and many others are examples of a global evangelical *oikoumene*, an evangelical ecumenical movement that has changed the face of world Christianity and world mission, an evangelical ecumenism that represents the global commitment of world Christians to bring the whole gospel to the whole world.

Once we see ourselves in this light, we can begin to understand that we are the universal Church of Jesus Christ, the global Koinonia, the missionary fellowship of the disciples of Jesus Christ, commissioned to participate in Christ's mission to the whole world.[246] This means we are fully the disciples of Jesus Christ only as we live out our faith in the midst of the World Church. There is an increasing

---

244. Küng 1967, 302–3.

245. See D. Bosch 1980, 181, 193; C. F. Henry and W.W. Mooneyham, eds., 1967; F. J. Verstraelen et al, eds., 1995, 6, 157; D. Bosch 1991, 457–67.

246. See Van Engen, *God's Missionary People*, 1991, 90–92.

myopia of North American Christians with reference to the rest of the world, and the rising emphasis on mission in our back yards. Commendable as that may be, when these are set over against global mission involvement they become counterproductive emphases that contradict the very nature of the gospel and of the Church. All disciples of Jesus Christ must live out their faith in participation with the Church that surrounds the globe. To be "worthy of our calling" is to be totally dedicated to being World Christians. American evangelicalism will only be true to its Lord as it participates on a global scale with the Church of Christ that surrounds the "oecumene," the whole inhabited earth. In this sense, to be "American" or "Western" (or Dutch, or Mexican—to pick on myself here) is to sell one's birthright. In this new millennium we must all learn to be first and foremost world Christians, disciples of the one Lord whose one Body circles the globe.[247]

One way we can do this is by a deep awareness and appreciation of one another's gifts for ministry, perceived globally. This brings us to our third word: diversity.

WE WORK TOGETHER BECAUSE TOGETHER WE EACH EXERCISE OUR SPIRIT-GIVEN GIFTS IN MINISTRY AS WE PARTICIPATE IN CHRIST'S MISSION: THE AGENCY OF MISSIONAL PARTNERSHIPS

In this third section I want to deal with the concept of diversity not so much in terms of a plurality of faiths, or a multiplicity of faith interpretations, but rather in terms of a variety of ministries, as Paul does in Ephesians 4.

A. The Biblical Text

Jesus Christ who fills the whole universe has given gifts: apostles, prophets, evangelists, pastors, and teachers. Paul's list of gifts here is only illustrative, and we know it is to be seen in conjunction with the lists at least in Romans 12, 1 Corinthians 12, and 2 Peter 3.

One of the major themes of our passage has to do with the juxtaposition of the concepts of "one," "all" and "fulness" with the repetition here of the word "some." "We all (will) reach unity in the faith" (Eph 4:13) as we exercise our gifts: some as apostles, some as prophets, some as evangelists, and so on. The one Body of Christ

---

247. See Costas 1988, 162–72.

is built up as each participates through the exercise of their gifts: "some" in one way, "some" in another way.

Now all this is familiar to us. But customarily we associate the gifts of the Holy Spirit in this passage with individual persons as they live out their ministries in the context of a local congregation. However, given the global emphasis in all of Ephesians and in the rest of this chapter, is it not legitimate also to apply Paul's concept of gifts here to the world church? In that case, the passage would be telling us that in relation to the church that surrounds the globe, some denominations and churches have certain gifts to offer, some mission boards have specific giftedness to bring, some one gift, some another.

Let's let our minds think of circling the globe; we might conceptualize 1.5 billion Christians spread over the entire globe, representing a multitude of languages, peoples, families, tribes and nations. We could think of them as groups of congregations, denominations, mission agencies, mission initiatives, NGO's, and a multitude of ministries circling the globe. Then I believe we begin to understand what Paul was really after. I believe Paul's frame of reference in Ephesians 4 was not only, maybe not primarily, the local congregation in a specific location. Rather, I believe he was thinking of all Christians everywhere who are disciples of Jesus Christ.

A global hermeneutic of this passage has transformed the way I think of the gifts of the Holy Spirit. Now we are talking about each group of believers anywhere on the globe offering their gifts to all other believers anywhere on the globe. Now we conceptualize a Body of Christ whose members are spread throughout the entire world, dedicated to participating in Christ's mission of evangelizing the other 5.5 billion who yet do not know Jesus Christ as their personal Saviour and Lord. Each member of the global Body has something unique to offer the Body's ministry in the world. And, conversely, the Body is incomplete without the contribution of each member.

Here, then, is a perspective of missionary partnership that is spiritually grounded, world-encompassing, and missionally oriented. This is the Body of Christ that wraps its arms around the whole *oikoumene* and loves all peoples and tries to reach all peoples because "God so loved the world that he gave his one and only Son" (John 3:16).

B. Missiological Concerns

There are a host of missiological implications we might draw from such a global picture of the one Body's gifts, given by the Holy Spirit. I will focus attention on just a couple. First, what the global Body image does not mean.

What a global Body of Christ image does not mean

It does not mean declaring an official or even an informal moratorium on mission partnerships. A very controversial initiative that sought to give concrete shape to the oneness of the church in mission was the ill-fated and misunderstood movement in Africa, Asia, and Latin America that called for a "moratorium" on mission sending from the Western churches and missions. The "moratorium" debate of the 1970s is especially instructive for us, given recent calls on the part of some Western evangelical mission leaders to drastically reduce or completely stop financial aid to Africa as a way to combat the dependencies they see on the part of African churches.[248]

In the early 1970s John Gatu of Africa and Emerito Nacpil of the Philippines, along with others, wanted to see their churches and missions in the two-thirds world become fully mature, adult, respected, and active participants in the world mission of the world church. One might say, they were anxious to create space for the churches in the majority world to be able to exercise their gifts of ministry and mission. Their deepest desires had to do with the churches and missions of the majority being taken seriously, being respected, and being accepted as full partners by the missions and churches in the West. The proposal was a response on the part of Christians, particularly in Africa, to the paternalism and dependency that had developed as a result of Western personnel and finances being offered to African churches. I believe the initial motivation was laudable. Johannes Verkuyl suggested that the original impetus behind the talk of "moratorium" was this question. "How can we by our interecclesiastical relations become a better instrument for completing the work [of world evangelization] which still needs doing?"[249]

A motive behind the call for "moratorium" could be viewed as a consistent outgrowth of churches and mission having taken to heart the "three-self"

---

248. For informative background on the debate concerning "moratorium," see, e.g., James Scherer 1964; Federico Pagura 1973; Emilio Castro 1973; Gerald Anderson 1974; Burgess Carr 1975; David Bosch 1978 in Daniel Rickett and Dotsey Welliver, editors,1997, 53–64; Johannes Verkuyl 1978, 334–40; Robert T. Coote 1993, 377.

249. Verkuyl 1978, 334.

formula of Henry Venn and Rufus Anderson. One might consider a moratorium on receiving mission support to be a necessary step for the receiving churches to become truly self-governing, self-supporting and self-propagating—as well as self-theologizing and self-directed in mission. As Johannes Verkuyl puts it, "[The call for "moratorium" in Africa] was also a positive indication of the deep African desire for self-expression and self-reliance."[250]

But the shape that the "moratorium" debate took—and the negative consequences it had for world evangelization—were most unfortunate. During the late 1960s and early 1970s this led to talk (and in some cases very real decisions) to reduce the mission vision and the commitment for mission sending on the part of churches and missions in both the West and in the majority World. Many receiving churches that had been taught that mature, indigenous churches should become "three-self" churches—simply became selfish and self-centered.

In my own case, the National Presbyterian Church of Mexico adopted the "moratorium" perspectives and in 1972, in celebration of its centennial, declared a "moratorium," stating it would no longer accept any expatriate personnel or financial support from anywhere outside of Mexico. The Mexican church may have needed a time of setting its own house in order and determining its own destiny as a church. However, the long-term result of that "moratorium" was an increasing myopia and insularity on the part of the Mexican church because of its total noninvolvement in world Christianity. It took over a decade to clarify the situation and recreate a format whereby the Mexican church was again able to participate in mission with the world Church—both in receiving and in sending.[251]

What a global Body of Christ image could mean.

The image of a global Body of Christ implies a new and renewed commitment to partnership on the part of churches and missions circling the globe. Paul's concept of the gifts of the Holy Spirit are stimulating and creative at this point. They call us to encourage an environment of mutuality, and complementarity among the members, a climate in which all members of the Body, everywhere in the world,

---

250. Verkuyl 1978, 337. Burgess Carr wrote, "Let it be clearly understood that selfhood and self-reliance are linked in a relationship of identity to mission. In a word, the real measure of our capacity to contribute significantly to the humanization of the world is directly dependent upon a rediscovery and perhaps even a redefining of our identity as African Christians" (quoted from Anderson & Stransky 1976, 163).

251. See Bosch 1978, 56–60.

may participate in God's mission in world evangelization, offering to the world church what the Holy Spirit has given to each of them uniquely and to all of us collectively. The concept of the gifts of the Holy Spirit, looked at globally, moves us all toward wanting to foster healthy forms of interdependence as a way of avoiding the creation of unhealthy dependencies.

As David Bosch wrote,

> The solution, I believe, can only be found when the churches in the West and those in the Third World have come to the realization that each of them has at least as much to receive from the other as it has to give. This is where the crux of the matter lies. . . . We know that in ordinary human situations, genuine adult relationships can only develop where both sides give and receive.[252]

The Congress on World Evangelization at Lausanne in 1974 said, "The dominant role of Western missions is fast disappearing. God is raising up from the young churches a great new resource for world evangelization."[253]

Partnership is partnership in world evangelization. The focus must not be on cooperation as such, but on the task of world evangelization.[254] Cooperation must be for something. Partnership should not be an "empty basket."[255] However, even when we may agree on the missional goal of our partnership, the way we treat one another is of utmost significance. As Bill Taylor has suggested, true global partnership in mission will include the following lessons:

- "Listen before entering a partnership, and be willing to learn from mistakes and try again. . . ."
- "Partnerships work best when there is shared ownership of the project, including finances. . . ."
- "Be balanced. Don't get sucked in by hard sells based solely on comparisons of cost-effectiveness. Take time to check out potential partners before signing up. . . ."

---

252. Bosch 1978; quoted in Daniel Rickett and Dotsey Welliver 1997, 60.
253. Lausanne Covenant, article 8; see also Costas 1982, 65.
254. See Verkuyl 1978, 339.
255. Skreslet 1995.

- "Wise churches recognize that they cannot do everything, and partner with those who can assist them in their long-range goals. . . ."

- "Surely there is some relationship between partnership in mission and the prayer of our Lord in John 17:11, 21–23. . . . The global body of Christ is learning about partnerships in every language and culture. Let us continue to grow, to expand, to please the heart of God without creating artificial structures. Let us now be true partners in the gospel."[256]

Phillip Butler states rightly that partnership is not optional. For nearly 200 years, the church in the West has prayed and invested in missions to see the birth of the church in Asia, Africa, and Latin America. Now the majority world church is taking its place alongside the Western church so that *together* they can reach the final segment of the world—the (over 5) billion who have never heard of Jesus' love. Working in partnership has been talked of for a long time, but today we have no other option![257]

A main reason why partnership is not optional is that we really do need each other in order to evangelize the world in our generation. Although the total percentage of Christians in relation to world population is higher today than it has ever been, the actual number of those who don't yet know Jesus Christ is larger than ever before: 5.5 billion! We need each other in order to evangelize the world for whom Christ died. No one church, no one mission agency, no single missionary movement can evangelize the world in our generation alone and by themselves. This has become increasingly obvious to those of us, for example, who are involved in mission in the city. In the complex metroplexes of the world of the twenty-first century, the only way the Church of Jesus Christ will impact the cities—any city—is by all the disciples of Jesus partnering together to present the gospel through word and deed in each city.

Is it not time for all of us to take seriously what was affirmed by the Lausanne Movement in Manila ten years ago?

---

256. Taylor 1999, 749–52.

257. Butler 1999, 753–58; See also Wilbert Shenk 1988; Frances Hiebert 1997; Chuck Bennett 1998; Daniel Rickett 1998; John Robb 1999; Paul Hiebert 1991; Stan Nussbaum 1999.

- We affirm that we who claim to be members of the Body of Christ must transcend within our fellowship the barriers of race, gender, and class.
- We affirm that the gifts of the Spirit are distributed to all God's people, women and men, and that their partnership in evangelization must be welcomed for the common good. . . .
- We affirm the urgent need for churches, mission agencies and other Christian organizations to cooperate in evangelism and social action, repudiating competition and avoiding duplication.[258]

For churches and mission agencies to partner together in world evangelization, they must be willing to listen to each other, learn from each other, and appreciate one another in their theological understanding of the gospel. This brings us to our final word: theological.

WE WORK TOGETHER BECAUSE WE GROW TOGETHER AS TOGETHER WE GROW INTO THE FULLNESS OF THE STATURE OF JESUS CHRIST: THE GOAL OF MISSIONAL PARTNERSHIPS

The Christological center of our passage is rather obvious. Although the chapter is about the Church and its growth in diaconal ministries, yet it is Jesus Christ who permeates the entire chapter.

A. The Biblical Text

Paul is a prisoner of Jesus Christ, his Lord (Eph 4:1). There is one Lord (4:5). Jesus Christ is the one who apportions the grace, who ascended on high and led captives in his train and gave gifts to humans (4:7–9). This is the Christ who fills the whole universe (4:10). He gives a variety of gifts (4:11). The Church is the body of Christ (4:12). The Body is built up in the knowledge of Jesus Christ the Son of God, and becomes mature, attaining to the whole measure of the fullness of Christ who is the Head (4:13, 15). Paul writes to the Ephesians insisting in the Lord (4:17). The Ephesians are not to live as the Gentiles do, because that is not how they had come to know Christ (4:20). The truth is to be found in Jesus (4:21). Therefore the Ephesian Christians are called to put off falsehood, speak the truth in love, not let any unwholesome talk come out of their mouths, not grieve the Holy Spirit of God,

---

258. Manila Manifesto, affirmations 13, 14, and 17.

be kind and compassionate to each other, forgive one another the way in Christ God has forgiven them (4:25–32). In short, they are to live a life of love just as Christ loved them and gave himself up for them, because Jesus Christ is a fragrant offering and sacrifice to God (4:32–5:2).

If we were to take out the Christological references in this passage, there would be little left. The center of Paul's missiological ecclesiology in Ephesians 4 is, in fact, Jesus Christ the Lord. Paul shows us a comprehensive approach to mission theologizing that includes both propositional and experiential content.

First, a comment about theological content. When we as evangelicals think of the word "theology," we tend to associate it with a set of propositions, a "statement of faith," that neatly spells out those with whom we agree and those with whom we disagree. This has been true since the Fundamentalist/Modernist debates of the 1920s and 1930s. And in terms of mission partnerships, our tendency has been to cooperate in specific missional action, as long as our theological propositions are not questioned. Discussion of our mission agency's or church's theological affirmations has been off-limits. In mission partnerships we evangelicals have tended to show a marked unwillingness to deepen, reexamine, and reflect on the theological assumptions that undergird our missional actions. And yet, it is also true that during the twentieth century evangelicals have demonstrated a "broadening vision" that included a degree of openness to reexamining the way they did their mission theology.[259] This has included a willingness to examine their theological method, bringing together their propositional reasoning with their experience of being encountered by Jesus Christ. I dealt with this issue more at length in an earlier chapter in this book.

Stanley Grenz offers a classical meaning of the term.

> Basically, systematic theology is the reflection on, and the ordered articulation of faith. . . . The word "theology" does not

---

259. By way of example, in "A Broadening Vision: Forty Years of Evangelical Theology of Mission," I examined evangelical theology of mission from the 1940's to the 1980s and offered the thesis that "as North American evangelicals experienced (1) new sociocultural strength and confidence, (2) changes in the ecumenical theology of mission, and (3) developments in evangelical partner churches in the Third World, they responded with a broadening vision of an evangelical theology of mission which became less reactionary and more wholistic without compromising the initial evangelical élan of the World Missionary Conference at Edinburgh in 1910." (Joel A. Carpenter and Wilbert R Shenk, eds., 1990, 204–5; reprinted in Van Engen 1996a, 128.)

appear in the biblical documents. . . . The word itself is formed
from two other Greek terms, theos (God) and logos (word,
teaching, study). Hence, etymologically "theology" means "the
teaching concerning God" or "the study of God." . . . Theology
is primarily the articulation of a specific religious belief system
itself (doctrine). But it also includes reflection on the nature of
believing, as well as declarations concerning the integration of
commitment with personal and community life."[260]

Donald Bloesch emphasizes that both the rational and the experiential, the
propositional and the mystical, are integral aspects of the theological task. "The
dogma of revelation," Bloesch writes, "consists in the unity of logos and praxis. . . .
Dogma is not just an external truth but an internal truth. It must take root in one's
inner being. It appeals not just to the mind but to the whole person. . . . An evangelical dogmatics is based on the supposition that God's Word is at the same time God's
act. This Word is both conceptual and personal, propositional and existential."[261]

Hendrikus Berkhof speaks of doing theology in terms of a relationship of love
that seeks sanctification.

The essence of the study of the faith is best grasped if we regard
it as an element in the sanctification of the church. In the faith
relationship God seizes us for himself with his love. We may
respond to that by loving him with our whole being and therefore with all our mind. The study of the faith is not the only
form, but certainly one of the forms of our loving God with
the mind . . . All right thinking about God arises out of the
encounter with God and is aimed at the encounter with God.
. . . The possibility of making this true and meaningful thinking
depends on the relationship which from the other side is established by the Holy Spirit.[262]

This leads to a comment on theological method. Grenz, Bloesch and Berkhof
present us with an approach to theologizing that seeks to bring us relationally closer
to Jesus Christ—and in so doing deepens our understanding of the truth of the gospel.

---

260. Grentz 1994, 2–4. H. Berkhof affirms a classical definition of theology as, "Theology
teaches God, is taught by God, and leads to God." (H. Berkhof 1979, 30.)

261. Bloesch 1992, 19–20.

262. H. Berkhof 1979, 29–30.

Lesslie Newbigin emphasized this when he suggested that we need to reverse Descarte's methodology and "believe in order to know."[263] Our passage in Ephesians 4 is both experience and objectification, both faith relationship with Jesus Christ and propositional reflection. It draws from the "Ten Blessings" of Ephesians 1:3–14, together with all the various propositional affirmations that weave their way through Ephesians. But it also calls for radical transformation of the spirituality of the disciples, growth toward a truer and clearer reflection of their Head. This is a growth in "knowing" in the biblical sense of an intimate relationship like the way the old King James English stated that "Adam knew Eve. . . . and she bore a son." (Gen 4:1). This is the sense of "knowing" that has to do with wisdom, rather than holding onto empirical facts.[264] It is the kind of thing the Psalmist was speaking of, saying, "The fear of the Lord is the beginning of wisdom." (Ps 111:10).

For us to be able to work together in mission partnerships in the midst of differences in our theological perspectives, we will need to learn to theologize comprehensively, including both propositions and experience as legitimate data for our theological task. And we will need to do this through a "centered-set" approach that asks about our growing proximity or distance from Jesus Christ our Lord. We can no longer use our theologizing primarily as a defense of our own boundaries by which we decide who is in and who is out. Rather, "speaking the truth in love" (Eph 4:15), we will need to receive from each other—on a global scale—the insights which draw all of us closer to our Lord, the Head of the Church. In this way we can learn to cooperate without compromise. We are centered in Jesus Christ, in the midst of the multiple cultures of the globe.

B. Missiological Concerns

Our biblical and theological reflection concerning the goal of mission partnerships suggests some missiological issues.

What theological growth does not mean.

Comprehensive theological and missiological growth of the Body of Christ means we all must struggle to avoid paternalism in missional partnerships. Paternalism was a major source of frustration on the part of receptor churches during the height of the "moratorium" debate. And we must not underestimate the destructive power of paternalism. Though it is beyond the limits of this chapter, let me

---

263. Newbigin 1991, 36.
264. See, e.g., Lesslie Newbigin 1986 and 1989.

illustrate what I mean by mentioning some of the "many faces" that paternalism might include:

- The Financier Syndrome[265]
- The Mothering/Smothering Syndrome[266]
- The Organization Syndrome[267]
- The Invasion Syndrome[268]
- The Isolation Syndrome[269]
- The Big Cheese Syndrome[270]
- The Prince and the Pauper Syndrome[271]
- The "Professional" Complex[272]

---

265. Giving money only if we can control its use; or not giving money because we feel it would not be good for them; or giving money in such a way that it makes the recipient totally dependent on us.

266. Deciding what the recipients really need and fomenting change accordingly; or hearing the recipients say they need something but deciding they really do not need it.

267. The sending agency designs programs on its own and then asks the recipients to take it or leave it; or manipulates the recipients in such a way that they have no choice but to receive their services; or they do nothing until they have been asked by recipients—and then only when the request is well-planned, in advance, and done right according to their own criteria.

268. We bring in services and people, we create programs or budget money and locate all the services in a setting without any consultation with the recipients.

269. This is an insidious double-think that wishes to assert the autonomy of the recipients but from a disconnected point of view. The sending agency decides independently of the recipients the arenas they will talk about, the arenas they will not deal with, and what arenas are the problem of the recipient, not of the sending agency—with little or no consultation with the recipients. The flip side of this is the co-opting syndrome that invites the recipients to join with the donors in joint committees, but the most basic and influential decisions have already been made before the recipients join the process.

270. Deciding not do something because the recipients could never carry it on or keep it up without the sending agency's help; or the sending agency thinking that its time and money is so valuable there are many day-to-day tasks which the recipients should do, and the really important ones are to be carried out only by the sending agency.

271. The sending agency's personnel live so far above the standard of living of the people they serve that they never experience life as the recipients live it; or "going native" in such an overly self-conscious way that the sending agency's personnel live in such poor conditions they spend all their time trying to survive.

272. The idea that the sending agency offers services to the recipients in an impersonal, removed fashion, avoiding "getting personal" or developing close relationships with the recipients.

- The "Fix It" Syndrome[273]
- The "Reproducing Ourselves" or "Cloning" Syndrome[274]

We all know that paternalism is an ever-present danger in mission and ministry. It appears mostly when we hold to some position or idea in a doctrinaire fashion, or take some action regardless of the circumstances, opinions, wisdom, and feelings of the recipients or partners with whom we have been called to serve. Can we escape paternalism altogether? Probably not. But maybe we can be aware of its traps.

And one of the most insidious traps of paternalism is a theological one. Because we are convinced of the theological propositions to which we hold, and because we are committed to the faith we have experienced, we too easily apply that unchanged to new situations. We assume that our understanding of the gospel is universally applicable in identical fashion to the way we learned and experienced it. We thus find it easier to contextualize the wrapping of the package of our theology than to reexamine our understanding of the actual contents of the package.

Thus for centuries Western European theologians have thought of their theology as applicable for all time and all cultures—and have imposed a theological hegemony on the world church, a theological quality control of which they have seemed to be mostly unaware. At times, this has been accompanied by an air of triumphalism and arrogance on the part of the sending agencies and churches who have supposed they already have all the theological answers necessary to respond to all the questions faced by the church everywhere. As Lesslie Newbigin and others pointed out with increasing force, Western theology itself represents a highly contextualized formulation of the gospel. Unfortunately, sometimes the excellent answers the missionary enterprise has offered have involved responses to what the recipients have considered to be the wrong questions. Thus Dean

---

273. The sending agency is interested in a quick fix to a problem that the receptors apparently have—and has little time to listen, learn from, and partner with the recipients who may not consider the situation a problem at all; the recipients may know better than the sender the depth, pervasiveness and difficulty the problem presents such that it is not possible to "fix it" in a short-term manner.

274. The sending agency or church is most deeply concerned in creating clones of itself in new locations; the only really authentic and acceptable mission and church structures become those that are exact replicas of the sending group's structures, "like we do it back home." The flip side of this is to think that all cultures are so unique and different that nothing in the former culture is applicable or helpful in the new setting.

Gilliland, for example, has suggested that in our contextual theologizing we need to begin by asking what are the operative questions of the culture?[275]

On the other hand, as seen in Ephesians 4, Paul would be adamantly opposed to speaking of a plural "theologies" like in Latin American Liberation Theology, Minjung Theology, African Theology, Dalit Theology, Asian Theology, and so forth. Rather, Paul states, "there is one hope, . . . one faith, . . . one baptism, one God and Father of all" (Eph 4:4–6). How, then, do we theologize as a world Church, as mission partners who circle the globe, as members of the one Body who represent radically different contexts of mission?

What global theological growth could mean.

I would like to suggest that our global theological task must involve growth—growth for all of us in our closeness to Jesus Christ, through the work of the Holy Spirit. I believe Paul offers us a way to do this in Ephesians 4. And it involves all of us together in each place growing into the fullness of Jesus Christ. And as we do so, we will, and must, grow closer together with each other, as disciples of the same Lord.[276]

As mission partners, we grow together as together we grow into the fullness of the stature of Jesus Christ. The size of the Head does not change. The Lordship of Jesus Christ, Christ's rule, the kingdom of God, does not change. And as the Church grows, it is the same Church. It was not less church before it grew, nor is it more Church after it has grown. But as it grows, it reflects to the world more completely, more clearly, more thoroughly the One who is the Head of the Church. It grows toward matching the "whole measure of the fullness of Christ." It grows because of Christ's work through the Holy Spirit, looking to the day when Christ will "present her to himself as a radiant Church, (the bride) without stain or wrinkle or any other blemish, but holy and blameless" (Eph 5:27). This organic picture of the Church involves a perspective of theological interdependence, complementarity, and mutuality.

And we need each other. The complexity of theological issues facing us in mission in the next century demands that we partner together in the theological task as well, seeking to understand in a new way the old, old story of Jesus and his love—in new contexts, facing new issues.

As I pointed out in "The New Covenant: Knowing God in Context," (Van Engen 1989) an organic view of the Church's theological growth in closeness to

---

275. Gilliland, "New Testament Contextualization," 1989, 52.
276. See Van Engen 1981, 438–41 and Barth 1958, 614–41.

the Lord Jesus Christ must now become a global perspective. In this millennium it will be the *world* church that together grows in its understanding of God's covenant with God's People. It is always the same covenant, always the same gospel, yet always new, and always deepening in its impact of transforming and sanctifying Christ's church. And this is now a global phenomenon. "As the gospel continues to take root in new cultures, and God's people grow in their covenantal relationship to God in those contexts, a broader, fuller, and deeper understanding of God's revelation will be given to the world church."[277]

This theological endeavor will entail all believers in Jesus Christ from all the continents, in the midst of each and every culture to come closer to Jesus Christ as they read the Bible for themselves, share what they see with all other Christians around the world, and grow together as together they grow into the stature of our one Head, Jesus Christ.

A graphic way to present this might be the following.

**The Global/Local Hermeneutical Community
Knowing God in Context**

FIGURE 10: Glocal Mission Theology

---

277. Van Engen, "The New Covenant: Knowing God in Context," 1989, 88–89; reprinted in Van Engen 1996, 88–89.

As we begin to listen to one another as theological mission partners we will deepen our relationship with Jesus Christ, want to learn from each other, and want to grow closer to our Head. Then we will begin to experience what Orlando Costas called "integral (or comprehensive) growth." Costas believed that the authentic Church of Jesus Christ was meant to grow in four dimensions simultaneously. I have added a fifth.[278]

I believe it will take us all together, working together, in theological mission partnership to begin together "with all the Lord's holy people, to grasp how wide and long and high and deep is the love of Christ, and to know this love that surpasses knowledge—that you may be filled to the measure of all the fullness of

---

278.   By SPIRITUAL GROWTH is meant the depth and breadth of the covenantal relationship of the people of God in intimate spiritual closeness with God, through faith in Jesus Christ by the Holy Spirit; i.e., the depth of spiritual maturity of leaders and members, their degree of immersion in Scripture, their living out of a lifestyle and ethics of the kingdom of God, their involvement in prayer, their dependence of God, their search for holiness, and their vibrancy in worship (Van Engen).

"By NUMERICAL GROWTH is understood the recruitment of persons for the kingdom of God by calling them to repentance and faith in Jesus Christ as Lord and Savior of their lives and their incorporation into a local community of persons who, having made a similar decision, worship, obey, and give witness, collectively and personally, to the world of God's redemptive action in Jesus Christ and his liberating power.

"By ORGANIC GROWTH is meant the internal development of a local community of faith, i.e., the system of relationships among its members—its form of government, financial structure, leadership, types of activities in which its time and resources are invested, etc.

"By CONCEPTUAL GROWTH is meant the degree of consciousness that a community of faith has with regard to its nature and mission to the world, i.e., the image that the community has formed of itself, the depth of its reflection on the meaning of its faith in Christ (understanding of Scripture, etc.), and its image of the world.

"By INCARNATIONAL GROWTH is meant the degree of involvement of a community of faith in the life and problems of its social environment; i.e., its participation in the afflictions of its world; its prophetic, intercessory, and liberating action on behalf of the weak and destitute; the intensity of its preaching to the poor, the brokenhearted, the captives, the blind, and the oppressed. (Luke 4:18–21)."

With the exception of the first paragraph, this material is taken from Orlando Costas, *The Church and its Mission: A Shattering Critique from the Third World* (Chicago: Tyndale, 1974) 90–91. This was later published in Spanish in Orlando Costas. *El Protestantismo en America Latina Hoy: Ensayos del Camino* (1972–1974) (San Jose, Costa Rica, Indef, 1975) 68–70. See also Orlando Costas, *The Integrity of Mission: The Inner Life and Outreach of the Church* (NY: Harper & Row, 1979) 37–60.

God" (Eph 3:18–19). Such is the integral growth of the disciples of Jesus Christ who circle the globe, committed to working together in the next millennium.

CONCLUSION

Some time ago my wife, Jean, and I were in our back yard, trimming the bushes. Normally, I do that by myself. But this time we were doing it together. I was cutting and chopping, she was breaking up the branches and putting them into the trash bin. And I was amazed at how quickly the job was getting done. I stopped and exclaimed to Jean, "This goes so much faster with two of us!"

I believe the evangelization of the world in our generation will go much faster if we work together. Even the writer of Ecclesiastes knew this: "Two are better than one, because they have a good return for their labor" (Eccl 4:9).

In this chapter we have considered the implications of working together amidst theological diversity. Our partnership in mission in this millennium must be centered in Jesus Christ, focused in the local congregation, shaped by a kingdom of God missiology, directed to a world in desperate need of Christ, recognizing that the gospel is for everyone, committed to cooperating together in mutuality and humility, celebrating the gifts given to each member of the global Community of the King, and growing together to become mature partners, attaining together to the whole measure of the fullness of Jesus Christ our Lord.

For us to be able to meet the challenges that will face us in world evangelization in this new millennium, we need to take to heart Billy Graham's words that appeared in the Epilogue of the NAE's Evangelical Manifesto in 1996.

> It is my fervent prayer that the evangelical community will take seriously the command of the Great Commission in the manner which Jesus described in his greatly priestly prayer—cooperating without compromise, so that the world might believe!
>
> The challenge before us calls for a strategic united evangelistic effort as we've never undertaken before. The world in our time is said to have made discipleship harder. But it has also made evangelism easier. Today's world is said to be multiplying crises all around us. But we must never forget that, for the gospel, each crisis is an opportunity. . . .
>
> We need to rededicate ourselves to the primary task of winning and making disciples of Jesus Christ in our generation.

Today's world waits to see our response to questions and challenges such as these.

Evangelicalism has a future to the extent that we evangelicals ourselves are drawn by the gospel, are defined by the gospel, and are declaring and demonstrating the gospel of our Lord and Savior, Jesus Christ, in word and deed. . . .

Our faithful witness may or may not result in new understanding of the name "evangelical" by the culture and media. Our faithful united witness might result in visible Christian worship of our Lord in the public celebrations of the year A.D. 2000 rather than merely a glorification of another epoch of human achievement and existence. But our faithful united witness will result in revival and reconciliation and renewal. Let us go forward in faith together—and the very gates of hell cannot prevail![279]

---

279. National Association of Evangelicals "An Evangelical Manifesto: A Strategic Plan for the Dawn of the 21st Century," NAE Web Site www.nae.net/sig_doc11.html (website inactive), 1996.

CHAPTER 12
FAITH, LOVE, HOPE: THESE THREE IN MISSION THEOLOGY

This chapter was originally published as, "Faith, Love and Hope: A Theology of Mission On-the-Way," in Van Engen, Gilliland, and Pierson, eds., *The Good News of the Kingdom: Mission Theology for the 3rd Millennium* Maryknoll: Orbis, 1993, 253–63. Available from Wipf and Stock Publishers, 150 West Broadway, Eugene, OR 97401 Reprinted in Van Engen *Mission on the Way*. Grand Rapids: Baker, 1996, 253–62. Used by permission.

THESIS

In this new millennium we need a trinitarian mission theology that (a) emanates from a deeply personal, biblical, and corporate faith in Jesus Christ (the King); (b) is lived out in the Body of Christ as an ecumenical fellowship of love (the central locus of Christ's reign); and (c) offers hope for the total transformation of God's world (as a sign of the present inbreaking of the coming kingdom of God).

INTRODUCTION

In this time between the times we live in the stressful dialectic of the kingdom of God, a kingdom that has already come in Jesus Christ, yet is still coming (Cullmann 1951). This reality becomes even more poignant when considered in the light of the unrest and anxiety that flows from the conflicts around the globe in the first decades of this new millennium.

The already and not yet character of God's rule means that the Church and its mission constitute an interim sign. In the power of the Holy Spirit the Church points all humanity backward to its origins in God's creation and forward to the present and coming kingdom in Jesus Christ.[280]

---

280. Verkuyl 1978, 203; Arthur Glasser 1985, 12; 1990, 250; and Glasser & McGavran 1983, 30–46. David Bosch (1991, 368–93 and 1980, 75–83, 239–48) has provided an excellent overview and critique of the "missio Dei" concept, especially as it was misused and unbiblically reshaped in the missiology of the World Council of Churches from 1965 to 1980.

Looking into this new millennium, we are filled with awe and no little fear. In *Transforming Mission* David Bosch laid out the broad parameters of our agenda for doing mission theology into the foreseeable future. In doing so, he attempted to describe for us what he considered to be some of the most important "Elements of an Emerging Ecumenical Missionary Paradigm" (1991, 368ff).[281] It will take a number of years, and a host of conversations to find a way to deal with, and cohesively integrate, the many diverse elements Bosch offered us. Although we reason like children and "see only a reflection as in a mirror" (1 Cor 13:11–12), yet we can at least look over the horizon, and search for a road map of what may lie ahead. At the risk of being simplistic, partial, and too general, I would offer the following thesis. Going into this new millennium we need a trinitarian theology of mission that:

- emanates from a deeply personal, biblical, and corporate *faith* in Jesus Christ (the King);
- is lived out in the Body of Christ as an ecumenical fellowship of *love* (the central locus of Christ's reign);
- and offers *hope* for the total transformation of God's world (as a sign of the present inbreaking of the coming kingdom of God).

In offering this thesis, I have borrowed an organizing framework from the Apostle Paul. As if it were a kind of signature, Paul salted his letters with references to a significant triad of missiological ideas: *faith, hope and love.* Mixing their

See, among others, Norman Goodall 1953, 195–97; James Scherer 1987, 126–34; Lesslie Newbigin 1977, 63–68; 1978, chapters 4 ,8, and 9; Wilhelm Andersen 1961; R. C. Bassham: 1979, 33–40, 67–71, 168–69; and Verkuyl 1978, 2–4, 197–204. The kingdom of God (and a biblical perspective of the *missio dei* within that) has become a major point of consensus in global missiology. See, for example, Esther and Mortimer Arias: 1980; Mortimer Arias 1984; Charles Van Engen 1981, 277–307; 1991a, 101–18; William Dyrness 1983; Robert Linthicum: 1991, 80–108; J. Blauw 1962; Hans Küng 1971, 46ff; G. E. Ladd 1974; John Bright 1953, 216, 231–38; Karl Barth 1958, 655ff; H. N. Ridderbos 1962; G. Vicedom 1965; W. Pannenberg 1969; C. Rene Padilla 1975, 1985; Orlando Costas 1979, 5–8; Orlando Costas 1989; Donald Senior and Carroll Stuhlmueller 1983, 141–160; Dempster, Klaus and Petersen 1991, 1–58; Robert Linthicum 1991; Emilio Castro 1985, 38–88; WCC 1980; George Peters 1981, 37–47; Edward Pentecost 1982; Paul Pomerville 1985; Ken Gnanakan:1989; C. Peter Wagner 1987, 35–55, 96–112; Gailyn Van Rheenen 1983, 1–20; and William Abraham 1989.

281. Bosch mentions mission as: the Church-With-Others, *Missio Dei*, Mediating Salvation, the Quest for Justice, Evangelism, Contextualization, Liberation, Inculturation, Common Witness, Ministry by the Whole People of God, Witness to People of Other Living Faiths, Theology, and as Action in Hope.

order, and interweaving them with other contextual agendas, Paul's triad gives us a glimpse of what might be called the "habitus"[282] or integrating idea of his mission theology.[283] In what follows, the order of Faith, Love, and Hope gives a sense of movement on the road to God's future. The first principle in the triad is faith.

FAITH: THE HOLY SPIRIT MOTIVATES THE CHURCH'S PARTICIPATION IN GOD'S MISSION

Roland Allen (1962) and Harry Boer (1961), among others, emphasized the fact that the coming of the Holy Spirit at Pentecost brought a radically new and deeply personal relationship with Jesus Christ that is essential to mission. The traditional Pentecostal Movement since the turn of the century (and the Wesleyans before that), the Charismatic Movement of the last fifty years, and the Orthodox traditions in their participation in the World Council of Churches have continually emphasized the role of the Holy Spirit, personal faith, and deep spirituality as foundational for Christian mission. In this vein, there is substantial agreement between, say, Protestant expressions of mission theology like those in Section I of *The San Antonio Report* (WCC 1990) and *The Manila Manifesto* (LCWE 1989) and Roman Catholic encyclicals such as *Evangelii Nuntiandi*, *Redemptoris Missio* and most recently *Evangelii Gaudium*. This being the case, faith plays a crucial role with reference to some of the most critical issues of our time. Six considerations center on faith as we look across the horizon of a new millennium.

First, in certain circles, faith, as trust in God's revelation in Jesus Christ, enscripturated in the Bible, and witnessed to by the Holy Spirit is sometimes questioned, and even at times rejected. But mission that is not based on biblical revelation, the text that declares the uniqueness of Jesus Christ and offers a new birth through the Holy Spirit, may be church expansion, or colonialist extension, or sectarian proselytism—but it is not God's mission (cf. Gnanakan 1992, 195ff).

God's mission emanates from the power of the resurrection (Eph 1), in "the power of the Spirit."[284] This also means that God's mission should be tested and tried. As John suggested, "Every spirit [and every enterprise of mission] that

---

282. Cf. Van Engen 1987, 524–25. Cf. D. Bosch 1991, 489.

283. See, for example, Rom 5:1–5; Rom 12:9–13; 1 Cor 13:13; Gal 5:5–6; Eph 1:15; Col 1:3–6; 1 Thes 1:3, 5:8; 2 Thes 1:3 with 2:13–17; 1 Tim 4:9–12; 2 Tim 1:5, 13–14; Phil 5–6; and—however we deal with its authorship—Heb 6:9–12.

284. Jürgen Moltmann 1977.

acknowledges that Jesus Christ has come in the flesh is from God, but every spirit that does not acknowledge Jesus is not from God" (1 John 4:2–3). A theocentric pluralist perspective that disavows the uniqueness of Jesus Christ may be polite conversation or even compassionate cooperation—but it is not the apostolate of Jesus Christ. For when we are involved in God's mission, then we are participating in Jesus' mission: "As the Father has sent me, I am sending you" (John 20:21; see Glasser 1976, 3). Jesus calls us to be ambassadors, calling the world to be reconciled to God through faith in Jesus Christ—and such reconciliation is impossible apart from personal and corporate faith in Jesus Christ (2 Cor 5).

Secondly, mission that derives from faith will take seriously the centuries of reflection by the people of God concerning their faith as revealed by God in the Scriptures and as understood by the community of faith since Abraham. This means that systematic and historical theology need to be given their appropriate place in filling out the meaning, scope, and implications of mission. But it also means that there can be no truly biblical development of systematic or historical theology unless these are thoroughly saturated with missional questions, intentions, and dimensions, as I mentioned in Section I of this book.

Thirdly, mission from faith means that conversation with people of other faiths will occur at the deepest levels of shared convictions. This entails a radical differentiation between religion and culture, faith and worldview. To confuse religion and faith on the one hand with culture and worldview on the other too often means that once one affirms cultural relativity, one must immediately take the next step and accept religious pluralism. Such a confusion is evident in the writings of Wilfred Cantwell Smith, Karl Rahner, John Hick, John Cobb, Paul Knitter, and Wesley Ariarajah. One of the future tasks of mission theology will be to more clearly distinguish these two aspects of human experience.[285]

It will also be important to distinguish between the Holy Spirit (as a unique part of the triune God) and the spirits (be these pantheistic, animistic, spiritist, New Age, or materialist). This would also help us differentiate the Holy Spirit from human spirituality—a crucial issue related to the difference between God's mission and our own expansionist agendas.

Fourth, mission from faith will mean a continued search for ways in which our faith may be public faith, based on the facts of revelation. Especially in the West, this involves wrestling with the straitjacket of the Enlightenment that has wanted to force the concept of faith into a privatist mold of individual taste, as Lesslie

---

285. See Van Engen 1991b, 189–90.

Newbigin has so aptly demonstrated (Newbigin 1986, 1989).[286] Missionary faith inevitably, rightly, and powerfully must be a public faith, interested in the inner, spiritual conversion of the person as part of a larger social, economic, political, and global reality. Each person's conversion on the microscale has implications for the transformation of society on the macroscale, and vice versa. No longer can we maintain a dichotomy between these two. Mission theology into this new millennium must find a way to speak to both these aspects as part of the same reality. This means that missiology must find a way to integrate spirituality, psychology, anthropology, and sociology in a wholistic understanding that more closely approximates reality.

Fifth, mission from faith will mean we are deeply concerned about the over five billion people and thousands of unreached people groups who have not yet experienced the transformation of the Spirit through faith in Jesus Christ. Our hearts will ache for them (Rom 9:1–3), we will consider ourselves their debtors (Rom 1:14), and we will yearn deeply to see them touched by the Holy Spirit and converted to Jesus Christ (Van Engen, 1981). This is a mission theology that cannot stop short of committed plans and action, a mission theology that understands that it exists for the sake of those who have not yet become part of the people of God. As Johannes Verkuyl said it, "Missiology may never become a substitute for action and participation . . . If study does not lead to participation, whether at home or abroad, missiology has lost her humble calling" (Verkuyl 1978, 6).

Lastly, mission from faith through the Holy Spirit will not only use the gifts of the Spirit for ministry in the world; it will occur when the fruit of the Spirit emanates through the lives of the people of God (Gal 5:22–26). Down through the history of mission one would wish that the motivations, means, and goals of mission had been more thoroughly washed with love, joy, peace, patience, kindness, goodness, faithfulness, gentleness, and self-control. For the Church to be believable, it will need to conduct its mission as an expression of the fruit of the Spirit, conscious of Christ's lordship in the midst of God's People. This brings us to our second major word in Paul's triad: love.

---

286. The October 1991, issue of *Missiology* is an excellent introduction to some of these issues.

LOVE: JESUS CHRIST ACTIVATES HIS BODY'S PARTICIPATION IN GOD'S MISSION

"By this everyone will know that you are my disciples, if you love one another" (John 13:35). Jesus calls for agape love as the supreme quality of the fellowship of missionary disciples. As never before, the Church of Jesus Christ must discover what it means to be a fellowship of love—especially now that the Church circles the globe, and its center of gravity has shifted from North and West to South and East. Never before in the history of humanity has the Christian faith been adhered to by people of so many cultures. Today we can empirically observe what we implicitly knew: that the gospel was infinitely "translatable" into all human cultures (Lamin Sanneh 1989). The theological implications of this fact are staggering. Only a few can be highlighted.

In the first place, a multicultural world church calls for a new paradigm that more closely relates church, unity, and mission. When we say, "church," for example, we need to carefully balance the local and the universal, as the Orthodox tradition so often reminds us. No longer can we mean *only* the older denominations with roots in Western Europe, nor even their daughter churches in Africa, Asia, and Latin America, as in the phrase, "World Council of Churches." New religious movements in Asia, indigenous independent churches in Africa, new ecclesial groups in Latin America, new denominations all over the world, metachurches of hundreds of thousands that are denominations in their own right—all these have developed since the 1960s, and they have given a whole new meaning to the word "church" (Walls 1976).

We need a new paradigm of ecumenicity. The July, 1992, issue of *International Review of Mission* provides an excellent starting point for discussing this matter.[287] Mission in love must first mean that we learn to love, understand, listen to, and be corrected by one another in the Christian church (cf. Van Engen 1990).[288]

This involves more than tolerance as the highest value, and more than the celebration of total diversity with little commonality. Mission in love is also deeper than "Learning about Theology from the Third World" (Dyrness 1990), although it clearly begins with such learning. Rene Padilla has said it well.

---

287. See also Willem Saayman 1990; and Bosch 1991, 457–67.
288. See also NCCC/DOM 1983, 9.

> From the perspective of wholistic mission, there is no place for the polarization between an ecumenical outlook and an evangelical one. To be an ecumenical Christian is to be a Christian who conceives of the whole oikoumene (the inhabited world) as the place of God's transforming action . . . To be an evangelical Christian is to be a Christian who conceives of the gospel as good news of the love of God in Jesus Christ, the living Word witnessed to by the Bible, the written Word of God. It is to confess and to live out the gospel of Jesus Christ as Lord of the whole of life in the power of the Holy Spirit. It is to work together in the proclamation of the gospel to all the peoples of the earth . . . and in the formation of local Christian congregations that nurture and share the faith. (Padilla 1992, 381–82)

Mission in love will hold tightly to the truth of the gospel as revealed in the Scriptures, and hold loosely to the provincial agendas of one's own particular Christian tradition, be that evangelical, ecumenical, Roman Catholic, Orthodox, pentecostal, or charismatic.

Secondly, mission in love will affect the way we do theology on a global, multi-worldview scale. The basis on which we do mission theology, the data we incorporate, the methodologies we use, the people we listen to, and the issues we address will probably undergo considerable change. World conferences, their pronouncements, and the studies and papers emanating from such conferences, will probably become less important for mission theology. Instead, we will need to listen carefully to the people of God in local contexts, and then strive to find ways in which local theologizing may impact the world church, and vice versa.

If the Church is the loving Body of Christ, a community of faith in love that exists for and in mission for the world, then neither local theologies nor a monolithic supercultural theology are viable for a mission theology that goes "beyond anticolonialism to globalism" (Paul Hiebert 1991, 263). Rather, we must find ways to affirm both the local and the universal (see Berkhof 1985, 71–73). Following Augustine (as well as the Vincentian Canon), truth is considered to lie in "what has everywhere, always, by all been believed" (cf. Van Engen 1981, 200–11).

As William Dyrness observes,

> If it is true that theology that matters will be a theology of the majority of Christians, then "theology in the Third World is

now the only theology worth caring about." If theology is to be rooted in the actual lives of Christians today, increasingly it will have to be from the poor to the poor, in Africa, Latin America, and Asia. And theology done in the West, if it is not to become increasingly provincial, [Walls] notes, will have to be done in dialogue with the theological leaders in the Third World." (Dyrness 1990, 13; quoting Walls 1976, 182)

If this way of theologizing were given its place in the world church, more weight might need to be ascribed to the theological principle of acceptance or reception, an idea articulated, for example, by Gamaliel in Acts 5:33–39. This principle calls for all new theological ideas to be tested by the people of God who over time (sometimes centuries) will determine whether the idea should ultimately be accepted or rejected by the Church.

A third implication of mission in love has to do with nuancing of our kingdom of God theology to include the strong covenantal perspectives found in Scripture. Kingdom thinking tends to support concepts of hierarchy and order. Covenant, on the other hand, tends to empower the weak and strengthen them through new relationships. The biblical idea of covenant is impossible without the broader concept of the reign of God in Jesus Christ. But we may discover that the "kingdom of God" perspective is best worked out through covenantal relationships that especially pick up the feminine images of God's care: giving birth, embracing, loving, self-giving, providing, and protecting.

Thus a covenantal/kingdom mission theology would take seriously the role of refugees, women, the poor, the marginalized, the weak, and the foolish in understanding a biblical hermeneutic of the Church's participation in God's mission. What is needed is a missiological theology that arises from and speaks to the entire community (see Hauerwas and Willimon 1991; Motte 1991). This is the mission wisdom of Hagar, Ruth, Esther, Daniel, and the widow of Sarapheth (see, e.g., Luke 4 and Matt 15:21–28). This is mission from weakness and foolishness (1 Cor 1:18–31). The Third Millennium may bring us back to a situation reminiscent of the early church, where our mission will necessarily be from weakness, foolishness, and poverty. This would entail a radical paradigm shift in mission theology. Neither option makes it more or less true. Truth can only be judged in terms of "centered sets" that examines our proximity or distance from Jesus Christ (Hiebert 1978). However, the shift would dramatically change the way we do mission.

This shift may not be optional. The drastic ecological, economic, political, social, religious, demographic, and other changes happening on our small globe are presenting us with a new reality that will call for a new paradigm of theology of mission. This shift in paradigm leads to the third dimension of Paul's triad: hope.

HOPE: GOD'S MISSION IS TO CREATE A NEW HEAVEN AND A NEW EARTH

First Peter places our evangelistic confession in the context of a missional encounter of church and world; and hope is the central motif. "But in your hearts set apart Christ as Lord. Always be prepared to give an answer to everyone who asks you to give the reason for the hope that you have. But do this with gentleness and respect" (1 Peter 3:15).

Hope is possibly the most explosive concept that missiology has to offer today. Oscar Cullmann recognized it thirty years ago.

> The genuine primitive Christian hope does not paralyze Christian action in the world. On the contrary, the proclamation of the Christian Gospel in the missionary enterpirse is a characteristic form of such action, since it expresses the belief that "missions" are an essential element in the eschatological divine plan of salvation. The missionary work of the Church is the eschatological foretaste; of the kingdom of God, and the Biblical hope of the "end" constitutes the keenest incentive to action. (Cullmann 1961)

Today we are a long way from the unbelievable optimism of a hundred years ago regarding Western civilization, technology, and culture-Protestantism. These proved themselves to be empty and misguided, precisely because they were centered on faith in technology and civilization rather than on Jesus Christ.

But such a recognition should not blind us to the influence that hope and hopelessness can have on the way people participate in God's mission. For example, during the exile, the Israelites seem to have wavered between hopelessness and hope—and the difference entailed a radically distinct hermeneutic of God's mission and their part in it. On the one hand, they were prone to moan, "How can we sing the songs while in a foreign land?" (Ps 137:4). But others followed the lead of Daniel, Esther, and their friends. This was a hope-filled approach that even the weeping prophet Jeremiah advocated.

> Build houses and settle down; plant gardens and eat what they
> produce. Marry and have sons and daughters . . . Increase in
> number there; do not decrease. Also seek the peace and pros-
> perity of the city to which I have carried you into exile. Pray
> to the Lord for it, because if it prospers, you too will prosper.
> (Jer 29:5–7)

Here is a perspective that offers, precisely in its hopefulness, the possibility of reconciliation in a deeply biblical sense.[289] It represents a mission paradigm that Sunday Aigbe of Nigeria has called the "prophetic mandate" (1991).

The last several years have convinced me that hope is probably the most important single concept that the Church of Jesus Christ has to offer the world today. Some years ago I experienced a particular period of about twenty-six days when for the first time in my life I thought we might actually live in a world of peace. The Berlin wall was coming down, Eastern Europe was changing, negoti-ations were going on in the Middle East, Latin America was beginning to find its way politically and economically, South Africa was beginning its tortuous process of change, Asia was exploding economically and technologically, China was on the move to new things, and African nations were beginning to find new paths. But the hiatus was short-lived.

Today as I sit and write these lines I am reminded of cities in which I have experienced the most terrible tragedy of all: the nearly total loss of hope. Be it Sao Paulo, Sarajevo, Mexico City, the Middle East, Los Angeles after the riots, or New Orleans after the hurricane—what I keep hearing is an almost complete loss of hope. Especially in Latin America, the demise of Marxism as a viable approach, along with the failure of democratization to offer anything new for the welfare of the poor masses have brought a spirit of hopeless resignation that deeply concerns me. When I was a child growing up in Southern Mexico there was always a degree of optimism. Tomorrow, next week, the next governor, the next president, more education, and better organization would eventually change things. That hope seems to have died.

---

289. See Robert Schreiter 1992.

A missiology of hope[290] is central to Paul's missiological praxis.[291] This hope is neither breezy escapism, nor empty optimism, nor blind conformism, nor unrealistic utopianism: all of which can be found in the missiologies of this century. Rather, Paul's missiology of hope includes at least the following three components.

First, a missiology of hope means that Christians care, and care so deeply that they will risk hoping for the new. They dare hope because they know that in Christ's kingdom God's grace through faith brings about a radical and total transformation. "Therefore, if anyone is in Christ, the new creation has come: The old has gone, the new is here!" (2 Cor 5:17).

Secondly, a missiology of hope means that Christians dare to believe that together they can change the world. (cf. David Barrett 1983, 51.) This is at the heart of mission. But we must remember the not-yet-ness of God's kingdom, along with its already-ness. We of the "baby boomer" generation of the United States believed we could change the world on our own. We followed J.C. Hoekendijk in his pessimism about the church, and thought we could change the world by ourselves through Lyndon Johnson's "great society," through the Peace Corps, and through computer technology. As a result, many of us today are indelibly marked with pessimism and cynicism. We discovered that we could not change even the cities in which we created Christian communes, much less the world. We missed the mark by failing to realize our own sinfulness and the true extent of the Fall, by failing to grasp that we can neither bring in the kingdom, nor create the utopias envisioned by the ideologues. Rather, as we participate in God's mission, God's reign comes when people accept Jesus as Lord—and in obedience begin to see God's will being done "on earth as it is in heaven" (Matt 6:10). This involves structural and societal change as well as personal. It involves the whole person, not only the spiritual aspects. It involves all of life, not only the ecclesiastical. [292]

Third, a missiology of hope means that Christians profess certainty in that which they do not see (Heb 11:1). It means participating with Jesus in being a

---

290. Although Jürgen Moltmann and others developed a theology of hope in the 1960's, the concept did not emanate in new missiological directions. A missiology of hope is at once individual, social, and structural; and it derives from a deep sense of identity, purpose, and the *missio Dei*. This needs further exploration. Cf. Bosch 1980, 234–238.

291. Cf., e.g., Eph 1:18; Col 1:5,23,27; Eph 2:12; 1 Thes 1:3; 2:19; 4:13; 2 Thes 2:16. See also Prov 13:12; 29:18; Heb 6:18; 10:23; 1 Pet 1:3; 3:15.

292. The papers and declaration of the Consultation on the Church in Response to Human Need held in Wheaton in 1983 are a good place to begin one's reflection on these issues. See Samuel and Sugden 1983.

"light to the Gentiles" (Acts 13:47–49; Luke 2:32; 4:18–21). Living in the time between Ascension and Parousia, we recognize the presence of God's kingdom, live out its ethics (Matt 5–8), and call people and structures to be reconciled with creation, with themselves, with each other, and with God (2 Cor 5:18–21). This missiology of hope is deeply and creatively transformational, for it seeks to be a sign of the present and coming kingdom of God. Through it we recognize our profound commitment to radical transformation when we pray, "your kingdom come" (Matt 6:10).

Yet at the same time we will remember that the kingdom of God is present and coming only as the King comes. Our mission does not hasten Christ's coming, nor does it create the kingdom. Rather, the kingdom of God defines our mission (Orlando Costas 1979, 8–9), for only Jesus the King can bring the kingdom. Our mission, like that of Jesus, is to "proclaim the good news of the kingdom of God to the other towns also, because that is why (we have been) sent" (Luke 4:43; Acts 13:46–49). Even so, come, Lord Jesus.

In this time between the times, our participation in God's mission in this millenium awaits us like an adventure, a journey in the midst of, and moving toward, the present and coming reign of God, a running forward to discover what we already know: Jesus Christ is King.

PART V

SAMPLES OF MISSION THEOLOGY

CHAPTER 13
THE CITY: NO FIT PLACE FOR THE CHURCH?

A version of this chapter was originally published in an abbreviated form as, "Can Older Churches Grow in the City?" in *Global Church Growth* XXVI:1 (Jan–March 1989) 15–16. Used by permission.

THESIS

Today we need a new commitment to making older churches in transitional neighborhoods (OCTNs) viable expressions of the Church in the city. It is counterproductive for us to spend time and energy multiplying suburban churches while the OCTNs continue to die. In this chapter I offer some tentative suggestions and questions that need to be examined if we are to bring about a new era of growth of the many OCTNs struggling to survive in the cities of North America: vision, research, commitment, cooperation, and leadership.

INTRODUCTION

Several years ago, I was speaking at a church in Minnesota. That church was located in an area of the city that some might say was, "no fit place for a church." Before Richard (not his real name) had come, the church had declined to just a handful of members. Then Richard came. Within six years he had turned the church around. They were just completing the building of a new sanctuary. They were hosting a second congregation of Cambodian Christians. And the English language congregation was up over 200 in Sunday morning worship.

After the worship service, Richard invited me to his home for dinner. He said he wanted to talk to me. Richard was a tall, lanky, slow-talking, teddy bear kind of a man who cared deeply about people, the church, and his Lord. After dinner I found myself in Richard's living room—and he had a question for me.

"Chuck, I'm bored," he told me.

"This church is back on its feet, everything is running smoothly, the members are having a great time doing ministry, the church is growing again—someone

306 *Transforming Mission Theology*

else can pastor this church now. Chuck, I've been invited to go down to a city in Iowa. There is a church there that is dying. There are only a few members left. The church has been given one more year before the denominational judicatory closes it. But I'm not so young, anymore. Do you think I should go?"

What was I to say? I didn't know, so I started asking Richard some questions about the dying church in Iowa.

The building was located in a declining neighborhood. The members who still attended had all moved out of the area. It was located in a part of town some might say was "no fit place for a church." The members were discouraged. The building was in poor shape. The church was in financial trouble.

"Do you think I should go?" Richard asked.

Richard did accept the challenge. Not long ago I visited that city, and I was amazed at what I heard. Not only had Richard turned that dying church toward growth, the church had more than doubled its membership, called additional staff, and was in the midst of a building program to more than double the square footage of the church's buildings. The church had over a dozen new ministries going on in that city—all being carried out by members of the church!

But how many success stories like this do you know?

How many Richards do we have in the church in North America? The good news is that most Protestant denominations in North America seem to have a few leaders like Richard, but the bad news is that there are not enough of them, and seldom are they empowered by their denominations to do what they do best—turn dying congregations around to new life.

It takes only a few minutes to drive around the center-city of any large metroplex in the United States to see the closed church buildings, the former church buildings which are now being used for other purposes, and the run-down condition of other church buildings where a bare handful of faithful hangers-on still worship together in dying congregations. The trend does not seem to have run its course. During the past twenty years or so, many attempts have been made to reinvent the church in the city. Various perspectives have been suggested with names: seeker-sensitive church, emerging church, organic church, simple church, missional church, liquid church, healthy church. Many of these attempts spawned entire movements of networks of new endeavors in starting and multiplying churches. A sample of related publications can be seen in the footnote below.[293]

---

293. Eddie Gibbs 2000; Mark Dever 2007; Michael Frost and Alan Hirsch 2003; Reggie McNeal 2003; Mark Driscoll 2004; William Easum and Dave Travis 2003;

While many of these attempts and their related publications offer helpful insights and constructive vision, it would appear that these movements have had little lasting impact on the actual metroplexes in which they are located—especially in relation to older churches in transitional neighborhoods. The situation has made many of us realize the urgency of asking, "Can older churches grow in the city?" Or is the city in fact "no fit place for a church?"

THE URGENCY

Some years ago, in *World-Class Cities and World Evangelization*, David Barrett gave us an excellent historical summary of the life of the church in the city. "[Until] 1700," Barrett wrote, "all the world's five largest cities were non-Christian and even anti-Christian capitals. Certainly, they were hostile to Christian missions. . . .

> By the year 1900, all the world's five largest cities had become strongholds of Christian life, discipleship, urban evangelism, urban missions, foreign missions and global missions: London, New York, Paris, Berlin, and Chicago. This represented a major achievement in urban missions since AD 1700.
>
> But by 1985, . . . we find that 2 of the 5 world's largest cities are non-Christian, in fact 97% so. By AD 2000 3 of the 5 will be cities hostile to Christian missions—and by AD 2050, 4 of the top 5 will be non-Christian and even anti-Christian giants of around 40 million inhabitants each: Shanghai, Beijing, Bombay, and Calcutta. The fortunes of urban mission have thus reversed since 1900 and have declined startlingly. . . .
>
> The plain facts are that disciples [of Jesus] are decreasing as a proportion of all urban dwellers. . . . In the year 1800, 31% of all urban dwellers in the world were Christians. [In 1900] this had risen spectacularly to 69%. Then the tide suddenly turned.

Michael Frost 2006; Alan Hirsch 2007; Bill Hybels and Mark Mittelberg 1994; Dan Kimball 2003; Robert Lewis and Wayne Cordeiro 2005; Gary McIntosh and R. Daniel Reeves 2006; Thom S. Rainer 2001; Thom Rainer 2003; Alan J. Roxburgh and Fred Romanuk 2006; Stephen Seamands 2005; Steven Sjogren 1993, 2003; Steve Sjogren ed., 2002; Steve Sjogren, Dave Ping and Doug Pollock 2004; Ed Stetzer and David Putman 2006; Leonard Sweet 2000; Leonard Sweet, ed., and Andy Crouch, Michael Horton, Frederica Mathewes-Green, Brian McLaren and Erwin McManus 2003; Pete Ward 2002.

Today that proportion has dropped to only 44%, and by AD 2050 less than 38%.

The picture promises to remain bleak. In fact, Barrett counted about 95,000 new non-Christian urban dwellers added to the world's cities every day: about 219 million new non-Christians per year added to the world's cities.[294] The situation today does not appear to differ in any marked sense.

Harvie Conn called attention to the urgency of our seeking new life and new mission of the church in our world's cities.

> Statistically alone, the city demands attention. Today the number of people living in cities outnumbers the entire population of the world 150 years ago.[295] And that growth has been especially rapid outside the Anglo-Saxon world of North America and Europe. Africa's urban population has jumped from 14.4% in 1950 to 35.7% in 1990. During the same time period Latin America's urban community has moved from 40.6% to 70.75, East Asia from 16 to 38.6%. . . . A prominent feature of this global shift has been the megacity phenomenon. At the beginning of this century only twenty cities in the world had passed the million mark in size. By 1980, that figure had reached 235, with 118 located in economically less developed areas. In the thirty-five-year period from 1950 to 1985, the number of cities with over ten million people has gone from two (greater London and New York) to fifteen. And only three of these were found in Europe and North America. . . . And demanding the Christian integrity that links justice and compassion, and compassion to evangelism is the "urban anguish" of these cities—human dysfunction in a time of rapid social change; the political domination of the powerful over the marginalized; the widening gap between rich and poor. The city places on the Christian agenda

---

294. David Barrett, *World-Class Cities and World Evangelization*, Birmingham, AL: New Hope, 1986, 10.

295. Conn is quoting from John J. Palen, *The Urban World*, 3rd edition. New York: McGraw Hill, 1987, 5.

of reflection and action such discrete issues as justice and mercy, power and powerlessness, the church and the world.[296]

If the city is *"no fit place for the church,"* then our cities are in trouble—and so is the church!

In his challenging book, *Seek the Peace of the City*, Eldin Villafañe said it this way. "As we enter the 21st century, there is no greater need for [Christians] in the cities than to articulate in both word and deed, a social spirituality. The twin phenomena of urbanization and globalization, which define the ethos of our great cities, demand no more and no less than an authentically biblical spirituality [in the city]."[297]

In the United States, this matter screams for our attention—especially as it impacts older churches in transitional neighborhoods. Most older Protestant denominations have many declining congregations that are now over twenty-five years old, worship in buildings located in transitional neighborhoods, and are on the verge of turning to survival-mode existence. Typically, OCTNs were once-flourishing churches, but usually the charismatic founder is no longer the pastor, many of the charter members are now older, there is a relatively small middle-aged population, and attendance is less than half of what it was in the heyday of the congregation's life. Most of the discouraged membership commutes over five miles for worship. Usually the membership is strongly committed to the survival of their congregation, but not very interested in the new people who have moved into the surrounding neighborhood. You can see the picture: an older building, chain-link fences around the property,[298] plexiglas in front of the stained glass windows, bars in front of the plexiglas, gates and doors locked most of the time during the week, paint cracking, a commuting congregation that comes together only on Sunday morning. As Ray Bakke said,

---

296. Taken from page 2 of Harvie Conn, "A Contextual Theology of Mission for the City," prepublication draft of Conn's article by the same title in Charles Van Engen, Dean S. Gilliland and Paul Pierson eds., *The Good News of the Kingdom: Mission Theology for the Third Millenium* NY: Orbis, 1993, 96–104. See also Stan Guthrie, "Urban Ministry No Longer Neglected Missions Stepchild," *Evangelical Missions Quarterly* XXXII:1 (Jan. 1996), 82–83.

297. Eldin Villafañe, *Seek the Peace of the City: Reflections on Urban Ministry,* Grand Rapids: Eerdmans, 1995, 12.

298. Kathy Mowry poignantly described this kind of situation in Kathy Mowry, "Do Good Fences Make Good Neighbors: Toward a Theology of Welcome"'in Charles Van Engen and Jude Tiersma eds., 1994/2009, 105–24.

> The apparent irrelevance of Christianity to so many in our
> cities suggests a failure on the part of the church. However, it
> quickly became clear to me that in many cases the church is not
> even trying to evangelize these areas.[299]

The neighborhood surrounding older Protestant churches in transitional neighborhoods is usually experiencing major transition in terms of rezoning from residential to commercial, or changes in the ethnic/linguistic make up of the inhabitants, or transitions in the economic range and cultural style of the newcomers to the neighborhood. Mostly, the type of people who populate the neighborhood are no longer like those who worship in the church building on Sunday morning. Thus, the OCTN will be forced to choose to continue to be a declining commuting church, choose to die and be reborn into something appropriate for the new people of the neighborhood, move out and give up on the city, merge with another congregation, or slowly die the painful death of irrelevance.[300]

During the last several decades in the US, we have seen a new kind of transition. This involves people moving into the center-city from the outer rings of the city. Often termed "gentrification," this movement, particularly of Generation X and Millenials, involves transforming older mostly abandoned or neglected buildings into high-end apartments, condos, or "lofts." The new renters or owners often have high-end white-collar jobs in the center city, have tired of commuting long distances from home to work, and love the city. The economic and cultural transformation of older neighborhoods that have been "gentrified" is remarkable. However, the sad downside of gentrification is that almost all, if not all, of those who once lived in those same buildings when they were mostly low-income housing or low-rent apartments can no longer live there. They often become homeless or are pushed out to other parts of the city. What might be the implications of gentrification for the older congregations located in the midst of gentrified segments of the city?

---

299. Ray Bakke, *The Urban Christian: Effective Ministry in Today's Urban World*, Downers Grove: InterVarsity, 1987, 45.

300. Ray Bakke mentioned this kind of typology in, *Ibid.*, 87. For a more complete description, see Charles L Chaney, *Church Planting at the End of the Twentieth Century*, Wheaton: Tyndale, 1987, 119 ff. (Reprinted, 1994.)

FACTORS CONTRIBUTING TO THE
NEGLECT OF THE OCTNS

What has brought about such a widespread neglect of the beloved and beleaguered OCTNs? Focusing on the United States, the death of OCTNs in the city might be related to two factors, among many others. The dramatic increase in interest in the city in the late 1960s and early 70s did not translate into much renewed vigor for the local congregations in the city. Instead, the urban activists mostly left the church, becoming part of large networks of social service agencies and "Great Society" organizations intent upon doing ministry in the city, carrying out ministries for the people of the city, with little linkage to the local congregations in the city.[301] Many city churches that did get involved in urban ministry often ended up giving themselves away in service, gathering very few new people or new resources to themselves in the process, and eventually burning themselves out.[302]

The 1980s saw the result of economic policies that had disastrous effects on the cities of the United States, as evidenced by the dramatic rise in the number of homeless "street people." During this same time the American Church Growth Movement concentrated its energies in Protestant church planting in the suburbs, predominantly among the white middle-class, and at the same time neglected the matter of planting churches in the middle city, as Charles Chaney pointed out.[303] So the middle city (where the older transitional neighborhoods are to be found) was neglected both by the social activists of the inner city in the 1960s and early '70s and by the suburban church planters of the 1970s and 80s.[304] Clearly, we are

---

301. This perspective is clearly illustrated in Donald Schriver and Karl Ostrom, *Is There Hope for the City?* Phil: Westminster, 1977, where the church figures predominantly as one more ethically–conscious social institution which might bring about social change—not uniquely as the Church. There is very little concern in the volume for the continued life of OCTNs.

302. See, e.g., Benton Johnson, "Is There Hope for Liberal Protestantism?" in Dorothy Bass, Benton Johnson and Wade Clark Roof, *Mainstream Protestantism in the Twentieth Century: Its Problems and Prospects,* Louisville, KY: Committee on Theological Education, Council on Theological Education, Presbyterian Church, USA, 1986, 13–26.

303. Charles Chaney 1987, 98. Chaney gives an excellent bibliography on OCTNs on pages 141–142 of this volume. However, it is significant that all but one title appeared before 1980, and mostly prior to, or during, the 1960's. See also Clinton Stockwell, "Barriers and Bridges to Evangelization in Urban Neighborhoods," in David Frenchak, Clinton Stockwell and Helen Ujvarosy, *Signs of the Kingdom in the Secular City,* Chicago: Covenant, 1984, 97.

304. A case in point may be found in David Claerbaut's excellent volume on *Urban Ministry,* Grand Rapids: Zondervan, 1983. In chapter 9, "The Urban Church and the Urban Minister,"

dealing with one of the forgotten arenas of missiology.[305] Mainline Protestantism, which represents a major share of the OCTNs, has not given much attention to them either. For example, in a work by Wade Clark Roof and William McKinney, *American Mainline Religion: Its Changing Shape and Future*, there is no separate treatment of the effect of urban transition upon mainline congregations. The chapter on, "The Social Sources of Denominationalism Revisited," mentions social class, ethnicity, region, and race, recognizing that they, "all have lost force in shaping religious and cultural identities." But the impact of urbanization and transitional neighborhoods upon these social factors is not mentioned at all.[306] Maybe it is time to call for a renewed commitment to understanding, transforming, and growing OCTNs in the North American context. If we continue to neglect the OCTNs of our cities, we may reproduce the same phenomenon evident in mainline Protestantism in much of continental Europe—large cathedrals with only a few people worshipping in them.

SUGGESTIONS FOR CREATING VIABLE OCTNS

What we need today is a new commitment to making OCTNs viable expressions of the Church in the middle city. It will not do for us to spend time and energy in

---

Claerbaut contrasts the "inner city" church with the "middle-class" church. However, a case could be made that OCTNs are neither "inner city" nor "middle-class," and in fact are impacted by dynamics derived from both categories.

305. Interestingly, when the Center for Urban Church Studies commissioned Larry L. Rose and C. Kirk to edit a book intended to, "inform and challenge the body of Christ, and in particular the part of the body called Southern Baptists, to the reality of urbanization in our world and the need to be better informed and equipped to minister in the urban context," the matter of OCTNs was forgotten. In an otherwise excellent work for ministry and church planting in the city, there is no acknowledgment of the presence, or importance, of OCTNs already present in the city. A recent notable exception is Raymond Bakke and Samuel Roberts, *The Expanded Mission of 'Old First' Churches*, Valley Forge: Judson Press, 1986. The most complete research I know of regarding OCTN's is the outstanding work done by Kathy Mowry in her PhD research in missiology, *Getting to Resurrection: Eschatological Imagination for Congregations Engaging Transitional Neighborhoods*, PhD dissertation done for the School of Intercultural Studies, Fuller Theological Seminary, 2011.

306. Cf. Wade Clark Roof and William McKinney, *American Mainline Religion: Its Changing Shape and Future*, New Brunswick: Rutgers U. Press, 1987, 145.

planting suburban churches, just to have the OCTNs continue to die.[307] Because of the dearth of relevant research concerning OCTNs, let me offer some tentative suggestions and questions which need to be examined if we are to bring about a new era of growth in the OCTNs of North America.: vision, research, commitment, cooperation and leadership.

A. Vision

David Roozen, William McKinney, and Jackson Carroll carried out a little-known, but nonetheless very significant study of the churches in Hartford, Connecticut.[308] Most of the congregations they studied were OCTNs. They began their study by stressing the essential role of the local congregation.

> The local congregation is the future of the church . . . A congregation, by virtue of its relationship to a religious or faith tradition, has the capacity, in a limited way, to transcend the determinative power of its context and the values and interests of its members so that it influences them as well as being influenced by them. . . . The local church is the best model for creating a bridge between the microcosm (personal, individual faith, commitment and vision), and the macrocosm (social, public belief, ethics, and action). . . . Relatively few institutions can 'mediate' effectively between society's megastructures and individuals, but congregations are clearly among them. They mediate in the sense that they intersect with both the "outer" world of structures, institutions, and social movements and the "inner" world of individual meaning and purpose. . . . Local congregations are spiritually, missionally, and socially responsible for the world, the society, and the people which surround them. . . . An essential element of ministry in the church involves ministry in, through, and to the socio-cultural context of the various 'communities' in which the local congregations is incarnated and directed in

---

307. My denomination, the Reformed Church in America, has been actively planting new suburban churches during the last twenty years, and yet the total number of congregations has remained relatively stable due to the number of OCTNs which disbanded during the same time period.

308. David Roozen, William McKinney, and Jackson Carroll, *Varieties of Religious Presence: Mission in Public Life,* NY: Pilgrim Press, 1984.

mission. . . . The meaning of "mission" for a local gathering of believers must be derived from and addressed to the needs, aspirations, perspectives, dreams, and future of the socio-cultural mosaic of peoples of the surrounding social context.

Through their research, Roozen, McKinney, and Carroll forcefully demonstrated that congregations tend to exhibit aspects of four major mission orientations in relation to their context: activist, citizen, sanctuary, and evangelist. The first step in turning an OCTN toward growth, may entail discovering its particular missional orientation to its city. And, given the context, one missional orientation may be more conducive to growth than another.

Many urban specialists have stressed the importance of a sense of vision, of a theology of hope, a firm grasp on eschatology, a sense of purpose and future for bringing new life to older congregations. This is especially true for OCTNs, and we need to discover how to allow such vision to arise from the membership of the OCTNs.

B. Research

Tony Campolo emphasized the unique "sociological nature of the urban church," in *Metro-Ministry: Ways & Means for the Urban Church* (Frenchak and Keyes).[309] It is increasingly clear that this uniqueness is also due in part to the special nature of transitional neighborhoods. We need more research here. We need to learn how the Richards in older denominations do what they do.

There is also insufficient research concerning the history, nature, and complex typology of OCTNs. A good example of such research was Robert Wilson's study of *The Effect of Racially Changing Communities on Methodist Churches in Thirty-Two Cities in the Southwest.*[310] And yet even that study focused primarily on racial (mostly black-white, white-black) transition, rather than economic, social, educational, or cultural transition, as we see it today. We need more people using available

---

309. Campolo, *Metro-Ministry: Ways & Means for the Urban Church*, Elgin, IL: David C. Cook, 1979, 26–42.

310. Robert Wilson, *The Effect of Racially Changing Communities on Methodist Churches in Thirty-Two Cities in the Southwest,* New York: Department of Research and Survey, National Division, Board of Missions of the Methodist Church, 1986. Walter Ziegenhals' work, *Urban Churches in Transition*. NY: Pilgrim, 1978, also looks at transition in primarily racial categories.

resources[311] to help OCTNs carry out detailed self-studies and begin to understand who they are and who they need to be in the midst of the massive changes they face in transitional neighborhoods.

C. Commitment

We cannot afford to give up on the thousands of OCTNs in this country. On the contrary, they are such a key part of the presence of the Body of Christ in the city, they know the city so well, and they have such a strong sense of survivability, that we need to let them inspire and guide us in mission in the city.[312]

D. Cooperation

Robert Linthicum, director of urban advance of World Vision, made a strong case for the need for networking in the city, and called for much more cooperation and unity of all churches struggling in the city.[313]

Although we are all aware of the incredible diversity of cultural units in the city, and the difficult barriers which exist between them, yet it seems that it may be time to begin helping the OCTNs become as ethnically comprehensive as the neighborhoods in which they minister. Thus we will need a theology derived from Ephesians 2 which recognizes that the middle wall of partition between people has been broken down, and all who are in Christ are re-created to be one new humanity in Him.

It may be time to take seriously the unity of the Church in a metroplex. We can no longer set the churches in one part of the city (like those in the suburbs, for example) over against the believing communities in another part of the city. Together they are all one Body of Jesus Christ, interdependent, and mutually-accountable for support and encouragement. Maybe it is time we challenge the megachurches of a city to be the catalysts for new things to happen in the OCTNs of their city. Or maybe new networks of OCTNs need to be created whereby a

---

311. Cf, e.g., Jackson Carroll, Carl Dudley, and William McKinney, eds., *Handbook for Congregational Studies*, Nashville: Abingdon, 1986; and E. Bruce Menning, *Shaping a Future Effectively*, Grand Rapids: RCA Synod of Michigan, 1985.

312. A good example of just such commitment is David Sheppard's work in London. See David Sheppard, *Built as a City: God and the Urban World Today*, London: Hodder and Stoughton, 1974.

313. Robert C. Linthicum, "Doing Effective Ministry in the City," *Together* (April–June, 1988), 1–2.

number of them together would form a loose network, a kind of decentralized megachurch, with its various cells and congregations distributed all over the city.

Although a number of very significant studies have been produced lately concerning mission in the city, few of them look carefully at the Church in the city, and the way local congregations interface with the whole metroplex system. As Harvie Conn has reminded us, we must not give in to the "secularization myth" of the city.[314] Rather, we need to be very creative in finding new ways of being the Church in the city in a way that is viable, dynamic, proclamational, and growing. And the rise of "home cell groups and house churches" demonstrates the possibility for such creativity.[315]

E. Leadership

In addition to vision, research, commitment, and cooperation, probably the greatest need at this time is for pastoral leadership which can turn OCTNs from slow death to dynamic new life. Tex Sample suggested a unique model of urban pastoral leadership which seems to be appropriate for this task.[316] He called it the "Ward-heeler" (heel, meaning the heel of a shoe, rather than having to do with health). A ward is a small area in a city, the phrase coming especially from the context of Chicago. In Chicago, the leader and caregiver walked the ward, knew everyone in the ward, provided whatever was necessary for the people of the ward—and, in turn, was followed by the people of the ward and led the ward. Unfortunately, we find few seminaries and leadership training programs that have taken Sample's suggestions seriously. Clearly we need many pastors like Richard who know how to turn dying OCTNs into viable, vibrant, growing churches in transitional neighborhoods.

We need women and men who like Richard

    a. *See* the city with new eyes;

    b. *Can be creative* in finding new ways of being the church in the city in ways that are viable, dynamic, proclamational, wholistic, and

314. Cf. Harvie Conn, *A Clarified Vision for Urban Mission: Dispelling the Urban Stereotypes*, Grand Rapids: Zondervan, 1987, 93 ff.

315. See, e.g., C. Kirk Hadaway, Stuart A. Wright, and Francis M. DuBose, *Home Cell Groups and House Churches*, Nashville: Broadman, 1987.

316. See Tex Sample, *Blue-Collar Ministry: Facing Economic and Social Realities of Working People*, Valley Forge: Judson Press, 1984.

transformational (the rise of home cell groups and house churches demonstrates the possibility of such creativity);

c. Are committed to being God's presence in the city;

d. Will cooperate together to encounter *together* the city; and

e. Will lead the church in the city in new and creative forms of ministry.

CONCLUSION

The church is not a social agency, but it is of social significance in the city. The church is not city government, but God called it to announce and live out his kingdom in all its political significance. The church is not a bank, but God called it to educate the people of the city concerning the gospel of love, justice, and social transformation. The church is not a family, but it is the family of God, called to be neighbors to all those whom God love. The church is not a building, but it needs buildings and owns buildings to carry out its ministries. The church is not exclusive, not better, but God specially called it to be different in the way it serves the city. The church is not an institution, but it needs institutional structures to effect changes in the lives of people and society. The church is not a community development organization, but the development of community is essential to the church's nature. [317]

Earlier in the book, I quoted Lesslie Newbigin. With reference to the topic of this chapter, I believe it merits repeating. Lesslie Newbigin spoke of the congregation in the city as "a hermeneutic of the gospel." This means that persons and institutions in the surrounding contextual environment read the gospel through the mediation of the local church. "I confess," wrote Newbigin in *The Gospel in a Pluralist Society*,

> that I have come to feel that the primary reality of which we have to take account in seeking for a Christian impact on public life is the Christian congregation . . . The only hermeneutic of the gospel is a congregation of men and women who believe it and live by it . . . This community will have, I think the following six characteristics:

---

317. Charles Van Engen, "Constructing a Theology of Mission for the City," in Charles Van Engen and Jude Tiersma, eds., *God So Loves the City: Seeking a Theology for Urban Mission*, Monrovia, CA: MARC, World Vision, 1994, 247–248.

It will be a community of praise . . .

It will be a community of truth . . .

It will be a community that does not live for itself . . .

It will be a community . . . sustained in the exercise of the priesthood in the world . . .

It will be a community of mutual responsibility . . .

It will be a community of hope.[318]

I am convinced that *the city is a fit place for the church.* Let's find more Richards
who can help us learn how the church can fit contextually, ecclesiologically, missionally and transformationally in the exploding cities of our world.

In *The Once and Future Church,* Loren Mead said it this way.

Congregations—like clergy, laity and executives—are living
in a time in which landmarks have been erased and old ways
have stopped working. We also live in a time when the answers
have not yet become clear. It is a time that calls for steadiness
and perseverance through uncertainty. Such a time generates
energy for change, but it also generates intense anxiety that
makes quick answers attractive, so long as they are quick.

The church—its laity, clergy, congregations, executives and
bishops—has organized and structured itself for one mission.
We have awakened to a world in which the mission frontier has
changed. The organization and the structures of church life,
formed for that one mission now need to be reoriented to face a
new frontier. The task ahead is the reinvention of the church.[319]

Let's invite the Richards of our Protestant denominations to show us how
the church can be transformed—reinvented, as it were—in such a way that the
church is once again, fit for the city. Is the city a fit place for the church? For the
sake of the city, I hope so. For the sake of Christ's church in the city, I pray it may
be so.

318. Lesslie Newbigin, *The Gospel* in a Pluralist Society, Grand Rapids: Eerdmans, 1989,
222–33.

319. Loren Mead, *The Once and Future Church: Reinventing the Congregation for a New Mission
Frontier.* NY: Alban Institute, 1991, 42.

CHAPTER 14
MISSION THEOLOGY WITH REGARD TO MIGRANTS

First published as the English translation of the original Spanish-language article as, "Biblical Perspectives on the Role of Immigrants in God's Mission," *Journal of Latin American Theology: Christian Reflections from the Latino South*, vol. 02 (2008), 15–38. An adapted form of this chapter was also published in Ekron Chan, Jeffrey Lu and Chloe Sun eds., *Logos for Life: Essays Commemorating Logos Evangelical Seminary 20th Anniversary.* Logos Evangelical Seminary: El Monte, CA, 2009, 285–318; and in *Evangelical Review of Theology* XXXIV:1 (Jan. 2010), 29–43. Adapted and used by permission.

THESIS

In the Bible there exists a clear emphasis on compassion toward, and care for, the migrant and stranger as a receptor of just and compassionate treatment on the part of the people of God, by other folks in general, and on the part of governments. However, the Bible also offers us other and different perspectives of migrants and strangers as partners, co-laborers, co-participants in the mission of God to the nations. In this chapter I will focus on the composite of viewpoints that see migrants as active agents of God's mission: God's instruments who contribute to the creation of human history and participate in the mediation of the grace of God to the nations. I will offer a wide panorama by following a thread of the tapestry of the Bible that will serve as a kind of outline signaling the way in which God uses migrants in God's mission to the nations.

INTRODUCTION

Some years ago, the United Nations estimated that there were around twenty-one million refugees and displaced persons around the globe at that time.[320] Clearly, this figure is now outdated and eclipsed by the huge migration of people from the Middle East to Europe and elsewhere during 2015–2016. And this figure also did not include those who migrated from rural areas to the cities of the world, nor those who voluntarily moved from one nation or region to another looking for

---

320. "2005 Global Refugee Trends," http://www.unhcr.org/statistics, 2006.

better living conditions today. Adding these categories together, one would estimate that, at any given moment today, there are at least fifty million people who have left one place of residence to migrate to another. So it is fair to assume that in this new century and new millennium we are seeing the greatest movement of humanity around the globe ever seen in human history. God is calling the Church of Jesus Christ—and presenting the Church with a marvelous opportunity—to join together in solidarity with immigrants, strangers, new-comers, and foreigners from all the nations that surround the Church in all parts of the world.

We know that throughout history we have seen great movements of peoples and groups from one place to another. This includes the Latin American continent where the history of many peoples, ancient and modern, tells the stories of periodic migrations of peoples from north to south, from east to west, from rural areas to the cities, from small towns to large cities, and so forth. There are migrants who have fled very negative economic and political situations. There are hundreds of thousands of people who have fled dictatorships, civil wars, and international conflicts. There are migrants who have been transported from one place to another by force as slaves. Many migrants voluntarily have left their homes seeking better living conditions. Some migrants have been forced to leave because of natural disasters. And many of these migrants have contributed in remarkable ways to the new nations to which they have gone, in terms, for example, of technology, science, industry, new cultural forms, the arts, education, and agriculture. The missions established by the missionary orders of the Roman Catholic Church in California during the nineteenth century are an example of the impact that migrants can have on their new environments.

As members of the Southern California chapter of the Latin American Theological Fraternity and in thinking about the subject of migrants and strangers (M/S),[321] we should remember that we are talking about ourselves. In Los Angeles we are all migrants and/or descendents of migrants. I am an example of this phenomenon. My grand parents emigrated as young people from the Netherlands to the central part of the United States, to the states of Nebraska and Iowa. My parents emigrated from the US to Chiapas, Mexico. And I emigrated from Mexico

---

321. In the rest of this chapter, to save space, I will use the initials M/S to refer to migrants and strangers of various types, categories and circumstances, including women and children. The femininization of poverty is one of the most critical aspects of the new reality of our world in the twenty-first century.

to Los Angeles. I am a migrant and the descendent of migrants who in our history represent at least three cultures and four languages.

A VARIETY OF BIBLICAL PERSPECTIVES CONCERNING THE STRANGER AND THE ALIEN.

The Bible presents various perspectives concerning the stranger and the alien.

A. The stranger as enemy

There are occasions when the Bible presents the stranger as an enemy of the people of God. See, for example, Isaiah 1:7; 2:6; 5:17; Matthew 17:25, 26; and Hebrews 11:39. More dominant is the perspective of the stranger and "the nations" (meaning all those peoples and cultures that are not a part of the people of God) as being unclean, sinful, and unholy and will cause the people of God to lose their true faith in YHWH. At times "the nations" are represented as those who will take possession of the land and belongings of Israel as God's punishment for the unfaithfulness of the people of God. See, for example, Genesis 31:15; Leviticus 22:12,13,25; Numbers 1:51; 3:10,38; 16:40; 18:4,7; Deuteronomy 17:15; 31:16; 25:5; Judges 19:12; Nehemiah 9:12; Job 15:19; Psalm 69:8; Proverbs 2:16; 5:10,17,20; 6:1; 7:7; 11:15; 14:10; 20:16; 27:2,13; Ecclesiastes 6:2; Isaiah 1:7; 2:6; 5:17; 61:5; 62:8; Jeremiah 2:25; 3:13; 5:19; 51:51; Lamentations 5:2; Ezekiel 7: 21; 11:9; 16:32; 28:10; 30:12; 31:12; 44:7,9; Hos 7:9; 8:7; Joel 3:17; Obadiah 11:12; Matthew 27:7; and John 10:5. In John 10:5 the stranger is the foreign shepherd whose unknown voice the sheep do not recognize and will not heed (see also Acts 17:21; Hebrews 11:39). It would seem that this perspective is affirmed over a long period of time.

B. The stranger is to obey the law of God

Alongside the perspective mentioned above, another viewpoint is strongly affirmed on the part of God: that the stranger who lives in the midst of the people of Israel is to obey the same norms and keep the same commandments that the Israelites were to keep. See, for example, Genesis 17:12, 27; Exodus 12:19–49; 20:10,20; 23:12; 30:33; Leviticus 16:29; 17; 18:26; 19:33; 20:2; 22:10, 18; 24:16,21–22; 25:6; Numbers 9:14; 15:15, 16, 26, 30; 19:10; 35:13; Deuteronomy 1:16; 5:14; 14:14–18,21,29; 16:11,14;24:14,17; 18:43; 19:11, 22; 26:11; 27: 19; 29: 11, 22; 31:12; Joshua 8:33,35; 20:9 (with reference to the cities of refuge); 1 Kings 8 (Solomon's prayer); 2 Chron 15:9; 30:25 (the prayer of Solomon); Psalm 18:44,45; Ezekiel 14:7; Acts 2:10.

For example, Leviticus 24:21–22 says,

> Whoever kills an animal must make restitution, but whoever kills a human being is to be put to death. You are to have the same law for the foreigner and the native-born. I am the Lord your God.

C. The care of the stranger who lives in the midst of the people of God

God does not only require that the stranger who lives in the midst of the People of Israel be treated fairly and equitably, but God also commands that the M/S is to receive the care and compassion of the people of God. In many texts the Bible couples the idea of the M/S with reference to the orphan and the widow. And compassion and intentional care is required, especially for the orphan, the widow and the stranger who lives in the midst of the people of God. See, for example, Leviticus 19:18; 19:33; 25; Deuteronomy 10:18 (together with the orphan and the widow); 14:21; 16:14; 26:12,13 (together with the orphan and the widow); 19:11; 27:19 (together with the orphan and the widow); Psalm 94:6 (together with the orphan and the widow); 146:9 (together with the orphan and the widow); Proverbs 3:19; Jeremiah 7:6; 22:3; Ezekiel 22:7,29; 47:22,23; Zechariah 7:10; and Malachi 3:5. The New Testament emphasizes the love of neighbor and enemy. See, for example, "you shall love your neighbor" in Matthew 5:43; 19:19; 22:39; Mark 12:31; Luke 10:27; Romans 12:20 (cf. Prov 25;21, 22; Ex 23:4; Matt 5:44; Luke 6:27); Romans 13:9; Galatians 5:14; 1 Timothy 5:10; Hebrews 13:2; James 2:8; 3 John 55.

D. Biblical perspectives of the instrumental role of the immigrant in God's mission

Generally speaking, when we think of the M/S we consider the marginalized, the needy, the minority groups, and those who are underrepresented in social, political, and economic arenas. In the Bible there exists a clear emphasis on compassion toward, and care for, the M/S's as receptors of just and compassionate treatment on the part of the people of God, by other folks in general, and on the part of governments. These biblical perspectives concerning the M/S's are well known and important.

However, in both testaments one finds an even stronger emphasis on the role of the people of God as special instruments of God's mission to impact and bless the nations. The Bible offers us other and different perspectives of the M/S's as partners, co-laborers, co-participants in the mission of God to the nations. In this chapter I will focus on the composite of viewpoints that see the M/S's as active agents of God's mission, God's instruments who contribute to the creation of human history and participate in the mediation of the grace of God to the nations.[322] It is not my intention to present an exhaustive biblical theology of the M/S's as found in the Bible, nor do I intend to present a detailed study or a minute examination of all the narratives or all the biblical passages having to do with this theme. Rather, I want to offer here a wide panorama by following a thread of the tapestry of the Bible[323] that will serve as a kind of outline signaling the way in which God uses the M/S's in God's mission to the nations.

This emphasis begins already with Abraham whose story is the story of all M/S's, including our own stories.

> My father was a wandering Aramean, and he went down into Egypt with a few people and lived there and became a great nation, powerful and numerous. But the Egyptians mistreated us and made us suffer, putting us to hard labor. Then we cried out to the Lord, the God of our ancestors, and the Lord heard our voice and saw our misery, toil and oppression. So the Lord brought us out of Egypt with a mighty hand and an outstretched arm, with great terror and with miraculous signs and wonders. He brought us to this place and gave us this land, a land flowing with milk and honey; and now I bring the firstfruits of the soil that you, O Lord, have given me. (Deut 26:5–10)

When the Bible first introduces us to Abram, he is presented as an M/S.

---

322. Here I follow the spirit of Paulo Freire who taught us the important transformational dynamism of conscientizing the people such that the poor and marginalized begin to catch a glimpse of the possibility that they may themselves be active agents of their own history and creators of their own destiny. See, for example, among other related works, Paulo Freire, *Pedagogy of the Oppressed* (New York: Herder and Herder, 1970).

323. In relation to reading the Bible as a tapestry that presents the *missio Dei* in narrative form, see Charles Van Engen, *Mission on the Way: Issues in Mission Theology,* Grand Rapids: Baker 1996, 17–43.

This is the account of Terah's family line. Terah became the father of Abram, Nahor and Haran. And Haran became the father of Lot. While his father Terah was still alive, Haran died in Ur of the Chaldeans, in the land of his birth. . . . Terah took his son Abram, his grandson Lot son of Haran, and his daughter-in-law Sarai, the wife of his son Abram, and together they set out from Ur of the Chaldeans to go to Canaan. But when they came to Haran, they settled there. Terah lived 205 years, and he died in Haran.

The Lord had said to Abram, "Go from your country, your people and your father's household and go to the land I will show you. I will make you into a great nation and I will bless you; I will make your name great, and you will be a blessing. I will bless those who bless you, and whoever curses you I will curse; and all peoples on earth will be blessed through you." So Abram went, as the Lord had told him; and Lot went with him. Abram was seventy-five years old when he set out from Haran. He took his wife Sarai, his nephew Lot, all the possessions they had accumulated and the people they had acquired in Haran, and they set out for the land of Canaan, and they arrived there. (Gen 11: 27–12:5)

The people of Israel recognized that an important aspect of their self-understanding, their identity as a special people, derived from being strangers, sojourners, aliens, migrants. (See, for example, Job 19:15; Psalm 69:8; Ephesians 2:12; and Colossians 1:21.) God says to Abram,

Know for certain that for four hundred years your descendants will be strangers in a country not their own, and they will be enslaved and mistreated there. But I will punish the nation they serve as slaves, and afterward they will come out with great possessions. You, however, will go to your ancestors in peace and be buried at a good old age. In the fourth generation your descendants will come back here, for the sin of the Amorites has not yet reached its full measure. (Gen 15:13–16; see also Gen 23:4; 28:4; Ex 3:13–15; 6:2–4)

Thus, an integral aspect of Abraham's missionary call to be an instrument of God's mission to the nations implied that he and his family would be strangers, aliens, sojourners, and migrants. See, for example, Genesis 12:10; 15:13; 17:8; 21:23,34; 23:4; 28:4; 36:7; 37:1; Exodus 6:4; 1 Chronicles 29:15; 37:1; Job 19:18; Psalm 39:12; 69:8; 119:19; Obadiah 11; Acts 13:17; Ephesians 2:12, 19; Colossians 1:21; Hebrews 11:13; and 1 Peter 1:1. Sharing this vision, Luke presents Jesus as a "stranger" in Jesus' encounter with the two who were walking to Emmaus after the passion week (Luke 24:18).

BIBLICAL PERSPECTIVES OF THE STRANGER/ ALIEN AS AN INSTRUMENT OF GOD'S MISSION

In this second section of the chapter we will examine the place of the M/S's in relation to the motivations, agents, means, and goals of the mission of God to the nations.

A. The motivations of the M/S's in the mission of God to the nations

There are numerous indications in the Bible that demonstrate how God used the very history of the people of Israel as a pilgrim, migrant people to motivate them to participate in God's mission to the nations. For example, in Exodus 22:21, God says, "Do not mistreat an alien or oppress him, for you were aliens in Egypt." In Exodus 23:9 God repeats, "Do not oppress an foreigner; you yourselves know how it feels to be foreigners, because you were foreigners in Egypt." In 1 Peter 2:9–11 the writer offers an echo of this same motivation to be instruments of God's mission to the nations, drawing his vision from Deuteronomy.

> But you are a chosen people, a royal priesthood, a holy nation, God's special possession that you may declare the praises of him who called you out of darkness into his wonderful light. Once you were not a people, but now you are the people of God; once you had not received mercy, but now you have received mercy. Dear friends, I urge you, as foreignersand exiles, to abstain from sinful desires, which war against your soul. Live such good lives among the pagans that, though they accuse you of doing wrong, they may see your good deeds and glorify God on the day he visits us.

In addition to participating in God's mission to the nations, the people of God were to treat the stranger who lived in their midst with compassion and justice precisely because they had themselves once been strangers and aliens in Egypt. Thus in Leviticus 19:33–34 it is precisely because the children of Israel had themselves been M/S's that they should be motivated to treat the stranger who lives in their midst with care and compassion. "When an alien lives with you in your land, do not mistreat him. The alien living with you must be treated as one of your native-born. Love him as yourself, for you were aliens in Egypt. I am the LORD your God" (Lev 19:33–34).

Having experienced the life of the pilgrim and sojourner, the people of Israel should also care for the land with a special sense of stewardship because the land belongs to God and not to Israel. "The land must not be sold permanently, because the land is mine and you are but aliens and my tenants" (Lev 25:22–23).

The judges were to judge the stranger on the same basis as the Israelite (Deut 1:16) and Israel was to love the M/S for two reasons: (1) because God loves the stranger and the alien; and (2) because Israel was also a foreigner and stranger in Egypt.

> For the LORD your God is God of gods and Lord of lords, the great God, mighty and awesome, who shows no partiality and accepts no bribes. He defends the cause of the fatherless and the widow, and loves the foreigner residing among you, giving them food and clothing. And you are to love those who are foreigners, for you yourselves were foreigners in Egypt. Fear the Lord your God and serve him. Hold fast to him and take your oaths in his name. He is the one you praise; he is your God, who performed for you those great and awesome wonders you saw with your own eyes. Your ancestors who went down into Egypt were seventy in all, and now the Lord your God has made you as numerous as the stars in the sky. (Deut 10:17–22)

In Deuteronomy 23:7 Israel is commanded, "Do not despise an Edomite, for the Edomites are related to you. Do not despise an Egyptian, because you resided as foreigners in their country."

This aspect of the self-understanding of Israel as a pilgrim people had profound spiritual and existential implications. In his prayer for the temple that his son Solomon would build, David recognizes the fact that the people of God are migrants and strangers.

> But who am I, and who are my people, that we should be able to give as generously as this? Everything comes from you, and we have given you only what comes from your hand. We are foreigners and strangers in your sight, as were all our ancestors. Our days on earth are like a shadow, without hope. (1 Chron 29:14–15)

The psalmist also emphasizes that precisely because they are immigrants and strangers God will hear their cry (Psalm 39:12; 119:19; see also Jer 35:7; 1 Pet 1:1 and 2:11).

How powerful could this motivation be to move our churches to participate in the mission of God locally and globally, participating in the movement of the Holy Spirit in mission, because we too were and are M/S's! It seems to me a great shame—and I consider it a sin of omission—that many migrants and descendents of migrants in southern California have forgotten who they are, that they themselves are also M/S's, a forgetfulness that appears to produce an attitude such that those of us who are M/S's and descendents of M/S's should demonstrate little or no compassion or receptivity, much less hospitality, for the new M/S's who have recently arrived in our neighborhoods and communities.

B. The M/S's as agents of God's mission to the nations

A second aspect of this missiological and instrumental perspective of the M/S's role in the mission of God has to do with the form in which various personalities are presented in the Bible as agents of God's mission precisely because they are M/S's. Let me highlight a few examples.

The first example we have already mentioned. Integral to his call to leave his homeland and his extended family clan and begin a pilgrimage to a new land that God would show him, and particularly as a stranger, pilgrim, foreigner and immigrant, Abraham would participate in God's mission to the nations. To be a stranger and an alien was such a fundamental aspect of the self-understanding of Abraham's family that Isaac also understood this quality as being an integral part of God's vision for him, a self-portrait that Isaac sees as fundamental to his being an instrument of God's mission to the nations. Thus God tells Isaac,

> Now there was a famine in the land—besides the previous
> famine of Abraham's time—and Isaac went to Abimelech king
> of the Philistines in Gerar. The Lord appeared to Isaac and
> said, "Do not go down to Egypt; live in the land where I tell
> you to live. Stay in this land for a while, and I will be with you
> and will bless you. For to you and your descendants I will give
> all these lands and will confirm the oath I swore to your father
> Abraham. I will make your descendants as numerous as the stars
> in the sky and will give them all these lands, and through your
> offspring all nations on earth will be blessed, because Abraham
> obeyed me and did everything I required of him, keeping my
> commands, my decrees and my instructions." So Isaac stayed
> in Gerar. (Gen 26:1–6)

This biblical perspective of the M/S as an agent of God's mission acquires
deeper roots and broader significance throughout the history of Israel. We can
see how the story of Joseph sheds light on this missional viewpoint. Sold as a slave
and sent to Egypt, Joseph is forced to become an alien, stranger, migrant. Joseph
suffers through deceit, mistreatment, false accusations, undeserved imprisonment,
and utter loneliness in being forgotten in prison, a situation which many of today's
M/S's have also experienced. But precisely as an M/S, Joseph saves his family
from famine, saves all of Egypt, and feeds all the peoples surrounding Egypt.
Egypt grows in its international influence and power because of the work of this
migrant in the halls of power in Egypt. Joseph adapts to the Egyptian culture
to such an extent that when his own brothers come asking for food they do not
recognize him. In the end, Joseph himself acknowledges his special role as an M/S
when he says to his brothers,

> Then Joseph said to his brothers, "Come close to me." When
> they had done so, he said, "I am your brother Joseph, the one
> you sold into Egypt! And now, do not be distressed and do not
> be angry with yourselves for selling me here, because it was to
> save lives that God sent me ahead of you. For two years now
> there has been famine in the land, and for the next five years
> there will not be plowing and reaping. But God sent me ahead
> of you to preserve for you a remnant on earth and to save your

lives by a great deliverance. So then, it was not you who sent me
here, but God. . . .

Joseph said to them, "Don't be afraid. Am I in the place of
God? You intended to harm me, but God intended it for good to
accomplish what is now being done, the saving of many lives. So
then, don't be afraid. I will provide for you and your children."
And he reassured them and spoke kindly to them. (Gen 45:4–8;
50:19–21)

The Bible develops this missiological perspective in a significant number of
narratives about persons whom God uses precisely as M/S's. We could mention
Daniel and his missional role in Babylon. A cross-cultural missionary sent against
his will to a strange land, Daniel as an administrator was a special agent of God's
mission even though initially he is an exiled prisoner. Daniel devoted his life to
serving as counselor and friend of the kings of Babylon and Persia for over 50
years, even though he was a foreigner.

We could also mention the two women whom Jesus highlights in Luke 4 as
special agents of God's mission. Both are M/S's. One was the widow of Seraphath
(1 Kings 1:8–16), the other a young Israelite girl taken captive serving as a slave in
the household of Naaman the Syrian. As an agent of God's mission, the little girl's
simple testimony brings about Naaman's healing from leprosy (2 Kings 5:1–4).
Precisely as foreign women, God uses them in God's mission to the nations.

During the exile in Babylon, the people of Israel found themselves having
to choose between two different perspectives. On the one hand, they could see
themselves as victims as expressed in Psalm 137:4 where the Israelites—as captives in Babylon—cry, saying, "How can we sing the songs of the Lord while in a
foreign land (or as foreigners in this land)?" On the other hand, they could choose
a self-understanding as active agents of the mission of God, even though they were
strangers in a new nation. It is fascinating that during the exact same moment in
history, with reference to the same persons experiencing the same exile, in the
same context, God says to them through Jeremiah,

Build houses and settle down; plant gardens and eat what they
produce. Marry and have sons and daughters; find wives for
your sons and give your daughters in marriage, so that they
too may have sons and daughters. Increase in number there;
do not decrease. Also, seek the peace and prosperity of the city

> to which I have carried you into exile. Pray to the Lord for it,
> because if it prospers, you too will prosper. (Jer 29:5–7)

This second perspective involves the Israelites seeing themselves as being sent to Babylon by God with a missional purpose as agents of God's mission for the well-being of the land to which they had been sent.

We could mention Esther, a woman who as a descendant of M/S's adapts so well to her new culture that she is chosen to be Queen of Persia. And even as an M/S, Esther allows God to use her both to save her people from being destroyed, and to be the catalyst through whom all Persia comes to know about the God of Israel. Mordecai the Jew, also a migrant, ends up exercising great influence in Persia.

If we had space, we could mention David, exiled among the Philistines, an M/S whom God uses among them. David becomes companions in arms with, and counselor to, Achish, king of Gath (1 Sam 27). Maybe this is why the New Testament writers seem to so easily and naturally take note that Jesus himself was an M/S, exiled as a child to Egypt.

This perspective of the M/S as an agent of God's mission appears to be so compelling that Ezekiel speaks of God using foreigners themselves in God's mission of judgment against Israel when Israel refuses to be an instrument of God's mission to the nations (Ezek 28:7). This vision is echoed in Habakkuk 1:5–6 where God says that God will use the Chaldeans in God's mission. It is surprising that Paul makes reference to this same passage from Habakkuk in his first major sermon in which he develops his mission theology (Acts 13:41). Isaiah echoes these sentiments when he states that, due to the infidelity of Israel, God will use other nations in God's mission (Isa 61:5).

Can we imagine what God would like to do through the Hispanic/Latino peoples as agents of his mission in the reread evangelization of North America and Europe?

C. The M/S's as means of God's mission to the nations

A third aspect of this missionary and instrumental perspective of the M/S in God's mission has to do with the way in which immigration itself is presented as a fundamental method of God's mission to the nations. There are indications in the Bible that on certain occasions God used immigration to fulfill certain important aspects of God's mission. Clearly there is an intimate relationship between the agents whom God uses in God's mission and the means by which God chooses to carry out that mission. Yet in this chapter I will make a distinction (though it may at the outset appear to be somewhat artificial) between these two aspects of God's mission in order to be able to read with new missiological eyes the history of God's mission as it is portrayed in the Bible.

When one thinks of migration—that is, the phenomenon itself of being a stranger/alien/foreigner—as one of the methods that God uses in God's mission, a number of biblical narratives come to mind. The first we might mention is the story of Moses. Raised in a bi-cultural and bi-lingual environment (Aramaic and Egyptian) Moses was still not a useful instrument for God's mission. It was necessary for Moses to spend forty years as an M/S among the Midianites, learning how to survive in the desert, learning how to shepherd sheep (God was preparing him to be able to shepheard a large human flock in the desert), and being shaped personally, emotionally, spiritually, and physically for the leadership role that would be his. Moses describes himself as an M/S. The narration in Exodus 18:1–3 tells us,

> Now Jethro, the priest of Midian and father-in-law of Moses, heard of everything God had done for Moses and for his people Israel, and how the Lord had brought Israel out of Egypt.
>
> After Moses had sent away his wife Zipporah, his father-in-law Jethro received her and her two sons. One son was named Gershom, for Moses said, "I have become a foreigner in a foreign land." (Ex 18.1–3; see also Ex 2:22; Acts 7:29)

The theme of the desert as the womb from which mission is born represents a strong and consistent emphasis in the Bible. John the Baptist came from the desert to begin his ministry. As another example, in Luke 4, Jesus begins his ministry surviving the temptations in the desert. And in the case of Saul of Tarsus, after being encountered by Jesus on the road to Damascus, Saul—known later as Paul—spends quite a few years in the desert rereading the Old Testament. In the desert, all are strangers. And in the desert they are shaped, formed, and reborn to participate in God's mission. It appears that God places people in situations of being M/S's with the purpose of forming them in preparation for their participation in God's mission.

A second figure we could mention is a woman, a widow, a Moabite, who precisely because she was an M/S was used by God to heal the bitterness of Naomi, her mother-in-law, illustrating in her person what God wanted to do for Israel. In the history of Ruth, the agent of God's mission is combined with the means of

God's mission. Here I want to emphasize an aspect of the narrative of Ruth having to do with migration itself as a means of God's mission.

The entire story derives from the way in which Boaz treats Ruth. Clearly the narrative is meant to be a love story in the midst of which the bitterness of Naomi (representing Israel) is healed by and through the love Ruth and Boaz have for each other. But the relationship of Ruth and Boaz flows from the faithfulness of Boaz as a righteous Israelite. He knows the Scriptures. He knows that in Leviticus 19:10 and again in Leviticus 23:22 God signals the way in which the people of Israel were to treat the M/S in their midst. Ruth describes herself as a "stranger" in Ruth 2:10, "At this, she bowed down with her face to the ground. She asked him, 'Why have I found such favor in your eyes that you notice me—a foreigner?'"

The form in which Boaz receives her and the compassion that Boaz shows to Ruth demonstrates that Boaz was a just and righteous Israelite who follows the levitical norms. "Do not go over your vineyard a second time or pick up the grapes that have fallen. Leave them for the poor and the foreigner. I am the Lord your God." (Lev 19:10) "When you reap the harvest of your land, do not reap to the very edges of your field or gather the gleanings of your harvest. Leave them for the poor and the foreigner residing among you. I am the Lord your God" (Lev 23:22; see also Deut 24:19–21; 26:12,13).

Let's remember what we have already noted: God's special care, compassion, and love for the stranger, widow, and orphan (see, for example, Psalm 94:6; 146:9). It is precisely because Ruth is a stranger, a widow, an alien, that God was able to use her in the environment of the faithfulness, compassion, and love of Boaz to bring about the healing of the bitterness of Naomi. The woman, the widow, the stranger is the means and the example of the compassion of God.

The New Testament offers us an echo. In Luke 17, when Jesus heals the ten lepers, only one returns to give thanks to Jesus and praise God for being healed. And that one was a Samaritan, considered a stranger and alien by the Jews at the time of Jesus. It is precisely because he was a stranger and alien (in the eyes of the Jews) that Jesus points him out as an example.

> Now on his way to Jerusalem, Jesus traveled along the border between Samaria and Galilee. As he was going into a village, ten men who had leprosy met him. They stood at a distance and called out in a loud voice, "Jesus, Master, have pity on us!"
>
> When he saw them, he said, "Go, show yourselves to the priests." And as they went, they were cleansed.

> One of them, when he saw he was healed, came back, praising God in a loud voice. He threw himself at Jesus' feet and thanked him—and he was a Samaritan.
>
> Jesus asked, "Were not all ten cleansed? Where are the other nine? Has no one returned to give praise to God except this foreigner?" Then he said to him, "Rise and go; your faith has made you well." (Luke 17: 11–19)

There are many other examples of this third aspect of migration as a means of God's mission to the nations. The exile itself was a means whereby God creates a great *diaspora* from which resulted the Septuagint, the synagogues, the continuing proselytism of Gentiles by Jews, and a network of human relationships that spread over the entire Roman Empire, contacts that Paul would later use as the pathways for his missionary journeys.

Later in this chapter I will highlight the Parable of the Good Samaritan as one more illustration of the way the stranger and alien are presented as examples of the means of God's mission to the nations.

Could this biblical perspective of immigration as a means of God's mission offer us a lens through which we might better understand what is happening in this century? Is it possible that God is using migration itself as a means to proclaim in word and deed the coming of the kingdom of God among the nations?

D. The M/S's as goals of God's mission to the nations

A fourth and final aspect of a missiological and instrumental perspective of the role of M/S's in God's mission sees migration in relation to the goals of God's mission among the nations. Migration seems to play an eschatological role that propels God's mission and the participation of the people of God in that mission toward the future. This futurist vision appears early in the Bible in the call of Abraham in Gen 17:8.

> Abram fell face down, and God said to him, "As for me, this is my covenant with you: You will be the father of many nations. No longer will you be called Abram; your name will be Abraham, for I have made you a father of many nations. I will make you very fruitful; I will make nations of you, and kings will come from you. I will establish my covenant as an everlasting covenant between me and you and your descendants after you for the generations to come, to be your God and the

God of your descendants after you. The whole land of Canaan, where you now reside as a foreigner, I will give as an everlasting possession to you and your descendants after you; and I will be their God." (Gen 17:3–8)

All migrants think and dream of going to a promised land that will offer better conditions of life. This hope of the future as a fundamental aspect of migration can be seen in numerous biblical narratives. For example, when God commands Moses to call the people of Israel to come out of Egypt, Moses speaks of their going to a new land. In Exodus 6:1–8, we read,

Then the Lord said to Moses, "Now you will see what I will do to Pharaoh: Because of my mighty hand he will let them go; because of my mighty hand he will drive them out of his country."

God also said to Moses, "I am the Lord. I appeared to Abraham, to Isaac and to Jacob as God Almighty, but by my name the Lord I did not make myself fully known to them I also established my covenant with them to give them the land of Canaan, where they resided as foreigners. Moreover, I have heard the groaning of the Israelites, whom the Egyptians are enslaving, and I have remembered my covenant.

"Therefore, say to the Israelites: 'I am the Lord, and I will bring you out from under the yoke of the Egyptians. I will free you from being slaves to them, and I will redeem you with an outstretched arm and with mighty acts of judgment. I will take you as my own people, and I will be your God. Then you will know that I am the Lord your God, who brought you out from under the yoke of the Egyptians. And I will bring you to the land I swore with uplifted hand to give to Abraham, to Isaac and to Jacob. I will give it to you as a possession. I am the Lord.'" (Ex 6:1–8)

God's mission toward the future is closely connected to his love of Israel as a pilgrim and immigrant people. In one of his psalms, David cries out,

He remembers his covenant forever, the promise he made, for a thousand generations, the covenant he made with Abraham, the oath he swore to Isaac. He confirmed it to Jacob as a decree, to Israel as an everlasting covenant: "To you I will give the land of Canaan as the portion you will inherit." When they were but few in number, few indeed, and strangers in it, they wandered from nation to nation, from one kingdom to another. He allowed no one to oppress them; for their sake he rebuked kings: "Do not touch my anointed ones; do my prophets no harm." Sing to the Lord, all the earth; proclaim his salvation day after day. Declare his glory among the nations, his marvelous deeds among all peoples. For great is the Lord and most worthy of praise; he is to be feared above all gods. For all the gods of the nations are idols, but the Lord made the heavens. (1 Chron 16:15–26)

This eschatological perspective of migration includes the hope that the nations will one day come to worship the God of Abraham, Isaac, and Jacob, creator of heaven and earth. This is the vision of Isaiah. For example, in Isaiah 56:3–7, we read the following. "Let no foreigner who is bound to the Lord say, 'The Lord will surely exclude me from his people.' And let not any eunuch complain, 'I am only a dry tree.' For this is what the Lord says: 'To the eunuchs who keep my Sabbaths, who choose what pleases me and hold fast to my covenant—to them I will give within my temple and its walls a memorial and a name better than sons and daughters; I will give them an everlasting name that will endure forever. And foreigners who bind themselves to the Lord to minister to him, to love the name of the Lord, and to be his servants, all who keep the Sabbath without desecrating it and who hold fast to my covenant—these I will bring to my holy mountain and give them joy in my house of prayer. Their burnt offerings and sacrifices will be accepted on my altar; for my house will be called a house of prayer for all nations.'"

The vision the Bible offers us is that all M/S's are invited to the great banquet of the Lamb (Matt 22:1–14; Luke 14:15–24). Every stranger is invited to the table of the Lord. This eschatological perspective of the M/S is emphasized also in Revelation. Repeatedly the author of the Revelation announces that a great multitude of every language, family, tribe, and nation will gather around the throne of the Lamb. (See, for example, Revelation 1:7; 5:8,13; 6:12; 10:6; 11:15; 14:6; 15:1; 19:6; 21.) This great gathering will occur as the result of a great migration to the holy city. In Revelation 21:1–2, 23–26, John describes the event:

Then I saw "a new heaven and a new earth," for the first heaven and the first earth had passed away, and there was no longer any sea. I saw the Holy City, the new Jerusalem, coming down out of heaven from God, prepared as a bride beautifully dressed for her husband. . . . The city does not need the sun or the moon to shine on it, for the glory of God gives it light, and the Lamb is its lamp. The nations will walk by its light, and the kings of the earth will bring their splendor into it. On no day will its gates ever be shut, for there will be no night there. The glory and honor of the nations will be brought into it.

What impact—and what changes might there be—in our Christian churches and ecclesiastical institutions if we really believed that in the final analysis, at the end of history, the M/S's are specially invited to the Great Banquet of the Lamb? (See Luke 14:15ff; Matt 22:1ff.) What are the implications for our nations and our Christian churches to think that the hope of the world resides with the migrants, aliens, strangers, and foreigners in our midst? And what if in their future we find our own global future?

CONCLUSION

The four aspects of this instrumental and missiological perspective of the role of M/S's in God's mission to the nations converge in the parable of the Good Samaritan. Luke places the parable within the narrative in which Jesus sends the 70 on a mission. They are sent as envoys of Jesus mission which is thus their mission. And the primary example of such a mission is the Samaritan.

In the parable we find the motivation for mission in Jesus' response to the question posed by the young noble as to how the young noble is to keep the law. As Jesus tells it, the "neighbor" in this story is not the one who stands beside the young noble. Rather, it is the one who acts neighborly. The "neighbor" is the one who lives out the norms of the Older Testament in being "neighborly" to others. In the parable, the one who demonstrates such a way of life is in fact the Samaritan. The Samaritan is the "neighbor."

The parable clearly presents the Samaritan stranger/alien as the agent of God's mission. And the way Jesus tells the parable shows that Jesus wants to highlight the alien Samaritan as the means by which Jesus can offer the young noble a new path of participating in God's mission.

The parable also focuses on the future. With the words, "Go and do likewise," Jesus points toward a future in which the young noble can fully receive God's mercy. The young noble himself will no longer be a stranger. And because of God's mercy the young noble also can begin to create a new reality in which M/S's are no longer excluded from his care, his compassion, and his love.

I believe that when we begin to fully understand the Bible's missiological and instrumental perspectives with regard to the migrant and stranger, we may possibly gain a better grasp of, and live more fully into, the missionary vision expressed in 1 Peter 2. If the church of Jesus Christ truly saw itself as a pilgrim community whose land and nation are not of this earth, then the Christian church would begin to understand that it is itself a community of migrants—ambassadors, yes (2 Cor 5)—but even so, migrants.

Out of all the nations of the earth, God has chosen the Christian church to be "a royal priesthood, a holy nation, a people belonging to God." This being our reality, it is not possible to reject the call of God to participate in God's mission in this world—especially God's mission because of, by means of, with the participation of, and on the way toward migrants and strangers. Is it possible, in this century, to express the canticle that gives concrete expression in real life to the vision of the psalmist in Psalm 146: 1, 5–10?

Praise the Lord. . . .

Blessed are those whose help is the God of Jacob, whose hope is in the Lord his God,

He is the Maker of heaven and earth, the sea, and everything in them—he remains faithful forever.

He upholds the cause of the oppressed and gives food to the hungry. The Lord sets prisoners free,

the Lord gives sight to the blind, the Lord lifts up those who are bowed down, the Lord loves the righteous.

The Lord watches over the foreigner and sustains the fatherless and the widow, but he frustrates the ways of the wicked.

The Lord reigns forever, your God, O Zion, for all generations. Praise the Lord.

CHAPTER 15
WHY MULTIPLY HEALTHY CHURCHES?

This chapter was originally published in Spanish as, "¿Por qué sembrar iglesias saludables? Bases bíblicas y misiológicas" in John Wagenveld, *Sembremos Iglesias saludables: un acercamiento bíblico y práctico al estudio de la multiplicación de iglesias*. Miami: FLET 2005, 43–94. English translation: Gary Teja and John Wagenveld, eds., *Planting Healthy Churches*, Sauk Village, IL: Multiplication Network Ministries 2015, 23–60. Used by permission.

THESIS

The biblical motivation for multiplying healthy churches resides in the loving and compassionate mission of the triune God (missio Dei), who desires for all men and women to be disciples of Jesus Christ, actively involved members of a local church, and committed agents of the transformation of their reality. As such, these congregations are witnesses to the coming reign of God for the honor and glory of God.

INTRODUCTION

Years ago, a large church in Monterrey, Mexico invited me to give a series of talks on the nature of God. Toward the end of this series of talks, after having concluded one of the papers, a short, elderly, and simply dressed woman came up to me.

"Sir, sir," she said to me, "I have a question I want to ask you."

"Yes, of course," I responded. "What is your question? Was something from the lecture not clear?"

Judging from her way of speaking, it seemed to me that this woman was not a member of any evangelical church and was not accustomed to the way Mexican evangelicals refer to each other as "brother" or "sister." It also seemed that she did not have a lot of biblical knowledge.

"No sir, that's not it," the woman commented, "there wasn't anything bad about what you just finished teaching. In fact, you spoke beautifully, very clearly, and you taught us what you think the Bible says about God. This was all very good.

"But sir," the woman continued, "that's where my problem is. Years ago, here in Monterrey, we were all Roman Catholics. We all believed what the Catholic church taught us and we were all in agreement. But now it's not like that at all. There are so many different churches, so many different preachers on the radio and so many religious centers! And they all have different opinions—they all teach and say different things about God. And that is my problem."

I ask myself: "Of all these people who are talking about God, of all these opinions that we hear, which one is the truth?"

This elderly lady from Monterrey hit the nail on the head. Her question was direct and profound. This is a major problem we are currently everywhere in the world. There are thousands of opinions regarding God: Which will be the truth? And how can we be sure? Upon which foundations will we build our theology and missiology today? Where this situation impacts us most is in regard to the topic of multiplying churches particularly in Latin America.

Over a decade ago, in the preface of David Martin's book, *Tongues of Fire: The Explosion of Protestantism in Latin America*, Peter Berger, well-known sociologist of religion, commented on the situation today in Latin America.

> This book deals with one of the most extraordinary developments in the world today—the rapid spread of evangelical Protestantism in vast areas of the underdeveloped societies, notably in Latin America. . . . If one looks at today's religious scene in an international perspective, there are two truly global movements of enormous vitality. One is conservative Islam, the other conservative Protestantism. . . . The potential impact of (the growth of conservative Protestantism) is likely to be very powerful indeed. . . . The growth of evangelical Protestantism in Latin America. . . . is the most dramatic case. (Martin 1990, vii)

In the twenty-first century in Latin America, it is essential that our thinking on multiplying new churches come from clear motives. Today we are confronted by a complicated and almost contradictory reality regarding this topic. The religiosity of Latin American people is a two-sided coin. On one side, 90 percent of the Latin American population considers themselves "Christian" in some way. Yet, within this large majority, there is a radical difference between the religion of the people and that of the official and formal churches; a small percentage of the population attends church regularly and secularization and nominalism grow every day. And although there is a marked difference from country to country, there is, nonetheless, in almost all of the republics, a general feeling among the people of disillusionment with the institutional church.

There is another side to this coin. In this new century in Latin America, we find an atmosphere of profound spiritual hunger in which it seems everyone is open to any religious subject, open to try out almost anything religious and believe all of it. We live in a time of phenomenal changes regarding religious loyalty. We are faced with changes so large and profound that the Reformation of the sixteenth century in Europe seems to pale in comparison, even though those Reformers, such as Luther, Calvin, Zwingli, Bucer, and others remain prominent in our minds. As Peter Berger mentioned above, we are navigating a time of great religious revolution in the creation of new religious forms, new church structures, and new spiritual expressions.

The two sides of this religious reality contribute to the creation of an atmosphere of competition and suspicion, all of which has a profound impact on multiplying new churches. In a place where there has been only one recognized church for centuries, a church that still dominates the religious reality for many republics, what does it mean to multiply new churches? In an atmosphere of such radical religious change and competition for new followers, it is of greatest importance to examine our motives. What are our motives for multiplying new healthy churches?

This chapter is focused primarily in the Latin American context. It has to do with the biblical bases and values that motivate us to spend our time and energy in multiplying new healthy churches, to look for creative ways to do so, and to pay the necessary price. Not only do we want our actions to glorify God, but also our motives. The reason behind multiplying churches is as important as the methods we use in multiplying them. And this is especially true in the religious atmosphere we find today in Latin America. In the end, as we will see later, the task of multiplying churches is not our own: it is God's. It is because of this that our motives must bring glory to our God.

Knowing this, it is perhaps important to examine ourselves and highlight some of our motives that might not be in line with the heart of God. In order to save space, these motives are presented in list form. The reader is invited to reflect on the following motives that are not consistent with the love of Christ. Why multiply healthy churches?

- NOT to extend the small kingdom, domain, or influence of our own denomination, mission organization, church, or pastor. In all of these cases, we are only establishing new branches of a religious corporation—not multiplying the Church of Jesus Christ.

- NOT because all the other churches in our city or nation are not truly Christ's churches. In this case we see ourselves as forced to prove that only we have the truth and all others are wrong before God. This kind of thinking means that our negative motivation focuses on other churches in place of positively pointing to Christ, the Head of the Church. On the contrary, Jesus invites us to examine the plank in our own eye before we try and remove the speck from our neighbor's eye (Matt 7:3–5).

- NOT because we want to forcefully impose one form of religiosity on all people. This type of church "multiplying" has already been tried in Latin America in the Colonial era, with disastrous results. On the contrary, the Bible calls us to extend an open, loving, tender, and gentle invitation to all who, by the power of the Holy Spirit, would come to confess their faith in Jesus Christ and based, on this faith, become members of Christ's Church.[324]

---

324. With regard to this wrong motive, I am beginning to see that in Latin America we should avoid using the word "plant" to refer to starting new churches. Latin American evangelicals have borrowed this word from English language usage where it has been used for the last forty years in reference to starting new congregations and churches in North America. However, in the context of Latin America, the word "plant" has certain historical roots and makes one think of the Spanish and Portuguese conquests during which churches were "planted" in a mostly brusque, forced, conquering, and destructive manner. I was born in Mexico City and raised in San Cristobal de Las Casas in the state of Chiapas in Southern Mexico. In both of these places the history of the Spanish conquest includes the killing of thousands and thousands of people from pre-Columbian cultures, all in the name of "planting" churches. This is a sad and disheartening history of the imposition of forms of "Christianity" in ways not consistent with a biblical understanding of mission. This same story was repeated in many parts of Latin America and the Caribbean. There have also been situations in some aspects of Protestant missionary work of the nineteenth and twentieth centuries where the imposition of foreign religious practices is alarmingly similar to the European conquest of the sixteenth century. Perhaps, with reference to our evangelization and mission in Latin America we should use the word "multiply" with more of a sense of humility and hope. Or if we use

- NOT because we are in a competition for more converts over against other churches, as if multiplying churches were a soccer championship. If our motivation is competition, what we would be doing is "recycling of the saints" or "stealing sheep." This is not God's mission.

- NOT because we want to manipulate the people of God in such a way that they would follow us so that we could gain a lot of money and prestige in our community and nation.

- NOT because multiplying churches gives us pride or recognition, making us great or famous. Although we do know that some church leaders have psychological leanings in this direction, it is imperative that we acknowledge this predisposition and "offer [our] bodies as a living sacrifice, holy and pleasing to God" so that our activities in multiplying new, healthy churches can be our "true and proper worship," our offering to God (Rom 12:1).

If we reject these motives that honor neither our Savior Jesus Christ nor the Holy Spirit, we then must focus on finding true and biblical motives that will lead us to multiply new, healthy churches. Biblical motivations for multiplying new, healthy churches need to be based on a trinitarian missiology (see Ajith Fernando 2000). And because of this, I suggest that the Bible presents us with at least the following five reasons why we should multiply new churches:

- Because God the Father seeks and finds the lost;
- Because the love of Christ obligates us;
- Because the Holy Spirit has been sent for all human beings (all flesh);
- Because the local congregation is the primary locus of the kingdom of God, the rule of the King;
- Because multiplying churches is for praise of the glory of God.

In this chapter there is only enough space to present the biblical foundation in a rather broad outline. This is presented here with the hope that this review will challenge the reader to study his/her Bible in a new way, allowing it to answer the

---

the word "plant," perhaps we need to conceptualize that as one who places a small seed in the ground and hopes the seed will die and that God would bring it to new life such that, with time, it may yield a harvest. (For example, see Mark 4:26–29; John 4:36–37; 1 Cor 3:6; 15:36–37).

question, "Why does God want us to multiply new, healthy churches around the world today?" The first reason is found in the nature and will of God.

BECAUSE GOD THE FATHER SEEKS AND FINDS THE LOST

The first biblical foundation for multiplying new, healthy churches is the most basic of all. It stems from the nature of God. Every effort within mission, including multiplying new churches, comes from and flows out of the will of God (*missio Dei*) who loved the world so much "he gave his one and only Son, that whoever believes in him shall not perish but have eternal life" (John 3:16).

Hendrikus Berkhof affirmed that the most basic attribute of God is that he is a God who reveals himself to us (See H. Berkhof 1979, 41–65). In 1 John 4:8 we read that God is *agape*, love that is self-giving. God is always the one who initiates the search to reach humans, looking to draw them in and receive them within a covenant relationship. "I will be your God, you will be my people, and I will dwell in your midst" is the fundamental biblical affirmation of the will of God. (See Van Engen 1996, 71–89).

The God of the Bible is neither the unmovable mover nor the original cause of the European Enlightenment of the fifteenth, sixteenth, and seventeenth centuries. The God of the Bible is not the god of the deists, a god who supposedly put the "laws of nature" into place and then removed himself in order to let "nature" govern the world. The God of the Bible is not merely the God of the "Omni's" (omnipresent, omniscient, omnipotent, etc.) as, for example he is described in the Westminster Confession, although these are included in God's characteristics. The God of the Bible is not just the creation of our own subjective experience as Schleiermacher presented; nor is God only part of categories of the mind as Emmanuel Kant expressed. The God of the Bible is neither an immanent God, a product of cultural world-and-life-views, nor the product of a psychological hunger for meaning. And He is also not the pure object of human religious searching.

On the contrary, the God of the Bible is loving, compassionate, slow to anger, benevolent, full of mercy who constantly and always desires to share his grace and love with humans and to enter into covenant with them. The Bible presents us with a God who is actively involved in his creation, who reveals God's self to humanity, who responds, even emotionally to the human rejection of God's love, and who—in Jesus Christ—preserves and sustains God's creation, as Paul says in the high Christology of Colossians 1. What follows is an outline of the biblical texts that speak to the missionary nature of the God of the Bible.

A. God created and cares for all human beings, even in spite of the fact that humanity rejects God.

- All human beings share the same origin in their creation by the God of the universe. (Gen 1–3; Job 38–42; Isa 41–46; Jonah; John 1; Acts 17:16–31; Rom 1; Ps 64:9; 65; 66:1,4,8; 67:3–5; 2 Pet 3:8–13; Rev 21:1). As such all people have common ancestors in Adam and Eve (Gen 1–5).
- All humanity is judged in the flood. Noah and his family are the ancestors of all people, and God established a covenant with all people, as evidenced by the rainbow (Gen 6:10).
- The "Table of the Nations" presents the idea that all people are descendants of the same race (Gen 10:5,6,20,31,32).
- The Tower of Babel affirms that all human beings have common ancestors in terms of language (Gen 11:1–9). Here we see different people groups within the universal love of God, a concept that is reaffirmed in the genealogy of Shem and Terah.
- God is the King of all the earth, creator, ruler, the "king of glory" (2 Sam 15:10; 2 Kgs 9:13; Isa 52:7; Ps 32; 47:8; see, for example, Jer 17:12 and the Christology of Eph 1, Col 1; Phil 2; Rev 4:9,10; 5:1,7,13; 6:16; 7:10, 15; 19:4).

The God of the Bible always takes the first step. He initiates the search and invites all humanity into a new relationship with God through reconciliation. This God has created and continues creating human beings with the intent that they would be in constant communion with God. With God's own hands, the God of creation formed human beings out of mud. Having breathed life into that lump of clay (Gen 2:7), God took it and lovingly, joyfully, and carefully formed humanity in the image of God—*imago Dei* (Gen 2:20–25). This is the God of the Bible who, after Adam and Eve sinned against God and hid themselves from God's face, cried out in pain and anguish, "Adam, Adam, where are you?" And this God of the Bible is the God who saved Noah and his family and promised to never destroy all people again (Gen 6–9).

As children of this creating and sustaining God, we must also learn to care for creation over which we have been given dominion. We must make the effort to affirm the value of human life and to safeguard it. With regard to multiplying healthy churches, this first truth suggests that we work so that every human being might come to know their creator. We invite all human beings, by faith in Jesus Christ, to join with us in praising and glorifying our creator. In this way members of our congregations can participate in God's work of caring for creation and the life of each human being, thus transforming the reality in which they live (see Bakke 2000 and Padilla and Yamamori, eds. 2003).

B.   God is a God of love and mercy.

Time after time the Bible affirms that God is loving and merciful. This triune God of the Bible, as mentioned earlier, is love (*agape*), one who reveals God's self to God's people. Moses found himself in the presence of God after he left Egypt. About that encounter, the Bible tells us the following: "And he passed in front of Moses, proclaiming, 'The Lord, the Lord, the compassionate and gracious God, slow to anger, abounding in love and faithfulness, maintaining love to thousands, and forgiving wickedness, rebellion and sin. Yet he does not leave the guilty unpunished; he punishes the children and their children for the sin of the parents . . . '" (Ex 34:6–7). This description of God's being is repeated innumerable times in the Bible. See, for example, Ex 22:27; Num 14:18; Deut 5:9–10; 7:9–10; 2 Chron 30:9; Neh 9:17; Psalm 51:1; 86:5,15; 103:8, 11:4; 112:4; 116:5; 145:8; Joel 2:13; Jonah 4:2; Micah 7:18; James 5:11.

The God of the Bible is the God of love spoken of in the Psalms. There are a multitude of Psalms that speak of God's love, mercy, and care. For example, Psalm 23 says, "The Lord is my shepherd, I lack nothing . . ."

In Isaiah 6, one finds the call of the prophet Isaiah. He is in the temple and encounters the missionary God, the God of Abraham, Isaac, and Jacob. In this encounter with the presence of God, all five of Isaiah's senses were engaged: he saw God high and lifted up, he heard the seraphim praising God, he felt the building shake, he smelled the smoke filling the temple, and he tasted the coal of God's forgiveness with which the seraphim touched his lips. The primary importance of this encounter is not limited to the relationship between Isaiah and his God. Additionally, there is a missionary element to it. The God of love and mercy cries out, "Whom shall I send? And who will go for us?" (Is 6:8). Isaiah's vocation is centered on this missionary God's desires to send Isaiah as his messenger to Israel and to all the nations. The moment will come when Isaiah will declare the following about Israel and the coming Messiah, words that, much later in the Gospel of Luke, Jesus of Nazareth will speak concerning his mission.

This is what God the Lord says—the Creator of the heavens . . . "I, the Lord, have called you in righteousness; I will take hold of your hand. I will keep you and will make you to be a covenant for the people and a light for the Gentiles, to open eyes that are blind, to free captives from prison and to release from the dungeon those who sit in darkness." (Is 42:5–7, compare with Is 49:6; 61:1–3; Luke 2:32; 4:18–19).

The messianic and missional prophecies in Isaiah form part of the background for the words of Mary, the mother of Jesus. The main emphasis of Mary's Magnificat in Luke 1:46–55 is God's loving and merciful nature towards Israel and all other nations.

Jesus stresses that this love is an attribute of his heavenly Father as well, who because of love, seeks to be in relationship with his people. Jesus said to Nicodemus the Pharisee, a member of the Sanhedrin (a council of 70 people who governed the people of Israel during Jesus' time), and leader of the Jews, "For God so loved the world he gave his one and only Son, that whoever believes in him should not perish but have eternal life." In his teaching Jesus again stressed God's loving nature. Another example of this is in the parable of the Tenants in Luke 20:9–17. God, represented as the owner of the vineyard, constantly tries to enter into a relationship with his workers (compare with Isaiah 5). Additionally, in the parable of the Great Banquet, God, who is characterized by the host of the dinner, sends his servant, "Go out quickly into the streets and alleys of the town and bring in the poor, the crippled, the blind and the lame . . . Go out to the roads and country lanes and compel them to come in, so that my house will be full" (Luke 14:15–24; Matt 22:1–10). In chapter 15 of his book, Luke combines three parables that show us how this God loves, seeks, and finds the lost. This God, as a shepherd, looks for and finds his lost sheep. He is like a woman who looks for and finds her lost coin. He is also like a father who anxiously waits for the day when his lost son will return home. Upon finding the lost, the God of the Bible throws a party with his angels and joyfully celebrates that the lost has been found. Concerning this point, the reader should note that in these parables the idea of being "lost" has to do with a break in a close relationship with God: with the shepherd on behalf of the sheep, with the woman on behalf of the coin, and with the father on behalf of the prodigal son.

In regard to this God of love, Paul asks, "He who did not spare his own Son, but gave him up for us all—how will he not also, along with him, graciously give us all things?" (Romans 8:32). Peter also affirms that God is a God of love and mercy and "he is patient with you, not wanting anyone to perish, but everyone to come to repentance" (2 Peter 3:9). In his first letter, John affirms this most basic characteristic of God as well: "God is love" (1 John 4:8). Additionally, in Revelation we see this God of love will bring people from every tribe, language, people, and nation together around the Lamb in the New Jerusalem (Rev 5:9; 7:9; 15:4; 21:24; 22:2).

In Christ we have become children of this loving and merciful father (John 1:12). Therefore, as his children, we must be involved and challenged to participate with our loving father in the search and rescue of the lost. It is not possible to be sons and daughters of this loving God and refuse to participate in this search for the lost. Additionally, when we as sons and daughters of God come together to worship this God of love, we are incomplete because we are missing those who have not yet come to know our loving and merciful father. Each time we come together to worship God is a challenge and call to invite others to join with us in praise to our God who loves all humanity.

C. God chooses his people to be his instruments of love in the search among the nations.

God is the God of particular people and at the same time is the God of all nations. In the Bible the word "nations" does not refer to a modern political entity like Mexico, for example. It refers to a particular group of people connected by language, culture, ancestry, and history. In the Old Testament the term "nations" speaks to the ethnic entities, people, and cultural groups of Israel's immediate environment. Israel is the *am*, the people of God, and "the nations" are the *goyim*, all the other people groups who are not part of God's *am*. Beginning with the call of Abraham, the Bible is clear that Abraham and Sarah's descendants, the people of God, exist in order to be God's instrument of love among the nations.

The God of Abraham, Isaac, and Jacob heard the cry of his people in Egypt and used Moses and his creation to bring about their deliverance from slavery in Egypt. This deliverance had two interrelated purposes. The first purpose was so that the people of Israel would come to know God in a new way and would worship the God of Abraham, Isaac, and Jacob at Mt. Sinai (Ex 6:2–7; 7:16; 8:1, 20; 9:1,13; 10:3,8; 14:31; 20:2). However, this was only part of what God wanted to teach his people through their deliverance from Egypt. His plan is much bigger, deeper, and more profound. Through the Exodus, God wanted all of Egypt and their surrounding "nations" to come to know that the God of Abraham, Isaac, and Jacob is the only true God, and he created and sustains all of life on earth

(Ex 5:2; 7:5; 17; 8:10; 9:14,16; 10:2; 14:4,18,31). God's use of his people as his instruments among the nations is so important that, centuries later, Paul cites one of these passages in his own description of the mission of God's love. During the Exodus, God used Moses to say to Pharaoh, "But I have raised you up for this very purpose, that I might show you my power and that my name might be proclaimed in all the earth" (Ex 9:16; Rom 9:17).

What follows is an outline of some of the texts that show the love of God and his desire to bring this love to "the nations."

- God gives specific commandments regarding the special care that Israel must offer to "the stranger that is among you" (Gen 12:10; 20:1; 21:34; 47:4; Ex 20:10; 22:21; Lev 18:26; 20:2; 25:40; Num 15:14–16; Deut 10:18–19; 26:5–11; 1 Kings 8:27,41–43; 2 Chron 6:18,32, The dedication of Solomon's Temple)

- The "nations" play an important role in God's activity (Deut 26:19; 1 Chron 16:8,31; Ps 9:1,19–20; 47:1,7–9; 64:9; 65; 66:1,4,8; 67:1–5; 72:17–18; 96:1–3,7,10,13; 97:5–6; 98:2–3,9; 102:13–15; 108:3; 113:4; Is 2:2–4, 40:5,17; 49:5–6; 52:15; 55:4–5; 56:6–7; 60:3,11; 62:2; 66:2; 66:19–20; Jer 4:2; Zeph 2:11–13; Amos; Jonah; Micah 1:1–7; 4:1–5).

- In Old Testament and in the words of Jesus, the "house of prayer for all the nations." Solomon's temple was a special place for prayer for the "stranger" (2 Chron 6:32–33; Mic 4:1–2; Is 56:7; Jer 7:11; Matt 21:13; Mark 11:17; Luke 19:46; Matt 25:32; compare with Acts 14:15–17).

- God chose Israel to "be among the nations" as his instrument of love for all people (Ex 6:6–8; 19:5–6; Deut 4:20; 7:6; 14:2; 26:1; Titus 2:14; 1 Pet 2:9–10). In his conversation with Nicodemus (John 3) and in the declaration of his messianic mission (Luke 4:18–19), Jesus mentions God's intention for his people. See also the following related passages: Isaiah 35:4–8; 61:1; Hebrews 1:9; Psalm 45:7; Matthew 11:1–6, John the Baptist; Psalm 145:14–21; Luke 1:46–55; I Sam 2:1–10; Matt 25:31–46; Acts 2:42–47.

- Paul understood the universal mission of God in such a way that he considered himself to be a debtor to all people (Romans 1:14) and was committed to participating in the "mystery of Christ" (Eph 2:11–3:21).

- The people of God are a sign of the universal love of God that he has for all nations (Is 11:12; 49:22; 62:10; Matt 5; John 3:14,15; 12:32; Romans 1:14).

The covenant that God makes with his people has within it the purpose of reaching out to the nations who do not already know their Creator. Emilio Nuñez, focusing on the covenant with Noah, helps us understand this missionary element of God's covenant. Nuñez explains the following:

> For the purpose of our missiological reflection, what we want to emphasize the most from God's covenant with Noah and other unconditional covenants that Yahweh establishes with humans is the divine interest in the salvation of all human beings. This salvation is not limited to the forgiveness of sins and the gift of eternal life. It also had to do with the spiritual (*shalom*) and physical well being of human beings. The promise covers everything from the animal kingdom (Gen 9:8–17) to the plant world (Gen 8:22–9:3). God has made a covenant with "the earth" (Gen 9:13). This blessing is also ecological. "As long as the earth endures seedtime and harvest, cold and heat, summer and winter, day and night will never cease" (Gen 8:22). The effects of the covenant are cosmic, as a blessing for all humanity. . . .
>
> The rainbow is mentioned in Ezekiel 1:28 and Revelation 4:3 as a symbol of God's majesty. The rainbow becomes an apocalyptic sign and symbol for humanity. Judgment day is coming . . .
>
> God does not want "anyone to perish, but everyone to come to repentance" (2 Pet 3:9). He "wants all people to be saved and to come to a knowledge of the truth" (1 Tim 2:4). He wants the biblical stories of the flood with the rainbow in the clouds to be a powerful incentive for all human beings to repent and believe in Christ for their salvation . . .
>
> Every time we participate in the Lord's Supper, in communion with our brothers and sisters in Christ, we remember the blood that was shed as a seal of this new covenant (Matt 26:26–29), taking on the sins of the world (1 John 2:2),

as a ransom for many (Matt 20:28; 1 Pet 1:18–19) and in order to reconcile the world with God (2 Cor 5:18–21; Eph 2:16; Col 1:20–21). We should remember that the blood of the Lamb was poured out to "take away the sin of the world!" (John 1:29) We must also remember that, in obedience to God, the Church must continue to come around the table of communion "until he comes again." In other words, until the Son of David returns to reign over all the earth . . .

God's covenant with Noah and those established with the people of Israel, attest to the divine interest in the salvation of all people. The covenants in the Old Testament provide a solid base to the universal Christian mission. They also serve as a foundation for the concept of holistic missions because the promises of the covenants include the spiritual as well as the material. They offer blessings for all human beings (Nuñez 1997, 181–82, 214; translation by Van Engen).

The reality of God's love for all people, as written above, shows us that all believers in Christ must by definition be involved in the search for the lost because of God's nature. In other words, to be children of God means that we must multiply new, healthy churches. Our heavenly Father seeks out the lost, and as his children we must do the same.

Those of us who have known Christ for some time and are members of an evangelical church probably know the above truths in our heads but too often we fail to live them out. The fundamental basis for multiplying new, healthy churches lies in the nature of God, a loving, merciful God who reveals God's self to humans and looks to be in covenant relationship with them. Because of this, multiplying churches is not optional. On the contrary, it is part of the essential nature of our faith. If we are children of this God, we must then do all that is possible in seeking out, finding, receiving and incorporating all human beings into the community of faith so that they can be reconciled with God (2 Cor 5). A biblical missiology recognizes that ultimately our motivation for multiplying new, healthy churches does not merely stem from the nature of the church, but flows from the will of God.

In the footnote below the reader will find a short list of supporting works that emphasize a similar perspective of a God who, because of his love and mercy, seeks and finds the lost.[325]

BECAUSE THE LOVE OF CHRIST COMPELS US

How God shows his love and mercy through seeking and saving the lost is the foundation for the mission of Jesus Christ, for the sending of the Holy Spirit, and for the Church's call to announce the Good News of God's reign to the whole world, bringing honor and glory to God. Therefore, in this second part, we will briefly examine the mission of Jesus Christ as one of the main motivations to multiplying new, healthy churches.

A. The Incarnation

"For God so loved the world that he gave his one and only Son, that whoever believes in him shall not perish but have eternal life" (John 3:16). "The Word became flesh and made his dwelling among us. We have seen his glory, the glory of the one and only Son, who came from the Father, full of grace and truth" (John 1:14). The love of God does not remain in theory or in speculation. On the contrary, God, because of his great love, became flesh. "He came to that which was his own . . ." (John 1:11). In Jesus, the Christ (the Messiah) God became human, flesh and bone, culturally a Jew, a man who lived in Palestine during the first century AD, under the rule of Caesar Augustus, while "Quirinius was governor of Syria" (Luke 2:2). God did not come in an abstract or purely mystical way. He came to be in relationship with human beings in concrete situations, in a visible and identifiable reality.

As with Jesus and his disciples, "the love of Christ compels us" to make the love of God visible through our interactions with all people. For "if anyone is in Christ, the new creation has come: The old has gone, the new is here! All this is

---

325. Karl Barth 1961; Johannes Blauw 1962; Richard de Ridder 1975; John Fuellenback 1995; Arthur Glasser, with Charles Van Engen, Dean S. Gilliland and Shawn B. Redford 2003; Ken R. Gnanakan 1993; Roger Hedlund 1985; Walter C. Kaiser, 2000; Gerhard Kittel and Gerhard Friedrich, eds. 1985; George E. Ladd 1959; Helen Barrett Montgomery 1920; Johannes Nissen 1999; Emilio A . Nuñez 1997; C. René Padilla 1998; Donald Senior and Carroll Stuhlmueller 1983; Norman Snaith 1944; John Stott 1981; Valdir R. Steuernagel 1991; Mark Strom 1990; Charles Van Engen, Dean Gilliland and Paul Pierson, eds. 1993; Gailyn Van Rheenen 1983; Gerhard von Rad 1962; and George Ernest Wright 1955, 1961.

from God, who reconciled us to himself through Christ and gave us the ministry of reconciliation that God was reconciling the world to himself in Christ, not counting people's sins against them. And he has committed to us the message of reconciliation." Therefore, as a new creation, we cry out to all people throughout the world: "Be reconciled to God" (2 Cor 5:14–20).

Just as God became flesh to dwell among humanity, Christ's disciples are part of communities, towns, and cities. Because of this, multiplying new, healthy churches guarantees that the Good News is born out of and grows in concrete places, particular cultures, and among specific people. And in reality these new, healthy congregations are the ambassadors of the presence and grace of God. Through these groups of Christ's followers, God invites everyone who comes to them to be reconciled with God.

During his ministry, Jesus had a number of followers (maybe even up to 120) who walked with him during the three years of his ministry. They walked together, ate together, prayed together, laughed together, cried together. That group of disciples was the first congregation of the New Testament. And just like the first group of Jesus' followers were the first congregation of the New Testament, Jesus' followers today make up a new congregation. As people become disciples of Jesus Christ, new congregations are born. The people who make up these groups are made of flesh and bone, influenced by their culture and context.

Multiplying new, healthy churches is the fruit of missionary activity that flows out of the nature of the church. Christ's love compels us to proclaim the salvation that he offers. And when people decide to follow Christ and come together in his name, a new congregation is born. Even more, Jesus promises that "Where two or three gather in my name, there am I with them" (Matt 18:20). Jesus promises to be present (through the Holy Spirit) in those moments and places wherever his followers come together in his name. Even more, "Anyone who loves me will obey my teaching. My Father will love them, and we will come to them and make our home with them" (John 14:23). In other words, when Jesus' disciples come together in his name and when they love each other, Jesus and God the Father are present through the presence of the Holy Spirit.

Why must we multiply new, healthy churches? Because Christ's love always is shown in a concrete way when his disciples come together in his name, in an atmosphere of love. This occurs in specific places: the countryside, a village, between people of flesh and bone who have their own particular language and culture.

And in these places "Christ's love compels us" to invite those around us to become disciples of the King of kings and the Lord of lords.

B. Contextualization

When Jesus' disciples come together, they gather in an atmosphere where he is present. In this atmosphere the gospel of Jesus Christ becomes natural to the cultural context of the church. The genius behind multiplying new, healthy churches is that they come from the people in that they reflect the culture in which they have been multiplied. In his ministry, Jesus responded differently to each person with whom He interacted. He offered living water to the Samaritan Woman. He gave food to hungry crowds. For Mary and Martha, he gave them life in bringing back Lazarus, their brother, from the dead. In Jesus' ministry his gifts were tailored for those who were receiving them. As such, each congregation should not just reflect their denomination, mission organization or mother church. They must also reflect the culture in which they have been multiplied in terms of economy, language, and world-and-life view. Healthy congregations must reflect the culture of their surrounding contexts. In other words they must not be like a foreign bush, planted among native shrubs. Instead they must be planted in their native soil where they can grow well. For more than one hundred years, missiologists have followed this concept, drawing from the thinking of Roland Allen, John Nevius, Mel Hodges, John A. Mackay, Orlando Costas, Rubén Tito Paredes, and others. The local congregation is where the gospel becomes contextualized.

C. The Calling into Mission

A healthy congregation is not only made up of followers of Christ who come together to think only about themselves. A congregation will not be healthy and mature if it does not reach outside of its surrounding culture. True followers of Jesus try to make new followers of Christ. One can clearly see this call in chapters 9 and 10 of Luke, in addition to the five Great Commissions (Matt 28:18–20—compare with Matt 10:5–15; Mark 16:15–16; Luke 24:46–49; Acts 1:8; John 15:12–17 with 21:15–17).[326]

---

326. Most missiologists write about a biblical basis for starting new churches by drawing from the Great Commission. In many of these cases, the authors pay little attention or put little effort into examining the hermeneutics behind, and the significance of, the Great Commission as it relates to the mission of God throughout the entire Bible. See, for example, Robert Logan 1989, 190–92; Robert Logan 2002, 15, 9; Aubrey Malphur 1992, 119–23;

Biblically speaking, making new disciples has never been a merely individual pursuit, but rather a collective activity. Since the birth of the Church in Acts, one can see that the disciples of Christ, by the fact of being his followers, came together with other disciples in collective congregations. As we saw before, Jesus says, "Wherever two or three are gathered in my name . . ." Exercising one's Christian faith always happens collectively.

A missionary christology does not separate Christ's personhood from his actions, his humanity from his divinity, nor does it separate the "Jesus of history" from the "Christ of faith." On the contrary, it emphasizes Jesus' missionary ministry as one who was sent from the Father to save the world. This holistic ministry includes his offices (prophet, priest, king) and his ministry as Savior, Liberator, and sage. Jesus transfers his mission to his disciples: "As the Father has sent me, I am sending you" (John 20:21). Jesus' mission and ministry are the basis for the calling and commitment of Christ's followers.

In his first sermon in Acts, Paul says, "For this is what the Lord has commanded us: 'I have made you a light for the Gentiles, that you may bring salvation to the ends of the earth'" (Acts 13:47; compare with Luke 2:32, with reference to Jesus). Jesus transfers his offices, his ministry and his mission to his disciples who, together, make up the Body of Christ, the physical presence of Christ in the world. It is in this way that we, as Christ's disciples, come to be prophets, priests, kings, healers, liberators and sages in mission. The local congregation as the Body of Christ exists to put into action the mission and ministry of Jesus in the world. Fundamentally speaking, the local congregation exists to invite other people—all human beings—to be disciples of Jesus Christ, just as it is seen in the message of the book of Acts (Van Engen 1991, 119–130).

Missiologists with a missionary mindset recognize that salvation is neither found in participating in church activities nor in simply being a member of a church. In this sense, our calling is not to simply "multiply" churches. At its most basic, our calling is to make disciples of Jesus Christ. In other words, multiplying new, healthy churches is making new groups of people who participate in Christ's mission by being his disciples.

Our message is not the superiority of our church or its creeds and confessions. Additionally, we do not exist to simply be instruments of socioeconomic or political change. Our message is simply and only Jesus Christ who lived, was crucified,

Marlin Nelson 2001, 39–47; Elmer Towns and Douglas Porter 2003, 11–25; C. Peter Wagner 1990, 19; and C. Peter Wagner 1980, 44–46.

and "rose again from the dead and is seated at the right hand of God the Father almighty where he will come to judge the living and the dead," as the Apostles' Creed states.

In Revelation John sees the future: "After this I looked, and there before me was a great multitude that no one could count, from every nation, tribe, people and language, standing before the throne and before the Lamb. They were wearing white robes and were holding palm branches in their hands. And they cried out in a loud voice: 'Salvation belongs to our God, who sits on the throne, and to the Lamb'" (Rev 7:9–10; see also 5:9; 10:11; 11:9; 13:7; 14:6; 17:15). This vision fulfills the promise that John had previously heard from Jesus when Jesus said, "And I, when I am lifted up from the earth, will draw all people to myself" (John 12:32). The local congregation is a sign and a symbol, a representation of that multitude around the throne of God, the Lamb. As we wait for the fulfillment of this time, during this time-between-the-times of his first and second comings, Jesus and our heavenly Father has sent us the Holy Spirit to build his church.

BECAUSE THE HOLY SPIRIT WAS SENT FOR ALL PEOPLE AND TO BUILD THE CHURCH

The third fundamental reason for multiplying healthy churches is because this action if the work of the Holy Spirit. Ultimately, we are not the ones who multiply churches. You and I do not grow the church. The church exists only because of the work of the Holy Spirit. There are three aspects to this truth.

A. The Holy Spirit was given for all people.

God the Father and his son Jesus Christ sent the Holy Spirit out of a desire that no one be lost and that all might be saved. In Acts 2 Luke narrates the events of the first Pentecost when the Holy Spirit came to Jesus' disciples: "they were all together in one place" (Acts 2:1). They formed a new local congregation. The Holy Spirit was sent in the form of fire and wind and the disciples "began to speak in other tongues" (Acts 2:4). Luke explains through Peter's words that "In the last days, God says, 'I will pour out my Spirit on all people'" (Acts 2:17). Luke offers us a list of the places where people were able to hear, in their own language, Peter's sermon, in order to emphasize the fact that the Holy Spirit was sent for all people (Acts 2:8). In Figure 11, the reader can appreciate Luke's genius in providing us a list of the main cultures and nations surrounding Jerusalem during this time.

People from these places heard the gospel of Jesus Christ in their own language. This was a miracle of hearing and was through the special work of the Holy Spirit.

In Acts 2:9–11 Luke mentions 15 places of origin for those who heard Peter's sermon on Pentecost. This "Table of Nations" in Acts echoes that of Genesis 10. In chapter 2, Luke seems to indicate that the confusion of tongues from Babel has been transformed and healed at Pentecost. The people present at Pentecost mainly came from the provinces of Asia (of the Roman Empire) and from the Empire of the Medes and Persians, as well as from Crete and Rome (see Figure 11). All of these people heard the gospel in their own heart language.

The New Testament "Table of Nations" at Pentecost

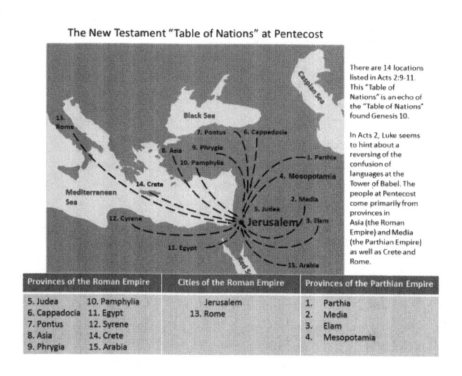

There are 14 locations listed in Acts 2:9-11. This "Table of Nations" is an echo of the "Table of Nations" found Genesis 10.

In Acts 2, Luke seems to hint about a reversing of the confusion of languages at the Tower of Babel. The people at Pentecost come primarily from provinces in Asia (the Roman Empire) and Media (the Parthian Empire) as well as Crete and Rome.

Provinces of the Roman Empire		Cities of the Roman Empire	Provinces of the Parthian Empire	
5. Judea	10. Pamphylia	Jerusalem	1.	Parthia
6. Cappadocia	11. Egypt	13. Rome	2.	Media
7. Pontus	12. Syrene		3.	Elam
8. Asia	14. Crete		4.	Mesopotamia
9. Phrygia	15. Arabia			

FIGURE 11: The NT "Table of Nations"
(Courtesy of Shawn Redford, used with permission.)

Why multiply new, healthy churches? Because through new congregations the Holy Spirit wants to continue transforming the lives of all people. In Acts, Luke tells us four more times, in four different places, representing four different cultures to which the Holy Spirit comes in a form identical to that of Pentecost in Acts 2. See chapter 4 (Judea), chapter 8 (Samaria), chapter 10 (Cornelius, a Gentile convert to Judaism, who feared God), and chapter 19 (the Gentiles of Ephesians, "to the ends of the earth"). The Holy Spirit wants to multiply new, healthy, local congregations made up of women and men who represent "all people." It is clear from Acts that in order to reach this goal, the Holy Spirit uses the Christ followers from local churches to multiply new, healthy churches. This process is the norm of the New Testament.

B. The Holy Spirit Builds New Healthy Congregations.

In the end, we need to recognize that as humans, we are not the ones who build the Church. In reality we are also not the ones who multiply new, local congregations. This is the work of the Holy Spirit. The book of Acts clearly teaches that the Holy Spirit is responsible for the growth, health, and development of a Church. In Acts, we see that the Holy Spirit does the following:

- Builds the Church.
- Reforms and transforms the Church.
- Gives power to the Church.
- Unifies the Church.
- Gives new knowledge and illumination to the words of Jesus.
- Sends the Church out.
- Creates within the Church a desire to grow.
- Accompanies the Church on its mission.
- Guides the Church.
- Prays through the church and intercedes for the Church.
- Gives the Church the words for testimony and proclamation.
- Facilitates communication.
- Develops and facilitates in the receptivity of the listeners.
- Convinces people of their sin, of justice, and of judgment.
- Converts people to faith in Jesus Christ.
- Brings together and unifies Christians so that together they can be the Church.
- Receives new believers.
- Sends the Church out into the world that God loves so much.

One of the Holy Spirit's most profound desires is to grow the Church. Even the best strategies cannot make the Church grow. The church is the "mysterious creation of God" (in the words of Karl Barth) and exists through the work of the Holy Spirit. We know this truth but often we forget it. Perhaps we forget the Holy Spirit's role because the Holy Spirit rarely works alone. The Holy Spirit enjoys using human instruments, Jesus' disciples, to accomplish the work of creating new, healthy churches.

This desire of the Holy Spirit is evident throughout Acts and the New Testament. It is emphasized in a notable way in Acts 13. After giving us a list of the church leaders in Antioch, Luke tells us that it was the Holy Spirit who said, "Set apart for me Barnabas and Saul for the work to which I have called them" (Acts 13:2). The rest of the book is the story of how the Holy Spirit used Paul, Barnabas, and many others in multiplying new, healthy churches in the different places Luke mentions in the second chapter. Accordingly, every congregation throughout the world must listen to the call of the Holy Spirit to be agents of the triune God in multiplying new, healthy churches. All healthy churches should be concerned about, and actively involved in, multiplying new churches through the power of the Holy Spirit.

C. The Holy Spirit gives gifts to and sends out the members of the Church so that they will multiply new congregations.

In order to carry out this multiplying, the Holy Spirit gives gifts to believers of Christ as a means of special grace. Surely, the reader is familiar with the New Testament passages that mention the different gifts the Holy Spirit gives to the members of the body of Christ (see Rom 12:1 Cor 12; Eph 4; 1 Pet 4:10–11). One could say that the Holy Spirit is like the central nervous system of the body. Just as the nerves in the human body carry electrical impulses from the brain to the muscles, so the Holy Spirit carries the commands from the Head of the Church (Christ) to the members of the Body and moves the muscles to action. That is, the Holy Spirit moves the members of the Body of Christ in their mission in the world. It is not possible to multiply new, healthy churches without the careful and efficient use of the gifts of the Holy Spirit.

A careful study of Ephesians 4 shows that the gifts of the Spirit are given with two complementary purposes. On the one hand, the gifts are used for the development and maturity of the members of the church. But the work of the Holy Spirit does not stop here. The members' development and maturity has a purpose beyond the confines of the church. They are given for mission in the world. In Ephesians 4:12 Paul says that the gifts have been given "to equip his people *for works of service, so that the body of Christ may be built up.*" The word Paul uses here, translated into English as "service," is *diakonia*. This word, from where we get our word "deacon," is a key word that Paul frequently uses as a synonym for *the mission of God*. For example, see Ephesians 3:1–7 where Paul says that he became a servant [deacon] of the "mystery" (Eph 3:6) that the Gentiles are "heirs together with Israel, members together of one body, and sharers together in the promise in Christ Jesus." The gifts are activities of ministry that are practiced as much outside as inside the church in order to bring to Christ those who do not yet know him as their Savior. When these gifts are carried out in this way, the church is "built up," that is, it grows in a holistic way: organically, spiritually, socially, and numerically (see Costas 1975; 1974; 1979). The gifts of the Spirit are missionary gifts that the Spirit wants to use to touch the lives of those who are not yet disciples of Christ, in order to transform them and bring them into the church of Christ, creating new, healthy congregations.

Because these gifts are given directly from the Holy Spirit, they must only be used in an atmosphere drenched by the fruit of the Spirit: love, joy peace, patience, kindness, gentleness, etc. (Gal 5:22–23; Eph 4:1–6). When these gifts are used biblically, the anticipated result is that new people will come to Christ and new, healthy churches will develop. The Holy Spirit does not give these gifts just to grow already established churches. Biblical growth results in the multiplication of believers and of new, healthy, congregations. Biblical growth should also result in the transformation of the society and culture of the neighborhoods surrounding these new congregations.

Currently, there are too many megachurches around the world who have not given birth to enough new congregations. It seems as if they want to hoard God's grace all for themselves and not share it with "all people." A healthy church looks to reproduce itself, multiplying new, congregations—locally, regionally, and globally. A healthy church participates in the mission of Jesus Christ through the power of the Holy Spirit as "witnesses in Jerusalem, and in all Judea and Samaria, and to the ends of the earth" (Acts 1:8). In this missionary activity, by the work of the Holy Spirit, a healthy church will multiply other new, healthy churches.

BECAUSE THE LOCAL CONGREGATION IS THE PRIMARY AGENT OF THE KINGDOM OF GOD

The exposition on the work of the Holy Spirit above drives us to consider the fourth fundamental reason why new and healthy churches should be multiplied. This fourth reason has much to do with the nature of the Church and its relationship with the kingdom of God. I want to suggest here that it is a natural and essential aspect of the very nature of the Church for it to reproduce itself into new congregations.[327] This is something that may be expected of every healthy congregation. We could also say it negatively: something is wrong with a local congregation that does not reproduce itself. We can think about this from three points of view.

We first must consider what the Bible teaches us about the nature of a healthy congregation. When we multiply new and healthy churches, what are we multiplying? That answer may be found in Acts 2 and I Thessalonians 1. In each passage we find a description of a new congregation less than a year old. Luke explains the characteristics of the congregation in Acts 2.43–47 with the purpose of proving that it is made up of messianic Jews who faithfully follow the Old Testament commandments and are also faithful followers of the Messiah, Jesus of Nazareth. In the case of the believers of Thessalonica, Paul mentions the characteristics of that church in order to prove that "he has chosen you" (1 Thess 1:4). How can one know that the believers of Thessalonica are chosen? It is known because they manifest the following characteristics.

Given the biblical context in which these characteristics appear, I believe that Luke, like Paul, offers us not only a description of a particular group of believers (written only in descriptive form), but he also is giving a summary of what he believes constitutes a true and authentic local church (written in normative form). In other words, our congregations and new, healthy churches should demonstrate the following characteristics:

- There are miracles and extraordinary signs.
- The congregation has an impact in its surrounding context.
- The members of the congregation have everything in common. They care for one another.
- They eat together and celebrate Communion and special unity.
- They praise and worship God.
- The Lord adds to their number each day those who have been chosen for salvation. (Acts 2:43–47)
- They confess Jesus as their Savior

---

327. One of the best resources I have encountered concerning the development of the biblical basis for multiplying healthy churches is the work of Fernando Mora, a pastor and biochemical engineer in Caracas, Venezuela. See Fernando Mora 2000, chapter 3. This book is self-published and may be found by contacting Fernando at: fmorac@cantv.net. Also, consider the work of Stuart Murray 1998, 36–65.

- The gospel arrives with power. There are miracles and special signs.
- The Word is preached.
- They experience a communion of love.
- They express an exemplary form of living.
- They suffer on behalf of the gospel.
- They show a spiritual joy.
- They show radical conversion.
- Their witness is known throughout the world.
- They demonstrate a new hope. (1 Thess 1:2–10)

There is much that could be said concerning these descriptions of healthy churches. However, here I only want to mention one issue. Both of these new churches are committed to evangelization, to mission and to the numerical growth of believers and congregations. There are occasions when we wish to emphasize one or two of these characteristics mentioned in the two passages. However, these characteristics describe a reality that takes shape when all are considered together. It is not possible to accept or emphasize one or two of these characteristics and pass over the rest. To do so would be to ignore the form in which Luke and Paul describe these two congregations. The description of each one is a complete package: organic and holistic. To emphasize unity, or worship, or signs and wonders means that one must also stress the missionary work of these congregations in announcing the gospel, the way they bring forth the numerical growth of believers and their attempts to multiply new and healthy churches (see Van Engen 1981, 178–90.)

Multiplying new churches is the penultimate goal of God's mission.

As the Body of Christ, the Church is the physical presence of God in this world for the blessing and transformation of the world (Rom 12; 1 Cor 12; Eph 4; 1 Pet 2 and 4). This truth obligates us to emphasize the ultimate importance of the Church. The universal Church, the Church in the world—of all times and cultures—is an idea, nothing more. Actually, this Church does not exist in concrete, visible form. What exists is a multitude of local congregations, local churches who are each a local manifestation of the Church universal. You and I and all the believers of Jesus Christ will never experience the universal Church. The base from which we are sent into the world is the local congregation, in which we experience the communion of saints and grow spiritually. As such, it is impossible to overestimate the importance of the local congregation of men and women who love Christ and worship God through the power of the Holy Spirit.

Nevertheless, the final goal of our mission cannot only be the local congregation. Multiplying, growing, and watching over the development of the local church is the penultimate goal of our mission, as Orlando Costas helps us see (Costas 1974, 90; 1979, 37–59; 1982, 46–48). The final goal our missionary labor is the glory of God, as we will see in the last part of this chapter.

The penultimate goal of multiplying healthy churches is essential. God has chosen the local congregation as his main instrument for his mission in the world. As such, in order to reach the final goal, it is of upmost importance to build thousands of new missionary congregations around the world. God is glorified when people's lives are changed and family, socioeconomic, and political structures of a city or nation experience a radical transformation. All this because the Holy Spirit used the local churches to announce the coming of the kingdom of God in Jesus Christ in a holistic way, through word and deed, and in a contextually appropriate and biblically sound manner.

BECAUSE MULTIPLYING NEW CHURCHES GIVES GLORY TO GOD

Why multiply new, healthy churches? The fifth reason is one that is over all the others. Multiplying new churches brings glory to God. At the end of the story, building new, healthy churches is not for the glory of a denomination or a missionary organization. It is not for the glory of a pastor or an evangelist. It is not for the glory of the mother church. Our fundamental motivation for multiplying new, healthy churches always must be a profound desire to give glory to God.

A. "The Ten Blessings" of Ephesians 1

All that has been said previously in this chapter can be summed up in the words of Paul in the first chapter of Ephesians. Upon beginning his letter to the Ephesians, his main letter regarding the Church and its mission, Paul uses the words of one of the oldest hymns of the primitive church. Although the music is not known, the words have been preserved because Paul used them to begin his letter. The hymn contains ten words that are verbs. These ten actions are divided into three verses, one for each of the three people of the Trinity. Because of this I have called this passage, "The Ten Blessings." Each verse emphasizes the work and special role of each person of the Trinity. This review of what God has done for us is beautiful, profound, and moving. Nevertheless, the most outstanding part of the hymn is a phrase that is repeated three times and serves as a chorus interwoven throughout the hymn. The phrase is: "For the praise of his glory." See the words of the hymn below.

Ephesians 1:1–14: "The Ten Blessings"

Through the Father
1. Chosen
2. Made saints
3. Predestined
4. Adopted

Chorus: For the praise of his glory.

Through the Son
5. Redeemed
6. Pardoned
7. Made participants of the mystery
8. United with Christ
9. Coheirs with Him

Chorus: For the praise of his glory.

Through the Holy Spirit
10. Marked with the seal of the promise through the Holy
Spirit who is the deposit (first payment) of our inheritance until
the redemption of God's possession

Chorus: For the praise of his glory

Centuries later we find an echo of Paul's emphasis in Ephesians in the writings of Gisbertus Voetius (1589–1676). A Dutch professor of theology, Voetius was one of the first protestant missiologists. Writing during the beginning of the seventeenth century, Voetius affirmed that biblically the mission of the Church has a three-part goal. He declared that the goal of God's mission in the Bible was *conversio gentili; plantatio ecclesiae; gloria Dei*: (a) the conversion of people to faith in Jesus Christ; (b) the multiplying of churches; and (c) the glory of God (see Bavinck 1960, 155ff). During the last five centuries, this perspective has been the most fundamental basis for missionary work among evangelical churches, descendants of the Protestant Reformation. In its most basic, these evangelical churches' motivation for church expansion was derived from this visionary goal: God wants men and women to become followers of Christ, responsible members of the church, and agents of the transformation of their contexts, to the glory of God.[328] Notice that all three parts of Matthew's articulation of the Great Commission (Matt 28:18–20) are to be found here ("disciple, baptize, and teach").

B. The vision in Revelation

The new, healthy church that stands out the most in the Bible is the congregation that comes together around the throne of Jesus Christ, the Shepherd of God in the New Jerusalem. What an amazing vision John describes in the last few chapters of Revelation! The angel tells John that he will show him "the bride, the wife of the Lamb" (Rev 21:9). This rhetorical figure, this verbal picture is one of the main representations of the Church of Jesus Christ, which Paul also describes as a bride ready to go to Jesus, her husband (Eph 5:23–27). How marvelous! The angel is presenting the Church as the New Jerusalem. The Church has become a city with twelve gates that will never close, made from the twelve stones from Aaron's vestments in the Tabernacle from the desert. The angel also makes him see that the "kings of the earth will bring their splendor into it." This vision is truly remarkable. The "kings of the earth" bring the splendor of their language, culture, history, civilization—bringing all of this to the New Jerusalem, which is the Church, whose temple is Jesus Christ, whose sun and light is Christ, whose doors never close so that they can constantly and eternally invite all people to wash in the blood of Christ. Then they can come together with all the saints around the throne of the Shepherd. Together, all the members of this new, healthy church, sing in a thousand languages, as if in answer to the miracle of Pentecost in Acts 2. All the nations, families, tongues, tribes of the world praise God with the hymn of eternity:

> You are worthy, our Lord and God, to receive glory and honor and power, for you created all things, and by your will they were created and have their being . . . To him who sits on the throne and to the Lamb be praise and honor and glory and power, forever and ever . . . Salvation belongs to our God, who sits on the throne, and to the Lamb . . . Amen! Praise and glory and

---

328. This phrase is an adaptation of the definition of mission from Donald McGavran 1970, 35.

wisdom and thanks and honor and power and strength be to
our God for ever and ever . . . Great and marvelous are your
deeds, Lord God Almighty. Just and true are your ways, King
of the nations . . . Let us rejoice and be glad and give him glory!
For the wedding of the Lamb has come, and his bride has made
herself ready" (Rev 4:11; 5:13b; 7:10b, 12; 15:3b; 19:7).

In this city that represents the Church, there is a very special tree: the Tree
of Life whose leaves are "for the healing of the nations" (Rev 22:2). To multiply
healthy churches is to participate in this vision, to be conduits, through the power
of the Holy Spirit, in moving towards this new reality, the new heaven and the
new earth—for the praise of the glory of our God. One of the ways in which we
represent, signal, prepare the way for, invite others to join in, and participate in
this vision is by multiplying new, healthy churches for the glory of God. The Bible
teaches us that the people of God, the Church, journeys from a garden to a new
city, the New Jerusalem.

C. The final goal: for the praise of the glory of God

Why should we devote all the money, time, energy, and personnel resources to
multiply healthy churches? In this essay I have suggested that most fundamentally,
such an endeavor flows from God's nature and mission: "for God so loved the
world." Love, God's initiative, his missionary action, forms the foundation, the
basis for all efforts in multiplying new, healthy churches. God's love, then, forms
the fountain from which flow the five reasons we have examined as to why we
should multiply new congregations:

- Because God the Father seeks and finds the lost;
- Because the love of Christ compels us;
- Because the Holy Spirit has been sent for all human beings (all
flesh);
- Because the local congregation is the primary agent of the
kingdom of God;
- Because multiplying churches is for the praise of the glory of God.

We could then express the mission of the church in the following way: it is the
will of God that men and women of all peoples of the earth be invited to become
followers of Jesus Christ, responsible members of Christ's Church, joined together
in faith communities, in the power of the Holy Spirit. These groups of believers, as

the agents of the kingdom of God, seek to transform the reality of their context in order to give praise to God.

The Church of Jesus Christ is therefore called to creative missionary action in the world as it seeks to proclaim the Good News of the kingdom of God in ways that are biblically faithful, contextually appropriate, and globally transformative. The Head of the Church is Jesus Christ, the Lord. From this point of view, the Church's existence has only one purpose: it exists for the praise of the glory of God.

What will be our motives for multiplying new, healthy churches? Will we choose the human, sinful, selfish, and oppressive motives? Or will we choose the motives—and the goals—that the Bible gives us? Will we multiply churches for our own glory? Or will we commit ourselves to participate in God's mission for the praise of his glory?

CONCLUSION

The elderly lady in Monterrey, Mexico who asked such a penetrating question deserves a careful answer. In the confusing multiplicity of diverse religious opinions, we need to give careful consideration to our own motives for multiplying churches. Ultimately our desire is that women and men become followers of Jesus, and only secondarily members of new churches. But, those who are new followers of Jesus need to be gathered into faith communities, the result of which is the expansion of new or existing churches. The hope of the world and the possibility to transform the reality that we face today resides in multiplying thousands of new, healthy churches in every city, town, and village throughout the world. These congregations are to be made up of sons and daughters of God, followers of Jesus Christ, blessed with the presence and gifts of the Holy Spirit, who intentionally and carefully look to be signs of the coming of the kingdom of God, for the praise of the glory of our God

Why multiply new, healthy churches?

1. Because God is a God of love; the mission is God's; the purpose is God's. Our God, the God of the Bible does not want, "anyone to perish, but everyone to come to repentance" (2 Peter 3:9).
2. Because we are chosen in order to serve; we are instruments in the hands of God; we are the Body of Christ, the physical presence of Jesus Christ in the world in order to be a blessing to the nations. As the Body of Christ one aspect of our nature is to raise up new

congregations as we would our sons and daughters. All mature congregations have to be mothers of other congregations.

3. Because we find ourselves to the extent to which we participate in being instruments of God's love for all the nations and all human beings (Matt 10:39). The Church does not exist to serve its members. On the contrary, the church is made up of members who, together as the people of God, exist in order to be instruments of the love of God to those who do not already know Jesus Christ.

4. Because we are specially called to participate in God's mission. One of the most appropriate and efficient ways to concretely express this election, consists of multiplying new, healthy churches.

5. Because always, in every place, we are the people of God, the God who loved the world so much he gave his one and only Son, that whoever believes in him shall not perish but have eternal life" (John 3:16). As such, we are a community of love, the community of the fruit of the Spirit, and we do not rest while there are still those who still do not know Jesus Christ through the work of the Holy Spirit—for the praise of the glory of our God.

CONCLUSION

In this book, we have examined what is involved in transforming mission theology as an activity of missiological reflection and self-examination on the part of believers, the Christian Church, mission agencies, and mission practitioners the world over. I have offered the examples found in this volume with the hope that these may stimulate and inspire others to explore ways in which they may also participate in transforming mission theology. The title of this book entails three related meanings.

First, mission theology has a transforming role with regard to the Christian thought and the missional action of churches and mission agencies. As Christians do mission theology in their contexts and in their historical moments, mission theology calls them to examine carefully their proximity or distance from Jesus Christ in whose mission they participate. It is vital that all of us as followers of Jesus examine the beam in our own eye (Matt 7:3–5) before we seek to eradicate the speck of dust in another's eye. We need to shine the light of the Bible on our motivations, perspectives, and practices of mission while we inspire one another to do Christ's mission.

This internal transforming function needs to change the way we read the Bible (our missional hermeneutic), the way we do historical theology, and how we do systematic theology. Mission theology needs to transform us in relation to the data, the agendas, and the paradigmatic filters (the plausibility structures) that we use in our reflection concerning the mission of the Church. As Andrew Kirk and others have reminded us, the issue is not that missiology needs to be more theological. The issue is that all Christian thought needs to be more missiologically informed in its proximity to the Bible's revelation of God's mission.

A second meaning of transforming mission theology entails how we do mission theology itself. As I pointed out in several of the chapters of this book, we can no longer afford to do mission theology merely as a self-justification to buttress our particular agenda in mission. Too often we have used mission theology to support our mission promotion. We have created our own version of mission theology merely to provide a foundation, a basis, a justification as to why our particular mission action is legitimate, important, and should be supported by people and money. But we know that mission is not our mission: it is Christ's mission.

This means that all Christians everywhere are called to rethink and reevaluate our mission theology itself. The Christian Church needs to be intentional and careful in transforming what we understand to be our mission theology. This is a constant process of reexamining the way we understand Christ's mission. We are challenged to rewrite our definition of mission at least every year. And we need to listen to each other locally and globally, interculturally and intercontinentally, so that together we may continually reshape and express anew how we understand our mission theology. Together we are called to be continually transforming our mission theology to grow closer to Jesus Christ, our Lord, the Head of the Church, in whose mission we participate as deacons and messengers.

A third meaning of the title of this book involves looking outward to the world. An essential and integral aspect of mission theology is that its motivation, purpose, and goal is to transform the world in which we live. As "ambassadors of reconciliation" (2 Cor 5:20) we are sent to call all humans everywhere to be reconciled to God, to self, to each other, and to creation. Mission theology's fundamental purpose is activist. It exists to be a transforming presence in a conflicted and hurting world so loved by God. Mission theology fulfills its purpose when the people of God commit themselves to proclaim in word and deed the gospel of the kingdom of God, inviting men and women to become followers of Jesus Christ the Lord.

Said another way, when mission theology is reduced to being merely mission studies, mere philosophical reflection, merely demoralizing critique that discourages missional action, then mission theology has lost its way. In that case, it desperately needs the inspiration of the Holy Spirit "to be transformed by the renewing of your mind . . . to test and approve what God's will is—his good, pleasing, and perfect will" (Rom 12:2). Mission theology's reason for existence is to be a missional agent of Christ mission to transform the world in which we live. I have offered the examples presented in the chapters of this book with the hope that they will inspire the reader to become actively involved in doing Christ's mission in the world.

It is my prayer that the thoughts presented in this book will encourage you, the reader, to join me in transforming mission theology for the salvation of the world and the glory of God.

APPENDIX

THEMATIC CONCORDANCE OF
DIAKONEW, DIAKONIA, AND *DIAKONOS*

Matthew

4:11   angels came and D him. (Mark 1:13)

8:15   she arose and D them (Mark 1:31; Luke 4:39)

20:26 whoever would be great must be your D (Mark 10:43; Luke 22:26)

22:13 the king said to the D

23:11 the elder among you shall be your D

25:44 Lord, when . . . and we did not D you?

27:55 many women who had D Jesus (Mark 15:41; Luke 23:49)

Luke

8:3   Joanna, Susanna and many others D him out of their own resources.

10:40 But Martha was preoccupied with much D (John 12:2)

10:40 my sister who lets me D alone?

12:37 his lord . . . shall gird himself and shall come and D them

17:8   Does he not say . . . D me?

22:26 he who leads shall be as the D

22:27 Who is the greater, he who sits at table or he who D?

22:27 But I am among you as one who D

John

12:26 If anyone would D me, follow me

12:26 and where I am, there also will be my D

12:26 If anyone D's me, my Father will honor him.

Acts

1:17   And had a part in the D
1:25   so that he may take part in this D
6:1   their widows were neglected in the daily D
6:2   It is not just that we should leave the word to D the tables
6:4   We will continue . . . in the D of the word
11:29 The determined to send D to the brethren
12:25 And Barnabas and Saul, having completed their D, returned
       to Jerusalem
19:22 And the sent two who could D them, Timothy and Erastus.
20:24 to finish my race with joy and the D which I received from the
       Lord Jesus.
21:19 He . . . described what God had done among the Gentiles
       through his D

Romans

11:13 Inasmuch as I am an apostle of Gentiles, I honor my D.
12:7   or if of D, in D
13:4   for it is God's D for your good.
15:8   Christ Jesus came to be D to the circumcision . . .
15:25 But now I go to Jerusalem for the D of the saints.
15:31 . . . and that my D to Jerusalem may be acceptable to
       the saints.
16:1   Phoebe, who is a D of the church. . . .

1 Corinthians

3:5   . . . What, then, is Paul, what Apollos? D's . . .
12:5   And there are diversity of D's
16:15 . . . they have devoted themselves for the D of the saints.

2 Corinthians

3:3   . . . you are the letter of Christ D by us.
3:6   he made us adequate as D of the new covenant
3:7   But if the D of death in letters engraved in stone . . .
3:8   how shall the D of the Spirit fail. . . . ?
3:9   Because if the D of condemnation . . .

3:9   much more does the D of righteousness . . .

4:1   Therefore, since we have this D, . . .

5:18   God, who reconciled us, and has given us the D of reconciliation . . .

6:3   giving no cause for offense . . . in order that the D may not be discredited.

6:4   commending ourselves as D of God

8:4   begging us . . . for the favor of participation in the D of the saints,

8:19   appointed . . . to travel with us in the grace (*xaris*) of this D of ours to you

8:20   that no one should discredit us in our D of this generous gift;

9:1   concerning the D of the saints;

9:12   For the D of this service

9:13   Because of the proof given by this D they will glorify God . . .

11:8   taking wages from them to D you

11:15   his D's also disguise themselves as D's of righteousness

11:23   Are they D's of Christ?

Galatians

2:17   is Christ, then, a D of sin?

Ephesians

3:7   of which I was made a D, according to the gift of God's grace . . .

4:12   for the equipping of the saints for the work of D . . .

6:21   Tychicus, the beloved brother and faithful D in the Lord . . .

Colossains

1:7   Epaphras, our beloved fellow bondservant (*sundoulou*) who is a faithful D of Christ

1:23   of which I Paul was made a D

1:25   of which I was made a D according to the stewardship (*oikonomian*) of God

4:17   And say to Archippus, "Take heed to the D . . .

1 Thessolonians

3:2   Timothy, our brother, D of God and . . .

1 Timothy

1:12   Christ Jesus . . . who . . . considered me faithful, appointing me into this D

3:8   The D's should also be

3:10   let these also first be tested; then let them serve as D's

3:12   The D's should be husbands of one wife . . .

3:13   For those who have served well as D's

4:6   If you teach these things to the believers, you will be a good D of Christ Jesus

2 Timothy

1:18   Onesiphorus . . . you know very well what D he rendered at Ephesus.

4:5   But you, . . . fulfill your D

4:11   Mark . . . he is useful to me for D

Philemon

13   that in your behalf he might D me

Hebrews

1:14   Are they not all serving *(leiturgika pneumata)* sent to D . . . ?

6:10   For God is not unjust so as to forget . . . in your having D and D-ing the saints

1 Peter

1:12   they were not D themselves, but you

4:10   Each one according to the gift . . . D one another, as good administrators *(oikonomoi)* . . .

4:11   whoever D, as by the strength which God supplies

Revelation

2:19   I know your deeds, love, faith, D, and . . .

BIBLIOGRAPHY

Abraham, William J. 1989. *The Logic of Evangelism*. Grand Rapids: Eerdmans.

AD 2000 and Beyond. 1999. "The PAD (Presidents and Academic Deans) Declaration," *EMQ* XXXV:3 (July), 321.

Aigbe, Sunday. 1991. "Cultural Mandate, Evangelistic Mandate, Prophetic Mandate: of These Three the Greatest Is . . ." *Missiology* XIX: 1 (January), 31–43.

Allen, Roland. 1962. *The Spontaneous Expansion of the Church*. Grand Rapids: Eerdmans.

———. 1962. *Missionary Methods St. Paul's or Ours?* Grand Rapids: Eerdmans.

Andersen, Wilhelm. 1961. "Further Toward a Theology of Mission," in: G. H. Anderson, ed., 1961, 300–13.

Anderson, Gerald H. 1974. "A Moratorium on Missionaries?" *Christian Century* (January 16); reprinted in Gerald H. Anderson, and Thomas F. Stransky, editors: 1974, 133–41.

——— 1988. "American Protestants in Pursuit of Mission: 1886–986" *IBMR* XII:3 (July), 98–118; reprinted in F. J. Verstraelen, et al 1995, 374–420.

Anderson, Gerald H., ed., 1961. *The Theology of Christian Mission*. Nashville: Abingdon.

———, ed., 1998. *Biographical Dictionary of World Mission*. Grand Rapids: Eerdmans.

Anderson, Gerald H. and Thomas F. Stransky, eds., 1974. *Mission Trends No. 1*. Grand Rapids: Eerdmans.

———. 1976. *Mission Trends No. 3*. Grand Rapids: Eerdmans.

Anderson, Gerald H., James Phillips, and Robert Coote eds., 1991. *Mission in the 1990's*. G. R.: Eerdmans.

Anderson, Justice. 1998, "An Overview of Missiology," in John Mark Terry, Ebbie Smith, and Justice Anderson, eds., 1998, 1–17.

Arias, Esther and Mortimer Arias. 1980. *The Cry of My People: Out of Captivity in Latin America*. New York: Friendship.

Arias, Mortimer. 1980. *Venga tu Reino: La memoria subversiva de Jesús*. México: Casa Unida—subsequently published in English as *Announcing the Reign of God: Evangelization and the Subversive Memory of Jesus*. Phil.: Fortress, 1984.

———. 1998. *Anunciando el Reino de Dios, Evangelización integral desde la memoria de Jesús*. San José, Costa Rica: Visión Mundial.

———. 2001. "Global and Local: A Critical View of Mission Models," in Howard Snyder, ed., 2001, 55–64.

———. 2003. *El Ultimo Mandato, la Gran Comisión, Relectura desde América Latina*. Bogotá: Visión Mundial.

Armerding, Carl, ed., 1977. *Evangelism and Liberation*. Nutley, N.J.: Presbyterian and Reformed.

Armstrong, H., M. McClellan, and D. Sills, eds., 2011 (Third Edition). *Introducción a la Misiología*. Louisville: Reaching and Teaching International Ministries.

Eddie Arthur. 2013. "Missio Dei and the Mission of the Church," *The World* [posted 06–2013]. at http://www.wycliffe.net/missiology?id=3960; downloaded June 30, 2016.

Baillie, John, ed., 1946. *Natural Theology*. London: Geoffrey Bles.

Bakke, Ray. 1987. *The Urban Christian: Effective Ministry in Today's Urban World*. Downers Grove: IVP.

———. 2002. *Misión Integral en la Ciudad*. Buenos Aires: Kairós.

Bakke, Ray and Samuel Roberts. 1986. *The Expanded Mission of "Old First' Churches*. Valley Forge: Judson Press.

Barrett, David B. 1983. "Silver and Gold Have I None: Church of the Poor or Church of the Rich?" *IBMR* VII:4 (Oct.), 146–51.

———. 1986. *World Class Cities and World Evangelization*. Birmingham, AL, New Hope Publ.

Barrett, David, ed., 1982. *World Christian Encyclopedia*. Oxford: Oxford U. Press. This was updated and reprinted in David Barrett, George Kurian and Todd Johnson, *World Christian Encyclopedia* 2nd ed. Oxford: Oxford U. Press, 2001.

Barrett, Lois, ed., Dale A. Ziemer, Darrell L. Guder, George R. Hunsberger, Walter Hobbs, Lynn Stutzman, Jeff Van Cooten. 2003. *Treasure in Clay Jars: Patterns in Missional Faithfulness*. Grand Rapids: Eerdmans.

Barrett Montgomery, Helen. 2000. *The Bible and Missions*. (1st Edition, The Central Committee on the United Study of Foreign Missions, 1920) Revised Edition published by Shawn B. Redford, ed., Pasadena, CA: Fuller Theological Seminary.

Barth, Karl. 1933. *Theologische Existenz Heute!* Munich: Chr. Kaiser (quoted in Bosch, 1991: 424).

———. 1936. *Credo: A Presentation of the Chief Problems of Dogmatics with Reference to the Apostles' Creed*, J. S. McNab, trans. N.Y.: Scribners.

———. 1958. *Church Dogmatics.* vol. 4, G.T. Thomson, trans. Edinburgh: T and T Clark.

———. 1961. "An Exegetical Study of Matt 28:16–20," in G. H. Anderson 1961: 55–71.

Bass, Dorothy, Benton Johnson and Wade Clark Roof. 1986. *Mainstream Protestantism in the Twentieth Century: Its Problems and Prospects.* Louisville, KY: Committee on Theological Education, Council on Theological Education, Presbyterian Church, USA.

Bassham, Rodger C. 1979. *Mission Theology: 1948–1975 Years of Worldwide Creative Tension, Ecumenical, Evangelical and Roman Catholic.* Pasadena: William Carey Library.

Bauckham, Richard. 2003. *Bible and Mission: Christian Witness in a Postmodern World.* Grand Rapids: Baker.

Bavinck, Herman. 1956. *Our Reasonable Faith: A Survey of Christian Doctrine.* Grand Rapids: Baker.

Bavinck, J. H. 1960. *An Introduction to the Science of Missions.* Phillipsburg: Presbyterian and Reformed.

———. 1977. An Introduction to the Science of Missions. N.J.: Presbyterian and Reformed.

Bediako, Kwame. 1995. *Christianity in Africa: The Renewal of the Non-Western Religion.* Maryknoll: Orbis.

Bennett, Chuck. 1998. "Is There a Spin Doctor in the House?" *EMQ* XXXIV:4 (Oct.), 420–25.

Bennett, John C. 1999. "Working Together to Shape the New Millennium: Dreams, Hopes, Concerns, Fears" (COSIM) *EMQ* XXXV:3 (July), 314–17.

———. 1990. "Foreword" in David Martin, 1990, vii–x.

Berkhof, Hendrikus. 1979. *Christian Faith: An Introduction to the Study of the Faith.* Grand Rapids: Eerdmans.

———. 1985. *Introduction to the Study of Dogmatics.* Grand Rapids: Eerdmans.

Berkhof, Louis. 1932. *Reformed Dogmatics.* Grand Rapids: Eerdmans.

Berkouwer, G.C. 1955. *General Revelation.* Grand Rapids: Eerdmans.

—————. 1976. *The Church.* Grand Rapids: Eerdmans.

Berney, James E., ed., 1979. *You Can Tell the World.* Downers Grove: InterVarsity.

Best, Ernest. 1955. *One Body in Christ.* London: SPCK.

Bettenson, Henry. 1956. *The Early Christian Fathers.* London: Oxford U. Press.

—————. 1947, 1963. *Documents of the Christian Church.* N.Y.: Oxford U. Press.

—————. 1970. *The Late Christian Fathers.* N.Y.: Oxford U. Press.

Bevans, Stephen. 1992. *Models of Contextual Theology* (Faith and Cultures Series). Maryknoll: Orbis; reprinted in *Models of Contextual Theology: Revised and Expanded Edition.* Maryknoll: Orbis, 2002.

—————.1993. "The Biblical Basis of the Mission of the Church in *Redemptoris Missio*" in Van Engen, et al, eds., 1993. 37–44.

Bevans, Stephen and Roger P. Schroeder. 2004. *Constants in Context: A Theology of Mission for Today.* Maryknoll: Orbis.

—————. 2009. *Teología para la Misión Hoy: Constantes en Contexto.* Estella, Spain: Verbo Divino. (Spanish Translation of 2004 *Constants in Context.*)

Blauw, Johannes. 1962. *The Missionary Nature of the Church.* Grand Rapids: Eerdmans.

—————. 1974. *The Missionary Nature of the Church.* Grand Rapids: Eerdmans; London: Lutterworth.

Bloesch, Donald G. 1992. *A Theology of Word & Spirit: Authority & Method in Theology.* Downers Grove: IVP.

Boer, Harry. 1961. *Pentecost and Missions.* Grand Rapids: Eerdmans.

Boff, Clodovis. 1987. *Theology and Praxis: Epistemological Foundations.* Maryknoll: Orbis.

Boff, Clodovis and Leonardo Boff. 1987. *Introducing Liberation Theology.* Maryknoll: Orbis.

Boff, Leonardo. 1979. *Liberating Grace.* Maryknoll: Orbis.

Bosch, David J. 1978a. "The Why and How of a True Biblical Foundation of Mission," in Jerald D. Gort, ed., 35–45. Reprinted as "Hermeneutical Principles in the Biblical Foundation for Mission," *Evangelical Review of Theology* 17:4 (Oct. 1993), 437–451.

—————. 1978b. "Toward True Mutuality: Exchanging the Same Commodities or Supplementing Each Others' Needs?" *Missiology* VI:3 (July); reprinted in Daniel Rickett and Dotsey Welliver, eds., *Supporting Indigenous Ministries: With Selected Readings.* Wheaton: Billy Graham Center, 1997, 53–64.

—————. 1980, 2006. *Witness to the World: The Christian Mission in Theological Perspective.* London: Marshall, Morgan & Scott.

―――. 1991. *Transforming Mission: Paradigm Shifts in Theology of Mission*. Maryknoll: Orbis.

―――. 1993. "Reflections on Biblical Models of Mission," in J. Phillips and R. Coote, eds., 175–92.

―――. 1995. *Believing in the Future: Toward a Missiology of Western Culture*. Valley Forge, PA: Trinity Press.

Braaten, Carl. 1985. *The Nature and Aim of the Church's Mission and Ministry*. Minn.: Augsburg.

―――. 1990. "The Triune God; The Source and Model of Christian Unity and Mission," *Missiology* XVIII:4 (Oct.), 415–28.

Branson, Mark and René Padilla, eds., 1984. *Conflict and Context: Hermeneutics in the Americas*. Grand Rapids: Eerdmans.

Brauer, Jerald C. 1971. *The Westminster Dictionary of Church History*. Phil.: Westminster.

Bria, Ion. 1991. *The Sense of Ecumenical Tradition: the Ecumenical Witness and Vision of the Orthodox*. Geneva: WCC.

Bright, John. 1953. *The Kingdom of God*. Nashville: Abingdon.

Bright, W. 1892. *The Canons of the First Four General Councils*. Oxford: Clarendon Press.

Bromiley, Geoffrey. 1978. *Historical Theology, an Introduction*. Grand Rapids: Eerdmans.

Brown, Robert McAfee. 1978. *Theology in a New Key: Responding to Liberation Themes*. Phil.: Westminster.

―――. 1984. *Unexpected News: Reading the Bible with Third World Eyes*. Phil.: Westminster.

Brunner, Emil. 1949. *The Christian Doctrine of God*. Phil.: Westminster.

Burkhalter, William. 1984, *A Comparative Analysis of the Roland Allen and Donald Anderson McGavran*. Ph.D dissertation; Southern Baptist Theological Seminary, Louisville, KY.

Butler, Phillip. 1999. "The Power of Partnership," in Ralph Winter and Steven Hawthorne, eds., 753–758.

Calvin, John. 1851. *Calvin's Commentaries*, Calvin Trans. Soc.

―――. 1949. *The Christian Doctrine of God*. Phil: Westminster.

―――. 1960. *Institutes of the Christian Religion*. (Ford Lewis Battles, trans.). Phil.: Westminster Press.

―――. 1975. *Institutes of the Christian Religion*. H. Beveridge, trans., Grand Rapids: Eerdmans.

Campbell, Evvy. 1999. "Working Together to Shape the New Millennium: Dreams, Hopes, Concerns, Fears" (AERDO) *EMQ* XXXV:3 (July), 311–14.

Camps, A., L. A. Hoedemaker, M. R. Spindler, and F. J. Verstraelen. eds., 1988. *Oecumenische inleiding in de missiologie. Teksten en konteksten van het wereldchristendom.* Kampen: Kok.

Cardenal, Ernesto. 1985. *Flights of Victory.* Maryknoll: Orbis.

Carpenter, Joel A. and Wilbert R. Shenk, eds., 1990. *Earthen Vessels: American Evangelicals and Foreign Missions, 1880–1980* Grand Rapids: Eerdmans.

Carr, Burgess. 1975. "The Relation of Union to Mission," *Mid-Stream: An Ecumenical Journal.* XIV:4 (Oct.); reprinted in Gerald H. Anderson and Thomas Stransky, eds., 1976, 158–168.

Carriker, Timóteo. 1992a. *Missão Integral: Uma Teologia Bíblica.* São Paulo: Editorial Sepal.

———. 1992b, Missões na Bíblia. Princípios gerais. São Paulo: Vida Nova.

———. 2000. *O Caminho Missionário de Deus: Uma Teologia Bíblica de Missões.* São Paulo: SEPAL. (Third edition; Brasília: Palabra: 2000,1992.

———. 2005. *A Visão Missionária na Biblia: Uma história de amor.* São Paulo: Editora Ultimato. (Spanish translation: *La visión misionera en la Biblia. Una historia de amor.* Série: Campañerismo em la misión de Dios. São Leopoldo and Quito: CLAI Ediciones and Editora Sinodal, 2011.

———. 2007. A missão apocalíptica de Paulo. (Paul's Apocalyptic Mission). São Paulo: Abba Press.

———. 2008, Proclamando Boas-Novas. Bases sólidas para o evangelismo. (Proclaiming Good News. Solid Foundations for Evangelism). Brasília: Palavra.

———. 2014. Teologia bíblica de criação. Passado, Presente e futuro. Série: Um livro, uma causa. (Biblical Theology of Creation. Past, Present and Future. One book, one cause) Viçosa: Ultimato.

Carroll, Jackson, Carl Dudley, and William McKinney, eds., 1986. *Handbook for Congregational Studies.* Nashville: Abingdon.

Castro, Emilio. 1973. "Editorial" *International Review of Mission* LXII: 248 (Oct.), 393–398. (This entire issue of the 1985 *Freedom in Mission: The Perspective of the Kingdom of God, an Ecumenical Inquiry.* Geneva: WCC. *IRM* was devoted to discussion of matters related to the "moratorium" debate.)

Chaney, Charles. 1987, 1991. *Church Planting at the End of the Twentieth Century.* Wheaton: Tyndale.

Chrispal, Ashish. 1995. "Contextualization," in Sunand Sumithra and F. Hrangkuma, eds., 1995. 1–15.

Chopp, Rebecca S. 1986. *The Praxis of Suffering: An Interpretation of Liberation and Political Theologies.* Maryknoll: Orbis.

Claerbaut, David. 1983. *Urban Ministry.* Grand Rapids: Zondervan.

Coe, Shoki. 1976. "Contextualizing Theology" in *Mission Trends No. 3.* Gerald Anderson and Thomas Stransky, eds., Grand Rapids: Eerdmans, 19–24.

Coggins, Wade. 1980. "COWE: An Assessment of Progress and Work Left Undone," *Evangelical Missions Quarterly* 16 (October), 225–32.

Cole, Neil. 2005. *Organic Church: Growing Faith Where Life Happens.* San Francisco: Jossey-Bass.

Conn, Harvie M. 1977. "Contextualization: Where Do We Begin?" in Carl Armerding, ed., 1977. 90–119.

———. 1978. "Contextualization: A New Dimension for Cross-Cultural Hermeneutic" *Evangelical Missions Quarterly* XIV: 1 (January) 39–46.

———. 1982. *Evangelism: Doing Justice and Preaching Grace.* Grand Rapids: Zondervan.

———. 1984. *Eternal Word and Changing World: Theology, Anthropology, and Mission in Trialogue.* Grand Rapids: Zondervan.

———, 1987. *A Clarified Vision for Urban Mission: Dispelling the Urban Stereotypes.* Grand Rapids: Zondervan.

———. 1993a. "A Contextual Theology of Mission for the City," in Charles Van Engen, Dean Gilliland and Paul Pierson, eds., 1993. 96–106.

———. 1993b. "Urban Mission," in James Phillips and Robert Coote, eds., 318–37.

Conn, Harvie M., ed., 1977. *Theological Perspectives on Church Growth.* Nutley, N.J.: Presbyterian and Reformed.

———. 1984. *Reaching the Unreached: The Old-New Challenge.* Phillipsburg, N.J.: Presbyterian and Reformed.

———. 1997. *Multiplying and Growing Urban Churches: From Dream to Reality.* Grand Rapids: Baker.

Cook, Guillermo. 1985. *The Expectation of the Poor: Latin American Base Ecclesial Communities in Protestant Perspective.* Maryknoll: Orbis.

Coote, Robert T. 1993. "Gerald H. Anderson: A Career Dedicated to Mission," in James M. Phillips and Robert T. Coote, eds., : 1993, 375–379.

Coote, Robert and John Stott, eds., 1980. *Down to Earth: Studies in Christianity and Culture.* Grand Rapids: Eerdmans.

Coote, Robert T., and James M. Phillips, eds., 1993. *Toward the 21st Century in Christian Mission.* Grand Rapids: Eerdmans.

Corrie, John, ed., 2007. *Dictionary of Mission Theology: Evangelical Foundations.* Downers Grove: InterVarsity Press.

Corrie, John and Cathy Ross, eds., 2012. *Mission in Context: Explorations Inspired by J. Andrew Kirk.* Farnham, UK: Ashgate.

Corwin, Gary and Kenneth Mulholland, eds., 2000. *Working Together With God to Shape the New Millennium.* Pasadena: William Carey Library

Costas, Orlando. 1974. *The Church and its Mission: A Shattering Critique from the Third World,* Wheaton: Tyndale.

———. 1975. El Protestantismo en América Latina Hoy. San Jose: IDEF.

———. 1976. *Theology of the Crossroads in Contemporary Latin America: Missiology in Mainline Protestantism, 1969–1974.* Amsterdam: Rodopi.

———. 1979. *The Integrity of Mission: The Inner Life and Outreach of the Church.* N.Y.: Harper & Row.

———. 1980. "The Whole World for the Whole Gospel," *Missiology* 8 (Oct., 1980), 395–504.

———. 1982. *Christ Outside the Gate: Mission Beyond Christendom.* Maryknoll: Orbis.

———. 1989. *Liberating News: A Theology of Contextual Evangelization.* Grand Rapids: Eerdmans.

Crane, William H. 1969. "Editorial," *International Review of Mission.* 58: 141–44.

Cullmann, Oscar. 1951. *Christ and Time.* London: SCM; Phil.: Westminster.

———. 1961. "Eschatology and Missions in the New Testament" in Gerald Anderson, ed., 42–54.

Daneel, Inus, Charles Van Engen, and Hendrik Vroom, eds., 2003. *Fullness of Life for All: Challenges for Mission in the Early 21st Century.* Amsterdam: Rodopi.

Davies, J. G. 1965. *The Early Christian Church.* London: Weidenfelf and Nicolson.

Dawson, David. 1997. "A Recurring Issue in Mission Administration" *Missiology* XXV:4 (Oct.), 457–65.

Dayton, Edward R. 1980. *That Everyone May Hear,* 2nd ed. Monrovia: MARC Publications.

Dayton, Edward R. and David A. Fraser. 1990. *Planning Strategies for World Evangelization*. Monrovia: MARC; Grand Rapids: Eerdmans.

Deferrari, Roy, ed., 1958. *The Fathers of the Church*: Saint Cyprian, Treatises. N.Y.: Fathers of the Church, Inc.

De Groot, A. 1966. *The Bible on the Salvation of Nations*. De Pere, Wisc.: St. Norbert Abbey.

De Gruchy, John W. 1994. "The Nature, Necessity and Task of Theology," in John De Gruchy and Charles Villa-Vicencio, eds., 1993. 2–14.

De Gruchy, John W. and Charles Villa-Vicencio, eds., 1994. *Doing Theology in Context*. Maryknoll: Orbis.

Demarest, Bruce A. 1982. *General Revelation*. Grand Rapids: Zondervan.

De Mesa, José M. 2000. *Inculturation as Pilgrimage*. Chicago: Catholic Theological Union.

Dempster, Murray, Byron Klaus and Douglas Petersen. 1991. *Called & Empowered: Global Mission in Pentecostal Perspective*. Peabody, MA: Hendrickson.

De Ridder, Richard. 1975. *Discipling the Nations*. Grand Rapids: Baker.

Dever, Mark. 2007. *What is a Healthy Church?* Wheaton, IL: Crossway Books.

Dollar, Harold. 2000. "Holy Spirit" in A. Scott Moreau, Harold Netland, and Charles Van Engen, eds., 2000, 450–452.

Douglas, J.D., ed., 1975. *Let the Earth Hear His Voice*. Minneapolis: World Wide Publications.

———. 1980. "Lausanne's Extended Shadow Gauges Evangelism Progress," *Christianity Today* 8 (August) 43–44.

———. 1990. *Proclaim Christ Until He Comes: Calling the Whole Church to Take the Whole Gospel to the Whole World*. Minneapolis: World Wide Publ.

Driscoll, Mark. 2004. *The Radical Reformission*. Grand Rapids: Zondervan.

Driver, Juan. 1998. *Imágenes de una iglesia en misión: Hacia una eclesiología transformadora*. Guatemala: Clara Semilla.

Drucker, Peter. 1993. *Post-Capitalist Society*. N.Y.: Harper Business.

Duerr, J. 1947. *Sendende und Werdende Kirche in der Missions-theologie Gustav Warneck*. Basel: Basler Missionbuchhandlung.

Dulles, Avery. 1992, 1995. *The Craft of Theology: From Symbol to System*. New York: Crossroad.

Dyrness, William A. 1983. *Let the Earth Rejoice: A Biblical Theology of Holistic Mission*. Pasadena: Fuller Seminary Press.

————. 1990. *Learning About Theology from the Third World*. Grand Rapids: Zondervan.

Easum, William and Dave Travis. 2003. *Beyond the Box: Innovative Churches that Work*. Loveland, CO: Group.

Eastman, Theodore. 1971. *Chosen and Sent, Calling the Church to Mission*. Grand Rapids: Eerdmans.

Eastwood, Cyril C. 1958. "Luther's Conception of the Church," *Scottish Journal of Theology* XI:1, 22–36.

Elliston, Edgar, ed., 2011. with Pablo Deiros, Viggo Søgaard and Charles Van Engen, *Introducing Missiological Research Design*, Pasadena: William Carey Library, 113–18.

Escobar, Samuel. 1987. *La Fe Evangélica y las Teorías de la Liberación*. El Paso: Casa Bautista.

————. 1998a. "Pablo y la misión a los gentiles," in C. René Padilla, ed., 307–50.

————. 1998b. *De la Misión a la Teología*. Buenos Aires: Kairos.

————. 1999. *Tiempo de Misión: América Latina y la misión cristiana hoy*. Guatemala: Semilla.

————. 2002. *Changing Tides: Latin America and World Mission Today*. Maryknoll: Orbis.

————. 2003. *The New Global Mission: The Gospel from Everywhere to Everyone*. Downers Grove: IVP.

Featherstone, Mike, Scott Lash, and Roland Robertson, eds., 1995. *Global Modernities*. Thousand Oaks, CA: Sage.

Ferm, Deane W. 1986. *Third World Liberation Theologies: An Introductory Survey*. Maryknoll: Orbis.

Fernando, Ajith. 2000. "Grounding our Reflections in Scripture: Biblical Trinitarianism and Mission," in William Taylor, ed., 2000. 189–256.

Flannery, Austin P., ed., 1975. *Documents of Vatican II*. Grand Rapids: Eerdmans.

Fleming, Bruce. 1980. *The Contextualization of Theology: An Evangelical Assessment*. Pasadena: William Carey Library.

Freire, Paulo. 1970. *Pedagogy of the Oppressed*. New York: Herder and Herder; London: Penguin 1972.

Frenchak, David, Clinton Stockwell and Helen Ujvarosy. 1984. *Signs of the Kingdom in the Secular City*. Chicago: Covenant.

Frost, Michael. 2006. *Exiles: Living Missionally in a Post-Christian Culture*. Peabody, MA: Hendrickson.

Frost, Michael and Alan Hirsch. 2003. *The Shaping of Things to Come: Innovation and Mission for the 21st Century Church.* Peabody, MA: Hendrickson.

Fuellenback, John. 1995. *The Kingdom of God: The Message of Jesus Today.* Orbis: Maryknoll.

Fuller, W. Harold. 1980. *Mission-Church Dynamics: How to Change Bicultural Tensions in Dynamic Missionary Outreach.* Pasadena: William Carey Library.

Gallagher, Robert. 1999. *Footprints of God: A Narrative Theology of Mission.* With Charles E. Van Engen and Nancy Thomas. Monrovia, CA: MARC/ World Vision.

———. 2004. *Mission in Acts: Ancient Narratives in Contemporary Context.* With Paul Hertig. American Society of Missiology Series, No. 34. Maryknoll, NY: Orbis Books.

———. 2009. *Landmark Essays in Mission and World Christianity.* With Paul Hertig. American Society of Missiology Series, No. 43. Maryknoll, NY: Orbis Books.

——— with Charles E. Van Engen and Nancy Thomas, eds., 1999. *Footprints of God: A Narrative Theology of Mission.* Monrovia, CA: MARC/World Vision.

Gallagher, Sarita. 2014. *Abrahamic Blessing: A Missiological Narrative of Revival in Papua New Guinea,* Eugene, OR: Wipf and Stock. Garden Valley Community Church. 2005. *Home Page,* Kelowna, British Columbia, Canada.

Gensichen, Hans-Werner. 1971. *Glaube für die Welt: Theologische Aspekte der Mission.* Gütersloh: Gerd Mohn.

Gibbs, Eddie. 1981. *I Believe in Church Growth.* Grand Rapids: Eerdmans.

———. 1986. "The Power Behind the Principles," in: C. Peter Wagner, Win Arn and Elmer Towns, eds., 189–205.

———. 1994. *In Name Only: Tackling the Problem of Nominal Christianity.* Kent, England: Monarch Publications.

———. 1999. *Transforming Transitions.* Pasadena: self-published. (Subsequently published as *ChurchNext: Quantum Changes in How We Do Ministry.* Downers Grove: IVP, 2000.)

Gibellini, Rosino, ed., 1979. *Frontiers of Theology in Latin America.* Maryknoll: Orbis.

Gilliland, Dean S. 1983. *Pauline Theology and Mission Practice.* Grand Rapids: Baker.

———. 1989a *The Word Among Us: Contextualizing Theology for Mission Today.* Waco: Word.

———. 1989b. "Contextual Theology as Incarnational Mission," in Gilliland, ed., *1989a*, 9–31.

———. 1989c. "New Testament Contextualization: Continuity and Particularity in Paul's Theology," in Gilliland, ed., 1989a, 52–73.

———. 2000. "Contextualization," in A. Scott Moreau, Harold Netland and Charles Van Engen, eds., 225–227.

Gilliland, Dean S. ed., 1989. *The Word Among Us: Contextualizing Theology for Mission Today.* Waco: Word,

Glasser, Arthur. 1972. "Salvation Today and the Kingdom," in Donald McGavran, ed., 33–53.

———. 1973. "Church Growth and Theology," in Alan Tippett, 52–65.

———. 1976. "The Missionary Task: An Introduction," in Glasser, Hiebert, Wagner and Winter, eds., 3–10.

———. 1979. "Help from an Unexpected Quarter or, The Old Testament and Contextualization," *Missiology* VII: 4 (Oct.) 401–9.

———. 1985. "The Evolution of Evangelical Mission Theology since World War II," *International Bulletin of Missionary Research* 9:1 January, 9–13.

———. 1989. "Old Testament Contextualization: Revelation and Its Environment," in Gilliland, ed., 32–51.

———. *1992. Kingdom and Mission: A Biblical Study of the Kingdom of God and the World Mission of His People.* unpublished syllabus, Pasadena: Fuller Theological Seminary.

Glasser, Arthur F, Paul Hiebert, Peter Wagner, and Ralph Winter, eds., 1976. *Crucial Dimensions in World Evangelization.* Pasadena: William Carey Library.

Glasser, Arthur with Charles E. Van Engen, Dean S. Gilliland y Shawn B. Redford. 2003. *Announcing the Kingdom: The Story of God's Mission in the Bible.* Grand Rapids: Baker.

Glasser, Arthur F. and Donald A. McGavran, eds., 1983. *Contemporary Theologies of Mission.* Grand Rapids: Baker.

Glover, Robert H. 1946. *The Bible Basis of Missions.* L.A.: Bible House of Los Angeles.

Gnanakan, Ken R. 1989. *Kingdom Concerns: A Biblical Exploration Towards a Theology of Mission.* Bangalore: Theological Book Trust.

———. 1992. *The Pluralist Predicament.* Bangalore: Theological Book Trust.

Gnanakan, Ken R., ed., 1992. *Salvation: Some Asian Perspectives*. Bangalore: Theological Book Trust.

Goheen, Michael W. 2000. *As the Father Has Sent me, I am Sending You: J.E. Lesslie Newbigin's Missionary Ecclesiology*. Zoetermeer, Netherlands: Boekencentrum, 2000 (dissertation done under Jan Jongeneel). Available in digital form at http://igitur-archive.library.uu.nl /dissertations /1947080/inhoud.htm.

————. 2011. *A Light to the Nations: The Missional Church and the Biblical Story*. Grand Rapids: Baker.

Goodall, Norman, ed., 1953. *Missions Under the Cross*. London: Edinburgh House and N.Y.: Friendship.

Gort, Jerald D., ed., 1978. *Zending Op Weg Naar de Toekomst*. Kampen: Kok.

Grenz. Stanley J. 1993. *Revisioning Evangelical Theology: A Fresh Agenda for the 21st Century*. Downers Grove: IVP.

————. 1994. *Theology for the Community of God*. Nashville: Broadman & Holman.

Grudem, Wayne. 1994. *Systematic Theology*. Grand Rapids: Zondervan.

Guder, Darrell L. 2000a. *Ser Testigos de Jesucristo: La misión de la Iglesia, su mensaje y sus mensajeros*. Buenos Aires: Kairós; published in English as *Be My Witnesses*. Grand Rapids: Eerdmans, 1985 with English preface to the edition by Charles Van Engen.

————. 2000b. *The Continuing Conversion of the Church*. Grand Rapids: Eerdmans.

Guder, Darrell, ed., 1998. *Missional Church: A Vision for the Sending of the Church in North America*. Grand Rapids: Eerdmans.

Guthrie, Stan. 1996. "Urban Ministry No Longer Neglected Missions Stepchild,' *EMQ* XXXII:1 (Jan) 82–83.

Gutierrez, Gustavo. 1974. *A Theology of Liberation* (fifteenth anniversary edition with a new introduction by the author). Maryknoll: Orbis.

————. 1984a. *We Drink from Our Own Wells*. Maryknoll: Orbis.

————. 1984b. *The Power of the Poor in History*. Maryknoll: Orbis.

Hadaway, C. Kirk, Stuart A. Wright and Francis M. DuBose. 1987, *Home Cell Groups and House Churches. Nashville: Broadman*.

Haight, Roger. 1985. *An Alternative Vision: An Interpretation of Liberation Theology*. N. Y.: Paulist.

Haleblian, Krikor. 1982. *Contextualization and French Structuralism: A Method to Delineate the Deep Structure of the Gospel*. (unpublished doctoral thesis). Pasadena: Fuller Theological Seminary.

————. 1983. "The Problem of Contextualization," *Missiology* XI:1 (Jan), 100–5.

Harr, Wilbur C., ed., 1962. *Frontiers of the Christian World Mission Since 1938*. N.Y.: Harper.

Hauerwas, Stanley and William Willimon. 1991. "Why Resident Aliens Struck a Chord," *Missiology* XIX: 4 (October), 419–429.

Hedlund, Roger. 1985. *The Mission of the Church in the World: A Biblical Theology*. Grand Rapids: Baker.

————. 1997. *God and the Nations: A Biblical Theology of Mission in the Asian Context*. New Delhi: ISPCK.

Henry, Carl. 1947. *The Uneasy Conscience of Modern Fundamentalism*. Grand Rapids: Eerdmans.

————. 1967. *Evangelicals at the Brink of Crisis*. Waco: Word.

Henry, Carl and W. W. Mooneyham, eds., 1967. *One Race, One Gospel, One Task*. Minn.: World Wide Publ.

Herron, Fred. 2003. *Expanding God's Kingdom through Church Multiplying*. N.Y.: Writer's Showcase.

Hertig, Paul. 1998. Matthew's Narrative Use of Galilee in the Multicultural and Missiological Journeys of Jesus. Lewiston, NY:Edwin Mellon Press.

Hesselgrave, David J. 1978. Communicating Christ Cross-Culturally: An Introduction to Missionary Communication. Grand Rapids: Zondervan.

————. 1999. "Redefining Holism," *EMQ* XXXV:3 (July), 278–84.

————. 2000. "Great Commission." Scott Moreau, Harold Netland and Charles Van Engen, eds., 412–14.

Hesselgrave, David and Edward Romen, eds., 1989. *Contextualization: Meanings, Methods, and Models*. Grand Rapids: Baker.

Hiebert, Frances F. 1997. "Beyond the Post-Modern Critique of Modern Mission: The Nineteenth Century Revisited," *Missiology* XXV:3 (July), 259–77.

Hiebert, Paul. 1978. "Conversion, Culture and Cognitive Categories," *Gospel in Context* I:3 (July), 24–29.

————. 1979. "The Gospel and Culture," in: Don McCurry, ed., 58–70.

————. 1982. "The Flaw of the Excluded Middle," *Missiology* X:1 (Jan.), 35–47.

————. 1983. "Missions and the Renewal of the Church," in Wilbert R. Shenk, ed., 157–167.

————. 1984. "Critical Contextualization," *Missiology* XI:3 (July 1), 287–296; reprinted in *International Bulletin of Missionary Research* XI:3 (July 1), 1987, 104–11; reprinted also in J. I. Packer, ed., *The Best in Theology*. Vol. 2. Carol Stream: CTI, 1989, 387–400; and in Paul Hiebert. *Anthropological*

Reflections on Missiological Issues. Grand Rapids: Baker, 1994, 75–92. Chapter 7 of Paul Hiebert. *Anthropological Insights for Missionaries* contains what I believe to be the earliest articulation of Hiebert's concept of "Critical Contextualization" (the title of the chapter) and includes a number of day-to-day examples of Gospel communication in context that Hiebert draws from India.

————. 1985. *Anthropological Insights for Missionaries*. Grand Rapids: Baker.

————. 1987. "Critical Contextualization," *International Bulletin of Missionary Research* XI:3 (July), 104–111. (Reprinted in J.I. Packer and Paul Fromer, eds., *The Best in Theology*, vol. 2. Carol Stream: Christianity Today, 1989, 396–99.)

————. 1989. "Form and Meaning in the Contextualization of the Gospel," in Dean Gilliland, ed., 101–120.

————. 1991. "Beyond Anti-Colonialism to Globalism," *Missiology*. XIX:3 (July), 263–81.

————. 1993. "Evangelism, Church, and Kingdom," in Charles Van Engen, Dean Gilliland and Paul Pierson, eds., 153–61.

————. 1994. *Anthropological Reflections on Missiological Issues*. Grand Rapids: Baker.

Hirsch, Alan. 2007. *The Forgotten Ways: Reactivating the Missional Church*. Grand Rapids: Brazos Press.

Hodges, Melvin. 1953. *The Indigenous Church*. Springfield, MO: Gospel Pub.

————. 1977. *A Theology of the Church and Its Mission: A Pentecostal Perspective*. Springfield, MO: Gospel Pub.

————. 1978. *The Indigenous Church and the Missionary*. Pasadena: William Carey Library.

Hoedemaker, L. A. 1995. "The People of God and the Ends of the Earth," in F. J. Verstraelen, A. Camps, L.A. Hoedemaker, and M.R. Spindler, eds., 157–71.

Hoekendijk, Johannes C. 1938. *The World Mission of the Church*. London: IMC.

————. 1952. *The Missionary Obligation of the Church*. London: Edinburgh House.

————. 1966. *The Church Inside Out*. Philadelphia, Westminster.

Hoge, Dean and David Roozen, ed., 1979. *Understanding Church Growth and Decline 1950–1978*. N.Y.: Pilgrim Press.

Hogg, William Richey. 1952. *Ecumenical Foundations: A History of the International Missionary Council and its Nineteenth-Century Background*. N.Y: Harper & Bros.

Howell, Richard. 1999. "An Overview and Plea: Christian Persecution in India," (AD2000 and Beyond Movement: email from Luis Bush, 7/19/99).

Hunsberger, George R. and Craig Van Gelder, eds., 1996. *Church Between Gospel & Culture: The Emerging Mission in North America.* Grand Rapids: Eerdmans.

Hunter, George G., III. 1979. *The Contagious Congregation.* Nashville: Abingdon.

Hybels, Bill and Mark Mittelberg. 1994. *Becoming a Contagious Christian.* Grand Rapids: Zondervan.

info@glocalforum.org. 2005. Web site of the Global Metro City-The Glocal Forum.

Jacobs, Donald. 1993. "Contextualization in Mission," in James Phillips and Robert Coote, eds., 235–44.

Jeganathan, W. S. Milton, ed., 2000. *Mission Paradigm in the New Millennium.* Delhi: ISPCK.

Jenkins, Philip. 2002. *The Next Christendom: The Coming of Global Christianity.* Oxford: Oxford U. Press.

Jewett, Paul. 1991. *God, Creation & Revelation.* Grand Rapids: Eerdmans.

Johnson, Benton. 1986, Is There Hope for Liberal Protestantism?" in Dorothy Bass, Benton Johnson and Wade Clark Roof. 1986, 13–26.

Johnson, Todd M. 1987. "Contextualization: A New-Old Idea," *The International Journal of Frontier Mission.* IV:1–4; available also from GEM World Christianity Collection, www.gem-werc.org/papers/papers005.htm.

Johnston, Robert K. 2014. *God's Wider Presence: Reconsidering General Revelation.* Grand Rapids: Baker.

Jongeneel, Jan A.B. 1997. *Philosophy, Science and Theology of Mission in the 19th and 20th Centuries: A Missiological Encyclopedia, Part II: Missionary Theology.* N.Y.: Peter Lang.

Jongeneel, Jan A.B., ed., 1992. *Pentecost, Mission and Ecumenism: Essays on Intercultural Theology.* Berlin: Peter Lang.

Jongeneel, Jan A. B. and Jan M. van Engelen, eds., 1995. "Contemporary Currents in Missiology," in F.J. Verstraelen et al, 1995, 438–57.

Kaiser, Walter C., Jr. 2000. *Mission in the Old Testament: Israel as a Light to the Nations.* Grand Rapids: Baker.

Kelly, J. N. D. 1960. *Early Christian Doctrines.* N.Y.: Harper & Row.

Kimball, Dan. 2003. *The Emerging Church: Vintage Christianity for New Generations.* Grand Rapids: Zondervan.

Kirk, J. Andrew. 1997. *The Mission of Theology and Theology as Mission*. Valley Forge: Trinity Press, Intl.

—. 1999 *What is Mission? Theological Explorations*. London: Darton, Longman & Todd.

Kittel, Gerhard and Gerhard Friedrich, eds., 1964–1976. *Theological Dictionary of the New Testament*, 10 vols. Grand Rapids: Eerdmans.

Köstenberger, Andreas J and Peter T. O'Brien. eds., 2001. *Salvation to the Ends of the Earth: A biblical theology of mission*. Downers Grove: IVP.

Kraft, Charles. 1979. *Christianity in Culture: A Study in Dynamic Biblical Theologizing in Cross-Cultural Perspective*. Maryknoll: Orbis.

—. 1983. *Communication Theory for Christian Witness*. Nashville: Abingdon; reprinted by N.Y.: Orbis, 1991.

—. 1992. "Allegiance, Truth and Power Encounters in Christian Witness," in Jan Jongeneel, ed., 215–30.

—. 1999a. "Contextualization in Three Dimensions," (Sun Hee Kwak Professor of Anthropology & Intercultural Communication, Inauguration Lecture). Pasadena: School of World Mission, Fuller Theological Seminary.

—. 1999b. *Communicating Jesus' Way*. Pasadena: William Carey Library

Kraft, Charles, ed., 2005. *Appropriate Christianity*. Pasadena: William Carey Library.

Kraft, Charles and Tom Wisely, eds., 1979. *Readings in Dynamic Indigeneity*. Pasadena: William Carey Library.

—. 1988. *The Church and Cultures*. Maryknoll: Orbis.

Küng, Hans. 1963. *The Living Church*. London and N.Y.: Sheed and Ward.

—. 1967. *The Church*. R. Ockenden, trans. N.Y.: Sheed & Ward.

—. 1971. *The Church*. London: Search Press.

Ladd, George E. 1959. *The Gospel of the Kingdom*. Grand Rapids: Eerdmans.

—. 1974. *The Presence of the Future: The Eschatology of Biblical Realism*. Grand Rapids: Eerdmans.

Latourette, Kenneth Scott. 1953. *A History of Christianity*. London: Harper & Row.

—. 1967. *A History of the Expansion of Christianity*. Grand Rapids: Zondervan.

Lausanne Committee for World Evangelization. 1974. "The Lausanne Covenant."

—. 1983. "Hindrances to Cooperation: The Suspicion about Finances," Pasadena: LCWE (Lausanne Occasional Papers 24); reprinted in Daniel Rickett and Dotsey Welliver, eds., 1987. 84–107.

———. Lausanne Committee for World Evangelization. 2016. www.lausanne. org/content/manifesto/the-manila-manifesto; downloaded Oct 3, 2016.

———. 1989. *The Manila Manifesto: An Elaboration of the Lausanne Covenant Fifteen Years Later.* Pasadena: LCWE.

Lewis, Robert and Wayne Cordeiro. 2005. *Culture Shift: Transforming Your Church from the Inside Out.* San Francisco: Jossey-Bass.

Liao, David C. 1972. *The Unresponsive: Resistant or Neglected?* Chicago: Moody.

Lightfoot, J.B. 1970. *The Apostolic Fathers.* Grand Rapids: Baker.

Lindsell, Harold. 1962. "Faith Missions since 1938" in Wilbur C. Harr, ed., : 189–230.

Linthicum, Robert C. 1988. "Doing Effective Ministry in the City, *Together* (April–June), 1–2.

———. 1991 *City of God, City of Satan: A Biblical Theology of the Urban Church.* Grand Rapids: Zondervan.

Loewen, Jacob A. 2000. The Bible in Cross-Cultural Perspective. Pasadena: William Carey Library.

Logan, Robert. 1989. *Beyond Church Growth: Action Plans for Developing Dynamic Church.* Grand Rapids: Baker.

———. 2002. "Church Reproduction: New Congregations Beyond Church Walls," in Steve Sjogren, ed., 159–73.

Love, R. 2000. "10/40 Window" in H. N. A. Scott Moreau, and Charles Van Engen. 938.

Luther, Martin. 1955. *Luther's Works.* Phil.: Fortress.

Luzbetak, Louis. 1989. *The Church and Cultures: New Perspectives in Missiological Anthropology.* Maryknoll: Orbis.

Mackay, John A. 1963. *The Latin American Church and the Ecumenical Movement.* N.Y.: NCC.

———. 1964. *Ecumenics: The Science of the Church Universal.* N.J.: Prentice-Hall.

———. 1998. *Choosing a Future for U.S. Mission.* Monrovia: MARC/World Vision.

———. 1999 "Working Together to Shape the New Millennium: Dreams, Hopes, Concerns, Fears" (EFMA) *EMQ* XXXV:3 (July), 306–8.

Malphurs, Aubrey. 1992, 1998, 2000. *Multiplying Growing Churches for the 21st Century.* Grand Rapids: Baker.

Martin, David. 1990. *Tongues of Fire: The Explosion of Protestantism in Latin America.* Oxford: Blackwell.

Mbiti, John. 1970. "Christianity and Traditional Religions in Africa," *International Review of Mission* LIX:236 (Oct.), 430–40.

———. 1979. "Response to the Article of John Kinney," *Occasional Bulletin of Missionary Research* III:2 (April), 68.

———. 2003. "Dialogue Between EATWOT and Western Theologians: A Comment on the 6th EATWOT Conference in Geneva 1983," in Inus Daneel, Charles Van Engen and Hendrik Vroom, eds., 91–104.

McCurry, Don., ed., 1979. *The Gospel and Islam*. Monrovia: MARC.

McGavran, Donald A. 1955. *The Bridges of God*. New York/London, Friendship/World Dominion.

———. 1959. *How Churches Grow*. N.Y.: Friendship.

———. 1965. "Homogeneous Populations and Church Growth," in Donald McGavran, ed., 69–85.

———. 1970. *Understanding Church Growth*. Grand Rapids: Eerdmans.

———. 1972. "Yes, Uppsala Has Betrayed the Two Billion, Now What?" *Christianity Today*. 16:19 (June 23, 1972), 16–18.

———. 1974. *The Clash Between Christianity and Culture*. Washington D.C.: Canon Press.

———. 1977a. *Ten Steps for Church Growth*. N.Y.: Harper & Row.

———. 1977b. "Wrong Strategy, the Real Crisis in Mission," in: Donald McGavran, ed., 97–107. This is reprinted from D. McGavran, "Wrong Strategy, the Real Crisis in Mission," *IRM*, 54, (October, 1965), 451–61.

———. 1977c. *The Conciliar-Evangelical Debate: The Crucial Documents, 1964–1978*. Pasadena: William Carey Library.

———. 1980. *Understanding Church Growth* (revised) Grand Rapids: Eerdmans.

———. 1981a. "Why Some American Churches are Growing and Some are Not," in Elmer Towns, John N. Vaughan and David J. Seifert, eds., 285–94.

———. 1981b. *Back to Basics in Church Growth*. Wheaton: Tyndale.

———. 1984a. "Ten Emphases in the Church Growth Movement," in Doug Priest Jr., ed., 1984, 248–59.

———. 1984b. *Momentous Decisions in Missions Today*. Grand Rapids: Baker.

———. 1990. *Understanding Church Growth* (3rd edition). Grand Rapids: Eerdmans.

McGavran, Donald, ed., 1965. *Church Growth and Christian Mission*. N.Y.: Harper and Row.

———. 1972. *Crucial Issues in Missions Tomorrow*. Chicago, Moody Press.

———. 1977. *The Conciliar-Evangelical Debate: The Crucial Documents, 1964–1976*. So. Pas.: William Carey Library.

McGavran, Donald A. and Win Arn. 1973. *How to Grow a Church: Conversations about Church Growth*. Glendale: ReGal

————. 1977. *Ten Steps for Church Growth*. N.Y.: Harper & Row.

————. 1981. *Back to Basics in Church Growth*. Wheaton: Tyndale.

McGavran, Donald A. and George G. Hunter III. 1980. *Church Growth Strategies that Work*. Nashville: Abingdon.

McGee, Gary B. 1986a, 1989, *This Gospel Shall Be Preached: a History of the Assemblies of God Foreign Missions*. (2 volumes). Springfield, Mo: Gospel Publishing House.

————. 1986b, "Assemblies of God Mission Theology: A Historical Perspective," *IBMR*. X, 166–70.

————. 2010. *Miracles, Missions, & American Pentecostalism*. Maryknoll: Orbis.

McGrath, Alister E. 1994. *Christian Theology: An Introduction*. Oxford: Blackwell.

McIntosh, Gary and R. Daniel Reeves. *Thriving Churches in the Twenty-First Century: 10 Life-Giving Systems for Vibrant Ministry*. Grand Rapids: Kregel, 2006.

McIntosh, Gary L. 2015. *Donald A. McGavran: A Biography of the Twentieth Century's Premier Missiologist*. Boca Raton, FL: ChurchLeaderInsights.

McIntosh, Gary L. 2916. "Donald A. McGavran, Life, Influence and Legacy in Mission," in Charles Van Engen, ed., 2016, 19–37.

McIntosh, John A. 2000. "Missio Dei," in A. Scott Moreau, Harold Netland and Charles Van Engen, eds., 631–33.

McKim, Donald K., ed., 1992. *Major Themes in the Reformed Tradition*. Grand Rapids: Eerdmans.

McNeal, Reggie. 2003. *The Present Future Six Tough Questions for the Church*. San Francisco: Jossey-Bass

McQuilkin, J. Robertson. 1973. *How Biblical is the Church Growth Movement?* Chicago: Moody.

Mead, Loren. 1991. *The Once and Future Church: Reinventing the Congregation for a New Mission Frontier*. N.Y.: Alban Institute.

Menning, Bruce. 1985. *Shaping a Future Effectively*. Grand Rapids: RCA Synod of Michigan.

Middleton, Vernon J. 1990. *The Development of a Missiologist: The Life and Thought of Donald Anderson McGavran, 1897–1965*. Pasadena: School of World Mission Ph.D. Dissertation, 1990 ; published as *Donald McGavran, His Early Life and Ministry: An Apostolic Vision for Reaching the Nations*. Pasadena: William Carey Library, 2011.

Miguez-Bonino, José. 1971. "New Theological Perspectives," *Religious Education* LXVI:6, 405–7.

———. 1975, 1984. *Doing Theology in a Revolutionary Situation* Phil: Fortress.

———. 1976. *Christians and Marxists: The Mutual Challenge of Revolution.* Grand Rapids: Eerdmans.

Miles, Delos. 1981. *Church Growth: A Mighty River.* Nashville: Broadman.

Miley, George. 1999. "The Awesome Potential of Mission Found in Local Churches," in Ralph Winter and Steven Hawthorne, eds., 729–32.

Miller, M. Rex. 2004. *The Millennium Matrix: Reclaiming the Past, Reframing the Future of the Church.* San Francisco: Jossey-Bass.

Minear, Paul. 1960. *Images of the Church in the New Testament.* Phil.: Westminster.

Moltmann, Jürgen. 1977. *The Church in the Power of the Spirit.* N.Y.: Harper & Row.

Montgomery, Helen Barrett. 1920. *The Bible and Mission.* Brattleboro, Vermont: The Central Committee on the Study of Foreign Missions; edited and republished in 2002 in Pasadena by Shawn Redford.

Mora C., Fernando A. 2000. *Manual de líderes de células.* Los Teques, Caracas, Venezuela: self-published.

Moreau, A. Scott, Gary R. Corwin, and Gary B. McGee, eds., 2004. *Introducing World Missions: A Biblical, Historical, and Practical Survey.* Grand Rapids: Baker.

Moreau, A. Scott, Harold Netland and Charles Van Engen, eds., 2000. *Evangelical Dictionary of World Missions.* Grand Rapids: Baker.

Motte, Mary. 1991. "The Poor: Starting Point for Mission," in Gerald Anderson, James Phillips and Robert Coote eds., 50–54.

Mulholland, Kenneth B. 1999. "Working Together to Shape the New Millennium: Dreams, Hopes, Concerns, Fears" (EMS) *EMQ* XXXV:3 (July), 317–20.

Murray, Stuart. 1998. *Church Multiplying: Laying Foundations.* London: Paternoster Press.

Myers, Bryant. 1992. "A Funny Thing Happened on the Way to Evangelical-Ecumenical Cooperation," *IRM* LXXXI: no. 323 (July) 397–407.

———. 1993. *The Changing Shape of World Mission.* Monrovia: MARC/World Vision. (Updated 1998).

———. 1999. "Another Look at Holistic Mission," *EMQ* XXXV:3 (July), 285–87.

National Association of Evangelicals. 1996. "An Evangelical Manifesto: A Strategic Plan for the Dawn of the 21st Century," NAE Web Site (www.nae.net/sig_doc11.html).

NCCC/DOM. 1983. *Mission and Evangelism: An Ecumenical Affirmation*. New York: NCCC.

Neill, Stephen. 1959. *Creative Tension*. London: Ediburgh House.

———. 1964. *A History of Christian Missions*. Harmondsworth/Baltimore, Penguin Books.

———. 1984. "How My Mind has Changed about Mission," Three-part video series taped at the Overseas Ministries Study Center, Atlanta: Southern Baptist Convention.

Neill, Stephen, Gerald H. Anderson, and John Goodwin, eds., 1971. *A Concise Dictionary of the Christian World Mission*. London: Lutterworth.

Nelson, Marlin. 1995, 2001. *Principles of Church Growth*. Bangalore: Theological Book Trust.

Newbigin, Lesslie. 1953. *The Household of God*. N.Y.: Friendship.

———. 1963. *The Relevance of a Trinitarian Doctrine for Today's Mission*. London: Edinburgh House.

———. 1977. *The Good Shepherd: Meditations on Christian Ministry in Today's World*. Grand Rapids: Eerdmans.

———. 1978. *The Open Secret*. Grand Rapids: Eerdmans.

———. 1986. *Foolishness to the Greeks: The Gospel and Western Culture*. Grand Rapids: Eerdmans.

———. 1989. *The Gospel in a Pluralist Society*. Grand Rapids: Eerdmans.

———. 1991. *Truth to Tell: The Gospel as Public Truth*. Geneva: WCC.

Nicholls, Bruce J. 1979. *Contextualization: A Theology of Gospel and Culture*. Downers Grove: IVP.

Nicholls, Bruce J., ed., 1985. *In Word and Deed: Evangelism and Social Responsibility*. Grand Rapids: Eerdmans.

Nida, Eugene. 1960. *Message and Mission*. N.Y.: Harper.

Niles, Daniel T. 1962. *Upon the Earth: The Mission of God and the Missionary Enterprise of the Churches*. N.Y. and London: McGraw-Hill/Lutterworth.

Nishioka, Yoshiyuki Billy. 1998. "Worldview Methodologies in Mission Theology: A Comparison between Kraft's and Hiebert's Approaches," *Missiology* XXVI: 4 (Oct.), 457–76.

Nissen, Johannes. 1999. *New Testament and Mission: Historical and Hermeneutical Perspectives*. N.Y.: Peter Lang.

Northwood Church. 2005. http://northwoodchurch.org/

Nuñez, Emilio A. 1997. *Hacia Una Misionología Evangélica Latinoamericana*. Miami: Unilit.

Nussbaum, Stan. 1999. "The Five Frontiers of Mission," *Global Mapping International Newsletter* (Winter/Spring), 1,5.

Oborji, Francis Anekwe. 2006. *Concepts of Mission: The Evolution of Contemporary Missiology.* Maryknoll: Orbis.

Okoye, James Chukwuma. 2006. *Israel and the Nations: A Mission Theology of the Old Testament.* Maryknoll: Orbis.

Orchard, Ronald K., ed., 1964. *Witness in Six Continents: Records of the Meeting of the Commission on World Mission and Evangelism of the World Council of Churches held in Mexico City, December 8th to 19th, 1963.* London: Edinburgh.

Orme, John. 2000. "Working Together to Shape the New Millennium: Dreams, Hopes, Concerns, Fears" (IFMA) *EMQ* XXXV:3 (July), 308–310.

Orr, J. Edwin. 1965 *The Light of the Nations.* Grand Rapids: Eerdmans, 1965.

———. 1975. *Evangelical awakenings in Eastern Asia.* Minneapolis: Bethany Fellowship.

———. 1975. *Evangelical Awakenings in Africa.* Minneapolis: Bethany Fellowship.

———. 1978. *Evangelical Awakenings in Latin America.* Minneapolis: Bethany Fellowship.

Osborne, Grant R. 1991. *The Hermeneutical Spiral: A Comprehensive Introduction to Biblical Interpretation.* Downers Grove: InterVarsity.

Ott, Craig, Stephen J. Strauss with Timothy C. Tennent, eds., 2010. *Encountering Theology of Mission: Biblical Foundations, Historical Developments and Contemporary Issues.* Grand Rapids: Baker.

Packer, J. I. and Paul Fromer, eds., 1989. *The Best in Theology*, vol. 2. Carol Stream: Christianity Today.

Padilla, C. René. 1985. *Mission Between the Times: Essays on the Kingdom of God.* Grand Rapids: Eerdmans. Published in Spanish as *Misión Integral: Ensayos Sobre el Reino y la Iglesia.* Grand Rapids: Nueva Creación, 1986.

———. 1992. "Wholistic Mission: Evangelical and Ecumenical," *IRM* LXXXI: 323 (July) 381–82.

Padilla, C. René, ed., 1998. *Bases bíblicas de la misión: Perspectivas latinoamericanas.* Buenos Aires: Nueva Creación and Grand Rapids: Eerdmans

Padilla, C. René, et al, eds., 1975. *El Reino de Dios y America Latina.* El Paso: Casa Bautista de Publ.

Padilla, C. René y Tetsunao Yamamori, eds., 2003a. *La iglesia local como agente de transformación: una eclesiología para la misión integral.* Buenos Aires: Kairós.

———. 2003b. "Introducción: Una eclesiología para la misión integral," in Padilla y Yamamori, eds., 2003:13–45.

Palen, John. J. 1987. *The Urban World*, 3rd Edition. NY: McGraw Hill.

Pannenberg, Wolfhart. 1969. *Theology and the Kingdom of God*. Phil.: Westminster.

Pagura, Federico. 1973. "Missionary, Go Home . . . Or Stay," *Christian Century* (April 11); reprinted in Gerald H. Anderson and Thomas F. Stransky, eds., : 1974, 115–116.

Pate, Larry D. 1987. *Misionología: nuestro cometido transcultural*. Miami: Editorial Vida.

Pelikan, Jaroslav. 1971. *The Christian Tradition: A History of the Development of Doctrine*. 1. Chicago and London: U. of Chicago Press.

————. 1978. *The Christian Tradition: A History of the Development of Doctrine, vol. 3*. Chicago and London: U. of Chicago Press.

Pentecost, Edward C. 1982. *Issues in Missiology: An Introduction*. Grand Rapids: Baker.

Peters, George W. 1972. *A Biblical Theology of Missions*. Chicago: Moody.

————. 1973. "Pauline Patterns of Church-Mission Relationships," *EMQ* IX (Winter), reprinted in Daniel Rickett and Dotsey Welliver, eds., 1997. 46–52.

————. 1981. *A Theology of Church Growth*. Grand Rapids: Zondervan.

Pierson, Paul E. 2000. "The Ecumenical Movement," in Scott Moreau, Charles Van Engen, and Harold Netland, eds., 2000. 300–303.

Piet, John. 1970. *The Road Ahead: A Theology for the Church in Mission*. Grand Rapids: Eerdmans.

Phan, Peter C. 2003. *Christianity with an Asian Face: Asian American Theology in the Making*. Maryknoll: Orbis.

Phillips, James M. and Robert T. Coote, eds., 1993. *Toward the 21st Century in Christian Mission*. Grand Rapids: Eerdmans.

Piper, John. 1993. *Let the Nations be Glad! The Supremacy of God in Missions*. Grand Rapids: Baker.

Plantinga, Alvin C. 1992. "The Reformed Objection to Natural Theology," in Donald K. McKim, ed., 66–75.

Pobee, J.S., ed., 1976. *Religion in a Pluralist Society*. Leiden: Brill

Pointer, Roy. 1984. *How do Churches Grow? A Guide to the Growth of Your Church*. London: Marshall Morgan & Scott.

Pomerville, Paul A. 1985. *The Third Force in Mission: A Pentecostal Contribution to Contemporary MIssion Theology*. Peabody, MA: Hendrickson.

Priest, Douglas Jr., ed., 1984. *Unto the Uttermost: Missions in the Christian Churches/ Churches of Christ*. Pasadena: William Carey.

Rainer, Thom. 1993. *The Book of Church Growth: History, Theology and Principles*. Nashville: Broadman.

Rainer, Thom S. 2001. *Surprising Insights from the Unchurched and Proven Ways to Reach Them*. Grand Rapids: Zondervan.

Rainer, Thom S. 2003. *The Unchurched Next Door: Understanding Faith Stages as Keys to Sharing your Faith*. Grand Rapids: Zondervan, 2003

Reapsome, J. 2000. "Carey, William," in H. N. A. Scott Moreau, Harold Netland and Charles Van Engen. eds., 162–63.

Redford, Shawn. 1999. "Facing the Faceless Frontier," in Charles Van Engen, Nancy Thomas and Rob Gallagher, eds., 215–24.

———. 2012. *Missiological Hermeneutics: Biblical Interpretation for the Global Church*. Eugene: Pickwick.

Reeves, R. Daniel and Ronald Jenson. 1984. *Always Advancing: Modern Strategies for Church Growth*. San Bernardino, CA: Here's Life Publishers.

Richardson, Don. 2000. "Redemptive Analogies," in Moreau, Netland and Van Engen, eds., 812–13.

Rickett, Daniel. 1998. "Developmental Partnering: Preventing Dependency," *EMQ* XXXIV:4 (Oct), 438–45.

Rickett, Daniel and Dotsey Welliver, eds., 1997. *Supporting Indigenous Ministries: With Selected Readings*. Wheaton: Billy Graham Center.

Ridderbos, Herman. 1962. *The Coming of the Kingdom*. Phil.: Presbyterian and Reformed.

Ro, Bong Rin and Ruth Eshenaur, eds., 1984, *The Bible and Theology in Asian Contexts: An Evangelical Perspective on Asian Theology*. Taichung: Asia Theological Association.

Robb, John. 1999. "Mission Leaders Propose New Framework." *MARC Newsletter* 99–2 (May), 1, 6.

Roxburgh, Alan J. 1997. *The Missionary Congregation, Leadership & Liminality*. Harrisburg, PA: Trinity Press, Int.

Roxburgh, Alan J. and Fred Romanuk. 2006. *The Missional Leader: Equipping your Church to Reach a Changing World*. San Francisco: Jossey-Bass.

Robertson, Roland. 1995. "Glocalization: Time-Space and Homogeneity-Heterogeneity," in Mike Featherstone, Scott Lash, and Roland Robertson, eds., 25–44.

Roof, Wade Clark and William McKinney. 1987. *American Mainline Religion: Its Changing Shape and Future*. New Brunswick: Rutgers U. Press.

Rooy, S. 1998. "La búsqueda histórica de las bases bíblicas de la misión," in C. R. Padilla, ed., 3–33.

Roozen, David, William McKinney and Jackson Carroll. 1984. *Varieties of Religious Presence: Mission in Public Life*. N.Y.: Pilgrim Press.

Rosenau, James N. 2003. *Distant Proximities: Dynamics Beyond Globalization*. Princeton: Princeton U. Press.

Rosin, H. H. 1972. *"Missio Dei:" An Examination of the Origin, Contents and Function of the Term in Protestant Missiological Discussion*. Leiden: Interuniversity Institute for Missiological and Ecumenical Research.

Rowley, H.H. 1955. The Missionary Message of the Old Testament London: Carey Kingsgate.

Saayman, Willem. 1990. "Bridging the Gulf: David Bosch and the Ecumenical/ Evangelical Polarisation," *Missionalia* XVIII: 1 (April) 99–108.

———. 2000. "Mission by its Very Nature," in. *Missionalia*. http://wwwgeocities. com/missionalia/ssayman00.htm?200521.

Sample, Tex. 1984. *Blue-Collar Ministry: Facing Economic and Social Realities of Working People*. Valley Forge: Judson Press.

Samuel, Vinay and Christopher Sugden, eds., 1983. *The Church in Response to Human Need*. Grand Rapids: Eerdmans.

———. 1991. *A.D. 2000 and Beyond: A Mission Agenda*. Oxford: Regnum Books.

———. 1999. *Mission as Transformation: A Theology of the Whole Gospel*. Oxford: Regnum.

Sanchez, Daniel R. with Ebbie C. Smith and Curtis E. Watke. 2001. *Starting Reproducing Congregations: A Guidebook for Contextual New Church Development*. Cumming, GA: Church Starting Network.

Sanneh, Lamin. 1989. *Translating the Message: The Missionary Impact on Culture*. Maryknoll: Orbis.

Santos, Angel. 1991. *Teología Sistemática de la Misión*. España: Editorial Verbo Divino.

Saracco, Norberto. 2000. "Mission and Missiology from Latin America," in William Taylor, ed., 357–66.

Sassen, Saskia. 2002. *Global Networks: Linked Cities*. London:Routledge.

Schaff, Phillip. 1950. *History of the Christian Church*. Grand Rapids: Eerdmans.

———. 1977. *The Creeds of Christendom*. N.Y.: Harper & Bros.

Schaff, Philip and H. Wace, eds., 1974. *Nicene and Post-Nicene Fathers*. Grand Rapids: Eerdmans.

Schaller, Lyle E. 1984. *Looking in the Mirror: Self-Appraisal in the Local Church*. Nashville: Abingdon.

Scherer, James A. 1964. *Mission, Go Home! A Reappraisal of the Christian World Mission Today—its Basis, Philosophy, Program, Problems, and Outlook for the Future*. Englewood Cliffs, N.J.: Prentice-Hall.

———. 1987. *Gospel, Church and Kingdom: Comparative Studies in World Mission Theology*. Minneapolis: Augsburg.

———. 1993a. "Church, Kingdom, and *Missio Dei*: Lutheran and Orthodox Correctives to Recent Ecumenical Mission Theology," in Van Engen, et al, eds., 1993, 82–88.

———. 1993b. "Mission Theology" in James Phillips and Robert Coote, eds., 193–202.

Schmemann, Alexander. 1961. "The Missionary Imperative in the Orthodox Tradition," in: G. H. Anderson, ed., 250–57.

———. 1979. *Church, World, Mission: Reflections on Orthodoxy in the West*. Crestwood, N.J.: St. Vladimir's Sem. Press.

Schreiter, Robert. 1985. *Constructing Local Theologies*. Maryknoll: Orbis.

———. 1992. "Reconciliation as a Missionary Task," *Missiology* XX: 1 (January) 3–10.

Schriver, Donald and Karl OstRom 1977. *Is There Hope for the City?* Phil.: Westminster.

Schwarz, Christian A. 1996. *Natural Church Development: A Guide to Eight Essential Qualities of Healthy Churches*. Carol Stream, IL: Church Smart Resources.

———. 1999. *Paradigm Shift in the Church*. Carol Stream, IL: Church Smart Resources.

Scott, Allen J., ed., 2001. *Global City-Regions: Trends, Theory, Policy*. Oxford: Oxford U. Press.

Scott, Waldron. 1980. *Bring Forth Justice: A Contemporary Perspective on Mission*. Grand Rapids: Eerdmans.

———. 1981. "The Significance of Pattaya," *Missiology* 9 (January), 57–75.

Seamands, Stephen. 2005. *Ministry in the Image of God: The Trinitarian Shape of Christian Service*. Downers Grove: IVP, 2005

Sedmak, Clemens. 2002. *Doing Local Theology: A Guide for Artisans of a New Humanity*. Maryknoll: Orbis.

Segundo, Juan Luis. 1975. *The Community Called Church*. Maryknoll: Orbis.

———. 1976. *The Liberation of Theology*. Maryknoll: Orbis.

Senior, Donald and Carroll Stuhlmueller. 1983. *The Biblical Foundations for Mission*. Maryknoll: Orbis.

Shaw, Daniel. 1988. *Transculturation: The Cultural Factor in Translation and Other Communication Tasks*. Pasadena: William Carey Library.

———. 1989. "The Context of Text: Transculturation and Bible Translation" in D. Gilliland, ed., 141–59.

Shaw, Daniel and Charles Van Engen. 2003. *Communicating God's Word in a Complex World: God's Truth or Hocus-Pocus?* Lanham, MD: Rowman & Littlefield Pub.

Shenk, Wilbert R. 1999. *Changing Frontiers of Mission*. Maryknoll: Orbis.

Shenk, Wilbert R., ed., 1980. *Mission Focus: Current Issues*. Elkhart, IN: Overseas Ministries, Mennonite Board of Missions.

———. 1983. *Exploring Church Growth*. Grand Rapids: Eerdmans.

———. 1988. *God's New Economy: Interdependence and Mission*. (A MISSION FOCUS pamphlet) Elkhart, IN: Overseas Ministries, Mennonite Board of Missions.

———. 1993. *The Transfiguration of Mission: Biblical, Theological & Historical Foundations*. Scottdale: Herald.

———. 1995. *Write the Vision: The Church Renewed*. Valley Forge, PA: Trinity Press, Int.

———. 1999. *Changing Frontiers of Mission*. Maryknoll: Orbis.

———. 2002. *Enlarging the Story: Perspectives on Writing World Christian History*. Maryknoll: Orbis.

Sheppard, David. 1974. *Built as a City: God and the Urban World Today*. London: Hodder and Stoughton.

Silvoso, Ed. 1994. *That None Should Perish: How to Reach Entire Cities for Christ Through Prayer Evangelism*. Ventura: ReGal

Sjogren, Steven. 1993, 2003. *Conspiracy of Kindness: A Refreshing New Approach to Sharing the Love of Jesus*. Ann Arbor: Servant.

Sjogren, Steve, ed. 2002. *Seeing Beyond Church Walls: Action Plans for Touching Your Community*. Loveland, CO: Group Publishing.

Sjogren, Steven, Dave Ping and Doug Pollock. 2004. *The Irresistible Evangelism: Natural Ways to Open Others to Jesus*. Loveland, CO: Group.

Skreslet, Stanley H. 1995. "The Empty Basket of Presbyterian Mission: Limits and Possibilities of Partnership," *IBMR*. XIX:3 (July), 98–106.

Smit, Dirkie. 1994. "The Self-Disclosure of God," in John De Gruchy and C. Villa-Vicencio, eds., 42–54.

Snoidderly, Beth and A. Scott Moreau, eds., 2011. *Evangelical and Frontier Mission: Perspectives on the Global Progress of the Gospel.* Oxford: Regnum Books.

Snaith, Norman. 1944. *The Distinctive Ideas of the Old Testament.* London: Epworth Press.

Snyder, Howard A., ed., 2001. *Global Good News: Mission in a New Context.* Nashville: Abingdon.

Snyder, Howard A. with Daniel V. Runyon. 2002. *Decoding the Church: Mapping the DNA of Christ's Body.* Grand Rapids: Baker.

Sobrino, Jon. 1984. *The True Church and the Poor.* Maryknoll: Orbis.

Spindler, Marc R. 1995. "The Biblical Grounding and Orientation of Mission," in Verstraelen, Camps, Hoedemaker and Spindler, eds., 1988. 123–56.

Spindler, Marc R. 1988. "Bijbelse fundering en oriëntatie van zending," in A. Camps, L. A. Hoedemaker, M. R. Spindler, and F. J. Verstraelen. eds., 132–54.

Spykman, Gordon and Cook, Dodson, Grahn, Rooy and Stam. 1988. *Let My People Live: Faith and Struggle in Central America.* Grand Rapids: Eerdmans.

Stackhouse, Max. 1988. *Apologia: Contextualization, Globalization, and Mission in Theological Education.* Grand Rapids: Eerdmans.

Stamoolis, James. 1986, 2001. *Eastern Orthodox Mission Theology Today.* Maryknoll: Orbis, Eugene, OR: Wipf and Stock.

Starling, Allan, ed., 1981. *Seeds of Promise.* Pasadena: William Carey Library.

Stetzer, E. a. D. P. 2006. *Breaking the Missional Code: Your Church Can Become a Missionary in Your Community.* Nashville: Broadman & Holman.

Steuernagel, Valdir R. 1991. "An Evangelical Assessment of Mission: A Two-Thirds World Perspective," in Vinay Samuel and Chris Sugden, eds., 1991, 1–13.

Stearns, Bill and Amy. 1991. *Al Servicio del Reino en América Latina.* Monrovia: Visión Mundial.

———. 1996. *Obediencia Misionera y Práctica Histórica.* Grand Rapids: Eerdmans—Nueva Creación.

———. 1999. "The Power of Integrated Vision," in Ralph Winter and Steven Hawthorne, eds., 724–28.

Stockwell, Clinton. 1984. "Barriers and Bridges to Evangelization in Urban Neighborhoods," in David Frenchak et al 1984, 13–26.

Stott, John. 1979. "The Living God is a Missionary God," in James E. Berney, ed., 20–32.

———. 1981. The Living God is a Missionary God," in: Ralph D. Winter and Steve Hawthorne, eds., 10–18; reprinted in Ralph D. Winter and Steve Hawthorne, eds., 4th edition, 2009, 3–9.

Stott, John R.W. and Robert T. Coote, eds., 1979. *Gospel and Culture.* Pasadena: William Carey Library.

Strom, Mark. 1990. *The Symphony of the Scripture: Making Sense of the Bible's Many Themes.* Downers Grove, IL: Inter Varsity Press.

Stults, Donald L. 1989. *Developing an Asian Evangelical Theology.* Metro Manila: OMF Literature.

Sumithra, Sunand and F. Hrangkuma, eds., 1995. *Doing Mission in Context.* Bangalore: Theological Book Trust.

Sunquist, Scott W. 2013. *Understanding Christian Mission: Participation in Suffering and Glory.* Grand Rapids: Baker.

Sweet, Leonard. 1999. *SoulTsumani: Sink or Swim in the New Millennium Culture.* Grand Rapids: Zondervan.

Sweet, Leonard. 2000. *Post-Modern Pilgrims: First Century Passion for the 21st Century World.* Nashville: Broadman & Holman.

Sweet, Leonard, ed., and Andy Crouch, Michael Horton, Frederica Mathewes-Green, Brian McLaren and Erwin McManus. 2003. *The Emerging Culture: Five Perspectives.* Grand Rapids: Zondervan.

Taber, Charles R. 1979a. "Hermeneutics and Culture: An Anthropological Perspective," in John Stott and Robert Coote, eds., 129–130.

———. 1979b. "Contextualization: Indigenization and/or Transformation" in Don McCurry, ed., 1979, 143–54.

———. 1979c. "The Limits of Indigenization in Theology," in Charles Kraft and Tom Wisley, eds., 1979, 372–99.

———. 1983 "Contextualization," in Wilbert Shenk, ed., 117–31.

———. 1980. "Structures and Strategies for Interdependence in World Mission," in Wilbert Shenk, ed., ; reprinted in Daniel Rickett and Dotsey Welliver, eds., 65–83.

Tai, Susan H. C. and Y.H. Wong. 1998. "Advertising Decision Making in Asia: 'Glocal' versus 'Regcal' Approach," *Journal of Managerial Issues,* Vo. 10 (Fall), 318–319.

Taylor, John V. 1972. *The Go-Between God: The Holy Spirit and the Christian Mission.* London: Student Christian Movement.

Taylor, William D. 1999. "Lessons of Partnership" in Ralph Winter and Steven Hawthorne, eds., 748–52.

―――. 2001. *Missiología Global para o século XXI: A consulta de Foz de Iguaçu.* Londrina: Descoberta Editora.

Taylor, William D., ed., 2000. *Global Missiology for the 21st Century: The Iguassu Dialogue.* Grand Rapids: Baker. Translated into Portuguese and published 2001 *Missiologia Glogal para o século XXI: A consulta de Foz de Iguaçu.* Londrina: Descoberta Editora Ltda.

Teja, Gary and John Wagenveld, eds., 2015. *Planting Healthy Churches,* Sauk Village, IL: Multiplication Network Ministries.

Tennekes, J. and H. M. Vroom. 1989. *Contextualiteit en christelijk geloof.* Kampen: J. H. Kok.

Terry, John Mark. 2000. "Indigenous Churches," in Moreau, Netland and Van Engen, eds., 483–85.

Terry, John Mark, Ebbie Smith and Justice Anderson, eds., 1998. *Missiology, An Introduction to the Foundations, History, and Strategies of World Mission.* Nashville: Broadman & Holman.

Thiselton, A. C. 1980. *The Two Horizons: New Testament Hermeneutics and Philosophical Description with Special Reference to Heidegger, Bultmann, Gadamer, and Wittgenstein.* Grand Rapids: Eerdmans

Thomas, Norman E., ed., 1995. *Classic Texts in Mission & World Christianity.* Maryknoll: Orbis.

Tiénou, Tite. 1993. "Forming Indigenous Theologies," in James M. Phillips and Robert T. Coote, eds., 245–52.

Tiplady, Richard, ed.,   2003. *One World or Many? The Impact of Globalisation on Mission.* Pasadena: William Carey Library.

Tippett, Alan R. 1969. *Verdict Theology in Missionary Theory.* Lincoln, IL: Lincoln Christian College Press; reprinted So. Pasadena: William Carey Library, 1973.

―――. 1970. *Church Growth and the Word of God.* Grand Rapids: Eerdmans.

―――. 1972. "The Holy Spirit and Responsive Populations," in D. McGavran, ed., 77–101.

―――. 1973. *God, Man and Church Growth.* Grand Rapids: Eerdmans.

―――. 1987. *Introduction to Missiology.* Pasadena: William Carey Library.

Torres, S. and V. Fabella, eds., 1978. *The Emergent Gospel: Theology from the Developing World*. London: Geoffrey Chapman.

Towns, Elmer, ed., 1995. *Evangelism and Church Growth: A Practical Encyclopedia*. Ventura: ReGal

Towns, Elmer and Douglas Porter. 2003. *Churches that Multiply: A Bible Study on Church Multiplying*. Kansas City: Beacon Hill Press.

Towns, Elmer, John N. Vaughan and David J. Seifert, eds., 1981. *The Complete Book of Church Growth*. Wheaton: Tyndale House.

Towns, Elmer, C. Peter Wagner and Thom S. Rainer, eds., 1998. *The Everychurch Guide to Growth: How Any Plateaued Church Can Grow*. Nashville: Broadman & Holman.

Van Dusen, Henry. 1961. *One Great Ground of Hope: Christian Missions and Christian Unity*. Phil.: Westminster.

Van Engen, Charles. 1981. *The Growth of the True Church: An Analysis of the Ecclesiology of the Church Growth Movement*. Amsterdam: Rodopi. Reprinted in 1995 by University Microfilms, Inc, Ann Arbor, MI.

———. 1987. "Responses to James Scherer's Paper From Different Disciplinary Perspectives: Systematic Theology," *Missiology* XV: 4 (October) 524–525.

———. 1989a. "The New Covenant: Knowing God in Context," in Dean Gilliland, ed., 74–100; reprinted in Charles Van Engen. 1996a, 71–89.

———. 1989b. "Can Older Churches Grow in the City?" in *Global Church Growth* XXVI:1 (Jan–Mar), 15–16.

———. 1990. "A Broadening Vision: Forty Years of Evangelical Theology of Mission, 1946–1986," in Joel Carpenter and Wilbert Shenk, eds., 203–34.

———. 1991a. *God's Missionary People*. Grand Rapids: Baker.

———. 1991b. "The Effect of Universalism on Mission Effort," in William Crockett and James Sigountos, eds., 183–94. (This was reprinted in Van Engen: 1996a, 159–68.)

———. 1993. "The Relation of Bible and Mission in Mission Theology" in Van Engen, Gilliland, and Pierson, eds., 27–36.

———. 1994. "Constructing a Theology of Mission for the City," in Charles Van Engen and Jude Tiersma, eds., 1994, 247–48.

———. 1996a. *Mission on the Way: Issues in Mission Theology*. Grand Rapids: Baker.

———. 1996b. "The Gospel Story: Mission of, in, and on the Way" (Installation address in the Arthur F. Glasser Chair of Biblical Theology of Mission), Pasadena: FTS; adapted and reprinted in *Theology, News and Notes* (June,

1998), 3–6 and 22–23; reprinted in Van Engen, Nancy Thomas and Robert Gallagher, eds., 1999. Introduction, xvii–xxviii.

————. 1998. "Reflecting Theologically About the Resistant" in J. Dudley Woodberry, ed., 22–78.

————. 2000. "Working Together Theologically in the New Millennium: Opportunities and Challenges," in Gary Corwin and Kenneth Mulholland, eds., 82–122.

————. 2001. "Toward a Theology of Mission Partnerships," *Missiology*, XXIX: 1 (January, 2001), 11–44.

————. 2004c "¿Por qué sembrar iglesias saludables? Bases bíblicas y misiológicas," in John Wagenveld, 2004/2005, 43–94. English publication: Van Engen, "Why Multiply Healthy Churches?" *Great Commission Research Journal*. 6: 1 (Summer, 2014), 57–90 and Gary Teja and John Wagenveld, eds., *Planting Healthy Churches*, Sauk Village, IL: Multiplication Network Ministries, 2015, 23–60.

————. 2005a. "Five Perspectives of Contextually Appropriate Mission Theology," in Charles Kraft, editor,

————. 2005b. "Toward a Contextually Appropriate Methodology in Mission Theology," in Charles Kraft, editor,

————. 2008. "Mission, Theology of," in William Dyrness and Veli-Matt i Kärkkäinen, eds., Global Dictionary of Theology. Downers Grove: IVP.

————. 2010. "'Mission' Defined and Described" one of three lead chapters in a discussion symposium book edited by David Hesselgrave and Ed Stetzer. *Missionshift: Global Mission Issues in the Third Millennium*. Nashville: B & H Publishing, 2010. 7–29.

————. 2011. "Biblical Theology of Mission's Research Method," in Edgar Elliston, ed., with Pablo Deiros, Viggo Søgaard and Charles Van Engen; *Introducing Missiological Research Design*; Pasadena: William Carey Library, 2011, 113–18.

Van Engen, Charles, Dean Gilliland and Paul Pierson, eds., 1993. *The Good News of the Kingdom: Mission Theology for the Third Millennium*. Maryknoll: Orbis.

Van Engen, C. and Jude Tiersma, eds., 1994. *God So Loves the City: Seeking a Theology for Urban Mission*. Monrovia: MARC; reprinted by Eugene, OR: Wipf and Stock, 2009.

Van Engen, C., Nancy Thomas and Robert Gallagher, eds., 1999. *Footprints of God: A Narrative Theology of Mission*. Monrovia: MARC, World Vision.

Van Engen, C., ed., 2016. *The State of Missiology Today: Global Innovations in Christian Witness*. Downers Grove: IVP.

Van Rheenen, Gailyn. 1983. *Biblical Anchored Mission: Perspectives on Church Growth*. Austin, TX: Firm Foundation Pub.

———. 2003. "The Missional Helix: Example of Church Planting" *Monthly Missiological Reflection # 26* Rhenen@Bible.acu.edu; see also www. missiology.org.

Verkuyl, Johannes. 1978. *Contemporary Missiology: An Introduction*. Grand Rapids: Eerdmans.

Verstraelen, F. J., A. Camps, L. A. Hoedemaker, and M. R. Spindler, eds., 1995. *Missiology: An Ecumenical Introduction: Texts and Contexts of Global Christianity*. Grand Rapids: Eerdmans. English translation of *Oecumenische Inleiding in de Missiologie: Teksten en Konteksten van het Wereld-Christendom*. Kampen: Kok, 1988.

Vicedom, Georg F. 1965. *The Mission of God: An Introduction to a Theology of Mission* (Trans. by A.A. Thiele and D. Higendorf from the German original, *Missio Dei*, 1957) St. Louis, MO: Concordia.

Vidales, Raul. 1979. "Methodological Issues in Liberation Theology," in Rosino Gibellini, ed., 34–57.

Villafañe, Eldin. 1995. *Seek the Peace of the City: Reflections on Urban Ministry*. Grand Rapids: Eerdmans.

Visser 't Hooft, W.A. ed., 1961. *The New Delhi Report*. Geneva: WCC.

Ward, Pete. 2002. *Liquid Church: A Bold Vision of How to Be God's People in Worship and Mission—A Flexible, Fluid Way of Being Church*. Peabody: Henderson.

Warren, Max. 1974. *Crowded Canvas*. London: Hodder & Stoughton.

———. 1978. "The Fusion of the I.M.C. and the W.C.C. at New Delhi: Retrospective Thoughts After a Decade and a Half," in J.D. Gort, ed., 1978, 190–202.

von Rad, Gerhard. 1962. *Old Testament Theology*. New York: Harper. (Vol.1.)

Wagenveld, John, ed., 2004, 2005. *Sembremos Iglesias saludables: un acercamiento bíblico y práctico al estudio de la multiplicación de iglesias*. Quito, Ecuador: FLET, 2004/Miami: FLET, 2005. English translation: Gary Teja and John Wagenveld, eds., *Planting Healthy Churches*, Sauk Village, IL: Multiplication Network Ministries, 2015.

Wagner, C. Peter. 1963. *Where in the World*. N.Y.: NCCC.

———. 1964. *What in the World*. N.Y.: NCCC. World Council of Churches

————. 1968. *The Church for Others and the Church for the World.* Geneva: WCC.

————. 1971. *Frontiers in Mission Strategy.* Chicago: Moody.

————. 1976. *Your Church Can Grow: Seven Vital Signs of a Healthy Church.* Ventura: ReGal

————. 1979. *Our Kind of People: The Ethical Dimensions of Church Growth in America.* Atlanta: John Knox.

————. 1981. *Church Growth and the Whole Gospel: A Biblical Mandate.* N.Y.: Harper & Row.

————. 1984. *Leading Your Church to Growth: The Secret of Pastor/People Partnership in Dynamic Church Growth.* Ventura: ReGal

————. 1984. *Your Church Can Grow.* Ventura: ReGal

————. 1986. "A Vision for Evangelizing the Real America," *IBMR;* X: 2, (April, 1986), 59–64.

————. 1987. *Strategies for Church Growth: Tools for Effective Mission and Evangelism.* Ventura: ReGal

————. 1989a. "Donald McGavran: A Tribute to the Founder," in C. Peter Wagner, ed., 16–18.

————. 1989b. *Church Growth: State of the Art.* Wheaton: Tyndale.

————. 1990. *Church Planting for a Greater Harvest.* Ventura: ReGal.

————. 1996. *The Healthy Church.* Ventura: ReGal. This is an update and reprint of C. Peter Wagner. *Your Church Can Be Healthy.* Nashville: Abingdon, 1969.

Wagner, C. Peter, Win Arn and Elmer Towns, eds., 1986. *Church Growth: State of the Art.* Wheaton: Tyndale.

Walls, Andrew F. 1976. "Toward an Understanding of Africa's Place in Christian History," in J. S. Pobee, ed., 180–189.

————. 1981. "The Gospel as Prisoner and Liberator of Culture," *Faith and Thought,* 108: 1–2) 39–52; also in *Missionalia* X:3 (Nov.), 93–105.

————. 1985. "Christian Tradition in Today's World," in F. D. Whaling, ed., 76–109.

————. 1996. *The Missionary Movement in Christian History: Studies in the Transmission of Faith.* Maryknoll: Orbis.

————. 2002. *The Cross-Cultural Process in Christian History.* Maryknoll: Orbis and Edinburgh: T&T Clark.

Warneck, Gustav. 1901. *Outline of a History of Protestant Missions.* N.Y.: Fleming H. Revell.

Whaling, F.D. ed., 1985. *Religion in Today's World,* Edinburgh: T & T Clark

Whiteman, Darrell L. 1997. "Contextualization: The Theory, the Gap, the Challenge," *IBMR*. (Jan.) 2–7.

———. 2003. *Anthropology and Mission: The Incarnational Connection*, Third Annual Louis J. Luzbetack Lecture on Mission and Culture, Chicago: Catholic Theological Union.

Wiles, Maurice and Mark Santer, eds., 1975. *Documents in Early Christian Thought*. London: Cambridge U. Press.

Williams, Colin. 1963. *Where in the World*. N.Y.: NCCC.

———. 1964. *What in the World*. N.Y.: NCCC/Geneva: WCC.

———. 1968. *The Church for Others and the Church for the World*. Geneva: WCC.

Wilson, Frederick, ed., 1990. *The San Antonio Report—Your Will Be Done: Mission in Christ's Way*. Geneva: WCC.

Winter, Ralph. 1971. "The Soils: A Church Growth Principle," *Church Growth Bulletin* VII: 5 (May), 145–47.

———. 1980. "1980: Year of Three Missions Congresses," *Evangelical Missions Quarterly* 16 (April), 79–85.

———. 1984. "Unreached Peoples: The Development of the Concept," in Charles Kraft and Tom Wisely, eds., 17–43.

Winter, Ralph and Steven C. Hawthorne, eds., 1981, 1999. *Perspectives on the World Christian Movement: A Reader* (Third Edition). Pasadena: William Carey Library.

Woodberry, J. Dudley, ed., 1998. *Reaching the Resistant: Barriers and Bridges for Mission*. Pasadena: William Carey Library.

World Council of Churches. 1961. *Evanston to New Delhi: 1954–1961*. Geneva: WCC.

———. 1968. *The Church for Others and the Church for the World*. Geneva: WCC.

World Missionary Conference, 1910 (9 vols.) N.Y.: Revell.

Wright, Christopher. 2006. *The Mission of God: Unlocking the Bible's Grand Narrative*. Downers Grove: InterVarsity Press.

———. 2010. *The Mission of God's People: A Biblical Theology of the Church's Mission*. Grand Rapids: Zondervan.

Wright, George Ernest. 1955. *The Old Testament Against Its Environment*. Chicago: Alec Allenson.

———. 1961. "The Old Testament Basis for the Christian Mission," in G. H. Anderson, ed., 17–30.

www.vbmb.org/glocalmissions/default.cfm. 2005.

Yesurathnam, R. 2000. "Contextualization in Mission," in W. S. Milton Jeganathan, ed., 44–57.

Zabatiero, Julio Paulo Tavares. 2000. Liberdade e Paixão. Londrina: Descoberta.

Ziegenhals, Walter. 1978. *Urban Churches in Transition. N.Y.: Pilgrim.*

Zunkel, C. Wayne. 1987. *Church Growth Under Fire.* Scottdale, PA: Herald Press.

Zwemer, Samuel. 1950. "Calvinism and the Missionary Enterprise," *Theology Today* VIII, 206–16.